SUSTAINABLE MARKETING

SUSTAINABLE MARKETING

Second Edition

Robert Dahlstrom
Miami University
BI Norwegian Business School

Jody L. Crosno
West Virginia University

CHICAGO
BUSINESS PRESS

CHICAGO
BUSINESS PRESS

ISBN-13: 978-0-9971171-9-6
ISBN-10: 0-9971171-9-2

To Susan, Meredith, and Patrick

To Jereme, Cole, and Liam

CONTENTS

PREFACE

Welcome to the Sustainable Marketing. We hope that this essay offers a fresh perspective on how marketers think about sustainability and its relevance to marketing.

Our interest in writing this book emerged in the early 2000's when we learned about the utility of wind power and other alternative energy sources. This experience prompted us to begin investigating influences of commerce on greenhouse gas emissions, natural resource conservation, and biodiversity. We began searching for a comprehensive approach to marketing and sustainability that addressed these issues. Although we noted some intriguing work in strategy and economics, these studies did not capture the sets of sustainability issues most germane to marketing management. As our interests grew, we began to develop ideas related to a number of divergent aspects of marketing management and their interactions with the environment.

Over time, we began to recognize that markets operate within ecosystems. Although this observation seems obvious, it has historically not been incorporated into many managerial decisions. For many years, marketers—those involved in buying, selling, and consuming—have been able to take the environment as a given. Increasingly, however, the scarcity of resources demands consideration of the environmental antecedents and consequences of marketing action. Thus, the marketer must consider how consumption influences greenhouse gas production; energy consumption; water, land, and air quality; and biodiversity. A sustainable marketing perspective adopts a triple bottom line perspective that addresses financial and social performance as well as ecological performance.

PHILOSOPHY

Our goal in developing this text has been to develop a theoretically-based and managerially-relevant perspective on sustainable marketing. In order to make this book meaningful to current and future marketing managers, we have simultaneously striven to incorporate state-of-the-art examples of business practice. In each chapter, we have sought scenarios and examples of environmental issues that managers face today. Each chapter begins with a short vignette designed to illustrate current efforts to interact successfully with the environment. Nothing works quite as well as a good theory, and the application of theory provides great insight to managers. The examples are designed to illuminate theory and pique the reader's interest in the topic.

Given the strong need to couch consumption within the ecosystem, the text investigates a number of theoretical approaches not typically incorporated into marketing textbooks. The treatment of the commerce-environment interface, for example, relies heavily on environmental perspectives accumulated by the United Nations (UN). The UN serves as a central clearinghouse for research in this vein, and it provides an opportunity to bring together logic developed within the natural sciences, social sciences, and industrial practice. We hope that this perspective is interesting and enlightening to the reader.

STRUCTURE OF THE TEXT

In developing this book, we tried to organize these ideas in a manner that was consistent with other marketing textbooks. The book has five sections. The first section provides an introduction to the subject matter of sustainable marketing. Chapter one defines sustainable marketing and outlines its importance to marketing management and practice. Chapter two illustrates how sustainable marketing is incorporated into strategic planning, and Chapter three indicates how sustainable marketing is germane to social responsibility and ethics.

Section two examines the promotion of sustainable value to consumers via sustainable promotional strategies. Chapter four describes consumer decision making and consumption, and Chapter five examines sustainability-based promotional efforts designed to influence consumption. Chapter six addresses the discovery of value via target marketing and segmentation, and Chapter seven addresses communicating value via promotional strategies. Chapter eight examines sustainable branding and labeling.

Section three examines the firm's efforts to deliver sustainable value throughout the supply chain. Chapter nine examines the declaration of value associated with sustainable pricing strategies. Chapter ten describes sustainable supply chains, and chapter eleven characterizes sustainable retailing. Chapter twelve examines new product strategies that provide value to consumers, and Chapter thirteen describes sustainable services marketing.

The fourth section of the book addresses the firm's efforts to report on sustainability. Chapter fourteen presents the essential tenets of sustainability reporting and reporting initiatives used across sectors of the global economy. This chapter underscores the relationship between marketing action and accounting. In addition, an understanding of these reporting procedures provides insight to financial markets.

Section five provides a series of appendices outlining macro-environmental factors related to sustainable marketing. Appendix A-1 describes the relationship between environmental factors and consumption whereas Appendix A-2 describes geo-political action designed to limit effects of consumption. Since four sectors of the economy are associated with more than ninety-five percent of greenhouse gas emissions, it is germane to consider issues endemic to each of these macro-economic sectors. Thus, the Appendices A 3-6 provide background on consumption in the household, services, transportation, and industrial sectors of the economy. Appendix A-7 provides a brief overview of ISO 14000 standards. These appendices are intended to inform readers of the ecological effects of consumption so that they can meaningfully incorporate ecological factors into sustainable marketing strategies.

We have incorporated a number of elements to enhance pedagogy. In addition to the vignettes presented at the beginning of each chapter, we provide numerous examples designed to illustrate the relevance of the subject to business practice. Key terms are provided at the end of each chapter, and these terms are highlighted in the accompanying text. Each chapter also offers a brief synopsis. In addition, we have provided ten questions at the end of each chapter. These questions can be used to stimulate understanding of the course subject matter within and beyond the classroom.

ACKNOWLEDGEMENTS

I would like to thank several people that had an influence on the development of this book. First, I would like to thank people in my home life that helped me to gain a broader understanding of the role sustainability. I thank Susan, my wife, Meredith, my daughter, and Patrick, my son, for helping me realize how we can incorporate sustainability into our daily lives.

I greatly appreciate the support and efforts of my co-author, Jody Crosno. She has provided an insightful approach to the development of the chapters addressing sustainable promotions and supply chains. Her understanding of business practice and her scholarship greatly enhanced the development of *Sustainable Marketing*.

I appreciate the encouragement of my colleagues who have made this text possible. Lisa Ellram has provided new perspectives on the role of sustainability in supply chains. Devon Delvecchio has similarly offered rich insights into branding and consumer decision making. Beyond the business school, I recognize the advice and support from colleagues affiliated with the Sustainability Committee at Miami University.

I would also like to thank my colleagues at BI-Norwegian Business School for their advice throughout the development of this work. Ragnhild Silkoset has offered many insightful perspectives on sustainability in international commerce. Torger Reve has continued to be an inspiration through his international strategy research. I am also indebted to Bendik Samuelsen for offering his perspectives on sustainable consumption.

I am also indebted to my colleague for more than a quarter century, Arne Nygaard, of the Oslo School of Management. Arne has offered tremendous insight into sustainability issues in retailing.

The editorial, production, and marketing staff at Chicago Business Press deserve tremendous praise for all the work they did to make this book a possibility. I would particularly like to thank Paul Ducham, for his guidance.

Robert Dahlstrom

First, I would like to thank my co-author, mentor, and friend, Robert Dahlstrom, for bringing me on this journey. His knowledge and hard work laid the foundation for *Sustainable Marketing*, and he provided me with tremendous guidance throughout the writing of this book. Second, I would like to acknowledge the support of my family, especially Jereme, Cole, and Liam Scribner; Joyce Sirota; Blanche Kilgore; Lee Scribner; and J.V. Crosno. I am also indebted to my colleagues at West Virginia University—Jim Brown, Annie Cui, and Paula Fitzgerald—each of whom provided insights on a range of topics pertinent to this book. Lastly, I would like to thank Paul Ducham and the staff at Chicago Business Press for their support of this book.

Jody Crosno

ABOUT THE AUTHORS

Robert Dahlstrom is the Joseph C. Seibert Professor of Marketing in the Farmer School of Business at Miami University. Prior to earning a PhD in marketing at the University of Cincinnati, Dr. Dahlstrom worked in sales, marketing, and system analysis in the computer industry. This experience and his interest in behavioral dimensions of interfirm relationships provide the background for a stream of research that examines sustainability in distribution channels, retailing, and supply chains. He has published articles in the *Journal of Marketing Research*, the *Journal of Marketing*, the *Journal of Retailing*, the *Journal of the Academy of Marketing Science*, and elsewhere.

Over the course of his career, Dr. Dahlstrom has worked extensively with colleagues in Norway. He has earned a Norwegian Marshall Fund Fellowship and two Fulbright-Hays research fellowships for his Nordic research. He has also worked for BI- Norwegian Business School where he has been active in research conducted with masters and doctoral students. Collaboration with scholars in Scandinavia has fueled a continuing interest in sustainable marketing.

Robert Dahlstrom previously served as the Bloomfield Professor of Marketing at the University of Kentucky. During his tenure, he established the Von Allmen Center for Green Marketing in the Gatton College of Business and Economics.

A passion for the classroom complements his interest in research. In a career that spans more than thirty years of instruction, he has taught business-to-business marketing, sales management, personal selling, international marketing, marketing management, marketing strategy, and sustainable marketing. In addition to his work in Ohio and Kentucky, he has taught in Austria, Norway, and Greece. Recognition of the need for programs of instruction in sustainability prompted him to develop courses in sustainable marketing at the undergraduate and masters' levels.

Jody L. Crosno is an Associate Professor of Marketing at West Virginia University. She earned her PhD in Marketing at the University of Kentucky. Dr. Crosno's research primarily focuses on the development and management of interfirm relationships in marketing channels. Her research draws on multiple theories and perspectives to gain a better understanding of how to maximize efficiency in channel relationships. Her research has been published in the *Industrial Marketing Management, Journal of the Academy of Marketing Science, Journal of Business-to-Business Marketing, Journal of Business and Industrial Management, Journal of Marketing Channels, Marketing Letters*, among others. Dr. Crosno serves on the Editorial Review Boards of *Journal of Business-to-Business Marketing* and *Journal of Marketing Theory and Practice*.

part one

Introduction

1

An Overview of Sustainable Marketing

In this chapter you will learn about:

Introduction to Sustainable Marketing

Adopting a Sustainable Approach to Marketing

Consumer Benefits Associated with Sustainable Marketing

Corporate Benefits Associated with Sustainable Marketing

Ecological Benefits Associated with Sustainable Marketing

How This Text Is Organized to Help Understand Sustainable Marketing

INTRODUCTION TO SUSTAINABLE MARKETING

Samso, Denmark

Our journey into sustainable marketing begins in Samso, Denmark, a tiny island located about four hours from Copenhagen.[1] Facing considerably high energy prices for diesel and coal, inhabitants of this island embarked on an effort to reduce their dependency on fossil fuels in 1997. The island won a state-sponsored contest to create a model community that combined wind and solar power for electricity and geothermal, plant-based energy for heating. The project has been successful on many fronts. The island reached energy independence in 2005, enabling the inhabitants to sell excess power to the national utility while bringing *income* to hundreds of residents who own shares in the island's land and sand sea-based wind farms (see Figure 1-1). Not only did the island eliminate its dependence on fossil fuels, but it did so via *renewable energy* sources with substantially lower carbon footprints than their fossil fuel counterparts. These renewable sources of energy will be employed rather than fossil fuels in the form of coal, oil, or natural gas.

The project will also demand long-term working relationships among residents of Samso. Throughout the island, public buildings and private homes connect to centralized heating plants. At these facilities, hay is burned to heat water, which circulates through underground pipes to provide heat and hot water for residents. Development of this technology provided new opportunities for plumbers to install

FIGURE 1-1

Wind turbines on the Danish island of Samso. Credit Erik Refner for *The New York Times.*[2]

---

[1] Cardwell, Diane (2015), "Green Inspiration off the Coast of Denmark," (August 27). www.nytimes.com/2015/01/18/business/energy-environment/green-energy-inspiration-from-samso-denmark.html (February 14, 2015).

[2] Cardwell, "Green Inspiration off the Coast of Denmark."

and service the new heat pump systems. Farmers on the island similarly found a new market that now accounts for 25 percent of hay production on the island.

The *Samso* success story exemplifies the potential of renewable energy sources. Energy needs are increasingly being met through wind, and it is the fastest-growing sources of energy around the world.[3] In 2011, renewable sources of energy supplied approximately 19 percent of global final energy consumption. Renewable energy provides many communities with a clean, local source of electricity rather than imported fossil fuels.

The story of Samso developing renewable energy is one example of sustainable marketing. In today's economy, each of us has the opportunity to engage in sustainable marketing. When we recycle aluminum cans, we are engaging in one form of sustainable marketing. Similarly, when we buy a hybrid automobile, we are acting with a sustainable approach to marketing. When General Electric invests in wind power, it is engaging in sustainable marketing. When General Motors invests in researching environmentally friendly technologies for the Chinese market, it is also engaged in sustainable marketing.

Each of these examples illustrates conditions under which people or institutions have chosen to act in a manner that is environmentally friendly. Nevertheless, we can each think of situations in which people do not engage in sustainable marketing. Many of us have been litterbugs, and most have on occasion failed to purchase environmentally sound products despite their availability. Similarly, we are aware of situations in which energy companies did not act in the best interests of the environment.

It is because the challenge to sustainable marketing is so great that it is important to study this subject. Indeed, the purpose of this book is to help individuals make informed decisions about choices that influence environmental, economic, and social performance. As we progress, however, we will find that many sustainable decisions are more complicated than they appear. Furthermore, the decision to use an environmentally friendly approach at one stage in a supply chain has environmental implications for another level of the supply chain. For example, compact fluorescent light bulbs use 25 percent of the energy and last 10 times longer than conventional bulbs, but the mercury in these bulbs complicates but the mercury in these bulbs complicates recycling.[4]

....

ADOPTING A SUSTAINABLE APPROACH TO MARKETING

In order for us to understand sustainable marketing, it is first important to have an appreciation of marketing. The American Marketing Association defines *marketing* as the "the activity, set of institutions, and processes for creating, communicating, delivering, and exchanging offerings that have value for customers, clients, partners, and society at large."[5] This definition recognizes that marketing

---

[3] International Energy Agency (2013), *Technology Roadmap: Wind Energy*, Paris, France; International Energy Agency.

[4] Hu, Yuanan, and Hefa Cheng (2012), "Mercury Risk from Fluorescent Lamps in China: Current Status and Future Perspective," *Environment International* 44 (1), 141–150

[5] http://ama-academics.communityzero.com/elmar?go=1712138.

is an organizational function and set of activities undertaken to bring about exchanges of goods, service, or ideas between people. The definition recognizes that marketing is a philosophical orientation to the practice of doing business. This philosophical orientation emphasizes the satisfaction and value that customers, clients, partners, and society realize due to marketing action.

As marketing has evolved, individuals operating in various parts of the field have adopted alternative definitions of sustainable marketing. Marketers have developed sustainable approaches that fundamentally emphasize ecological factors. Consumer researchers, for instance, have focused on the conditions that increase the potential for consumers to act in an ecologically responsible manner,[6] and they recognize marked variety among consumer interpretations of this responsibility.

Retailers and developers of sustainable products emphasize product offerings that are environmentally friendly.[7] Thus, products such as organic vegetables, recycled paper, and phosphate-free detergents are referred to as sustainable products. This definition of sustainable marketing emphasizes product offerings that are not harmful to the environment, but it does not address the production processes employed to prepare the products.

Social marketing adopts a different vantage point and defines sustainable marketing as the development and marketing of products designed to minimize negative effects on the physical environment. In contrast to the retailing perspective, the social orientation recognizes the pre-consumption and post-consumption costs to the environment. Thus, automobile manufacturers attempt to raise production efficiency while simultaneously decreasing costs associated with disassembly and reuse after consumption.[8]

These marketing perspectives underscore the relationship with the environment, but they do not address other salient outcomes desired by the firm. Firms that seek to become sustainable should augment these green marketing approaches with broader consideration of the firm's triple bottom line. Organizations increasingly must incorporate the environment into decision making, but this orientation cannot come at the expense of supply chain relationships and financial goals. By contrast, a sustainability-oriented approach incorporates ecological concerns into a more holistic view of marketing.

Our treatment of sustainable marketing is based on the eclectic approach to achieving social, economic, and ecological outcomes. The United Nations is an organization that has led the way in this recognition of the multiple interdependencies among nature, economy, and society. In December 1983, the United Nations commissioned research on development and the environment. The

---

[6] Sheth, Jagdish N., Nirmal K. Sethia, and Shanthi Srinivas (2011), "Mindful Consumption: A Customer-Centric Approach to Sustainability," *Journal of the Academy of Marketing Science* 39 (1), 21–39.

[7] Lai, Kee-hung, T. C. E. Cheng, and Ailie K. Y. Tang (2012), "Green Retailing: Factors for Success," *California Management Review*, 52(2), 6–31.

[8] Johnson, M.R., and M.H. Wang (1998), "Economical Evaluation of Disassembly Operations for Recycling, Remanufacturing and Reuse," *International Journal of Production Research*, 36 (12), 3227–3252.Pigosso, Daniela C. A., Evelyn T. Zanette, Américo Guelere Filho, Aldo R. Ometto, and Henrique Rozenfeld, (2010), "Ecodesign Methods Focused on Remanufacturing." Journal of Cleaner Production 18, (1), 21–31.

1987 report summarizing this research defined *sustainability* as development that "meets the needs of the present without compromising the ability of future generations to meet their own needs."[9] Importantly, this edict recognizes that there are at any time limits on the ability of the biosphere to absorb human activity. There are also limits imposed by the state of technology and social organizations, but both of these factors can be managed and improved to foster economic growth.

Since the publication of this report by the United Nations, industry practice has embraced the notion that sustainability derives from focusing on the *triple bottom line*.[10] Figure 1-2 outlines the pursuit of sustainability. The sustainable organization must generate acceptable levels of economic performance, or it will not survive. It must also nurture social performance in its interaction with customers, suppliers, consumers, and other interest groups. Survival is also contingent on the firm's ability to achieve acceptable levels of environmental performance throughout the supply cycle from raw material procurement to post-consumption disposal. Figure 1-2 illustrates that these alternative bottom lines are not always compatible. For example, the firm can raise its short-term financial performance by ignoring the costs of waste produced in its manufacturing facilities. The sustainable organization, however, simultaneously works toward achieving heightened performance in the economic, social, and environmental realms.

Samso and its operations illustrate a developing effort to achieve sustainability through triple bottom-line performance. Samso and the landowners benefit financially from the sale of renewable energy, and they must develop and maintain working relationships to ensure financial performance. As they nurture these financially rewarding relationships, they are also contributing markedly to the environment by using renewable sources of energy.

We, therefore, define *sustainable marketing* as the study all efforts to consume, produce, distribute, promote, package, and reclaim products in a manner to achieve ecological, economic, and social objectives. The inclusion of "all efforts to consume" recognizes that many entities are involved in sustainable marketing.

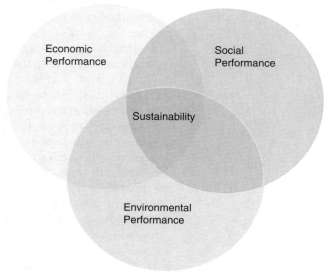

FIGURE 1-2
Sustainability and the triple bottom line.[11]

Economic Performance

Social Performance

Sustainability

Environmental Performance

---

[9] Brundtland, Gro (1987), *Our Common Future, The World Commission on Environment and Development*, Oxford University Press, New York, 1987, p.24.

[10] Waddock, Sandra A., Charles Bodwell, and Samuel B. Graves (2002). "The New Business Imperative," *Academy of Management Executive*, 16 (2), 132–148.Savitz, A. (2012), *The Triple Bottom Line: How Today's Best-Run Companies Are Achieving Economic, Social and Environmental Success--and How You Can Too*. San Francisco, CA: John Wiley & Sons.

[11] Carter, Craig R., and Dale S. Rogers (2008), "A Framework of Sustainable Supply Chain Management: Moving Toward New Theory," *International Journal of Physical Distribution & Logistics Management* 38(5), 360–387.

Sustainable marketing is not limited to government or nongovernment organizations, nor is it solely an activity undertaken by consumers. Manufacturers, wholesalers, retailers, and services firms each have opportunities to contribute to sustainable marketing. This definition also recognizes the need to consider the production, distribution, and reclamation of products as integrated components of the marketing effort. Efficiency at one stage of this process (e.g., distribution) may offer advantages in the channel, but the goal of sustainable efforts is to limit the total ecological influence associated with consumption. Finally, sustainable marketing must consider the promotional efforts employed to gain consumer support of ecologically-friendly products.

We define *sustainable marketing management* as the process of planning and executing the marketing mix to facilitate consumption, production, distribution, promotion, packaging, and product reclamation in a manner that is sensitive or responsive to ecological, economic, and social concerns. The management of sustainable marketing activity continues to evolve as companies incorporate new thinking about climate change throughout their organizations. Initial sustainable marketing efforts focused on the recycling of products such as aluminum cans and photocopier toner cartridges. Over time, firms have begun to consider ways to *modify inputs* to production that limit the influence of the products on the environment. For example, Staples reduced store operating overhead through centralized controls for lighting, heating, and cooling at its 1500 stores. Staples saved $6 million over two years by controlling this production input into its value chain.[12] As this Staples' example illustrates, development is at the core of a sustainable marketing approach. The study of sustainable marketing reflects an interest at becoming more aware of the ecological and sustainability issues and consistently working to achieve higher levels of sustainability.

Increasingly, firms are also recognizing that outputs from the production process should be viewed under scrutiny of climate change as well. Savvy management recognizes that everything coming out of a production facility is a *product*, *by-product*, or *waste*.[13] Sustainable products are recognized nationally or internationally through certification and eco-labeling. For example, the U.S. Environmental Protection Agency provides Energy Star labels for electronics and appliances that are environmentally friendly. In the United States, personal computers account for 3 percent of residential electricity consumption.[14] Adoption of these new personal computers with the EPA's new Energy Star labels would save more than $1 billion in annual energy costs while reducing annual greenhouse gas emissions by 15 billion pounds—equivalent to the emissions from more than 1.4 million vehicles[15].

Firms also are viewing by-products of production in novel ways. Shell Oil is pumping carbon dioxide, a refinery by-product, into 500 Dutch greenhouses. This action reduces emissions by 325,000 tons per year and saves greenhouses from having to burn millions of cubic meters of gas needed to produce carbon

---

[12] Varachaver, Nicholas (2004), "How to Kick the Oil Habit,' *Fortune*, August 23, 2004.

[13] Esty, Daniel C., and Andrew S. Winston (2006), *Green to Gold*, New Haven, CT: Yale University Press.

[14] www.eia.gov/analysis/studies/demand/miscelectric/pdf/miscelectric.pdf (February 15, 2015).

[15] www.energystar.gov/products/certified-products/detail/computers (February 15, 2015).

dioxide.[16] The pursuit of waste reduction is a third aspect of the production process undergoing a sustainable transformation. Companies recognize that efforts to constrain waste influence profitability. For example, Fetzer Vineyards took an aggressive approach when it set a goal of zero waste.[17] It has a companywide waste reduction programs that involves recycling of bottles, cardboard, plastic, aluminum, paper, antifreeze, waste oil, fluorescent tubes and glass. The firm has reduced the amount of waste it sends to landfills by 96 percent since 1990.

Each of these activities represent a form of sustainable marketing employed at various points in the supply chain. Increasingly, however, organizations recognize the interdependencies operating throughout an economy. Efforts to control costs and enhance productivity at one stage cannot occur at the expense of other stages.

Sustainability initiatives are being developed to address a host of situations in which effort is focused on current development without repercussions to future generations. The agricultural, manufacturing, and retailing sectors offer different examples of sustainability. In the agricultural sector, Costa Rica is making progress toward production of sustainable bananas. Small-scale producers grow bananas without heavy agrochemical inputs. These locally controlled agricultural systems are supportive of local people, economies, and cultures.[18] In the manufacturing sector, the U.S. Department of Energy and the Aluminum Association have formed a long-established partnership designed to improve technology competitiveness through collaborative planning and research.[19] This private-public partnership seeks to make the industry profitable and ecologically sustainable. In the retail sector, Wal-Mart has publicly committed to employing renewable energy sources and will expand the development of onsite and off-site solar, wind, fuel cells, and other technologies on its properties.[20] As part of its effort to gain logistical sustainability, the firm developed a packaging scorecard to monitor supplier performance.[21]

Together these examples from a broad range of industries underscore the common interest in establishing sustainable marketing initiatives. Firms may be hesitant to recognize the long-term merits of sustainable marketing, but they cannot deny the short-run financial incentives established by regulators, trading partners, and consumers.

CONSUMER BENEFITS DERIVED FROM SUSTAINABLE MARKETING

Sustainable marketing has positive influences on multiple participants in the economy. *Consumer*, *corporations*, and the *ecological environment* can benefit from sustainable marketing. Consider first the consumer benefits from sustainable marketing.

---

[16] Deliser, H. (2006), "Gas for the Greenhouse," *Nature* 442, 499PP.

[17] Kadleck, Chrissy (2007), "Calif. Vineyard Cuts Environmental Impact," *Waste News*, 13 (7) 12.

[18] www.awish.net/NA/banana_project.htm.

[19] www.nrel.gov/docs/fy01osti/29340.pdf (February 15, 2015).

[20] www.corporatereport.com/walmart/2014/grr/_pdf/Walmart_2014_GRR.pdf (February 15, 2015).

[21] Falkman, Mary Ann (2007), "Sustainability: The Wal-Mart Way," *Packaging Digest,* 44 (20) 12.

Consumers benefit in several important ways through sustainable marketing. These benefits often influence consumer decision making, and consumers will vary in the extent to which they value these benefits. Initially, consumers benefit from the knowledge that they are doing their part to reduce climate change. These consumers are likely to favor corporate efforts to reduce pollution over efforts to raise corporate profitability.[22] A nascent industry is developing that enables consumers to offset adverse effects of their action. For example, TerraPass enables consumers to purchase carbon offsets for their auto, air, or home emissions.[23]

Consumers also value the opportunity to be associated with environmentally friendly products and organizations.[24] For instance, the Body Shop's retail ambience prompts customer to associate their consumption with an environmentally friendly organization.[25]

Although sustainable product initiatives may independently convince some consumers to buy, evidence suggests that ecologically based products alone will not be substantial drivers of sales.[26] Consumers want ecologically friendly products without sacrificing other valuable features. Current marketing efforts, however, enable some firms to offer sustainable products that provide initial product savings, lower energy costs, and access to new technologies.[27] For example, current LED-based television monitors offer substantial savings over the LCD monitors currently being phased out of the product line.[28] These new monitors are less expensive and employ the more recent computer display technology. The LED monitors are also more energy efficient over time. Although sustainable products in every industry will not enjoy the technological benefits similar to those for televisions, ecological benefits of products will augment or complement other product features valued by consumers.

It is critical to recognize that the incorporation of product benefits must reflect a genuine value for the relevant-consuming public. Thus, sustainable products must offer customer satisfaction and be cost effective in addition to offering ecological merit. For example, Westinghouse developed an energy efficient refrigerator in 1994 that was 30 percent more efficient than U.S. Department of

---

[22] D'Souza, Clare, Mehdi Taghian, and Rajiv Khosla (2007), "Examination of Environmental Beliefs and Its Impact on the Influence of Price, Quality and Demographic Characteristics with Respect to Green Purchase Intention," *Journal of Targeting, Measurement & Analysis for Marketing*, 15(2), 69–78.

[23] Kotchen, Matthew J. (2009), "Offsetting Green Guilt," *Stanford Social Innovation Review*, 7(2), 26.

[24] Lee, Eun Mi, Seong-Yeon Park, Molly I. Rapert, and Christopher L. Newman (2012), "Does Perceived Consumer Fit Matter in Corporate Social Responsibility Issues?" *Journal of Business Research* 65 (11), 1558–1564.

[25] Kent T., and D. Stone (2007), "The Body Shop and the Role of Design in Retail Branding," *International Journal of Retail and Distribution Management*, 35 (7), 531–543.

[26] Esty, Daniel C., and Andrew S. Winston (2006), *Green to Gold*, New Haven, CT: Yale University Press.

[27] *Consumer Reports Buying Guide 2015.*

[28] Park, Won Young, Amol Phadke, Nihar Shah, and Virginie Letschert (2013), "Efficiency Improvement Opportunities in TVs: Implications for Market Transformation Programs," *Energy Policy* 59, 361–372.

Energy standards.[29] Despite receiving a $30 million government award for consumer rebates, the elimination of CFC in the coolant system did not offset the price premium associated with the new product.

Sustainable products have a greater likelihood of succeeding, however, when environmental benefits augment consumer value assessments. Most value assessments, regardless of whether the product is sustainable, center on price, quality, and performance. Sustainable attributes rarely stand on their own and must complement other benefits to increase consumer value and ultimately consumption.[30] Rechargeable batteries offer convenience benefits that make them more attractive than their single-use counterparts. The reduced landfill benefit augments the convenience benefit to consumers. Although the initial price of rechargeable batteries exceeds the costs of the disposable units, many consumers understand the complete value offered by the multiple-use batteries.

The battery example underscores another benefit to sustainable marketing, and that benefit lies in considering the value of the product throughout its life rather than the absolute initial cost. Auto purchasers who consider the relative lifetime operating costs of a hybrid versus internal combustion engine note marked disparities across brands. Consumers seeking to lower the overall cost of personal transportation must weigh the higher sticker price of the hybrid against the higher operating costs of the conventional engine. Increased fuel prices, longer driving distances, and reduced cost disparities with models using conventional engines are likely taken into consideration when the buyer evaluates the lifetime cost of the hybrid auto.

Developing economies.

Consumers living in nations that have relatively low GDP per capita can also substantially benefit from sustainability. The low income, underdeveloped assets, and economic vulnerability endemic to these economies results in high dependence on the agricultural sector. Inhabitants in these markets, however, face increased exposure to drought, intense storms, floods, and environmental stress that limit the ability to enhance quality of life. Research performed by the United Nations indicates that inhabitants of these countries are much more likely to be affected by natural disasters than inhabitants in high-income countries[31]. Climate change limits agricultural productivity, increases water stress, raises sea levels, negatively transforms ecosystems, and thwarts human health. These factors do not operate in isolation—interactively, they contribute to hunger and poverty in developing markets. Sustainable marketing and production stand to reduce climate change and consequently limit hunger and poverty.

As these developing economies progress, there will be increasing pressure on urban areas. More than half of world's population currently lives in urban areas, and the number is expected to increase over the next few decades. In China, a 13 percent increase in the number of urban inhabitants over the past 10 years has

---

[29] Lee, A. D., and R. Conger (1996), "Market Transformation: Does It Work? The Super Efficient Refrigerator Program," *ACEEE Proceedings* 3.69–3.80.

[30] Esty, Daniel C., and Andrew S. Winston (2006), *Green to Gold*, New Haven, CT: Yale University Press.

[31] Watkins, Kevin (2007/2008), "Team for the Preparation of Human Development Report 2007/2008," *United Nations Development Programme*.

resulted in a majority of citizens now living in cities.[32] Since the consumption of resources is a global issue, the extent to which consumers and industries adopt sustainable marketing practices influences the global environment. Marketing sustainable technologies enables firms operating in these countries to leapfrog antiquated operations with efficient and environmentally friendly designs. For example, Nigeria upgraded analog telecommunications products with wireless phone systems and fiber optic technologies.[33] New sustainable technologies enable such economies to bypass antiquated technologies previously employed in mature market economies.

CORPORATE BENEFITS DERIVED FROM SUSTAINABLE MARKETING

The strategies, workforce, markets served, products, production processes, and supply chains of firms benefit from adopting sustainability-based strategies.[34] Companies incorporate ecological consciousness into their mission statements and *strategy* enhance their images among consumers, employees, investors, insurers, and the general public. As previously outlined, some consumers have strong affinities toward sustainable products, and approaching the market with an ecological focus enhances brand image among these consumers.

Corporate initiatives that emphasize a sustainable orientation to markets have several implications for the *workforce*.[35] First, potential employees may decide whether to interview with a firm based on the company's environmental image. For example, Philips has developed a corporate culture that fuses sustainability within a culture that fosters creativity, entrepreneurship, and collaboration. This positioning enables the firm to be an employer choice in labor markets for highly skilled talent.[36]

The image further influences employee action after hiring.[37] General Electric, for instance, engages employees to come up with novel solutions for the environment. The solutions include energy-efficient appliances, compact fluorescent lighting, and wind turbine power. Genzyme, a biotechnology firm, recently moved into a state-of-the-art sustainable building complete with all-glass facades, 18

---

[32] Peng, Xizhe (2011), "China's Demographic History and Future Challenges," *Science* 333 (6042), 581–587.

[33] Tella, Adeyinka, Niran Adetoro, and Paul Adesola Adekunle (2009), "A Case Study of the Global System of Mobile Communication (GSM) in Nigeria," *The Spanish CEPIS Society*, 5 (3), 2–7.

[34] Rothenberg, Sandra (2012), "Sustainability through Servicizing," *MIT Sloan Management Review* 48 (2), 83–91.

[35] Fox, Adrienne (2007), "Corporate Social Responsibility Pays Off," *HR Magazine*, August, 52 (8) 2.

[36] www.philips.com/about/sustainability/oursocialapproach/employee-engagement/index.page (Accessed May 27, 2015).

[37] Muros, John P. (2012), "Going after the Green: Expanding Industrial–Organizational Practice to Include Environmental Sustainability," *Industrial and Organizational Psychology* 5 (4), 467–472.

gardens, and conversational seating areas. After the firm moved into the facility, employees reported higher levels of job satisfaction. Moreover, employees reported that their increased sense of pride about Genzyme's commitment to the environment was their number one reason behind the new sense of productivity. Thus, enhanced corporate image augments recruiting, employee engagement in the firm's activities, and productivity.

Sustainable marketing also enables companies to *redefine markets*. General Electric has committed to the need for cleaner, more efficient sources of energy, reduced emissions, and abundant sources of clean water. This commitment resonates throughout its product line and enables channel partners to refine markets. For instance, aircraft technology has enabled GE to develop engines that are 15 percent more fuel efficient than comparable engines used in Boeing and Airbus planes.[38]

Sustainable business practices can enhance the benefits that products offer to consumers as they can enhance the tools, devices, and knowledge in throughput technology designed to facilitate manufacturing and logistics.[39] For example, a hybrid engine is a product innovation, whereas a just-in-time inventory system is a process innovation.

Sustainable products, in many instances, enable manufacturers to differentiate their products while also enabling consumers to take advantage of the latest technological development. The BMW i3, for instance, is distinguished from other products in its class by the fuel efficiency of its electric engine.[40] The fuel performance of this auto complements the styling and the performance features that attract consumers to the Cooper.

In addition, sustainable marketing prompts manufacturers to reassess the product packaging. Packaging protects products during shipping, enhances product desirability, and offers convenience in product handling. Marketers are pursuing ways to achieve these goals with fewer plastics and other petrochemical products. Procter & Gamble, for example, has reduced the packaging material for the Gillette Fusion ProGlide razor. A plant fiber-based razor tray and recycled polyethylene replace the plastic clamshell plastic, yielding a 57 percent reduction in plastic and a 20 percent weight reduction. Elimination of this packaging decreases the amount of solid waste produced by consumers.[41] An important factor related to packaging is the cost of disposal of the product after consumption. In the personal computer market, manufacturers and retailers have developed programs to recycle e-waste regardless of the producer. Retailer locations collect items at no cost to the consumer and then process the computers for reuse or recycling.[42]

---

[38] www.gereports.com/post/99568939810/a-short-flight-for-a-jet-a-giant-leap-for-a-jet. (Accessed May 27, 2015).

[39] Griffin, A. (1997,) "The Effect of Project and Process Characteristics on Product Development Cycle Time," *Journal of Marketing Research*, 34(1), 24–35.

[40] Ramsbrock, Jens, Roman Vilimek, and Julian Weber (2013), "Exploring Electric Driving Pleasure–The BMW EV Pilot Projects," in *Human-Computer Interaction: Applications and Services*, 621–630. Springer: Berlin Heidelberg, 2013.

[41] Agarwal, Raveesh, and Monica Thiel (2013), "P&G: Providing Sustainable Innovative Products through LCA Worldwide." *South Asian Journal of Business and Management Cases* 2 (1), 85–96.

[42] Tanskanen, Pia (2013), "Management and Recycling of Electronic Waste," *Acta Materialia*, 61(3), 1001–1011.

Production process benefits.

Production processes focus on organizational efforts to produce the highest quality products at the lowest possible cost. Process benefits accrue for handling of products, by-products, and waste. The material costs associated with sustainable manufacturing techniques can be reduced in number of ways. Advanced Composite Structures, for instance, was able to reduce costs, lower facility size, and reduce scrap waste while more than doubling production[43]. Material costs can also be reduced via just-in-time (JIT) inventory procedures.[44] JIT enables companies to carry optimal levels of inventory that save space and energy.

By-product considerations also serve as incentives to engage in sustainable production. Over the past 15 years, the chemical industry has developed a green chemistry perspective that seeks to develop products that are benign by design.[45] Green chemistry focuses on the efficient use of raw materials, the elimination of waste, and the avoidance of toxic or hazardous solvents and reagents and solvents in the manufacture and application of chemical products. The craft beer industry has developed procedures for using the spent grain that is a by-product of the brewing process. The high-protein and fiber-content grain has many applications ranging from biofuel and bioplastics to agricultural uses human food, animal feed, and compost material.[46]

Supply-chain benefits.

Sustainable marketing influences relationships among the firms that make up the channel from raw material mining to consumption. Sustainable strategies that seek to eliminate waste in the supply chain result in firms analyzing truck loading and route planning in the delivery process.[47] Routing that seeks to eliminate fuel costs can maximize truck capacity utilization and improve customer service.

Increasingly, partners in the supply chain seek the ability to trace products throughout the supply chain. European Union law refers to traceability as "the ability to trace and follow food feed, or food-producing animal or substance intended to be or expected to be incorporated into food or feed, through all stages of production, processing and distribution."[48] Companies that adopt sustainable strategies for the production and distribution of food products provide a level of insurance of product quality. The ability to trace components throughout the

---

[43] www.epa.gov/sustainablemanufacturing/case-studies.htm (Accessed June 1, 2015).

[44] Chan, Hing Kai, Shizhao Yin, and Felix T. S. Chan (2010), "Implementing Just-in-Time Philosophy to Reverse Logistics Systems: A Review," *International Journal of Production Research* 48 (2), 6293–6313.

[45] Sheldon, Roger A. (2012), "Fundamentals of Green Chemistry: Efficiency in Reaction Design," *Chemical Society Reviews* 41 (4), 1437–1451.

[46] Acacio, Kevin, et al. (2011), "Business Study of Alternatives Uses for Brewers' Spent Grain (Semester Unknown) IPRO 340."

[47] Colicchia, Claudia, Marco Melacini, and Sara Perotti (2011), "Benchmarking Supply Chain Sustainability: Insights from a Field Study." *Benchmarking: An International Journal* 18 (5), 705–732.

[48] Canavari, Maurizio, Roberta Centonze, Martin Hingley, and Roberta Spadoni (2010), "Traceability as Part of Competitive Strategy in the Fruit Supply Chain," *British Food Journal* 112 (2), 171–186.

distribution process is not limited to food as the automotive and computing industries have also adopted forms of traceability.

ECOLOGICAL BENEFITS DERIVED FROM SUSTAINABLE MARKETING

The obvious benefactor of sustainable marketing is the ecological environment. Appendix 1 of this book characterizes current conditions and trends in climate change, air, water, soil conservation, and biodiversity. Sustainable marketing can have an influence on climate change in several substantial ways. Fossil fuel consumption is a major source of greenhouse gases associated with *climate change*. Two leading sources of climate change are the burning of coal for electricity and gasoline burned for automobile transportation. Sustainable marketing initiatives focused on product development strategies reduce the need to rely on these forms of energy. For example, new appliances are designed with fuel efficiencies that markedly reduce energy consumption.

The consumer must incorporate concern for the environment with multiple other considerations. For example, potential consumers of the Chevrolet Volt must reconcile zero fossil fuel consumption with the price differential for this car versus less expensive cars that produce more carbon dioxide. Sustainable marketing initiatives contribute to the environment by incorporating sustainable marketing strategies into superior value propositions for consumers.

Sustainable marketing reduces *air pollution* in multiple ways. For example, New York Mayor Bloomberg called for one-third of the city's taxi fleet to be electric vehicles by 2020. These autos will reduce New York City carbon dioxide emissions by 55,000 tons of CO_2 and decrease total CO_2 emissions from taxis by 18 percent.[49] Provided the energy comes from renewable sources, this efficiency means fewer emissions and lower air pollution. Similarly, agricultural run-off of fertilizer is a significant source of *water pollution*, but farming methods that eliminate inorganic fertilization reduce the amount of excess nutrients contaminating groundwater.[50]

Soil degradation is a rising concern due in part to contaminants discarded in personal technological components. The need for remediation of pollution without removing soil is an increasingly important issue in industry.[51]

A related consequence of environmental change is the number of *endangered species*. Current rates of extinction are estimated to be about 1000 times the likely background rate of extinction.[52] Their numbers increase every year due to deforestation, development, and climate change. Efforts to develop and consume environmentally friendly products, however, offer the potential to reduce the number of species on the endangered list.

---

[49] www.nyc.gov/html/tlc/downloads/pdf/electric_taxi_task_force_report_20131231 .pdf (February 15, 2015).

[50] Schoumans, O. F., et al. (2014), "Mitigation Options to Reduce Phosphorus Losses from the Agricultural Sector and Improve Surface Water Quality: A Review," *Science of the Total Environment* 468, 1255–1266.

[51] Liu, Jun, et al. (2015), "Ecological Effects of Combined Pollution Associated with E-Waste Recycling on the Composition and Diversity of Soil Microbial Communities," *Environmental Science and Technology* 49 (11), 6438–6447.

[52] Pimm, S. L., et al. (2014), "The Biodiversity of Species and Their Rates of Extinction, Distribution, and Protection," *Science* 344 (6187), 1246752.1–1246572.10.

HOW THIS TEXT IS ORGANIZED TO HELP UNDERSTAND SUSTAINABLE MARKETING

The goal of this text is to drive marketing decision making toward action that is sensitive to the ecological, social, and economic outcomes associated with triple bottom-line performance. Our general model of the context surrounding marketing action is provided in Figure 1-3. Marketing action is at the core of this model, and it is surrounded by environmental considerations, industrial activity, and marketing strategy. We define *marketing action* as any behavior associated with the procurement, purchasing, sales, consumption, and post-consumption of product offerings. Note that all this marketing action reflects situations in which there is some sort of exchange between two parties. The purchase of a cup of coffee in a reusable thermos, for instance, involves the exchange of currency for a beverage. Both entities that are involved in exchange activity are driven by the desire to increase value. The value of an exchange can be expressed in terms of the three related outcomes. To varying degrees, exchange activity provides economic, social, and environmental value. The coffee consumer, for example, may identify economic and environmental value from purchasing coffee in a reusable container, whereas the ambiance and service offered by the restaurant employees may yield social value to the consumer. It is not only meaningful to consider the triple bottom line of the consumer, but it is increasingly essential for companies to recognize that they must pay attention to economic, social, and environmental value of their product offerings.[53]

The definition of marketing action is broadly defined to include all action associated with sourcing environmentally sensitive products as well as the activity endemic to using and discarding products. Thus, this definition encompasses all action associated with the supply chain from the procurement of raw materials to the post-consumption treatment of products that have outlived their utility. For example, marketing action includes Pepsi's efforts to incorporate clean water into the syrups it sells to local bottlers in India. It also incorporates all the effort to make this product available for sale in the country, and it further includes all efforts to reuse or recycle the packaging of the product.

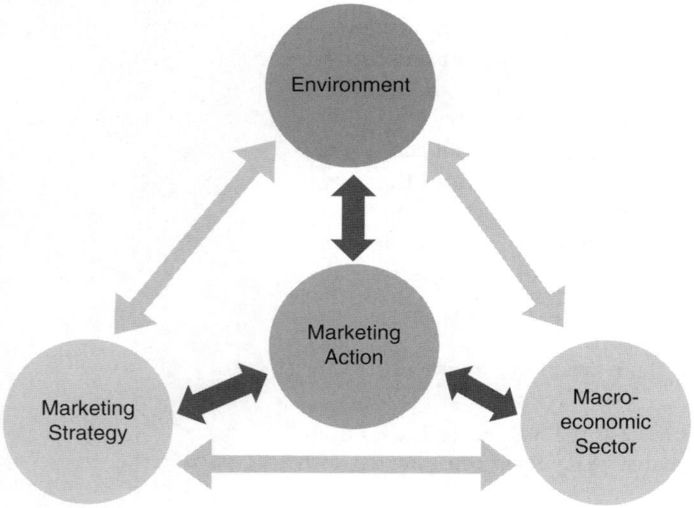

Importantly, the marketing action undertaken in a supply chain is influenced by and influences three factors. First, the action undertaken by individuals is influenced by the environment. The environment refers to physical and social context that provide the potential for marketing activity to occur. In the

FIGURE 1-3

Factors surrounding marketing action.

[53] Peters, Glen (1999), *Waltzing with the Raptors*, New York: John Wiley. Elkington, John (1998), *Cannibals with Forks*, Gabriola Island, BC: New Society Publishers.

remainder of Part I, we examine the relationship between corporate strategy and the environment. Chapter 2 provides a framework for incorporating sustainable into marketing planning and strategy. In Chapter 3, we examine the relationship between sustainable marketing and corporate social responsibility.

In Part II, we examine facets of marketing strategy designed to promote sustainability. The central factor in the pursuit of sustainability is the value that market offerings provide to consumers. Sustainable value emerges from analysis of the economic, relational, and ecological returns sought in a market. Consequently, each chapter in our discussion of sustainable promotion and value enhancement focuses on strategies that generate value. Chapter 4 provides a perspective on the processes by which consumers understand and recognize sustainable value. In Chapter 5, we outline specific strategies designed to influence action throughout the consumption process. Chapter 6 outlines a process for analyzing target markets. Promotional efforts by which firms communicate value are examined in Chapter 7. Chapter 8 illustrates how firms signal value via brands and labeling.

In Part III, we focus on the firm's effort to provide value. Chapter 9 provides an overview of the mechanisms by which the firm proclaims value via its pricing strategy. The set of processes by which the firm produces value are addressed in the analysis of supply cycles in Chapter 10 whereas the central role of retailing is addressed in Chapter 11. In Chapter 12, we explore the pursuit of value via innovation. The marketing of services is examined in Chapter 13.

In Part IV, we address procedures by which firms monitor and report the pursuit of value. Chapter 14 addresses sustainability reporting and the Global Reporting Initiative (GRI).

In the appendices, we examine the macroeconomic issues related to energy consumption. Appendix 1 examines influences of consumption on the ecological environment, and Appendix 2 addresses legal and administrative regulations designed to influence sustainable consumption. Across the globe, energy consumption and greenhouse gas emissions are associated with four industrial contexts: manufacturing, households, services, and transportation (See Figure 1-4). Consequently, Appendices A3–A6 address the major sources and uses of energy for each of these industrial contexts. Appendix A7 provides a brief overview of ISO14000.

FIGURE 1-4

Global total final energy consumption by sector in 2014.[54]

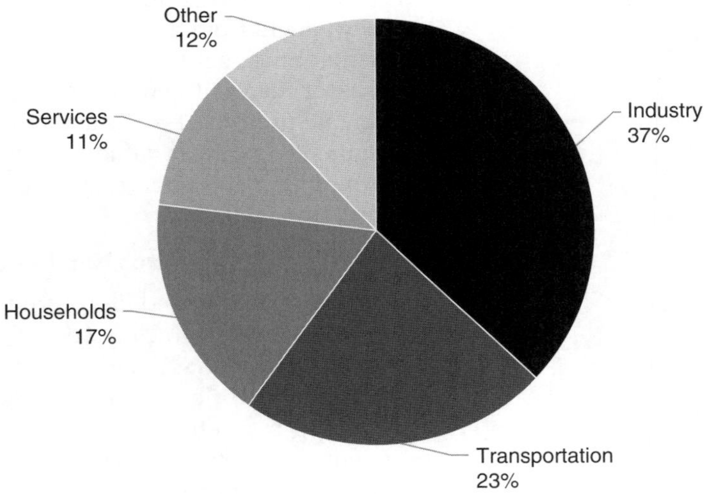

Other 12%
Services 11%
Households 17%
Industry 37%
Transportation 23%

---

[54] International Energy Agency (2016), *Key World Energy Trends—International Energy Agency*, Paris: International Energy Agency.

SUMMARY

Introduction to Sustainable Marketing

The purpose of this chapter has been to introduce the study of sustainable marketing. We defined sustainable marketing as the study of all efforts to consume, produce, distribute, promote, package, and reclaim products in a manner that is sensitive or responsive to ecological concerns. We described an incremental process by which firms evolve in their efforts to pursue sustainable marketing, and we subsequently defined sustainability as development that meets the needs of the present without compromising the ability of future generations to meet their own needs. Firms pursue sustainability via a triple bottom-line perspective focused on achieving economic, relational, and ecological outcomes.

Adopting a Sustainable Approach to Marketing

Adopting a sustainable approach requires that one adopt a strategy that focuses on securing the ecological, social, and economical returns associated with triple bottom-line performance. Sustainable marketing is approached when the firm adopts an orientation that seeks to examine all efforts to consume, produce, distribute, promote, package, and reclaim products in a manner to achieve ecological, economic, and social objectives.

Consumer Benefits of Sustainable Marketing

Consumers benefit in several important ways through sustainable marketing. They benefit from the knowledge that they are doing their part to reduce climate change. Sustainable marketing also provides consumers with the opportunity to be associated with environmentally friendly products and organizations. Sustainable products are more likely to succeed when the environmental benefits augment consumer value assessments. Emerging economies have potential to curb hunger and poverty by engaging in sustainable marketing.

Corporate Benefits that Accrue from Sustainable Marketing

In addition to the need for consumers and government to understand sustainable marketing, we characterized multiple benefits that accrue to firms that employ sustainably oriented marketing strategies. Corporate initiatives that emphasize a sustainable orientation to markets increase the likelihood of employing and retaining marketing talent. Sustainable marketing also enables companies to redefine markets, enhance the benefits that products offer to consumers, and differentiate their products. Production processes and supply chains also can enjoy heightened efficiency from sustainable production and distribution strategies.

Ecological Benefits Derived from Sustainable Marketing

Sustainable marketing can have an influence on climate change in several substantial ways. Sustainable marketing initiatives in product development reduce the amount of greenhouse gases produced by the firm. Sustainability reduces air and pollution, and it can help reduce the number of endangered plant and animal species.

How This Text Is Organized to Help Understand Sustainable Marketing

This book seeks to outline the relationship among marketing strategy, marketing action, macroeconomic sectors, and the environment. In Part I, we examine the relationship between corporate strategy and the environment. Part II examines facets of marketing strategy designed to promote sustainability, whereas Part III focuses on the firm's effort to provide value. The final section of the book examines procedures by which firms monitor and report the pursuit of value.

KEY TERMS

marketing
sustainable marketing

sustainable marketing
management

sustainability
triple bottom line

DISCUSSION QUESTIONS

1. What is the difference between green marketing and sustainable marketing?
2. Is sustainable marketing something done solely by corporations, or can anyone engage in sustainable marketing?
3. Think about a local grocery store operating in your community. To what extent do they consume, produce, distribute, promote, package, and reclaim products in a manner that is sensitive or responsive to ecological, economic, and social concerns?
4. An entrepreneur claims not to focus on sustainability because attention to such matters results in poorer financial performance. How might one address such a statement?
5. Provide some examples of how consumers might act in a sustainable manner that meets the needs of the present without compromising the ability of future generations to meet their needs. How does this perspective influence how people shop, consume, and dispose of the things they buy?
6. Provide examples of companies that have acted in a sustainable manner whereby they met the needs of the present without compromising the ability of future generations?
7. How might individuals and companies based in emerging economies benefit from the study of sustainable marketing?
8. If sustainable marketing draws attention to the way things are consumed, then how is the study of sustainable marketing relevant to production and supply chains?
9. Why is sustainable marketing relevant to supply chain managers?
10. Since everyone cares about the environment, shouldn't every marketing campaign focus on sustainability?

2

Sustainability-Based Strategic Planning

In this chapter you will learn about:

Planning for Sustainable Marketing

Firms that Need to Incorporate Sustainability-Based Strategic Planning

Incorporating a Sustainability Perspective into the Vision of the Firm

Incorporating a Sustainability Perspective into Mission of the Firm

Integrating Sustainability into Objectives, Strategy, and Marketing Tactics

PLANNING FOR SUSTAINABLE MARKETING

Timberland Inc.

On January 12, 2010, Haiti was struck with one of the world's deadliest disasters. This terrifying 7.0 magnitude earthquake shook the nation for 35 seconds. The catastrophe killed more than 316,000 people and left more than 1.5 million people homeless.[1] This earthquake permanently changed the social, political, and economic conditions faced by this island country.

A notable part of Timberland's response to this disaster is the commitment to plant 5 million trees in Haiti over a five-year period.[2] Begun in 2011, this effort enabled inhabitants to begin rebuilding their homes and lives. The tree planting project helped the firm offset its ecological impact, but by working in markets where they both buy and sell goods, the project offered value to suppliers and customers. Timberland has been making shoes in the Dominican Republic, Haiti's neighbor on the island of Hispaniola, for over 30 years. Timberland executives recognized a responsibility to give back to the community. In addition, they recognized that consumers are likely to choose companies that share their values over firms that do not.[3]

The decision to engage in this tree planting initiative is part of Timberland's long-standing commitment to the environment. The corporate strategy is based on a sustainability perspective that permeates everything it does. On a corporate level, the company has a commitment to corporate social responsibility that focuses on four themes. First, the company seeks to protect the outdoors. The firm approaches this goal by reducing its greenhouse gas inventories, purchasing renewable energy where possible, and generating its own renewable energy where clean energy is not available.

The second sustainability theme of the firm is to innovate responsibly. The firm pursues innovations that require fewer chemicals, leather, and raw materials. Timberland is striving to create lower cost products that are not only less harmful to the environment but can also become revenue generating products after the productive life of the shoe.[4]

The third theme of the Timberland's sustainability mission focuses on improving the lives of workers. Since it realizes the finished Timberland product is the result of efforts throughout the supply cycle, it monitors the entire supply chain for human rights issues and sustainable business practices. When the company began assessing the energy content of its footwear, they were surprised to find that more than half of the energy used in making a pair of shoes comes from processing and producing the raw materials. The second biggest energy drain is at the retail level, followed by factory operations. Transportation, the factor the company believed was the biggest producer of greenhouse gases in

[1] Schuller, Mark, and Pablo Morales (2012), *Tectonic Shifts: Haiti Since the Earthquake*. Sterling, VA: Kumarian Press, 2012.

[2] www.forbes.com/sites/eco-nomics/2013/01/30/timberland-helps-plant-2-2-million-trees-in-haiti/ pdf (Accessed June 8, 2015).

[3] www.forbes.com/sites/francisvorhies/2013/02/21/why-is-timberland-planting-trees-in-haiti/ (Accessed June 8, 2015).

[4] Frazier, Mya (2007), "Timberland 'Walks the Walk,'" Advertising Age, 78 (24), 8.

FIGURE 2-1
Timberland ad for Mountain
Athletics footwear.[5]

the supply cycle, turned out to be the lowest contributor to energy usage and carbon emissions.

The fourth sustainability theme that permeates the organization concerns the environment and the surroundings of the community workplaces in which the company operates. Timberland sponsors service events in which it works to strengthen communities by improving green spaces and access to the outdoors. Furthermore, it encourages employees to engage in community service in their communities.

The Timberland example illustrates how a firm can take a sustainability strategy and incorporate it throughout its marketing strategy. To make this transition from the plan to its implementation, every organization needs a roadmap outlining the direction the firm is pursuing. As organizations grow, each employee should have an understanding of the markets the firm serves, the customers within each market, and the product offerings designed to meet these consumers' needs. Strategic market planning is the process that outlines the manner in which a business unit competes in the markets it serves.[6] Strategic market decisions are based on assessments of product markets and provide the basis for competitive advantage in the market (see Figure 2-1). The plan developed through this process provides a blueprint for the development of the skills and resources of a business unit and specifies the results to be expected.

The planning process involves anticipating future conditions and establishing strategies to achieve objectives. The planning process demands that the firm establish a vision and a mission that are supported by strategy and culture.[7] Interestingly, the planning process necessarily involves relating the marketing

[5] design.northeaststandard.com/uploaded_images/gofast- 743676.jpg.

[6] www.marketingpower.com/_layouts/Dictionary.aspx.

[7] Lipton, Mark (1996), "Demystifying the Development of an Organizational Vision," *MIT Sloan Management Review* 37 (4), 83–92.

objectives of the firm to the environment.[8] Although strategists have long recognized the interaction between the firm and its environment, much of the research and planning process focuses on the influence of the environment on corporate decision making. Firms that incorporate sustainability concerns into strategic planning recognize that the activities and programs developed by the firm simultaneously influence the environment. For example, Toyota recognizes that gasoline prices represent a facet of the environment that influences consumer purchase decisions. In addition, Toyota also considers the influences of automobile production and operations on the environment.

A sustainability-based planning process must explicitly examine the interaction of the ecological, economic, and social context with the corporate strategy. We, therefore, define *sustainability-based planning* as the process of creating and maintaining a fit between the ecological, economic, and social environment and the objectives and resources of the firm. "Fit" refers to the effort to understand how these environments both influence *and are influenced* by marketers. In Chapter 3, we will examine the interaction of firms, consumers, and individuals with the environment. The planning process begins with an in-depth analysis of the internal and external environment of the firm. Based on this situational analysis, the firm establishes its mission, objectives, strategy, implementation, and evaluation.

As outlined in Figure 2-2, the planning process is a dynamic process that relies heavily on interaction with the environment. This environment is not only ecological, but it also includes the social, economic, competitive, political, and legal setting of the firm.

Strategic marketing planning should accompany planning throughout all functional areas of the firm such as financial planning, production, and research and development.[9] The output of the planning process is a *marketing plan* that provides an analysis of the current marketing situation, opportunities and threats analysis, marketing objectives, marketing strategy, action programs, and projected income statements.[10] This plan serves as the blueprint outlining how the organization will achieve its objectives. In addition, the plan informs employees regarding their functions and roles in the implementation of the plan. The plan also provides insight into the allocation of resources and the specification of tasks, responsibilities, and the timing of marketing action.[11]

The mission statement should be formulated and articulated by upper management

FIGURE 2-2

The strategic planning process

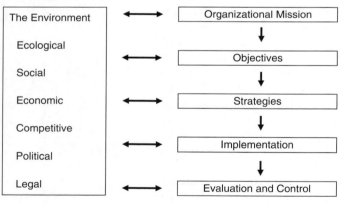

---

[8] Thompson, J.D., and W.J. McEwen (1958), "Organizational Goals and Environment: Goal-setting as an Interactive Process," *Administrative Science Quarterly* 23, 23–31.

[9] Daniel, Carroll (1979), "How to Make Marketing Plans More Effective," *Management Review*, 68 (10), 60–61.

[10] www.marketingpower.com/_layouts/Dictionary.aspx.

[11] Greenley, Gordon E. (1989), "An Understanding of Marketing Strategy," *European Journal of Marketing*, 23 (8), 45–58.

within the firm. The process of developing this statement and strategy demands buy-in by top management. In addition, articulation of the plan by senior executives signals to employees, customers, and stakeholders that the planning process is of central importance to the activity of the firm.

FIRMS THAT NEED TO INCORPORATE SUSTAINABILITY-BASED STRATEGIC PLANNING

Organizations increasingly recognize that sustainability should be incorporated into their strategic planning. Several conditions increase the need for firms to address sustainability in their planning efforts. The ecological reputation, human capital, brand exposure, market power, degree of industry regulation, and dependency on natural resources each can influence the need for a firm to attain to sustainability.[12]

Companies with established ecological reputations.
Companies that have been singled out as standard bearers for sustainable marketing expect significant scrutiny and publicity from environmentally questionable activity. For example, the Body Shop has a stellar record as a green-oriented firm, but it can anticipate substantial criticism if it fails to keep this orientation in all markets they serve. By contrast, companies such as Exxon that have been singled-out for nefarious acts against the environment must address sustainable marketing issues if they seek to change their reputations.

Companies highly dependent on scarce human capital.
Services refer to intangible activities that organizations provide to consumers. In the United States, services account for over 75 percent of the activity in the economy.[13] The intangible services are provided through human capital, and firms that operate in this sector of the economy must increasingly incorporate sustainable marketing into their product offerings. In Las Vegas, for example, dentists provide services to hotel and casino employees via mobile vans situated near the entertainment district.[14] The proximity of these facilities reduces fuel emissions by eliminating the need for employees to travel to the dentist. Consumer dental hygiene and worker productivity benefit from this ecoconscious service design.

Companies with high brand exposure.
In their annual reports on the best 100 global brands, Interbrand provides an annual estimate of the earnings attributable to the brand.[15] As brands increase in appeal, they simultaneously increase the amount of scrutiny they incur. In contrast to reports of brands that have little brand equity, stories that indicate the activity of brands with high brand equity are likely to be viewed as more newsworthy. For example, newspaper articles critical of the processing of chickens will be

---

[12] Esty, Daniel C., and Andrew S. Winston (2006), *Green to Gold*, New Haven, CT: Yale University Press.

[13] data.worldbank.org/indicator/NV.SRV.TETC.ZS (Accessed June 4, 2015).

[14] Flanigan, James (2006), "Parking-Lot Dentistry Is Finding Its Niche," *The New York Times*, August 17, 1.

[15] www.bestglobalbrands.com/2014/ranking/ (Accessed June 5, 2015).

of greater interest to the public when they refer to KFC rather than any other brand in this industry. Firms with strong brand equity must address sustainable marketing to limit the scrutiny experienced by the brands.

Companies with low market power.

Companies that rely on other firms for substantial amounts of output must attend to the sustainable-marketing constraints leveled by the supplier. General Mills, one of the largest companies in the packaged grocery business, recently modified the shape of Hamburger Helper on the request of Wal-Mart.[16] The retailer pointed out that the once-curly noodles in Hamburger Helper should be straight. This ecologically driven product modification reduced thousands of pounds of packaging and lowered the product's price. As buyers become more attuned to sustainability, suppliers reliant on these suppliers must also increase their understanding of sustainable marketing.

Companies operating in highly regulated industries.

Government implements regulations to control the manner in which an industry operates. Industries that employ hazardous materials (e.g., chemical industry) are subject to substantial regulations, and the increasing interest in sustainable marketing fuels the need for industrial standards. Similarly, utilities, automobile producers, and airlines must address multiple stringent regulations. The electronics industries face increased scrutiny in the European Union due to "takeback laws" that require manufacturers to handle product disposal after consumer usage. In each of these industries, firms that take a proactive stance toward environmental regulation can implement regulations before adherence is required.[17]

Companies dependent on natural resources.

Industries that are highly reliant on natural resources recognize the absolute limits in the availability of natural resources. These industries include oil, fish, and forestry. Natural production limits demand that firms understand economic marketing activity that can conserves scarce resources.

....

INCORPORATING A SUSTAINABILITY PERSPECTIVE INTO THE VISION OF THE FIRM

The long-term viability of the firm is dependent on leadership's ability to create a vision and craft a mission. The planning process begins with consideration of a vision and a mission that are pursued via strategy and corporate culture. These interconnected terms address essential questions about the nature of the firm and its potential for success.

The *vision* identifies what the firm seeks to become. Firms that establish a long-term vision generally outperform those who do not.[18] The vision promotes

---

[16] Neff, Jack (2007), "Eco Wal-Mart Costs Marketers Green," *Advertising Age*, 78 (39), 3,42.

[17] López-Gamero, María D., José F. Molina-Azorín, and Enrique Claver-Cortés (2010), "The Potential of Environmental Regulation to Change Managerial Perception, Environmental Management, Competitiveness and Financial Performance," *Journal of Cleaner Production* 18 (10), 963–974.

[18] Lipton, Mark (1996), "Demystifying the development of an organizational vision," *MIT Sloan Management Review* 37 (4), 83–92.

the need for change and provides the basis for the mission, strategic plan, and corporate culture.

The firm activates its vision via a vision statement. This statement is typically a one-sentence description of the firm's aspirations.[19] For example, IKEA's vision is to "To create a better everyday life for the many people.[20]" The vision enables the firm to take a long-term perspective and set a broad direction for the firm. Importantly, as many managers as possible should be involved in the development of the vision. Participation in the process enhances managerial understanding of the firm's goals and enables these leaders to commit to the vision. An articulated vision helps keep decision making in context and enables individuals to focus on what is important to the firm.[21] In the process, these individuals identify and eliminate a myriad of unproductive activities.

In short, the vision is a compass that provides direction for the firm. It serves as an organizing mechanism that enables managers to align resources and establish priorities. The declaration of the vision via the vision statement provides a public document that outlines the firm's commitments.

INCORPORATING A SUSTAINABILITY MISSION INTO THE MISSION OF THE FIRM

While the vision addresses what the firm hopes to become, the mission addresses why the firm exists. The *mission statement* describes a firm's fundamental, unique purpose indicating what the organization intends to accomplish, the markets in which it operates, and the philosophical premises that guide action.[22] The mission statement is an inspirational tool that provides insight into the company's character.[23] For example, Figure 2-3 provides the mission statement and values of Dole Foods. Importantly, the mission of the firm must consider the organization's history, its distinctive competencies, and its environment.[24]

The Dole Foods passage encompasses many traits associated with effective mission statements.[25] The mission is clearly articulated, relevant, and enduring. In establishing the mission, senior management provides a sense of direction to the organization. Employees and business partners are inspired to pursue specific action because the action is consistent with the message outlined in the mission.

---

[19] David, Fred, and Forest R. David (2016), *Strategic Management: A Competitive Advantage Approach, Concepts and Cases*.

[20] www.ikea.com/ms/en_CA/the_ikea_story/working_at_ikea/our_vision.html (September 29, 2016).

[21] Lipton, Mark (1996), "Demystifying the development of an organizational vision," *MIT Sloan Management Review* 37 (4), 83–92.

[22] Ireland, Duane, and Michael A. Hitt (1992), "*Mission Statements*: Importance, Challenge, and Recommendations for Development," *Business Horizons*, 35 (3), 34–42.

[23] Amabile, Theresa M., and Steve J. Kramer (2012), "To give your employees meaning, start with mission," Harvard Business Review 9 (2012).

[24] Kotler, Philip (1994), *Marketing Management: Analysis, Planning, Implementation, and Control*, Englewood Cliffs, NJ: Prentice-Hall.

[25] Stone, Romuald A. (1996), "Mission Statements Revisited," *SAM Advanced Management Journal* 61(1), 31–37.

FIGURE 2-3
Dole Food mission statement

> Dole Food Company, Inc. believes that in order to perpetuate sustainability, it is of the utmost importance to treat our people, resources, environment and community as our most precious assets. Business can be an important actor and agent for change through creating products and services that society values, establishing primary jobs, and efficiently using resources. As a company dedicated to making the world a better place to live both today and in the future, Dole's mission is to:
>
> Provide the world with healthy and nutritious foods.
> Offer employees competitive wages, ample benefits, and a safe work environment. Honor our employees' rights.
> Enhance and empower our communities to advance and prosper.
> Protect our natural resources and actively seeking ways to reduce our environmental impact.

Note that the contrary is also true—constituents are unlikely to pursue activities that do not reflect the values expressed in the mission statement.

Although the mission statement should underscore the firm's commitment to sustainability, it is critical for this statement to be consistent with the level of sustainability currently pursued by the firm. For example, in 2000 BP developed a new symbol along with a media message that claimed the firm was moving "beyond petroleum.[26]" The firm outlined a strategy that identified efforts to pursue energy sources other than fossil fuels, but oil and gas accounted for approximately 98 percent of the firm's revenue. *Greenwashing* refers to situations in which there is a significant gap between the expressed and genuine commitments to sustainability. Firms that market energy are accused of greenwashing when their investments in renewable energy sources are small compared with the money that goes on their oil and gas divisions.[27] Chapter 8 identifies mechanisms employed to reduce greenwashing.

Purposes of the Mission

Mission statements serve many purposes for a firm. These statements project a public image, motivate staff, assert leadership, and enable the firm to manage volatility.[28] Consider how firms address each of these issues in their design of sustainable marketing strategies.

Public Image. The proclamation of a mission is a means by which companies project how they would like to be seen by their stakeholders and the general public. For example, Adidas calls attention to sustainability efforts via the following:

> "We are a global organisation that is socially and environmentally responsible, that embraces creativity and diversity and is financially rewarding for our employees and shareholders.[29]"

---

[26] Esty, Daniel C., and Andrew S. Winston (2006), *Green to Gold*, New Haven, CT: Yale University Press.

[27] *Economist* (2005), "Consider the Alternatives," April 30, 375 (8424), 21–24.

[28] Klemm, Mary, Stuart Sanderson, and George Luffman (1991), "Mission Statements: Selling Corporate Values to Employees," *Long Range Planning*, 24 (3), 73–78.Verma, Harsh V. (2009), "Mission Statements-A Study of Intent and Influence," *Journal of Services Research*, 9(2), 153–172.

[29] www.adidas-group.com/en/group/profile/ (September 9, 2016).

The role of stakeholders is addressed in greater detail in Chapter 3. Financial markets are the most important stakeholders during the development of the mission.[30] In some cases, however, firms view the mission statement as a way to attract new employees. For example, the Tata Strive division of the Tata Group states their mission as:

> The mission of Tata Strive is to enable the youth of India to be skilled for employment, entrepreneurship and social sector impact.[31]

Motivate Staff. The mission statement enables the firm to garner greater support from its employees in a number of ways.[32] First, the statement enables companies to communicate managerial philosophies and intentions to staff. Thus, the Patagonia mission statement reads:

> Build the best product, cause no unnecessary harm, use business to inspire and implement solutions to the environmental crisis.[33]

Staff are also motivated by the firm's efforts to identify its beliefs about its distinctive competencies. For example, Bayer's mission statement underscores the role of innovation via the following:

> Bayer is a world-class innovation company with a 150-year history. Our scientific successes are intended to help improve people's lives. At the same time, our innovations form the basis for sustainable and profitable business[34] activity and are the key to maintaining or achieving leadership positions in all of our markets.

The mission statement can also incorporate expectations concerning standards of behavior expected from employees. For example, the renewable energy firm SMA sustainable mission statement calls for the following:

> We want to firmly anchor sustainability concepts into our daily working lives this turning our vision into reality. To do this, we have to develop objectives, strategies and key figures for all fields of activity relevant to sustainability and integrate them into an overall concept. These will be examined regularly and disclosed in a sustainability report. Within this context, all decisions made must take into consideration economic, environmental and social aspects.[35]

Statements that elucidate why the firm is in business and what it is trying to achieve raise the level of commitment to the firm. When employees understand

---

[30] Klemm, Mary, Stuart Sanderson, and George Luffman (1991), "Mission Statements: Selling Corporate Values to Employees," *Long Range Planning*, 24 (3), 73–78.

[31] www.tata.com/article/inside/tata-strive-skill-development-programme (September 9, 2016).

[32] Klemm, Mary, Stuart Sanderson, and George Luffman (1991), "Mission Statements: Selling Corporate Values to Employees," *Long Range Planning*, 24 (3), 73–78.

[33] www.patagonia.com/company-info.html (September 9, 2016).

[34] www.bayer.com/en/mission---values.aspx (September 9, 2016).

[35] www.sma-america.com/fileadmin/content/global/Company/Media/Leitbild_Nach-haltigkeit_EN.pdf (October 4, 2016).

the underlying logic derived from the firm's strategy, they are inclined to work toward achieving objectives.[36] In addition, as employees identify with the shared goals within the firm, there is less need for monitoring and control.[37]

Assertion of Leadership. The mission statement serves as an empowering tool that enables executives to oversee and direct operations.[38] It serves as a way for management to assert its legitimate authority. The mission also defines the scope of the business and provides direction that transcends departmental, departmental, individual, or transitory needs. For example, Toyota's philosophy is reflected in the following:

> Toyota Striving to create outstanding earth-friendly products for sustainable growth, Toyota honors the laws, customs and cultures of all nations.[39]

Documenting the objectives of the firm provides an opportunity for management to take the firm in a new direction. Mission statements can generate new ideas and serve as the basis for challenging old ideas. Interface Carpet illustrates this perspective via their mission:

> What drives us? A positive vision of the future and the determination to make it come true. The moral courage to do what is right, despite all obstacles. An abiding commitment to show that sustainability is better for business. We believe that change starts with us and is transforming Interface from a plunderer of the earth to an agent of its restoration. Through this process of redesigning ourselves, we hope to be a catalyst for the redesign of global industry.[40]

By outlining the nature of the business and its objectives, leaders are equipped with some direction concerning the selection and recruitment of personnel. For example, the Fairmont Hotel mission states:

> We know that even the best locations and offerings would be meaningless without outstanding guest service. Our skilled and motivated staff is equipped with the tools and the mindset to naturally deliver on this promise. Within a Fairmont experience, every guest is offered a warm welcome and is made to feel special, valued and appreciated.[41]

---

[36] Frazier, Gary L., and John O. Summers (1984), "Interfirm Influence Strategies and Their Application within Distribution Channels," *Journal of Marketing* 48 (3), 43–55.

[37] Gençtürk, Esra F., and Preet S. Aulakh (2007), "Norms- and Control-based Governance of International Manufacturer-Distributor Relational Exchanges," *Journal of International Marketing* 15 (1), 92–126. Paswan, Audhesh K., and Joyce A. Young (1999), "An Exploratory Examination of the Relationship between Channel Support Mechanisms and Relational Norms in an International Context," *Journal of Business & Industrial Marketing* 14 (5/6), 445–455.

[38] Klemm, Mary, Stuart Sanderson, and George Luffman (1991), "Mission Statements: Selling Corporate Values to Employees," *Long Range Planning*, 24 (3), 73–78.

[39] www.toyota-global.com/investors/ (September 9, 2016).

[40] www.interface.com/US/en-US/about/mission (September 9, 2016).

[41] www.fairmont.com/about-us/ourphilosophy/ (September 9, 2016).

This proclamation underscores the type of experiences customers can anticipate and the level of service expected of its employees.

Manage Volatility. When properly designed, the mission can provide direction when faced with uncertainty.[42] Leaders can refocus the organization during a crisis. When management has a clear focus concerning the business it is in and the objectives it hopes to achieve, it can retain focus in turbulent or unpredictable markets.[43] Understanding of the firm's mission provides a basis for the allocation of resources.

Mission Development Questions

The development of the mission requires substantial reflection during which time leaders identify contingencies that influence its ability to succeed. Managers examine the following questions during development:

1. **What business are we in?** It is instrumental for firms to recognize the needs fulfilled by their product offerings and alternative ways that consumers can satisfy these needs.[44] For example, transportation has been transformed by the advent of ride-share programs such as Uber. These ride-share services offer ecological advantages by reducing the number of vehicles on the road.[45] Wyndham Hotels present its business via the following:

   "Wyndham Worldwide strives to become the widely-recognized service leader in the hospitality industry. We have a service-oriented culture in which each associate strives to be responsive, be respectful and deliver great experiences to our customers, guests, partners and communities as well as to each other."[46]

2. **What is our fundamental reason for being?** This question focuses on the essence of the mission by outlining why the firm exists. Responses to this question can be tailored to address triple bottom-line considerations. Corporate renewal and assessment of purpose benefits when firms augment financial objectives with social and ecological factors.

3. **What types of products or services do we provide?** Answers to this question enable firms to consider the needs met by their offerings and

---

[42] Klemm, Mary, Stuart Sanderson, and George Luffman (1991), "Mission Statements: Selling Corporate Values to Employees," *Long Range Planning*, 24 (3), 73–78.

[43] Baetz, Mark C., and Christopher K. Bart (1996), "Developing Mission Statements Which Work," *Long Range Planning*, 29 (4), 526–533.

[44] Levitt, Theodore (1960), "Marketing Myopia" *Harvard Business Review* 38 (4), 24–47.

[45] Burns, Lawrence D. (2013), "Sustainable Mobility: A Vision of Our Transport Future," *Nature* 497 (7448), 181–182.

[46] www.wyndhamworldwide.com/category/mission-culture (September 13, 2016).

[47] www.statista.com/statistics/274823/ibms-global-revenue-by-segment/ (September 13, 2016).

design products and services that meet these needs. For example, the global services segment of IBM's business has generated more revenue than any other business sector since 2010.[47] Continuous assessment of customer needs and corporate resources has enabled the firm to enhance its mix of products and services. Redefinition of its products and services enables IBM to augment triple bottom-line performance within the firm and among its customers.

4. **How do we define the customers we serve?** Careful analysis of the customers served is essential to development of the mission. Management should be able to identify the largest customers by sales volume but also be able to distinguish consumers based on the needs derived from the firm's product offerings. Chapter 6 offers an in-depth investigation of target markets.

5. **What unique value do we bring to customers?** *Sustainable competitive advantage* refers to the extent to which a firm's strategy cannot be easily duplicated. Note that the term "sustainable" does not necessarily refer to sustainability derived for a triple bottom-line orientation. The unique value accrues from assessing the way a firm competes through marketing tactics (e.g., pricing), the places where it competes, and the bases for competition[48]. As firms incorporate social and ecological concerns into planning, they are positioned to devise product offerings that uniquely provide triple bottom-line value to consumers[49].

6. **Who benefits from our efforts?** The firm examines its relationships with stakeholders and assesses the value that they derive from the corporation. The firm can use triple bottom-line logic to assess multiple facets of financial and nonfinancial performance. For example, the owners of fashion brands examine the social, ecological, and financial performance of their supply chains.[50]

7. **What do we need to survive?** In all cases, the firm must identify the critical resources necessary for its existence. It is imperative that the firm accurately projects how its action will lead to triple bottom-line performance. Moreover, the firm should recognize what is absolutely essential in each facet of performance. Sustainable practice is essential to the firm's survival because a strategy of targeted enduring action enables the firm to develop a competitive advantage.[51]

---

[48] Aaker, David A. (1989), "Managing Assets and Skills: The Key to a Sustainable Competitive Advantage," *California Management Review*, 31 (2), 91–106.

[49] Benn, Suzanne, Dexter Dunphy, and Andrew Griffiths (2014), *Organizational Change for Corporate Sustainability*. Routledge. Arseculeratne, Dinuk, and Rashad Yazdanifard (2014), "How Green Marketing Can Create a Sustainable Competitive Advantage for a Business," *International Business Research* 7 (1), 130–137.

[50] Ly, Ting Ting, Cornelis Baardemans, and Inês Bernardes (2015), "Improving Triple Bottom Line through Reverse Logistics: A Study of Fashion Companies Operating in Sweden," Working paper, Linnaeus University.

[51] Lloret, Antonio (2016), "Modeling Corporate Sustainability Strategy," *Journal of Business Research* 69 (2), 418–425.

Potential Components of the Mission

The critical review of the firm via the developmental questions equips the firm to develop the mission. Although the components of the mission vary based on the corporate profile and industry, mission statements may contain the following:[52]

1. Identification of the target customers and markets,
2. Specification of principle products and services,
3. Core technologies integral to the firm,
4. Commitments to triple bottom-line performance,
5. Specification of the geographic domain,
6. Core elements of the company's philosophy,
7. Identification of the firm's self-concept, and
8. Specification of the company's desired public image.

The firm augments the vision and the mission statement by stating the corporate strategy and culture necessary to approach its objectives.[53] The strategy is not presented in detail. Nevertheless, it should outline the firm's basic approach to achieving its mission and the competitive advantage that it brings to the market. The final component of the planning process is the recognition of corporate culture. Management describes a leadership and collaborative style designed to achieve objectives. In addition, the firm identifies values that are central to performance.

The firm that has taken the effort to craft a vision, mission, strategy, and corporate culture is groomed to implement sustainable programs that are welcomed by customers. For example, Proctor & Gamble (P&G) incorporates a sustainability perspective into its manufacturing and marketing strategy.[54] First, P&G has adopted a sustainability perspective focused on improving lives for years to come. Second, the firm has a product safety initiative designed to enhance the environmental quality of products, packaging, and operations across the globe. Third, P&G has implemented a commitment to the environment. Since detergents and other products that the firm manufactures have a significant influence on water and water treatment plants, P&G requires all ingredients to pass an environmental risk assessment before they can be integrated into products. These commitments to the environment flow from a corporate mission that emphasizes environmentalism and sustainability.[55]

[52] Rajasekar, James (2013), "A Comparative Analysis of Mission Statement Content and Readability," *Journal of Management Policy & Practice* 14 (6), 131–147. Pearce, John A., and Fred David (1987), "Corporate Mission Statements: The Bottom Line," *The Academy of Management Executive* 1 (2), 109–115.

[53] Lipton, Mark (1996), "Demystifying the Development of an Organizational Vision," *MIT Sloan Management Review* 37 (4), 83–92.

[54] www.pg.com/en_US/company/purpose_people/pvp.shtml (Accessed June 8, 2015).

[55] Procter and Gamble (2014), *P&G Sustainability Report*. www.pg.com/en_US/downloads/sustainability/reports/PG_2014_Sustainability_Report.pdf (Accessed June 8, 2015).

INTEGRATING SUSTAINABILITY INTO OBJECTIVES, STRATEGY, AND MARKETING TACTICS

If the mission statement incorporates a discussion of sustainability, there is a much greater likelihood that the objectives and strategy will be poised to consider the interaction of the firm with its environment. Figure 2-4 uses Timberland apparel to illustrate the planning process. The firm's mission is to equip people to make a difference in their world.[56] Timberland pursues this mission by creating outstanding products and by trying to make a difference in the communities where employees live and work. Importantly, the firm views volunteering in communities and designing ecologically friendly products as ways to reduce the company's influence on the environment.

Organizational objectives are time dependent[57] and emerge from the development of the mission statement. For Timberland, one objective is environmental stewardship whereby the company is committed to a 95 diversion rate for waste

FIGURE 2-4
The Timberland planning process

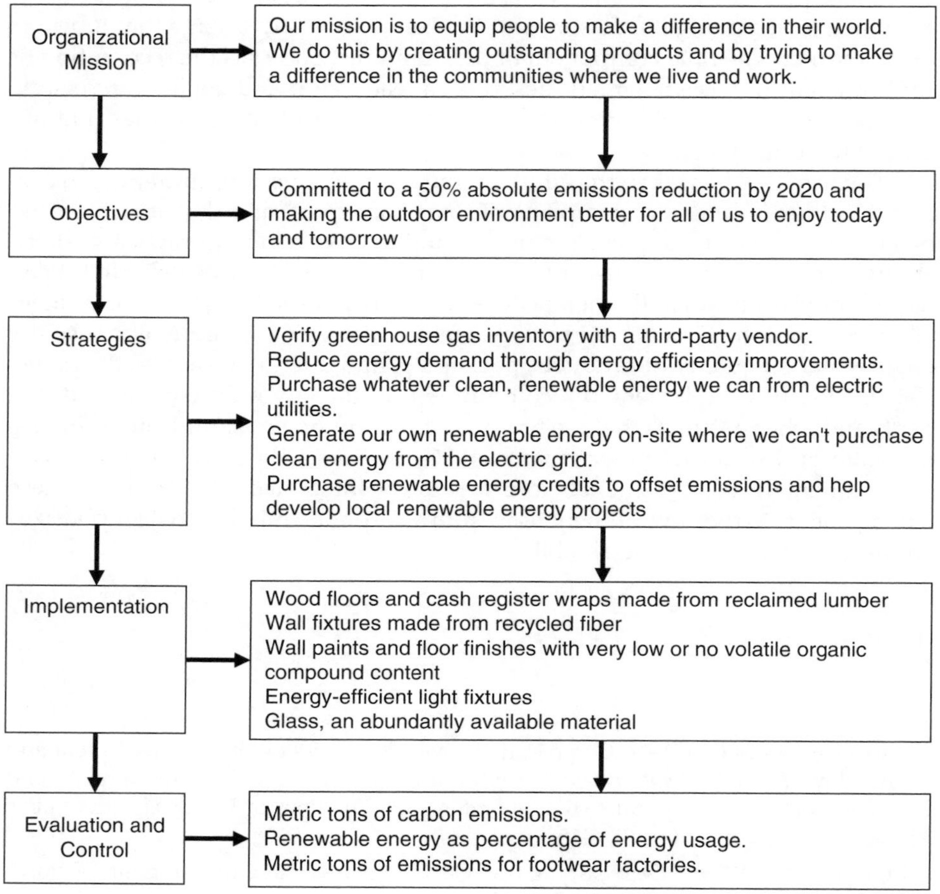

[56] www.timberlandonline.co.uk/en/about_timberland_our_story.html (accessed June 8, 2015).

[57] www.marketingpower.com/_layouts/Dictionary.aspx.

produced in its facilities by 2020.[58] This goal embodies three essential elements of objectives.[59] First, the objective precisely specifies the goals of the organization. If the objective is not precise and clear, employees will be less likely to achieve the desired outcome. Second, the objective is measurable, and in this case, it leads to exact mechanisms for assessing the pursuit of this objective. Objectives must be measurable if the firm is to assess the level of success in a meaningful way. Third, the objective must entail action commitments specifying the behaviors associated with the achieving the objective. If the relevant action is understood, management can covert the objective into specific action associated in the marketing plan and strategy.

Corporate strategy outlines the direction the firm will pursue within its chosen environment and guides the allocation of resources and effort.[60] For Timberland, the strategy emphasizes third-party verification of energy use, efficient operations, the use of clean renewable energy, and the purchase of energy credits to offset emissions.

Clearly articulated strategies based on measureable objectives enable management to develop specific implementation plans. The implementation process refers to the stage at which the firm directs specific effort to the realization of objectives. Although senior management establishes objectives and strategy, they are rarely involved in the implementation process. Thus, it is essential that management relay a message of sustainability throughout the strategic planning process.

Implementation includes determination of action plans and related tactics designed to enable the firm to realize objectives.[61] The action plan provides schedules and milestones, whereas the tactics refer to the specific activities that the firm will engage in to ensure that objectives are realized. For Timberland, some of these tactics include the types of fixtures installed at retail locations.

The strategic planning process concludes in the evaluation and control phase. At this point, management takes stock of the degree to which the firm has realized objectives. Importantly, the criteria that emerge from the plan are the factors incorporated into evaluation. These evaluative criteria should logically complement the mission and objectives. Again, if the mission and objectives do not incorporate sustainability, then the evaluation and control systems will not address these concerns. The commitment to sustainability must therefore accompany every phase of the strategic planning process.

The presentation of strategic planning process as a static step-by-step process facilitates presentation of the model. Nevertheless, the step-by-step process does not capture the manner by which planning occurs in many organizations. The multiple phases of this process are going on simultaneously. Senior management is re-evaluating the tactical plans while their employees are implementing specific facets of the plan.

---

[58] https://www.timberland.com/responsibility.html (April 23, 2017).

[59] Peter, J. Paul, and James H. Donnelly (2003), *A Preface to Marketing Management*, New York: McGraw Hill.

[60] www.marketingpower.com/_layouts/Dictionary.aspx (accessed June 8, 2015).

[61] Pinto, Jeffrey K., and John E. Prescott (1990), "Planning and Tactical Factors in the Project Implementation Process," *Journal of Management Studies*, 27 (3), 305–327.

A primary need for constant reassessment of strategic planning is the interaction with the environment. Entities in the firm ranging from CEO to field sales representative monitor changes in the environment and modify their behavior to accommodate this action. For example, as energy prices escalate, senior management must consider the costs of reimbursement to sales representatives while sales representatives likely re-assess their sales call schedules and routes. Because the environment is subject to change that has a significant influence on marketing activity, it is essential for the marketing organization to monitor the environment. Thus, marketers evaluate the ecological, competitive, economic, social, political, and legal environments.

SUMMARY

Sustainability-Based Strategic Planning

The purpose of this chapter has been to provide an overview sustainability-based strategic planning. We began by defining strategic market planning as the process that outlines the manner in which a business unit competes in the markets it serves.

Firms that Need to Incorporate Sustainability-based Strategic Planning

Companies increasingly recognize the need to incorporate sustainability into their strategic planning. The need to monitor sustainability issues is particularly important for firms with (good or bad) ecological reputations or firms who operate industries characterized by scarce human capital, high brand exposure, low market power, extensive regulation, and heavy dependence on natural resources.

Incorporating a Sustainability Perspective into the Vision of the Firm

The vision identifies what the firm seeks to become. Firms that establish a long-term vision generally outperform those who do not. The vision promotes the need for change and provides the basis for the mission, strategic plan, and corporate culture. It serves as an organizing mechanism that enables managers to align resources and establish priorities.

Incorporating a Sustainability Perspective into Mission of the Firm

The mission statement describes a firm's unique purpose, indicating what the organization intends to accomplish, the markets in which it operates, and the philosophical premises that guide action. If the firm is to have a strategy that meaningfully incorporates sustainability, the mission statement must incorporate sustainability.

Integrating Sustainability into Objectives, Strategy, and Marketing Tactics

Organizational objectives are results to be achieved by a specific time and emerge from the development of the mission statement. The objectives precisely specify the goals of the organization. If objectives, strategies, and tactic are measurable and specific with respect to sustainability goals, management are poised to achieve triple bottom line performance.

KEY TERMS

sustainability-based planning	vision statement	mission statement
marketing plan	mission	greenwashing
vision		

DISCUSSION QUESTIONS

1. Why would a firm such as Timberland elect to develop a sustainable strategy when it could effectively compete based on price?

2. How does the strategy of Timberland reflect an effort to achieve sustainability as defined in Chapter 1?

3. To what extent does the incorporation of a sustainability-based perspective into the mission statement change how the firm will operate and be viewed in the market?

4. What is difference between vision and mission? Why are both necessary to the firm?

5. Explain why multiple managers should be involved in the development of the vision?

6. In the development of strategy, firms must ask "what business are we in?" Provide an example of a firm that has redefined the business in which it operates. How has this reassessment affected its performance?

7. What is meant by the term "fit" as it is used in sustainable planning?

8. Describe a situation in which the general public has had an influence on a company's attitude toward sustainability. What events lead the public to become concerned about sustainability in this context?

9. How does the mission statement help to control the action undertaken by employees?

10. Why should a firm's planning process incorporate discussion of corporate culture?

3

Sustainability and Ethical Decision Making

INTRODUCTION

The wardrobe of most consumers contains many products made from cotton. Cotton represents almost half of the fiber used to make textiles and clothing in the $1 trillion (€885 billion) clothing industry.[1] Cotton producers, like most firms, are in business to generate revenue. To varying degrees, however, they augment financial concerns by addressing ecological and social performance. The natural environment faces multiple consequences associated with the manner by which crops are cultivated. Cotton, for instance, accounts for 24 percent of global insecticide use and 11 percent of pesticide use.[2] These chemicals are applied to enhance yields, but the detriments of their usage can surpass the benefits. The excess run-off is harmful to fish and other wildlife, and the application (i.e., spraying) of these chemicals kills millions of birds annually. Furthermore, cotton is a water-intensive crop that typically requires 20,000 liters (5283 gallons) to produce 1 kilogram (2.2 pounds) of cotton.[3]

Cotton also has appreciable consequences for individuals involved in its production and processing. Chronic exposure to pesticides is associated with infertility,[4] and it has also been linked to chest tightness, headaches, dizziness, fatigue, insomnia, and other symptoms.[5] Once a crop has been harvested, there is sizable potential health risk to employees that process cotton. The chemical processes associated with bleaching, dyeing, and finishing products use large amounts of chemicals.[6] Formaldehyde, chlorine bleach, and heavy metals are among the chemicals employed during processing, and these chemicals are problematic when discarded in waste water.

In addition to the ecological risks, workers face substantial socioeconomic risks. Workers may face low wages, long working hours, health and safety risks, restricted participation in organized labor, discrimination, and child labor. These issues are particularly acute in developing countries that increasingly supply more of the world's cotton.

Given the challenges associated with this industry, how can firms devise strategies that enable them to achieve financial, ecological, and social

---

[1] www.statista.com/statistics/279757/apparel-market-size-projections-by-region/ (June 23, 2016).
[2] wwf.panda.org/about_our_earth/about_freshwater/freshwater_problems/thirsty_crops/cotton/ (June 23, 2016).
[3] www.nwf.org/News-and-Magazines/National-Wildlife/Green-Living/Archives/2006/Cotton-and-Pesticides.aspx (June 23, 2016).
[4] Alavanja, Michael C. R., Jane A. Hoppin, and Freya Kamel (2004), "Health Effects of Chronic Pesticide Exposure: Cancer and Neurotoxicity* 3," *Annual Review of Public Health* 25, 155–197. Hanke, Wojciech, and Joanna Jurewicz (2004), "The Risk of Adverse Reproductive and Developmental Disorders Due to Occupational Pesticide Exposure: An Overview of Current Epidemiological Evidence," *International Journal of Occupational Medicine and Environmental Health*, 17 (2), 223–243.
[5] Kamel, Freya, and Jane A. Hoppin (2004), "Association of Pesticide Exposure with Neurologic Dysfunction and Disease," *Environmental Health Perspectives* 112 (9), 950-958.
[6] www.organiccotton.org/oc/Cotton-general/Impact-of-cotton/Risk-of-cotton-processing.php (June 23, 2016).

performance endemic to sustainability? Boll & Branch is a firm making great strides to achieve triple bottom-line performance. First, it uses only cotton that has been certified to meet Global Organic Textile Standards.[7] Cotton produced without pesticides means that fewer of these chemicals leach into fields and streams. Use of organic cotton keeps pesticides out of our food supply. Although 35 percent of cotton is used to make clothing, the remainder is used as ingredients in human food and livestock provisions.[8] Second, Boll & Branch works with Chetna Organic, a firm that works with cotton farmers in India.[9] Farmers who work with Chetna Organic grow their crops without pesticides or genetically modified seeds, and they use substantially less water than conventional farmers. The processing of cotton is performed by a certified fair trade producer, Rajlakshmi Cotton Mills, operating in Kolkata, India. Fair trade seeks to improve the well-being of producers, promote opportunities for disadvantaged producers, raise awareness of the consequence of international trade, campaign for changes in conventional international trade, and protect human rights.[10]

Boll & Branch also has incorporated a strategy that enables it to give back to the communities in which it operates.[11] It has an alliance with Not for Sale, an international organization that rescues children and women from human trafficking. Not for Sale also promotes the freedom and independence of disadvantaged women and children by providing rehabilitation services, housing, counseling, and education. Boll & Branch has agreed to contribute 5000 days' worth of care for rescued victims.

The use of organic cotton and fair trade labor has more than doubled the expenses. Consequently, Boll & Branch has modified its distribution system by marketing directly to the consumer. This strategy eliminates the markup associated with conventional retailers. The firm also relies heavily on online advertising to communicate its message. Since its inception in 2014, the firm has grown substantially, and sales have grown rapidly.

The Boll & Branch example illustrates how a firm can successfully achieve strong financial, ecological, and social performance. In this chapter, we examine several factors related to achieving triple bottom-line performance. We begin by describing the ethical context and the ethical stakes associated with sustainable performance. We subsequently describe individual and organizational factors that influence the pursuit of ethics and sustainable performance.

[7] www.nytimes.com/2016/06/19/business/with-organic-cotton-and-online-ads-boll-branch-helps-indian-farmers.html (June 23, 2016).
[8] www.nwf.org/News-and-Magazines/National-Wildlife/Green-Living/Archives/2006/Cotton-and-Pesticides.aspx (June 23, 2016).
[9] www.nytimes.com/2016/06/19/business/with-organic-cotton-and-online-ads-boll-branch-helps-indian-farmers.html (June 23, 2016).
[10] Moore, Geoff (2004), "The Fair Trade Movement: Parameters, Issues and Future Research," *Journal of Business Ethics*, 53 (1-2), 73–86.
[11] www.forbes.com/sites/lydiadishman/2014/02/05/how-boll-branchs-conscious-e-commerce-aims-to-make-customers-sleep-better/#31acafb99d32 (June 23, 2016).

ETHICAL LANDSCAPE

An understanding of ethics is essential to achieving a sustainable performance that enhances financial, social, and ecological outcomes. The Boll & Branch example illustrates a situation in which the firm achieves acceptable levels of triple bottom-line performance. In most settings such as this one, firms must weigh the trade-offs among facets of sustainable performance. These trade-offs can lead to ethical dilemmas for marketing decision makers.

In order to understand these decision makers, it is germane to recognize the motivations surrounding decisions and action. *Morals* refer to an individual's personal philosophy about what is right and wrong.[12] Importantly, morals are *individual* sets of values that relate to one person. *Business ethics*, however, refer to the organizational values, principles, and norms that guide group and individual behavior.[13] Values refer to the enduring ideals and beliefs that are socially reinforced. The level of trust operating in a supply chain, for instance, is an ethical value that is enriched by the communication strategies employed in the supply chain.[14] Principles refer to the pervasive and specific boundaries for behavior and may include a sense of equity, responsibility, and commitment.[15] For example, retailers' sense of fairness influences whether they are inclined to take advantage of suppliers.[16]

Since the values and principles inherent to ethical decision making are socially constructed, one must consider how the level of action and stakeholders influence ethical judgments. Consider each in turn.

Level of Action

The level of action refers to the number of entities associated with marketing behavior. Many analysts of marketing activity address the behavior of individuals, organization, and supply chains.[17] All action ultimately derives from the behavior of individuals. Boll & Branch, for instance, did not begin giving back to communities until an executive made the decision to do so. Our understanding of individual action is often driven by examination of the cognitive action and

---

[12] Ferrell, O. C., John Fraedrich, and Linda Ferrell (2017), *Business Ethics: Ethical Decision Making & Cases*, 11th edition, Stamford, CT: Cengage Learning.

[13] Ferrell, O. C., John Fraedrich, and Linda Ferrell (2017), *Business Ethics: Ethical Decision Making & Cases*, 11th edition, Stamford, CT: Cengage Learning.

[14] Morgan, Robert M., and Shelby D. Hunt (1994), "The Commitment-Trust Theory of Relationship Marketing," *Journal of Marketing*, 58 (3), 20–38.

[15] Gundlach, Gregory T., and Patrick E. Murphy (1993), "Ethical and Legal Foundations of Relational Marketing Exchanges," Journal of Marketing 57 (4), 35–46. Ferrell, O. C., John Fraedrich, and Linda Ferrell (2017), *Business Ethics: Ethical Decision Making & Cases*, 11th edition, Stamford, CT: Cengage Learning.

[16] Crosno, Jody L., Chris Manolis, and Robert Dahlstrom (2013), "Toward Understanding Passive Opportunism in Dedicated Channel Relationships," *Marketing Letters* 24 (4), 353–368.

[17] Pfeffer, Jeffrey, and Gerald R. Salancik (1978), *The External Control of Organizations: A Resource Dependence Approach*, New York, NY: Harper and Row Publishers. (1978). Elkington, John (1997), *Cannibals with Forks: The Triple Bottom Line of 21st Century*. Mankato, MN: Capstone Publishing.

decision making.[18] When a consumer visits an auto repair shop, for instance, she may favor the shop's services because the manager offered to recycle a used auto battery. Corporate action is observed as the collection of multiple individual acts. In many cases, understanding of corporate action is derived from analysis of the corporate culture operating within the firm.[19] The auto battery buyer, for instance, may be aware of a company policy whereby the seller agrees to take care of used parts. The collection of activities undertaken by associated firms comprises a value system.[20] The interaction of multiple firms provides the value generated in a supply chain. For example, Tesla Motors has established a closed-loop system that includes battery manufacturing, assembly, usage and recycling.[21] It is important to recognize that these levels of action are highly interdependent. Innovations, for instance, can emerge from an individual's idea to a multifirm entity. Similarly, the design of the value chain influences the corporate culture and individual action.

Stakeholders

Recognition that external forces affect sustainable efforts in the supply chain warrants consideration of those who can influence activity at the individual, corporate, and value system levels. *Stakeholders* include all those who influence the firm's operations. A stakeholder approach frames the firm in terms of all entities that influence its behavior and performance.[22] This perspective views the firm as a constellation of competitive and cooperative interests.[23] The firm with a stakeholder approach simultaneously attends to the interests of multiple stakeholders. It encourages managers to articulate the sense of value they create and the role of various business relationships in the delivery of this value.[24]

Stakeholders are characterized by the type of interest they have in a company and by whether the firm has an interest in them. For example, stakeholders who provide financial resources do so in anticipation of financial gain. The firm necessarily has an interest in them. By contrast, a *nongovernmental organization* (NGO) may become interested in the action of a firm. The Environmental Defense Fund (EDF), for instance, began monitoring packaging and waste issues at McDonald's in the late 1980s. Collaboration between EDF and

---

[18] Athanasopoulou, Andromachi, and John W. Selsky (2015), "The Social Context of Corporate Social Responsibility Enriching Research with Multiple Perspectives and Multiple Levels," *Business and Society*, 54 (3), 322–364.

[19] Athanasopoulou, Andromachi, and John W. Selsky (2015), "The Social Context of Corporate Social Responsibility Enriching Research with Multiple Perspectives and Multiple Levels," *Business and Society*, 54 (3), 322–364.

[20] Elkington, John (1997), *Cannibals with Forks: The Triple Bottom Line of 21st Century*. Mankato, MN: Capstone Publishing.

[21] www.teslamotors.com/blog/teslas-closed-loop-battery-recycling-program (July 18, 2016).

[22] Freeman, R. Edward (2010), *Strategic Management: A Stakeholder Approach*. Cambridge University Press.

[23] Donaldson, Thomas, and Lee E. Preston (1995), "The Stakeholder Theory of the Corporation: Concepts, Evidence, and Implications," Academy of Management Review 20 (1), 65–91.

[24] Freeman, R. Edward, Andrew C. Wicks, and Bidhan Parmar (2004), "Stakeholder theory and 'the corporate objective revisited'" *Organization Science* 15 (3), 364–369.

McDonald's has subsequently led to a 30 percent reduction in waste produced by the restaurateur.[25]

As Figure 3-1 illustrates, one can distinguish between primary and secondary stakeholders.[27] *Primary stakeholders* include entities that provide resources and associations that are necessary for a firm's survival. Investors, employees, customers, suppliers, governments, and communities are each primary stakeholders with contrasting vantage points on the role of the firm. They have discriminant perspectives on the importance of sustainable, triple bottom-line outcomes. They each possess an intrinsic interest in the firm.[28] *Secondary stakeholders* are less likely to be involved in the financial resource flows of the firm and, therefore, less important to the firm's survival. Special interest groups (including NGOs), trade associations, competition, and media are typical secondary stakeholders. These organizations can have powerful effects on firms through their influences on primary stakeholder or directly to the firm. For example, Greenpeace influenced Unilever's decision to explore the sourcing of palm oil used in its production process.[29]

The flow of value through the supply chain represents a portion of the overall stakeholder model outlined in Figure 3-1. Sustainable marketing activity primary addresses this facet of the stakeholder model yet simultaneously recognizes the other stakeholders and the obligations of the firm. Marketing efforts at each level of the supply chain need to take stock of the stakeholders of the focal firm.

To varying degrees, firms will attend to the concerns of stakeholders. A *stakeholder orientation* refers to the processes and activities within a system of social institutions that maintains and facilitates value via exchange relationships with multiple stakeholders.[30] This orientation strengthens relationships with stakeholders and describes most external influences on the firm. To establish a stakeholder orientation, the firm must generate stakeholder intelligence and distribute this intelligence. The firm initially identifies its relevant stakeholders. Companies effectively assess the power possessed by stakeholders and the power associated with the relationships among stakeholders. Sustainably oriented firms will recognize the diverse financial, social, and ecological objectives of stakeholders. Suppliers and customers, for instance, may have divergent views concerning the financial and ecological objectives of the firm. Recognition of

---

[25] www.edf.org/partnerships/mcdonalds (July 18, 2016).

[26] Donaldson, Thomas, and Lee E. Preston (1995), "The Stakeholder Theory of the Corporation: Concepts, Evidence, and Implications," *Academy of Management Review* 20 (1), 65–91. Ferrell, O. C., John Fraedrich, and Linda Ferrell (2017), *Business Ethics: Ethical Decision Making & Cases,* 11th edition, Stamford, CT: Cengage Learning.

[27] Hult, G. Tomas M., Jeannette A. Mena, O. C. Ferrell, and Linda Ferrell (2011), "Stakeholder Marketing: A Definition and Conceptual Framework," *AMS Review* 1 (1), 44–65.

[28] Donaldson, Thomas, and Lee E. Preston (1995), "The Stakeholder Theory of the Corporation: Concepts, Evidence, and Implications," *Academy of Management Review* 20 (1), 65–91.

[29] Sonne, Paul (2010). "To Wash Hands of Palm Oil Unilever Embraces Algae." *Wall Street Journal* 7 .

[30] Hult, G. Tomas M., Jeannette A. Mena, O. C. Ferrell, and Linda Ferrell (2011), "Stakeholder Marketing: A Definition and Conceptual Framework," *AMS Review* 1 (1), 44–65.

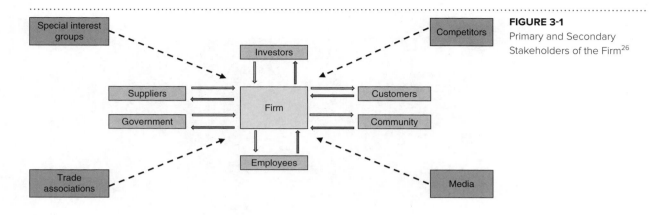

FIGURE 3-1
Primary and Secondary
Stakeholders of the Firm[26]

these divergent objectives enables the firm to prioritize among the goals of multiple stakeholders.

Once the stakeholder objectives have been established, the firm must then ensure the proper communication of these objectives to all stakeholders. The distribution of this information should indicate how the company's action addresses the sustainable objectives of stakeholders. Many firms illustrate their pursuit of sustainability via an annual sustainability report. The Global Reporting Initiative provides a metric for capturing the economic, ecological, and social performance of the firm.[32] An important aspect of the reporting process is the inclusion of multiple stakeholders. For example, Figure 3-2 outlines how Coca-Cola incorporated stakeholders into its assessment of strategic priorities. The pursuit of water stewardship, active healthy living, packaging, human rights, and product and ingredient safety as its top priorities was driven by stakeholders.

SUSTAINABLE CAPITAL AND CHALLENGES

The pursuit of triple bottom-line performance requires firms to consider how they achieve economic, social, and ecological performance.[33] In order to achieve multifaceted outcomes, a firm must take stock of the capital at its disposal. The available capital provides the opportunity to achieve levels of economic, social, and ecological performance. *Economic capital* is traditionally focused on the value of assets minus associated liabilities. This form of capital is traditionally described in terms of the financial capital and physical capital in the form of plants and machinery. In addition, human capital that manifests in skills, experience, and other knowledge-based assets are also forms of economic capital. The relationship between economic capital and performance is well established in

---

[31] www.coca-colacompany.com/content/dam/journey/us/en/private/fileassets/pdf/2015/09/2014-2015-sustainability-report.pdf.

[32] www.globalreporting.org/Pages/default.aspx (July 18, 2016).

[33] Elkington, John (1997), *Cannibals with Forks: The Triple Bottom Line of 21st Century.* Mankato, MN: Capstone Publishing.

FIGURE 3-2
Strategic Priorities
Assessment at Coca-Cola[31]

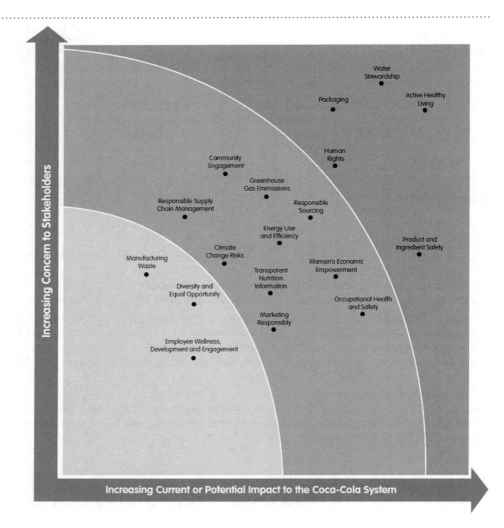

FIGURE 3-2
Strategic Priorities
Assessment at Coca-Cola[31]

accountancy. The for-profit firm must necessarily attend to achieving desirable economic performance given available resources.

Although accountancy captures economic performance, the treatment of other forms of capital receives less scrutiny. *Social capital* refers to a capability that arises from the prevalence of trust.[34] Relationships built on the basis of trust enable companies to work together toward a common purpose.[35] Social capital emerges from investments in education and health for stakeholders. For example, organizations that extensively train sales agents are doing so to ensure that agents attend to the long-term needs of customers. An assessment of social

---

[34] Fukuyama, Francis (1995), *Trust: The Social Virtues and the Creation of Prosperity*. New York: Free Press.
[35] Dwyer, F. Robert, Paul H. Schurr, and Sejo Oh (1987), "Developing Buyer-Seller Relationships," *Journal of Marketing* 51 (2), 11–27.

capital examines influences of an organization on its primary and secondary stakeholders. When firms report on their product safety efforts, training and education, community outreach, and charitable donations, they are describing facets of their social capital. These investments enhance the quality of working relationships with stakeholders.

Ecological capital refers to the availability of natural resources.[36] One challenge in assessing this form of capital lies in determining the value of natural elements that support an ecosystem. Consider, for example, the challenge associated with determining the ecological capital that supports the supply chain for a local grocery store. One can distinguish critical ecological capital and renewable ecological capital. Critical ecological capital refers to that which is essential to life and ecosystem integrity.[37] For example, honey bee pollination is essential to humans and biodiversity.[38] By contrast, renewable ecological capital refers to resources that can be repaired renewed, substituted, or replaced.[39] For example, fossil fuel can be replaced with solar cells.

If the realms of economic, social, and ecological capital were not related, pursuit of triple bottom-line performance would be much less complicated. Marketers face a *sustainability challenge* where the pursuit of two or more facets of sustainability are incompatible. A *socioeconomic challenge* refers to a situation in which the firm tries to achieve social and economic goals simultaneously. Thus, the cotton manufacturer wants to maximize performance of the firm but concurrently invests in training for suppliers.

An *ecoefficiency challenge* occurs when trying to achieve financial and ecological goals simultaneously. For example, manufacturers of cotton clothing face a trade-off between sourcing of responsibly produced, pesticide-free cotton and levels of consumer prices. Boll & Branch resolves this challenge through direct-to-the consumer online shopping that avoids retailer markups.

Firms encounter a *socioecological challenge* when they seek to achieve social and ecological goals simultaneously.[40] These challenges may be *intragenerational* concerning equity among those currently alive. Manufacturers of cotton clothing, for instance, may face suppliers that seek to convert habitat to residential areas. By contrast, *intergenerational* challenges refer to balances in advantages between different generations. For example, the 1970s recognition of the diminishing ozone layer stimulated worldwide adoption of new technologies.[41] Manufacturers necessarily adopted these technologies to the benefit of future consumers.

[36] Elkington, John (1997), *Cannibals with Forks: The Triple Bottom Line of 21st Century*. Mankato, MN: Capstone Publishing.
[37] Chiesura, Anna, and Rudolf De Groot (2003), "Critical Natural Capital: A Socio-Cultural Perspective," *Ecological Economics* 44 (2), 219–231.
[38] Brown, Mark J. F., and Robert J. Paxton (2009), "The Conservation of Bees: A Global Perspective," *Apidologie* 40 (3), 410–416.
[39] Elkington, John (1997), *Cannibals with Forks: The Triple Bottom Line of 21st Century*. Mankato, MN: Capstone Publishing.
[40] Elkington, John (1997), *Cannibals with Forks: The Triple Bottom Line of 21st Century*. Mankato, MN: Capstone Publishing.
[41] Schrope, Mark (2000), "Successes in Fight to Save Ozone Layer Could Close Holes by 2050," *Nature* 408 (6813), 627–627.

When the firm acknowledges these challenges among economy, society, and economy, they are examining the sustainability of the enterprise. Boll & Branch has adopted a lucrative business model that enables it to achieve sustainable outcomes for relevant stakeholders.

INFLUENCES ON ETHICAL DECISION MAKING

Since the challenges endemic to sustainability necessarily involves trade-offs, it is germane to consider how individuals operating within firms approach problem solving. Our discussion examines cognitive moral development, individual moral philosophy, corporate action, socioethical intensity. These relationships are outlined in Figure 3-3.

Cognitive Moral Development

It is important to recognize that moral philosophy is acquired over time. Thus, the desire to engage in fair trade with cotton producers emerges as individuals begin to recognize the importance of good working relationships with suppliers. Research in *cognitive moral development* characterizes the acquisition of moral evaluations over time.[42] Individuals pass through a series of stages in their moral development. They tend to be consistent in their action at each stage, and thinking at advanced stages always incorporates logic from earlier stages. People move forward throughout the stages and generally do not regress to prior conditions. Thus, executives that develop sustainable supply chains are not inclined to eliminate such practices at a later date.

Moral development can be characterized by the following levels and stages:[44]

Preconventional Level. In this initial level, individuals respond to cultural rules concerning right or wrong, but they do so in terms of authority figures.[45] Avoidance of punishment is central to ethical concerns. The two stages at this level are:

Stage 1: Punishment and obedience. At this stage, individuals act obediently through their literal obedience to authority and rules.

Stage 2: Individual instrumental purpose. In this second stage, the ethicality of action is based on serving one's needs or the needs of others. Fairness and reciprocity are present but in a pragmatic physical way.

---

[42] Kohlberg, Lawrence, and Richard H. Hersh (1977), "Moral Development: A Review of the Theory," *Theory into Practice* 16 (2), 53–59.

[43] Ferrell, O. C., Larry G. Gresham, and John Fraedrich (1989) "A Synthesis of Ethical Decision Models for Marketing," *Journal of Macromarketing* Fall: 55–64. Jones, Thomas M. (1991), "Ethical Decision Making by Individuals in Organizations: An Issue-Contingent Model," *Academy of Management Review, 16* (2), 366–395.

[44] Kohlberg, Lawrence, and Richard H. Hersh (1977), "Moral Development: A Review of the Theory," *Theory into Practice* 16 (2), 53–59. 46 Goolsby, Jerry R., and Shelby D. Hunt (1992), "Cognitive Moral Development and Marketing," *Journal of Marketing* 56 (1), 55–68.

[45] Goolsby, Jerry R., and Shelby D. Hunt (1992), "Cognitive Moral Development and Marketing," *Journal of Marketing* 56 (1), 55–68.

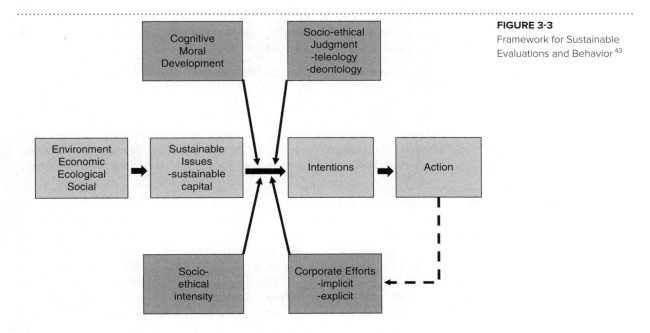

FIGURE 3-3
Framework for Sustainable
Evaluations and Behavior [43]

Conventional Level. At the conventional level, individuals begin to value the expectations of groups, including families, organizations, and institutions, for their own sake.[46] Conformity is replaced with loyalty and respect for order. The two stages of this level include:

> Stage 3: Mutual interpersonal expectation. At this stage, good ethical behavior is manifest in action that is approved by others or is pleasing to others. The need for social approval is paramount at this stage. The influence that decisions have on others is central to ethical judgements.[47]

> Stage 4: Social system and conscience maintenance. When individuals reach this level, ethical behavior consists of showing respect for authority and doing one's duty. Adherence to authority, fixed rules, and social order are central to ethical judgments. Duty to society, rather than just other people, factors into decision making.

Principled Level. At this final level, decision making focuses on values and principles that are valid beyond groups holding these principles by decision makers who are distinct from an affiliation with these groups.[48] The two stages at the principled level include:

---

[46] Goolsby, Jerry R., and Shelby D. Hunt (1992), "Cognitive Moral Development and Marketing," *Journal of Marketing* 56 (1), 55–68.

[47] Nowak, Linda I., and Thomas K. Clarke (2003), "Cause-Related Marketing: Keys to Successful Relationships with Corporate Sponsors and their Customers," *Journal of Nonprofit & Public Sector Marketing* 11 (1), 137–149.

[48] Christensen, Sandra L. (2008), "The role of law in models of ethical behavior," *Journal of Business Ethics*, 77 (4), 451–461.

Stage 5: Social contract. At this stage, people recognize that they have a social contract with society, and that contract requires them to uphold the rights, values and legal contracts of society.

Stage 6: Universal ethical principle. At this ultimate level, people determine what is the appropriate or the right behavior based on universal ethical principles that they should follow. Laws, social agreements, and norms are adhered to because they are universal in nature. The right to free speech, for instance, is viewed as an inalienable right applicable to all. Principles of justice, reciprocity and equality, human rights, and respect for human dignity are some of the universal principles invoked at this stage.

The messages used to influence decision makers should change over the three stages. At the pre-conventional level, decision makers are primarily concerned with their own outcomes. Marketers can, therefore, focus on the immediate benefits derived from decision making. At the conventional level, decision makers not only recognize the need for order, but they actively maintain this sense of order. Marketing messages that emphasize a desire to act in accordance with the expectations of family and society should foster sustainable action. At the post-conventional level, decision makers value principles beyond their own identification with authority figures. Since decision makers become increasingly less egocentric at this level, relevant promotional campaigns focus on an increasingly strong personal commitment to self-selected universal principles. Influence strategies that emphasize concepts such as fairness and equity should emphasize the universal nature of these concepts rather than their relevance to the conditions faced by the decision maker.

Moral Philosophy

Moral philosophy refers to the principles and values people use to determine what is right and wrong.[49] While business ethics derive from decisions made by groups or to achieve business goals, moral philosophy refers to the specific principles and values of an individual. Moral philosophies provide standards to judge intentions, behavior, and consequences of behavior.[50] They serve as guidelines for establishing resolutions to challenges and conflicts.

Moral philosophies are classified into two orientations—teleology and deontology. *Teleology* focuses on the consequences of action.[51] Evaluations that use a teleological approach focus on generating the greatest good. The construction of dams, for instance, is often based on the overall benefits accrued to society. The benefit of additional water supplies has historically been deemed more important than the loss of habitat. The number of people affected by a decision qualifies two forms of teleological judgements. *Egoists* make decisions that maximize their self-interests. An egoist, for instance, may not recycle because the temporal and financial costs greatly outweigh the personal benefit. By contrast, the *utilitarian* seeks the greatest good for the greatest number of people. The utilitarian may use

---

[49] Ferrell, O. C., John Fraedrich, and Linda Ferrell (2017), *Business Ethics: Ethical Decision Making & Cases*, 11th edition, Stamford, CT: Cengage Learning.

[50] Ferrell, O. C., Larry G. Gresham, and John Fraedrich (1989) "A Synthesis of Ethical Decision Models for Marketing," *Journal of Macromarketing* Fall: 55–64.

[51] Malhotra, Naresh K., and Gina L. Miller (1998), "An Integrated Model for Ethical Decisions in Marketing Research." *Journal of Business Ethics* 17 (3), 263–280.

a cost-benefit analysis to determine the consequences of alternatives and select the outcome that has the greatest benefit. Communities faced with limited water resources may use this approach to justify new reservoir and dam construction.

Ecosystem modifications designed to enhance the availability of water to humans may have detrimental effects on other living things. For example, the Three Gorges Dam has been touted due to its benefits relative to flood control, irrigation, navigation, and energy supply.[52] It simultaneously brings some negative consequences such as displacement of humans, disease, drought, and habitat loss.[53] An alternative to weighing the costs versus benefits of a decision is to make a decision based on principles of justice. Thus, the importance of caring for the natural environment could be the basis for decision making.

Deontology refers to a family of philosophies focused on the moral commitments or obligations that should be necessary for proper action.[54] Individuals who employ a deontological approach look for guiding principles or rules to guide behavior. Justice, for instance, is a principle designed to protect all participants in business or nonbusiness activity. When decision makers reference obligations such as justice and fidelity, they are engaged in a deontological process. Immanuel Kant's categorical imperative, for instance, maintains that an individual's behavior should be consistent with universal truths.[55] The *golden rule* (i.e., do unto others as you would like them to do to you) is another example of deontological reasoning.

The recognition that individuals employ a teleological or deontological approach has implications for those who seek to augment the decision-making process. Teleological approaches can be augmented by illustrating how the benefits associated with an action outweigh the losses. By contrast, deontological approaches can be influenced by indicating how the action is consistent with the rightness or wrongness outlined in a moral norm.

Socioethical Intensity

The sustainable and ethical judgments of marketers are influenced by the cognitive moral development and the moral philosophy of the individual. The likelihood that individuals will engage in an action that raises economic, social, and ecological outcomes is also influenced by the nature of an action and its consequences. As the consequences become more severe, individuals are more inclined to make ethical decisions.

Socioethical intensity refers to the decision maker's perceptions of the magnitude of a moral issue. As the perceived intensity of the ethical situation increases, decision makers are more likely to act ethically.[56] For example, consumer and

---

[52] Li, Kaifeng, Cheng Zhu, Li Wu, and Linyan Huang (2013), "Problems Caused by the Three Gorges Dam Construction in the Yangtze River Basin: A Review," *Environmental Reviews* 21 (3), 127–135.

[53] www.scientificamerican.com/article/chinas-three-gorges-dam-disaster/ (July 18, 2016).

[54] Ferrell, O. C., John Fraedrich, and Linda Ferrell (2017), *Business Ethics: Ethical Decision Making & Cases*, 11th edition, Stamford, CT: Cengage Learning.

[55] Kant, Immanuel (1785), *Foundations of the Metaphysics of Morals*. Indianapolis, IN: Bobbs-Merrill.

[56] Singhapakdi, Anusorn, Scott J. Vitell, and George R. Franke (1999), "Antecedents, Consequences, and Mediating Effects of Perceived Moral Intensity and Personal Moral Philosophies," *Journal of the Academy of Marketing Science* 27 (1), 19–36.

corporate awareness of the merits of water conservation have raised the moral intensity associated with maintaining this natural resource.

Socioethical intensity consists of the following factors:[57]

A. **Magnitude of Consequences**. Different ethical situations vary based on the magnitude of the consequences. For example, a greenfield retail development that transforms habitat on 10,000 square meters has greater consequences than a development that transforms 100 square meters. This magnitude of the consequences is expressed as the sum of the harm (or benefit) done to victims (or beneficiaries) of a potential act.

B. **Social Consensus**. Social consensus refers to the extent of social agreement that an act is good or evil.[58] While there is social agreement concerning the merits of recycling,[59] there is less consensus concerning the carbon footprint of alternative automobile engines.[60] Consensus increases the likelihood of ethical and sustainable action.

C. **Probability of Effect**. This facet of socioethical intensity examines the likelihood that an act will take place and the harm (or benefit) it will generate. For example, pharmaceutical firms must assess the potential patient reactions to drugs as well as the harm incurred by patients. A drug formula that has a low likelihood of harmful side effects is preferred to one that has a greater likelihood of side effects.

D. **Temporal Immediacy**. Temporal immediacy refers to the time between the present and the consequences of a particular act.[61] As this time period extends, consumers are less likely to engage in sustainable consumption. While there is general consensus among many scientists concerning the extent to which global warming is affecting living conditions, consumers are not at the same level of agreement.[62]

E. **Proximity**. The nearness of the victims (or beneficiaries) of a particular act is also central to socioethical intensity.[63] The degree of nearness can be captured as the physical, psychological, social, or cultural distance between one who commits an act and those who incur the consequences of the act. Consumers are more likely to have reservations about the use of pesticides in their home town versus their application in a distant setting.

---

[57] Jones, Thomas M. (1991), "Ethical Decision Making by Individuals in Organizations: An Issue-Contingent Model," *Academy of Management Review*, 16 (2), 366–395.

[58] Jones, Thomas M. (1991), "Ethical Decision Making by Individuals in Organizations: An Issue-Contingent Model," *Academy of Management Review*, 16 (2), 366–395.

[59] keepitoutofthelandfill.com/category/attitudes-toward-recycling/ (August 12, 2016).

[60] Prevedouros, Panos, and Lambros Mitropoulos (2016), "Life Cycle Emissions and Cost Study of Light Duty Vehicles," *Transportation Research Procedia* 15, 749–760.

[61] Jones, Thomas M. (1991), "Ethical Decision Making by Individuals in Organizations: An Issue-Contingent Model," *Academy of Management Review*, 16 (2), 366–395.

[62] Stocker, Thomas F., et al. (2014), "Climate Change 2013: The Physical Science Basis," (2014). www.skeptic.com/eskeptic/12-02-08/?gclid=CKO4nt_qvs4CFZKHaQod9u4KVA#feature (August 13, 2016). www.gallup.com/poll/161645/americans-concerns-global-warming -rise.aspx (August 13, 2016).

[63] Godos-Díez, Jose-Luis, Roberto Fernández-Gago, and Laura Cabeza-García (2015), "Business Education and Idealism as Determinants of Stakeholder Orientation," *Journal of Business Ethics* 131 (2), 439–452.

F. **Concentration of Effect**. The concentration of effect concerns the amount of people or habitat affected by an act.[64] Concentration of effect can be operationalized as the number of people, organisms, or habitat affected by an act of given magnitude. For example, a change in a warranty policy that denies coverage to five people with claims of $5000 is more concentrated than a change denying 5000 people claims of $5. Research indicates as the concentration of negative effects increases, marketers are more likely to recognize an ethical problem.[65]

Organizational Efforts to Augment Sustainable Action

To this point, our discussion has examined individual factors that influence the likelihood of sustainable action among marketing decision makers. These factors include cognitive moral development, judgmental philosophy, and socioethical intensity. The firm is not an idle bystander to the deliberations of these decision makers. Top management seeks to influence marketing decision makers to act in a sustainable fashion. Management's commitment to sustainability and the communication of this commitment to all stakeholders is vital to the performance of the firm.

Firms take multiple steps to ensure that sustainability is incorporated into decision making.[66] These measures can either be *explicit* attempts to clarify the sustainable duties and responsibilities of employees or *implicit* efforts to enhance sustainability. Explicit action includes proclamations of the firm's intent to act sustainably. In subsequent chapters, we discuss the role of sustainable marketing communication to internal and external stakeholders. The general proclamation of a desire to engage in sustainable commerce, however, is a specific recognition of the role of sustainability to the firm. Many Fortune 500 and smaller firms include proclamations of this nature on their websites, and they augment these proclamations via detailed sustainability reporting. For example, the Target Corporation's corporate web page outlines their commitment to sustainability and elaborates on the sustainability of its products and operations. Marketing management can take advantage of multiple tactics that augment these proclamations. Sales and marketing training should complement the company's commitments via policy manuals, training materials, and orientation programs that explicitly address the firm's commitment to sustainability.

Implicit efforts to enhance sustainability do not codify sustainable business practices. Nevertheless, they provide important mechanisms designed to ensure sustainable marketing and operations. The organizational culture is perhaps the most visible form of implicit action designed to enhance sustainability among marketers. The *corporate culture* operating within the firms consists of the shared norms, assumptions, and values that drive corporate action.[67]

[64] Jones, Thomas M. (1991), "Ethical Decision Making by Individuals in Organizations: An Issue-Contingent Model," *Academy of Management Review*, 16 (2), 366–395

[65] Singhapakdi, Anusorn, Scott J. Vitell, and Kenneth L. Kraft (1996), "Moral Intensity and Ethical Decision-Making of Marketing Professionals," *Journal of Business Research* 36 (3), 245–255.

[66] Jose, Anita, and Mary S. Thibodeaux (1999), "Institutionalization of Ethics: The Perspective of Managers," *Journal of Business Ethics*, 22 (2), 133–143.

[67] Schein, Edgar H. (1996), "Culture: The Missing Concept in Organization Studies," *Administrative Science Quarterly*, 41 (2), 229–240.

Culture operates at three levels, including the observable culture, espoused values, and underlying assumptions.[68] The *observable culture* refers to the behaviors, processes, and structures operating in a firm. The *espoused values* are embodied in the philosophies, goals, and strategies of the firm. *Underlying assumptions* of a company contain the perceptions and unconscious beliefs that drive behavior and values.

Some strategies undertaken by Patagonia illustrate how its culture radiates throughout its operations. The underlying assumption inherent to the firm is the belief that a throw-away society is not sustainable. A throw-away society is one where consumers do not think of repair or re-use of a garment. When consumers do not take this perspective, they can lower the carbon footprints by purchasing fewer garments. The espoused values of the firm are reflected in the "Worn Wear" strategy that provides guidelines on the repair of numerous clothing products.[69] Promotions associated with this strategy underscore how garment repair can lower one's carbon footprint. Patagonia's observed culture is visible in the form of the Patagonia Worn Wear team travelling coast-to-coast. The trip is choreographed so that Patagonia personnel can meet with consumers and retailers to promote product reuse. Consumers can either select a garment that Patagonia has repaired or bring a garment for the company to repair.

The implicit action of the firm also includes the incentive systems and leadership. When sustainable action is associated with financial compensation or promotion, marketing and sales employees are inclined to act sustainably. Similarly, leaders who champion sustainable culture foster sustainable action among employees. At Procter & Gamble, for instance, top management acted to ensure that all employees understood the sustainable objectives of the firm.[70] Innovation and creativity subsequently emerged that addressed consumer markets while simultaneously achieving other sustainable returns for the firm.

SUMMARY

The goal of this chapter has been to examine the role of ethical decision making in sustainable marketing. Sustainability and ethical decision making are highly interrelated given that sustainable action must account for ecological, social, and financial capital. The trade-offs among these forms of capital must be assessed by the sustainable marketer.

This interrelationship between sustainability and ethics provides the opportunity to describe the role of ethical decision making. We began by outlining the importance of ethical judgments within the firm and the roles of primary and secondary stakeholders. The analysis of capital presented social, ecological, and financial capital and provided the occasion to examine sustainable challenges. As the pursuit of one form of capital increases, there is the potential to encounter

[68] Linnenluecke, Martina K., and Andrew Griffiths (2010), "Corporate Sustainability and Organizational Culture," *Journal of World Business* 45 (4), 357–366.

[69] http://www.patagonia.com/worn-wear.html (August 13, 2016).

[70] Epstein, Marc J., Adriana Rejc Buhovac, and Kristi Yuthas (2010), "Implementing Sustainability: The Role of Leadership and Organizational Culture," *Strategic Finance* 91 (10), 41.

losses of other forms of capital. Resolving these trade-offs become the basis for making sustainable, ethical decision making.

We presented a model that identifies environmental influences on sustainable capital and decision makers' intents to act sustainably. These intentions are influenced by the cognitive moral development, judgmental philosophy, socioethical intensity, and corporate action. Cognitive moral development characterizes the maturity of decision makers, ranging from a pre-conventional punishment and obedience orientation to a post-conventional universal ethical orientation. Judgmental philosophy considers whether decisions are driven by consideration of the consequences of an act or through an attempt to remain consistent with general principles. Socioethical intensity captures the decision maker's perceptions of the magnitude of a moral issue. Finally, corporate action refers to explicit and implicit measures taken by the firm to increase the likelihood of sustainable action by marketers.

KEY TERMS

morals
business ethics
stakeholder
nongovernmental organization
primary stakeholders
secondary stakeholders
stakeholder orientation
economic capital
social capital
ecological capital
sustainability challenge
socioeconomic challenge

ecoefficiency challenge
socioecological challenge
intragenerational socioecological
   challenge
intergenerational socioecological
   challenge
cognitive moral development
pre-conventional level
conventional level
principled level
teleology
egoists

utilitarian
deontology
socioethical intensity
explicit corporate action
   to influence sustainable
   decisions
implicit corporate action
   to influence sustainable
   decisions
corporate culture
espoused values
underlying assumptions

DISCUSSION QUESTIONS

1. What is necessary to examine when making decisions that influence the triple bottom line performance of the firm?

2. Who are the primary and secondary stakeholders for Boll & Branch?

3. Why is it necessary to incorporate secondary stakeholders into the sustainable decision making by the firm?

4. What are the sustainability challenges facing Boll & Branch? How does the pursuit of one form of capital limit the ability to increase other forms of capital?

5. What is the difference between an intragenerational and intergenerational socioeconomic challenge?

6. How can knowledge of a decision maker's level of cognitive moral development enable a marketer to influence decision making?

7. What is basis for teleological versus deontological decision making? To what extent do these orientations seem to be operative in decision making at Boll & Branch?

8. How are decisions made by individuals at the principled level similar to deontological judgments?

9. Why would a decision maker deliberate more over the flow of toxins into a river rather than the disposal of one plastic bottle in a landfill? How can marketers distinguish among the level of intensity of marketing action?

10. How can the firm explicitly and implicitly influence sustainable decision making? Which of these influence strategies is more effective?

part two

Sustainable Promotional Strategies

4

Understanding the Consumption Process

RECOGNIZING THE CENTRAL IMPORTANCE
OF THE CONSUMPTION PROCESS

One thing that all automobile drivers have in common is the reality that their vehicles need frequent attention to ensure that they run well. Beyond refueling and periodic oil changes, cars at some point need further maintenance to ensure that they provide safe means of transportation. As the car ages, consumers have some difficulty determining whether repairs should be made or a new means of transportation should be pursued. In the United States, for instance, the average car is over 11 years old, and estimates suggest that the average car age will continue to increase in the foreseeable future.[1]

Auto repair experts often have customers who ask whether it is worth putting money into their current car or selling the car and looking for a new vehicle.[2] On a relatively new car of five years of age, owners may (perhaps begrudgingly) justify repairs on a large item such as a transmission or blown engine. As the auto ages, the challenge becomes more difficult. Repairs in one part of the car will typically not correct other car problems, and guarantees on repairs are typically not lengthy. Mechanics that know a car and its owner may weigh a new purchase against making a repair, but the decision whether to fix the car is entirely the consumer's decision. Automobile experts can help assess the utility of an automobile by checking its mechanical systems—brakes, steering and suspension, engine, and transmission. Failures or near failure in of any these components increases the potential savings from selling a vehicle rather than repairing it.

The financial costs of operations run parallel to the ecological costs. Proper maintenance of a car saves drivers money while making their cars more efficient and environmentally friendly. Properly inflated tires are safer, last longer, and improve gas mileage, whereas underinflated tires lower gas mileage.[3]

If the automobile only offered instrumental utility, the decision about trading in a car would be relatively simple. Beyond this instrumental utility of a car, however, an automobile also provides consumers with affective feelings of sensation, superiority, arousal, and symbolic rewards such as social status and self-esteem.[4] Some car buyers view ownership as a personal accomplishment or a realization of a lifelong dream.[5] Initial hybrid car offerings such as the Prius had modest styling and pricing that owners may not associate with a sense of accomplishment. New products such as the Mercedes S500 and the Porsche

---

[1] www.forbes.com/sites/jimhenry/2014/06/30/average-car-on-the-road-still-getting-older-but-for-the-right-reasons/ (July 20, 2015).

[2] autorepair.about.com/od/autonrepair12/a/aa020301a_2.htm (July 20, 2015).

[3] www.fueleconomy.gov/feg/maintain.jsp (July 20, 2015).

[4] Steg, Linda (2005), "Car Use: Lust and Must. Instrumental, Symbolic and Affective Motives for Car Use," *Transportation Research Part A: Policy and Practice,* 39 (2), 147–162. Steg, Linda, Charles Vlek, and Goos Slotegraaf (2001), "Instrumental-reasoned and symbolic-affective motives for using a motor car" *Transportation Research Part F: Traffic Psychology and Behaviour* 4 (3), 151–169.

[5] Lezotte, Chris (2013), "Women with Muscle: Contemporary Women and the Classic Muscle Car," *Frontiers: A Journal of Women Studies,* 34, (2), 83–113.

FIGURE 4-1
The Panamera E-Hybrid
and other New Cars are
Changing Consumer Views
of Hybrids.[6]

Panamera E-Hybrid, however, are changing impressions of hybrid automobiles (see Figure 4-1).

When the consumer makes a decision that it is time look for a new car, their decision incorporates economic and aesthetic considerations. Beyond the financial cost and the aesthetic value of a car, many consumers incorporate environmental costs into their auto purchases. Fuel efficiency standards have improved over time, and novel technologies have greatly reduced the carbon footprint of an automobile. The consumer considering whether to buy a new car can consider a myriad of fuel choices using battery electric, hydrogen fuel cell, compressed natural gas, hybrid, plug-in hybrid, or gasoline alternatives.[7] Newer technologies lower carbon emissions and often enjoy lower mileage costs, yet consumers may be reluctant to purchase such technologies.

This automobile example illustrates a consumption process and triple bottom-line considerations at the consumer level. To varying degrees, consumers recognize the financial costs, the aesthetic value, and the ecological costs inherent to automobile transportation. Many consumers are driving cars, but few are in the market to purchase at any time. Thus, there are sustainability issues inherent to the pre-purchase and purchase stages of consumption, and there are sustainability considerations after purchase.

In this chapter, we characterize the processes by which consumers search for information and make purchases. We subsequently describe post-purchase product use and divestment. After outlining the consumption process, we implicate the factors that influence consumption. These include psychological, demographic, situational, and social influences on the consumption process.

---

[6] insideevs.com/porsche-panamera-s-e-hybrid-featured-fully-charged/ (January 20, 2016).

[7] Hirsch, Jerry (2015) "What kind of car is the most green, fuel efficient and budget friendly?" *Los Angeles Times,* July 12. www.latimes.com/business/autos/la-fi-hy-green-car-emissions-20150713-story.html#page=2.

AN OVERVIEW OF THE CONSUMPTION PROCESS

To influence behavior consistently, it is essential to be able to understand and predict how consumers act. If we want consumers to shop, buy, use, and divest themselves of products in an ecoconscious manner, then it is essential to understand their behavior. The *consumption process* refers to the series of steps that buyers make before, during, and after consumption. Marketers have the opportunity to influence consumer decision making at each stage of the consumption process. Figure 4-2 provides an overview of the various stages of the process from pre-purchase evaluation to post-purchase product disposal.

The process that a consumer goes through when deciding to trade-in a currently owned car for a new automobile provides the opportunity to examine all phases of this decision-making process. The first stage of the decision-making process is the *pre-purchase stage*. The first phase of this stage is *need recognition*, or the point at which a consumer senses a difference between an ideal state of affairs and the current state.[8] The auto example at the beginning of this chapter, for instance, indicates that some customers will contact their mechanics to help them decide whether to repair a car. The driver of a 2004 Camry, for example, may talk to her mechanic and realize that the cost of recurring repairs for this car puts her in a less than desirable situation. Marketers dedicate substantial energy to help consumers recognize needs. For example, Nissan claims the low cost of operating its Leaf auto are likely to prompt some consumers to reflect on the inefficiency of their current cars.

Once consumers realize a gap between current and ideal conditions, they begin to search for alternatives. Thus, *search* refers to efforts to acquire information and solutions that satisfy unmet needs.[9] Consumers engage in search behavior to bridge the gap between current conditions and an ideal state of affairs. For example, the owner of the Camry may search for new cars that have warranties that suggest consumers will not have to invest time or money in auto repairs.

The third phase of the pre-purchase stage is the *evaluation of alternatives*. In this phase, consumers evaluate options identified during the search process. Thus, the owner of the Camry may evaluate current Toyota and General Motors cars based on price, style, fuel efficiency, and other attributes.

After consumers engage in the pre-purchase evaluations, they enter into the second stage. The *purchase stage* refers to point at which the consumer decides whether to buy and the conditions under which to buy the product. The owner of the Camry, for instance, may elect to go to the local Toyota dealer to purchase a new Prius automobile.

The third stage of the consumer decision process refers to the *consumption* of a product offering. This stage refers to the manner in which the product is used by the consumer. The owner of a new Prius, for example, may decide to use the automobile in a variety of ways that have repercussions for the environment. For example, if the tires on the car are not properly inflated, the fuel efficiency the car will suffer dramatically.

---

[8] Blackwell, Roger D., Paul W. Miniard, and James F. Engel (2006), *Consumer Behavior*, Mason, OH: Thomson Higher Education.

[9] Blackwell, Roger D., Paul W. Miniard, and James F. Engel (2006), *Consumer Behavior*, Mason, OH: Thomson Higher Education.

Stage of the Process	Phase of the Decision-making Process	Example
Pre-purchase	**Need recognition:** Point at which a consumer senses a difference between an ideal state of affairs and the current state.	The driver of a 2004 Camry realizes that the cost of recurring repairs car puts her in a less than desirable situation.
	Search: Effort to acquire information and solutions that satisfy unmet needs. Consumers engage in search behavior to bridge the gap between current conditions and an ideal state of affairs.	The Camry owner searches for new cars that have warranties that suggest consumers will not have to invest time or money in auto repairs.
	Pre-purchase evaluation: Consumers evaluate options identified during the search process.	The Camry owner evaluates current Toyota and General Motors cars based on price, fuel efficiency, and other attributes.
Purchase Stage	**Purchase decision:** Consumer decides whether to purchase and the conditions under which to buy the product.	The Camry owner buys a new Prius at the local Toyota dealership.
Consumption	**Product usage:** The manner in which the consumer uses the product.	The owner of a Prius regularly changes the oil, checks the tire pressure, and otherwise maintains the car.
Post Consumption	**Post-consumption evaluation:** Refers to evaluation of a product after consumption has occurred.	The Prius owner is no longer satisfied with the car. The car's value is exceeded by that of a newer model Prius.
	Divestment: Disposal of products after they no longer offer utility to the consumer.	The old Prius is traded-in to the dealer in purchase of a newer model.

FIGURE 4-2
The Consumption Process[10]

The fourth and final stage of the consumer decision-making process is the *post-consumption stage*. After consumption begins, the consumer makes periodic evaluations of product performance in light of expectations before the purchase. *Post-consumption evaluation* refers to the evaluation of a product after consumption has occurred. At some point, the consumer recognizes that the value of a currently owned product is substantially lower than alternatives. The Prius owner has evaluated that the car's value is exceeded by a newer model.

Divestment refers to the disposal of products after they no longer offer utility to the consumer.

If sustainable marketers are to have an influence on the entire consumption process, then it is essential that they understand the nature of decision making throughout the consumption process. In the remaining sections of this chapter, we consider influences on the decision-making process. Psychological factors influence decision making and judgment. Consumers also vary based on demographic,

---

[10] Kerin, R. A., Hartley, S. W., & Rudelius, W. (2011). *The Core Marketing*, New York: McGraw Hill.

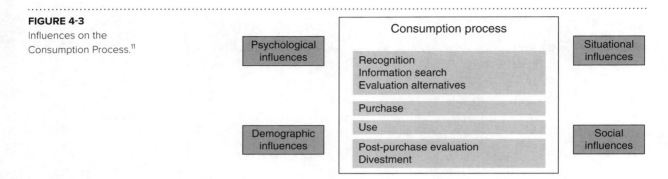

FIGURE 4-3
Influences on the
Consumption Process.[11]

situational, and social factors. These influences are outlined in Figure 4-3. Consider first how psychological conditions influence decision making.

PSYCHOLOGICAL INFLUENCES ON THE CONSUMPTION PROCESS

Psychology examines the mental activity and behavior of individuals. We begin this discussion by highlighting the influences of involvement and effort on sustainable attitudes and preference. We subsequently characterize influences of personality, motivation, and lifestyle.

Consumer Involvement and Effort

The elaborate consumption process outlined above may describe the decision-making process associated with automobile ownership, but, of course, this series of stages does not describe many purchase and consumption decisions. Consider, for instance, the length of time that each consumer could spend at a vending machine making a mundane purchase. In most cases, consumers are not heavily involved in such purchases, nor do they engage in much effort to make the purchase.

Psychologists suggest that decision making can be characterized based on the level of involvement and effort associated with a purchase. *Involvement* refers to the level of perceived interest and importance evoked by a stimulus within a specific situation.[12] Consumers are involved when a product or a service has economic, social, or personal significance. The degree to which consumers are involved in a purchase is also related to experience, interest, perceived risk, social visibility, and situational factors.[13] The automobile purchaser is typically highly involved in the purchase, but their interest may not last beyond a purchase.

[11] Kerin, R. A., Hartley, S. W., & Rudelius, W. (2011). *The Core Marketing*, New York: McGraw Hill.

[12] Blackwell, Roger D., Paul W. Miniard, and James F. Engel (2006), *Consumer Behavior*, Mason, OH: Thomson Higher Education.

[13] Kerin, Roger A., Steven W, Hartley, and William Rudelius (2011), *Marketing: The Core* New York: McGraw Hill.

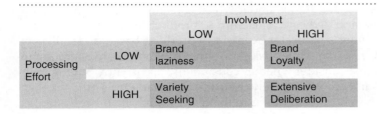

FIGURE 4-4
Involvement and Processing
Effort.

Most individuals have a *situational* (temporary) interest in new cars during the time they make a purchase, yet their interest in automobiles wanes after their purchase.[14] By contrast, involvement can be *enduring* whereby the consumer has interest in a product over a long period of time. Involvement also has cognitive and affective components.[15] *Affective* involvement indicates that a consumer is willing to spend emotional energy and has heightened feelings about an offer or activity. The buyer of a video game, for instance, may have considerable affective involvement in the purchase. *Cognitive* involvement indicates that a consumer is willing to think about or process information about some product or service. Many automobile consumers, for instance, will collect voluminous information and deliberate considerably prior to making a purchase.

The amount time and energy associated with a purchase also varies along the *effort continuum*.[16] Some decisions can be characterized by *routine problem-solving* whereby the consumer considers no new information while making a decision and repeats choices made previously. A consumer's at-home consumption of water, for example, is typically not a decision that requires any thought. Influencing routine behavior of this nature can be challenging. Research indicates, however, that drawing consumer awareness to issues such as water conservation can decrease consumption.[17] *Intermediate problem-solving* refers to a search that involves limited information search and deliberation. The purchaser of a replacement printer for a personal computer, for example, will often seek little information and spend little time on the search. Consumers may rely on rules or heuristics to help them make such decisions. *Extensive problem-solving* refers to situations in which a consumer engages in a prolonged deliberation and extensive search designed to minimize the negative consequences of a wrong choice. The auto example outlined earlier in this chapter reflects this type of setting given that the purchaser normally engages in extensive search to avoid making a poor decision.

Simultaneous consideration of involvement and processing effort enables us to describe four types of consumer decision types, depicted in Figure 4-4.[18]

---

[14] Hoyer, Wayne D., Deborah J. MacInnis, and Rik Pieters (2013), *Consumer Behavior*, Mason, OH: Cengage.

[15] Hoyer, Wayne D., Deborah J. MacInnis, and Rik Pieters (2013), *Consumer Behavior*, Mason, OH: Cengage.

[16] Kardes, Frank, Maria Cronley, and Thomas W. Cline (2011), *Consumer Behavior*, Mason, OH: Cengage.

[17] Middlestadt, Susan, et al. (2001), "Turning minds on and faucets off: Water conservation education in Jordanian schools," *The Journal of Environmental Education* 32 (2), 37–45.

[18] Kardes, Frank, Maria Cronley, and Thomas W. Cline (2011), *Consumer Behavior*, Mason, OH: Cengage.

Brand laziness refers to conditions under which consumers are marginally involved in a purchase and dedicate little effort to product selection. This behavior reflects the consumer's natural movement to products based on familiarity and convenience. When a marketer recognizes that consumers are operating in this manner, they must consider whether consumers are currently buying their product. If the consumer repeatedly buys a sustainable marketer's product, then effort should be focused on continuing to make this purchase process simple. If the consumer is not currently buying a firm's products, and consumers are engaged in brand laziness behavior, the marketer must find some motivation to augment the buyer's current rationale. While the marketer may prefer to emphasize sustainable and ecological product benefits, these consumers are not motivated to make such considerations. In many cases, the sustainable marketer may emphasize product convenience. *Variety seeking* refers to a consumer's desire to choose new alternatives over familiar ones. These consumers are low in involvement but process information in the pursuit of variety. Sustainable marketers can draw awareness to the merits of their products, and some consumers who process this information should be inclined to switch preferences to the more sustainable product.

Two other decision types are characterized by varying levels of processing but high levels of involvement. *Brand loyalty* reflects a consumer's intrinsic commitment to a brand based on the benefits it provides to consumers. These consumers are heavily involved in purchases, but they do not spend much time deliberating among alternatives. When a sustainable marketer's brand is preferred by these consumers, the marketer uses promotions that reinforce consumer preferences. When another brand is preferred, the marketer is challenged to draw awareness to the firm's product offerings. It can be challenging to draw awareness to sustainable and ecological merits of a product when the consumer is not willing to evaluate additional information. By contrast, *extensive deliberation* refers to decision making characterized by high involvement and high information processing. Promotional appeals to these customers can underscore how the sustainable alternatives offer the advantages beyond the consumer's current products.

Personality and Personality Traits

Social psychology has repeatedly illustrated how personality affects performance across a wide array of occupational groups and decision-making contexts. *Personality* refers to a person's consistent manner of responding to the environment in which she or he lives, whereas a *personality trait* is a consistent characteristic way of behaving.[19] Psychologists enumerate five personality traits, including a person's extraversion, emotional stability, agreeableness, conscientiousness, and openness to experience.[20] *Extraversion* addresses the degree to which a person can be characterized as sociable, gregarious, talkative, and assertive, whereas *emotional stability* refers to the extent to which an individual can be described

---

[19] Sheth, Jagdish N. and Banwari Mittal (2004), *Customer Behavior: A Managerial Approach*, Mason, OH: Southwestern.

[20] Barrick, Murray R., and Michael K. Mount (1991), "The Big Five personality dimensions and job performance: A meta-analysis," *Personnel Psychology*, 44, 1–26.

as anxious, depressed, angry, worried, and insecure. *Agreeableness* embodies the degree to which a person is courteous, flexible, trusting, cooperative, and good natured, and *conscientiousness* refers to the extent to which individuals are careful, thorough, organized, and responsible. *Openness to experience* captures the degree to which an individual is imaginative, curious, broad-minded, and artistically sensitive. Research suggests that individuals with strong levels of agreeableness, conscientiousness, and openness to experience are more likely to act in an environmentally friendly way.[21]

Motivation

Patagonia founder Yvon Chouinard decided to begin selling salmon jerky at Patagonia stores in 2012.[22] In the development of this product, he found it necessary to inform the industry about the toxins inherent to farm-raised fish. He has committed Patagonia to being a responsible company that seeks to make money without inflicting undue social harm. His methods have gained the attention of several larger firms such as Nike, Levi's, and Wal-Mart. His passion for sustainable excellence—achieved through triple bottom-line performance—offers a strong example of how a motivated person can enhance profits while minimizing ecological impact.

Yvon Chouinard is clearly motivated to work in unison with his natural environment. *Motivation* is defined as the state of drive or arousal that compels behavior toward a goal-object.[23] A drive is a state of tension within the individual that prompts action to alleviate the tension, whereas a goal-object is a something whose acquisition will reduce tension. Maslow's compelling hierarchy of needs classifies five levels of drives that influence behavior.[24] These include physiological, safety, social, self-esteem, and self-actualization. The appearance of one need rests on the satisfaction of lower level needs. Safety needs must be met, for example, prior to pursuing social needs. Consequently, marketers should appreciate where targeted consumers likely fall within the hierarchy and institute sustainability-oriented promotional campaigns that reflect motivations.

Lifestyle

During the 1996 U.S. presidential election, members of both the Democratic and Republican parties dedicated considerable energy to a group of swing voters described as "soccer moms." Women who fit this description drove sports utility vehicles or minivans and carried snacks and juice drinks for their children. They could be full-time homemakers or work outside the home, and they could be

---

[21] Milfont, Taciano L., and Chris G. Sibley (2012), "The big five personality traits and environmental engagement: Associations at the individual and societal level," *Journal of Environmental Psychology* 32 (2), 187–195.

[22] Stevenson, Seth (2012) "Patagonia's Founder Is America's Most Unlikely Business Guru," *The Wall Street Journal*, April 26.

[23] Sheth, Jagdish N., and Banwari Mittal (2004), *Customer Behavior: A Managerial Approach*, Mason, OH: Southwestern.

[24] Maslow, Abraham Harold (1943), "A theory of human motivation," *Psychological Review* 50 (4), 370–396.

working class or upper middle class suburbanites.[25] Campaign appeals focused on self-sacrificing women who always placed the needs of family above personal needs and interests. By understanding the needs and conditions of people within this soccer mom lifestyle, politicians sought to illustrate how their policies would enhance living conditions for these women and their families.

Lifestyle refers to a as a mode of living identified by how people spend their time, what their interests are, and what they think of themselves and the world around them.[26] For example, research indicates that many modern farmers incorporate a strong, ecological orientation to the way they live, and this orientation is incorporated into much of their decision making.[27] Understanding the priorities of consumers and their attitudes provides insight into their behavior, and marketers increasingly consider lifestyle issues when developing sustainability-oriented campaigns. Chapter 6 elucidates on these issues by describing sustainability-related lifestyles and their influences on market segmentation.

DEMOGRAPHIC INFLUENCES ON THE CONSUMPTION PROCESS

Demography refers to the size, distribution, structure, and change of populations. It examines gender and age group as well as ethnic considerations (race, legal nationality, and first language) and economic characteristics (economic activity, employment status, occupation, industry, and income).[28] These factors can heavily influence attitudes and behaviors associated with sustainability. Research suggests, for instance, that women are more likely than men to express concern about consumption's broader influences and act on social and environmental concerns.[29] Age affects consumer expectations that global warming effects will occur. Senior citizens are the age group that is least likely to believe that global warming will happen during their lifetimes. These differences are not solely a function of seniors' recognition of age, as individuals 65 and older are also the most skeptical that the effects of global warming have already begun.[30]

---

[25] Carroll, Susan J. (1999), "The disempowerment of the gender gap: Soccer moms and the 1996 elections," *PS: Political Science & Politics* 32 (1), 7–12

[26] Burgess, Steven Michael, and Jan-Benedict E. M. Steenkamp (2006), "Marketing renaissance: How research in emerging markets advances marketing science and practice," *International Journal of Research in Marketing* 23 (4), 337–356.

[27] Coldwell, Ian (2007), "New farming masculinities 'More than just shit-kickers', we're 'switched-on' farmers wanting to 'balance lifestyle, sustainability and coin'," *Journal of Sociology* 43 (1), 87–103.

[28] Shryock, Henry S., Jacob S. Siegel and Associates (2013) *The methods and materials of demography.* San Diego, CA: Academic Press.

[29] Luchs, Michael G., and Todd A. Mooradian (2012), "Sex, personality, and sustainable consumer behaviour: Elucidating the gender effect," *Journal of Consumer Policy* 35 (1), 127–144.

[30] www.gallup.com/poll/167879/not-global-warming-serious-threat.aspx (September 10, 2015).

Ethnicity has been implicated as a factor influencing American attitudes toward sustainability-related policies. For example, a recent national poll indicated that 30 percent of Americans favored the regulation of carbon dioxide as a pollutant. While 40 percent of Hispanics favored such regulation, less than 30 percent of African American and non-Hispanic white consumers favored this legislation.[31] Industry further has an effect on attitudes toward climate change. Industries seem to vary based on the ways they seek to neutralize stakeholder perceptions regarding their climate commitments.[32]

SITUATIONAL INFLUENCES ON THE CONSUMPTION PROCESS

The decisions made throughout the consumption process do not occur in a vacuum. On the contrary, they are influenced by the situation faced by the consumer.[33] The purchase task, social surroundings, physical setting, temporal conditions, and antecedent conditions affect consumption of all products. Consumers may be inclined to buy Toms Shoes when they are purchasing a product for an environmentally sensitive friend. Similarly, when consumption is a social process, such as in restaurant selection, consumers may prefer to dine at restaurants such as Chipotle that have a strong reputation for using healthy ingredients.[34] Marketers often use sales promotions to shape the physical surroundings to entice sustainable behavior. For example, Boots' Botanics shampoo marketed in the United Kingdom (see Figure 4-5) provides information on the retail shelf indicating the carbon footprint of the product. Point-of-sales items can have a strong influence at the moment of purchase, and similar promotions at the point of consumption can also enhance product usage. For example, the WWF poster in Figure 4-6 asks people to consider whether printing a document is necessary. Estimates indicate that companies can save 20 percent of their costs by being more efficient in their use of paper.[35]

Temporal effects refer to the timing of a purchase. Marketers often provide incentives to make purchases designed to prompt action at the current time. For

---

[31] Leiserowitz, Anthony, and Karen Akerlof (2010), *Race, Ethnicity and Public Responses to Climate Change.* Yale University and George Mason University. New Haven, CT: Yale Project on Climate Change.

[32] Talbot, David, and Olivier Boiral (2014), "Strategies for climate change and impression management: A case study among Canada's large industrial emitters," *Journal of Business Ethics* 1–18.

[33] Belk, Russell W. (1974), "An exploratory assessment of situational effects in buyer behavior," *Journal of Marketing Research* 11(2), 156–163. Kerin, Roger A., Steven W, Hartley, and William Rudelius (2011), *Marketing: The Core.* New York: McGraw Hill.

[34] Jang, Yoon Jung, Woo Gon Kim, and Mark A. Bonn (2011), "Generation Y consumers' selection attributes and behavioral intentions concerning green restaurants," *International Journal of Hospitality Management* 30 (4), 803–811.

[35] d2ouvy59p0dg6k.cloudfront.net/downloads/final_paper_saving_tips_1.pdf (September 10, 2015).

FIGURE 4-5

Boots' Reduced Carbon
Footprint Botanics
Shampoo[36]

instance, retailers may have limited-time offers that entice consumers to buy four LED light bulbs for the price of three. Antecedent effects concern the consumer's prior experiences and their influences on consumption. For example, research suggests that only 35 percent of hybrid automobile owners choose to purchase a hybrid again when they return to market.[37]

SOCIAL INFLUENCES ON THE CONSUMPTION PROCESS

Our discussion to this point underscores how psychological, demographic, and situational factors influence consumer decision making. In this section, we characterize several social influences, including culture, subculture, social class, and reference groups, that affect the consumption process.

Culture

German consumers have been recycling glass for decades. In cities such as Cologne, for instance, large depository receptacles are positioned strategically throughout

---

[36] www.pef-world-forum.org/2007/ (September 9, 2015).

[37] articles.latimes.com/2012/apr/09/business/la-fi-mo-repeat-hybrid-car-buyers-20120409 (September 10, 2015).

FIGURE 4-6
World Wildlife Federation
Paper Conservation Poster

town. Commuters using public transportation know that they can recycle glass and paper products before boarding trolleys or buses. The impetus to recycle is further enhanced by a government mandate that producers are responsible for the entire life cycle of packaging.[38] The desire to recycle is due in part to economic and political circumstances, but it also is due to cultural tradition and developments in German culture. The nation's culture reflects changes in social values and attitudes toward the environment. Moreover, it also participates in the construction of perceptions of nature through its art and literature.[39]

This German example offers some insight into the role of culture in the consumption process. *Culture* refers to a set of basic values and assumptions, orientations to life, beliefs, policies, procedures, and behavioral conventions shared by a group of people that influence each member's behavior and interpretations of

[38] www.economist.com/node/9249262 (September 11, 2015).

[39] Goodbody, Axel (2002), *The culture of German environmentalism: Anxieties, visions, realities*. Vol. 5. Berghahn Books.

the meaning of other people's behavior.[40] Culture is pervasive in that it operates throughout a society, and it is also functional, learned, and dynamic.[41] Figure 4-7 illustrates multiple levels at which culture manifests itself. Culture is revealed by understanding the underlying assumptions, values, and artifacts produced within a group. *Underlying assumptions* are ordinarily unconscious factors that influence the way in which people think, perceive, and feel. For example, the notion that businesses should be profitable or that medicine should prolong life are assumptions that are typically not questioned within a culture.[42]

Although these underlying assumptions are essential to understanding a culture, by their nature they are taken for granted, invisible, and pre-conscious. The underlying assumptions lead to the values that govern behavior. A *value* refers to a socially preferred mode of conduct that persists over time.[43] For instance, psychologists recognize that American values generally emphasize achievement, freedom, progress, individualism, and materialism.[44]

Values give rise to specific fruits of labor including artifacts, visible and audible behavioral patterns, technology, and art. *Artifacts* refer to the objects made by human beings. For example, single-use products such as plastic water bottles exemplify one type of artifact. The audible and visible behavioral patterns capture, among other things, the role of language in culture. Visible behavioral patterns also capture the myths, laws, customs, and rituals within a society. For example, U.S. retailers and shoppers have created Black Friday as a big shopping day prior to the December holidays.

Language can have a strong effect on perceptions and consumer learning. *Languages* vary based on the manner by which sounds are written, and these differences may be associated with different decision making processes.[45] In phonographic languages (e.g., English), symbols (letters) are used to represent sounds, whereas in syllabic languages (e.g., Burmese), symbols represent syllables. By contrast, in logographic languages (e.g., Japanese), symbols represent words.[46]

Technology refers to the application of knowledge for practical purposes. Cultures vary in how they employ technologies. For example, hydropower is a

[40] Spencer-Oatey, Helen (2008), *Culturally Speaking: Culture, Communication, and Politeness*, London: Continuum.

[41] Cateora, Philip R., Mary C. Gilly, and John L. Graham (2011), *International Marketing*, New York: McGraw Hill.

[42] Schein, Edgar (1984), "Coming to a New Awareness of Organizational Culture," *Sloan Management Review*, 25 (2), 3–16.

[43] Rokeach, Milton (1973). *The nature of human values* (Vol. 438). New York: Free Press.

[44] Spence, Janet T. (1985), "Achievement American style: The rewards and costs of individualism," *American Psychologist* 40 (12), 1285. Morris, Michael H., Ramon A. Avila, and Jeffrey Allen (1993), "Individualism and the modern corporation: Implications for innovation and entrepreneurship," *Journal of Management* 19 (3), 595–612.

Pelled, Lisa Hope, and Katherine R. Xin (1997), "Work values and their human resource management implications: A theoretical comparison of China, Mexico, and the United States," *Journal of Applied Management Studies* 6 (2), 185.

[45] Fillmore, Lily Wong, and Catherine E. Snow (2000), "What teachers need to know about language," U.S. Department of Education's Office of Educational Research and Improvement.

[46] Zhang, Shi, and Bernd H. Schmitt (2001), "Creating Local Brands in Multilingual International Markets," *Journal of Marketing Research* 38 (3), 313–325.

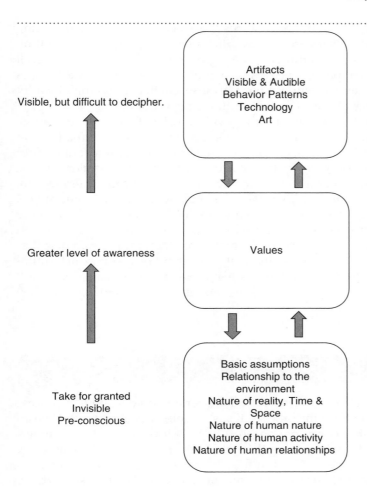

Visible, but difficult to decipher.

Greater level of awareness

Take for granted
Invisible
Pre-conscious

Artifacts
Visible & Audible
Behavior Patterns
Technology
Art

Values

Basic assumptions
Relationship to the
environment
Nature of reality, Time &
Space
Nature of human nature
Nature of human activity
Nature of human relationships

FIGURE 4-7
The levels of Culture and
their Interaction.[47]

source of energy in 150 countries around the world, yet its use is highly concentrated in a few regions. Africa has the least hydropower of all continents, yet it has the greatest capacity for increased production.[48]

Art refers to human activity whereby one person consciously hands on to others feelings experienced, and other people are infected by these feelings and experience them.[49] This definition provides broad latitude to encompass a wide range of human expression, including music, literature, architecture, sculpture, and visual arts. The forms of expression preferred by a society offers insight into the priorities and the objectives of people within the culture. Artists not only craft works of art to reflect sustainability issues, but they also use sustainable methods in production.

---

[47] Schein, Edgar (1984), "Coming to a New Awareness of Organizational Culture," *Sloan Management Review*, 25 (2), 3–16.

[48] www.worldwatch.org/use-and-capacity-global-hydropower-increases-0 (September 11, 2015).

[49] Tolstoy, Leo, Richard Pevear, and Larissa Volokhonsky (1899), *What is art?* New York: Thomas Y. Crowell & Company.

An important facet of culture concerns the social organizations operating within a society. *Subcultures* are groups differentiated from the rest of culture based on values, ideas, and attitudes. These groups may vary from the overall culture based on geography, ethnicity, race, or other demographic characteristics such as religion and family composition.[50] To the extent that individuals identify with a subculture, the effects of overall culture may be diminished.

Social class represents a subgrouping within society based on the prestige and esteem associated with economic success and the wealth accumulation.[51] In the United States, for instance, social class is often broken down into four groups: upper class, middle class, working class, and lower class.[52] Categorization into one of these groups is in part based on occupation, income, education, and wealth. The appeals that resonate with each class are unlikely to have the same appeal to other consumers. For instance, the marketing of Tesla automobiles and the prices of these cars has necessarily focused on wealthier consumers.[53] Although middle income consumers may favor the fuel technology, the price point makes the vehicle infeasible for this class. Finally, the consumption process can be influenced by a *reference group* that influences an individual's purchasing behavior.[54] These groups serve as information sources and influence perceptions, and they can also affect an individual's aspiration levels.

SUMMARY

The purpose of this chapter has been to characterize the consumption process and identify constraints on the process. If sustainable marketers are to have an influence on the entire consumption process, then it is essential they understand the nature of decision making throughout the product purchase and use. The consumption process outlined in this chapter refers to the series of steps that buyers make before, during, and after consumption. The first stage of the decision-making process is the pre-purchase stage, which includes need recognition, search, and evaluation of alternatives. The purchase stage refers to point at which the consumer decides whether to buy and the conditions under which to buy the product. The third stage of the consumer decision-making process refers to the consumption of a product offering. The final stage of the consumer decision-making process is the post-consumption stage. This process is influenced by psychological, demographic, situational, and social factors.

[50] Douglas, Susan P., and C. Samuel Craig (1983), *International Marketing Research*, Englewood Cliffs, NJ: Prentice-Hall.

[51] Weiss, Yoram, and Chaim Fershtman (1998), "Social status and economic performance: A survey" *European Economic Review* 42 (3), 801–820.

[52] Snarey, John R., and George E. Vaillant (1985), "How lower- and working-class youth become middle-class adults: The association between ego defense mechanisms and upward social mobility," *Child Development* (1985): 56 (4), 899–910.

[53] inrater.com/company/tesla-motors-inc/ (September 11, 2015).

[54] Bearden, William O., and Michael J. Etzel (1982), "Reference Group Influence on Product and Brand Purchase Decisions," *Journal of Consumer Research* 9 (2), 183–194.

KEY TERMS

consumption process
pre-purchase stage
need recognition
search
evaluation of alternatives
purchase stage
consumption
post-consumption stage
post-consumption evaluation
divestment
involvement
affective involvement

cognitive involvement
effort continuum
routine problem-solving
intermediate problem-solving
extensive problem-solving
brand laziness
variety seeking
brand loyalty
extensive deliberation
personality
personality traits
motivation

lifestyle
demography
culture
underlying assumptions
value
artifact
technology
art
subcultures
social class
reference group

DISCUSSION QUESTIONS

1. Why would baby boomers express interest in sustainable automobiles?

2. How do companies benefit from examining the decision-making processes for sustainable products?

3. What are the four stages of the consumption process?

4. Do all consumers engage in each phase of the consumption process? What psychological processes influences their likelihood of spending time on a consumption decision?

5. How does personality influence consumption?

6. What is the difference between brand laziness and extensive deliberation?

7. Describe a marketing organization that focuses on consumer use of their product.

8. Offer an example of how the five situational characteristics influence specific purchases.

9. Why should marketers consider demographic factors when making promotional campaigns?

10. What factors increase the likelihood that consumers will divest themselves of a product in a sustainable manner?

5

Influencing Consumer Choice

INTRODUCTION

Levi's

Consider the last time that you cleaned out a closet and eliminated some clothing items from your wardrobe. One of the surest ways to promote product reuse/recycling is by giving these discarded items to a charity such as Goodwill. For many of us, however, worn or used garments from our closets are not given to charity but end up in landfills. Consumers in the United States annually generate about 25 billion pounds (11 billion kilograms) of waste or approximately 82 pounds (37 kilograms) per person. A total of 85 percent of this *waste* ends up in landfills, accounting for 5.2 percent of municipal solid waste.[1] This rate of textile recycling is among the poorest recycling rate for any reusable material.[2] A total of 95 percent of recycled clothing can be reused, and nearly half of the recycled garments can be worn again as secondhand clothing.[3]

The need to increase the amount of garment recycling is increasing in importance, as American consumers may buy five times as much clothing as they did in 1980.[4] The fashion industry uses more water than any other industry except agriculture.[5] Thousands of chemicals are used to turn raw materials into textiles, and 25 percent

FIGURE 5-1
Levi Strauss Clothing
Recycling Initiative

[1] www.weardonaterecycle.org/about/issue.html (July 30, 2015).

[2] www.epa.gov/osw/nonhaz/municipal/pubs/2012_msw_fs.pdf (July 30, 2015).

[3] www.theatlantic.com/business/archive/2014/07/where-does-discarded-clothing-go/374613/ (July 30, 2015).

[4] www.theatlantic.com/business/archive/2014/07/where-does-discarded-clothing-go/374613/ (September 26, 2015).

[5] Ninimäki, Kirsi (2014), "Consumer Behavior in the Fashion Industry," *Handbook of Sustainable Apparel Production*, S. S. Muthu (Ed.) 271–288, Boca Raton, FL: CRC Press.

of the pesticides used in the United States are applied to grow nonorganic cotton.[6] This chemical use in production may yield irreversible damage to people and the environment. While the production process may be taxing on the environment, two-thirds of a garment's carbon footprint occurs after a product is purchased.[7]

The Levi Strauss Company has undertaken a program that enables consumers to reduce their carbon footprint while also lowering their clothing costs. Levi's has announced that customers who drop off a clean, dry item of clothing or a pair of shoes at any Levi's store—of any brand—will receive a voucher worth 20 percent off the purchase of a regular-priced, in-store Levi's item.[8] The company launched this garment take-back program in partnership with Switzerland-based I:CO, a company that specializes in reuse and recycling of apparel, footwear, and textiles. After clothing is dropped in the in-store collection boxes, I:CO plans to sort the garments into wearable for resale and not-so-wearable items repurposed for insulation, padding, cleaning cloths, or other uses.

This program addresses the consumer's sustainability at the moment of purchase and at the point of divestment. Previously worn products have lower processing and production costs than new garments, and the recycling of these products at divestment reduces the size of landfills. Providing financial incentives (as Levi's does) lowers customers' costs, enhances relationships with consumers, and reduces the buyer's ecological influence.

The fashion industry illustrates how consumer purchases influence climate change and sustainability. In this chapter, we look closely at the efforts to influence the consumption process. *Promotion* refers to all communication from the marketer designed to persuade, inform, or remind potential buyers of a product in order to elicit a response of influence an opinion. The *promotional mix* includes advertising, personal selling, public relations, sales promotion, and direct marketing. *Advertising* refers to one-way, impersonal mass communication about a product or organization that is paid for by a marketing organization, whereas *personal selling* refers to personal, face-to-face interaction with a potential customer. *Public relations* involves the use of publicity and other nonpaid forms of promotion and information to influence attitudes about a company, its products, or about the values of the organization. *Sales promotion* includes all marketing communication action other than advertising, personal selling, public relations, and direct marketing designed to influence consumer purchases and relationships with intermediaries in distribution channels. *Direct marketing* refers to direct efforts to target an audience through the Internet, direct mail, telemarketing, direct-action advertising, and catalog selling. To varying degrees, firms use each of these forms of promotion over the consumption process.

We begin by examining efforts to influence consumers before they purchase and subsequently consider efforts to influence consumers at the point of purchase. We then examine how marketers influence the manner of consumption followed by an investigation of processes by which consumer divest products via recycling or other means.

---

[6] www.organicconsumers.org/news/care-what-you-wear-facts-cotton-clothing-production (September 26, 2015).

[7] greenhomeauthority.com/eco-friendly-fashion/ (September 26, 2015).

[8] www.levistrauss.com/wp-content/uploads/2015/07/ICO-Recycling-Expansion-Release .pdf (September 26, 2015).

SUSTAINABLE MARKETING ACTION DESIGNED TO INFLUENCE PRE-PURCHASE DECISIONS

As described in Chapter 4, consumers may pass through three phases before they are ready to make a purchase, and sustainable marketing initiatives can play an important role throughout the pre-purchase stage. The first phase, *need recognition*, occurs when the consumer recognizes a discrepancy between current and desired conditions. Several inherent conditions can influence consumer perceptions of the current state of affairs. For example, someone buying groceries for a home knows that the passage of time influences food quality. Although the consumer may realize a discrepancy between current conditions and desired states, the marketer can have a strong influence on both facets of need recognition. Marketers often stimulate demand by altering consumer perceptions of currently owned products. For example, the GE Silicone III ad depicted in Figure 5-2a informs consumers that up to 40 percent of the energy used to heat and cool a home may be lost due to leakage associated with tiny cracks and holes in the home's exterior. The current state, the porous exterior, is less desirable than the desired state, the silicone-sealed home. The second way in which to influence need recognition is to increase the perceived value of alternative products. For example, the ad depicted in Figure 5-2b informs consumers that Osram bulbs last several years at normal usage.

When a firm elects to stimulate need recognition, it has two essential means by which to do so. First, the organization may employ a *generic need recognition strategy* that seeks to stimulate demand by drawing attention to the entire product class.[9] Since many environmentally based product offerings are in their infancy, it is not uncommon for advertisers to promote the product class rather than a specific product. Advertisers promoting sustainable marketing and sustainability projects may be sellers of the product, but they may also represent some other interest group. These groups may include industry-wide advocacy groups, nongovernment organizations (NGOs), governmental agencies, utilities, industry foundations, or other parties. For example, utility companies and NGOs may share the costs of campaigns to promote efficient lighting. Each of these groups has motivations to limit the amount of energy consumed, and fluorescent lighting helps them achieve this objective.

Brand-specific need recognition refers to efforts to stimulate demand for a specific branded product rather than for the industry or technology. For example, the Cree LED light bulb packaging in Figure 5-3 emphasizes the benefits of the brand rather than the product class. In some industries, the need to draw awareness of a product category is essential prior to marketing the merits of a single purveyor. For example, utility company ads for LED lightings increase awareness of the product before the exposure to ads calling attention to Cree's brand-specific offering.

Once consumers identify unmet needs, they begin to engage in search activities to satisfy the need. The search activities can be internal and external to the consumer. *Internal search* refers to retrieving knowledge from memory, whereas *external search* refers to collecting information from outside sources.[10] In many

---

[9] Chakravarti, Amitav, and Chris Janiszewski (2004), "The Influence of Generic Advertising on Brand Preferences," *Journal of Consumer Research*, 30 (4), 487–502.

[10] Hoyer, Wayne D., Deborah J. MacInnis, and Rik Pieters (2013), *Consumer Behavior*, Mason, OH: Cengage.

FIGURE 5-2

Need Recognition by Altering Consumer Perceptions of Currently Owned Products (a) or Increasing The Perceived Value of Alternative Products (b).

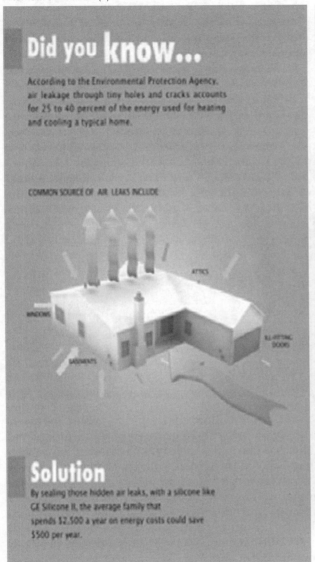

cases, consumers rely solely upon previous experiences in their search efforts. Consumer psychology indicates that reliance on prior experiences is dependent on the degree of confidence in the decision making, satisfaction with prior decisions, and the ability to retrieve knowledge.[11]

---

[11] Cacioppo, John T., and Richard E. Petty (1984), "The Elaboration Likelihood Model of Persuasion," *Advances in Consumer Research*, 11 (1), 673–675. Kiel, Geoffrey C., and Roger A. Lyon (1981), "Dimensions of Consumer Information Seeking Behavior," *Journal of Marketing Research*, 18 (2), 233–239.

FIGURE 5-3

Brand-Specific Need
Recognition [12]

The strategic implication of the internal search lies in recognizing the extent to which a consumer relies on personal past experiences to frame judgments. Consumers who express high levels of confidence in brands that offer high levels of satisfaction will be reluctant to consider new information in their purchasing decisions. If the marketer has the luxury of this consumer as a client, then the marketing effort should emphasize how new product offerings retain attributes that yield high satisfaction yet provide new environmental benefits that exceed prior product offerings. When this consumer is not currently a firm's client, the task of promotion is much more challenging, as it may be necessary to persuade the consumer to seek additional information.

External search efforts draw information from the environment so that evaluations can be made about product offerings. Family, friends, the media, and opinion leaders are sources of information not controlled by marketers of a product. This information may come via word of mouth, or increasingly consumers receive information by word-of-mouse. Word-of-mouth communication has been shown to be an important source of influence in the purchase of household goods.[13]

---

[12] cleantechnica.com/2014/07/29/cree-soft-white-led-bulb-review-exclusive/ (September 26, 2015).

[13] Katz, Elihu, and Paul F. Lazarsfeld (1955), *Personal Influence: The Part Played by People in the Flow of Mass Communications*. Glencoe, IL: The Free Press.

In addition, research indicates that advice from other consumers about a service exerts more influence than all marketer-generated information combined.[14] Word-of-mouse communication enables consumers to nurture relationships, refine evaluations of brands, develop an understanding of marketer efforts to influence decisions, and reflection upon the consumption experience.[15]

External search efforts provide an opportunity for nonmarketing entities to influence consumer decision-making processes. Nongovernment organizations can be informative to consumers engaged in search activities. Greenpeace, for example, annually publishes a *Guide to Greener Electronics* that evaluates electronics companies based on chemical usage, e-waste, and energy consumption. Similarly, *Consumer Reports* has published evaluations of the degree to which products are environmentally friendly, biodegradable, and gentle on the Earth.[16]

Marketers must make several considerations based on these external sources of information. First, they must examine the degree to which the consumer is involved in the purchase, as involved consumers are inclined to spend more time evaluating alternatives and collecting information.[17] Consumers are more likely to collect more information about an auto purchase, for example, than the purchase of paper towel. Second, the marketer should consider the degree to which the consumer is likely to rely on the information provided by the third party. Given the amount of information available today, there are likely to be many credible sources of information that are not incorporated into search activities. Underwriters Laboratories and the United Nations, for example, publish substantial amounts of product information, but it is questionable whether consumers use this information during their external search efforts. While it would be reckless for the marketer to ignore these sources of information, the sources are not frequently incorporated into decision making.

The third consideration for sustainable marketing strategy concerns the nature of the evaluations by the external source. When positive evaluations are provided by third parties, they can become effective parts of a marketing campaign. For example, the Honda Motor Company uses data from the U.S. Environmental Protection Agency to support its claim as the most fuel efficient car company in North America. When evaluations of company products are not favorable, the firm should investigate the evaluation process. To the extent that the evaluation is flawed, marketers should be explicit in expressing concerns for the basis for evaluation. Furthermore, evaluations that indicate limitations in current product offerings provide impetus for new product designs. For example, the Chevrolet announcement of the Volt electric car was motivated in part by the less than favorable evaluations of older models of General Motors cars.[18]

---

[14] Alreck, P. L., and R. B. Settle (1995), "The Importance of Word-of-Mouth Communication to Service Buyers," *AMA Winter Educators' Proceedings*. D. W. Stewart and N. J. Vilcassim, eds. Chicago: American Marketing Association.

[15] Hung, Kineta H. M., and Li Yiyan (2007), "The Influence of eWOM on Virtual Consumer Communities: Social Capital, Consumer Learning, and Behavioral Outcomes," *Journal of Advertising Research*, 47 (4), 485–495.

[16] *Consumer Reports* (2007), "It's Not Easy Being Green," *Consumer Reports*, 72 (9), 9.

[17] Celsi, Richard L., and Jerry C. Olson (1988), "The Role of Involvement in Attention and Comprehension Processes," *Journal of Consumer Research*, 15 (2), 210–224.

[18] Sherman, Don (2008), "G.M. at 100: Is Its Future Electric?" *New York Times*, September 14, AU1.

After consumers engage in search activities, they make their initial *pre-purchase evaluations*.[19] Although the merits of sustainable marketing initiatives may be known to the consumer, these product benefits are rarely the primary motivations for purchase decisions. The sustainable marketer must necessarily assess the value of a product offering in its entirety rather than solely on the environmental value. In their book examining sustainability strategies, Daniel Esty and Andrew S. Winston emphasize that sustainable benefits of a product are typically at least the third benefit offered by a product.[20] Thus, hybrid automobiles provide a family of benefits beyond fuel efficiency that must be considered by marketing strategy. Japanese researchers, for instance, report that drivers understand the deleterious influences of greenhouse gases, but recognition of the problem does not lead to purchases of fuel efficient cars.[21] In the Japanese market, researchers discovered that price constraints made purchases of some hybrid or fuel efficient infeasible. The marketer who wants to influence sustainable consumption must have a product offering with comparable value to the consumer that also provides environmental benefits. When consumers realize the total value offered by products developed through sustainability efforts, the likelihood of purchase should also increase.

SUSTAINABLE MARKETING ACTION DESIGNED TO INFLUENCE PURCHASES

The second stage of the decision-making process is the point at which the consumer decides to make a purchase. Sales promotion is particularly influential at the moment of purchase. *Sales promotion* refers to the marketing communication activities beyond advertising, personal selling, and public relations, in which a short-term incentive motivates a purchase.[22] In many cases, consumers need to make a purchase but need an immediate incentive to act. Sales promotion tends to be preferred over advertising when the marketers want to stimulate short-term demand, induce trail usage, encourage brand switching, obtain immediate short-term results, or promote a price orientation.

There are several forms of sales promotions frequently used to induce sustainable purchases. These promotions can be distinguished based on the type of incentive employed by the marketer. *Price reduction promotions* provide a financial saving to the customer that buys a product. A *coupon* refers to a document that entitles consumers to an immediate price reduction.[23] For example, Figure 5-4 illustrates how Seventh Generation uses coupons. By contrast, a *rebate* such as the one by Energy Smart Colorado in Figure 5-5 refers to a cash refund realized after a purchase.

[19] Blackwell, Roger D., Paul W. Miniard, and James F. Engel (2006), *Consumer Behavior*, Mason, OH: Thomson Higher Education.

[20] Esty, Daniel C., and Andrew S. Winston (2006), *Green to Gold*, New Haven, CT: Yale University Press.

[21] Kishi, Kunihiro, and Keiichi Satoh (2005), "Evaluation of Willingness to Buy a Low-Pollution Car in Japan," *Journal of the Eastern Asia Society for Transportation Studies*, 6, 3121–3134.

[22] O'Guinn, Thomas C., Chris T. Allen, and Richard J. Semenik (2006), *Advertising and Integrated Brand Promotion*, Mason, OH: Thompson Higher Education.

[23] Kerin, Roger A., Steven W, Hartley, and William Rudelius (2011), *Marketing: The Core*, New York: McGraw Hill.

FIGURE 5-4
Coupon use by Seventh
Generation.[24]

Product-based promotions refer to sales promotion in which the marketer rewards the customer in the form of merchandise. A *premium* refers to an additional item offered to the consumer after a purchase of some other item. Buy one, get one free promotions are forms of premiums. *Sampling* involves promotional programs that enable consumers to try a product for free. These products may be made available by direct mail to the consumer or via in-store offerings. In some cases, a product may be packaged with another product to enhance consumer use. For example, lithium batteries are often packaged with cameras and other consumer electronics products.

Some product-based promotions involve some sort of competition designed to draw awareness to a firm and its products. *Contests* are game-based promotions that require consumers to use their skills to compete for prizes. Thus, the Inhabitat spring greening contest asked consumers to develop designs that involved recycled or reclaimed products (Figure 5-6). *Sweepstakes* are similar to contests, but they rely on chance—rather than skill. For example, Nature's Own bakery goods recently offered a sweepstakes in which 20 contestants were randomly chosen to win a green egg grill. Game-based promotions do not necessarily reward customers with a firm's products. The Nature's Own promotion, for instance, provides consumers with barbecue grills rather than the firm's baked goods.

Relationship-building promotions use a variety of incentives to nurture long-term relationships with customers. *Loyalty marketing programs* offer premiums to consumers when they make repeat purchases. Credit card companies, for example, enable loyal customers to redeem points (collected through repeat

[24] www.blogher.com/enter-win-1000-or-trip-blogher-09-seventh-generation (September 26, 2015).

FIGURE 5-5

Rebate use by Energy Smart Colorado.[25]

FIGURE 5-6

Spring Greening Contest at Inhabitat.[26]

---

[25] www.energysmartcolorado.com/summer-rebate/ (September 29, 2015).

[26] inhabitat.com/vote-now-in-the-spring-greening-design-competition/ (September 29, 2015).

purchases) for airfare, hotel accommodations, and other incentives. Similarly, *frequent buyer programs* reward loyal consumers for making multiple purchases. Retailers, for instance, use programs in which loyal coffee purchasers get a free cup of coffee after a number of purchases.

   On-site promotions are sales incentives offered in a firm's retail space to increase sales. *Point-of-purchase* displays are on-site promotions that provide advertising, product background information, and in many cases, products. The Bulbrite light bulbs displayed in Figure 5-7 exemplifies the use of point-of-purchase displays in a store. In addition to advertising the brand, these displays can build traffic and induce impulse buying.

FIGURE 5-7
Bulbrite Point-of-Purchase Display.[27]

----

[27] www.sptpkg.com/Point-of-Purchase-Displays.html (September 29, 2015).

It is essential to recognize the objectives of a sales promotion and the target of the promotion before implementing any tactic. Price-sensitive shoppers and consumers who frequently switch brands are likely to be enticed by price-based promotions such as coupons and rebates. When loyal customers of a firm are targeted in sales promotions, the goal is typically to reinforce their behavior and increase consumption. Loyalty marketing programs and premiums can be particularly effective with these consumers. By contrast, targeting the loyal customers of other firms seeks to persuade the consumer to switch brands. Sampling, contests, premiums, and sweepstakes can be effective ways to influence consumers to try alternative products.

SUSTAINABLE MARKETING ACTION DESIGNED TO INFLUENCE CONSUMPTION

The consumption process continues as the consumer makes the transition from purchase to usage. The consumer who buys the product must decide the time, place, and manner by which to consume.[28] Socially responsible marketing can direct each of these facets of consumption in a manner that promotes sustainability. First, consider the timing of consumption.

Timing. The timing of consumption is related to the timing of purchasing, but these temporal concerns often occur at different times. Consumers ordinarily have some flexibility regarding the time at which they buy products. In the food sector, for example, consumers buying produce and groceries often monitor the expiration dates when making purchases. In one study, consumer psychologists found evidence that up to 12 percent of products bought for the pantry are never consumed.[29] Among food products that are stored in a consumer's pantry before consumption, this same research indicates that 57 percent of these stockpiled purchases are thrown away. Consequently, the environmental cost to manufacture and distribute the product is realized, but there is no consumer benefit from the purchase. Purchase without consumption, therefore, raises the carbon footprint of the consumer without added value. One marketing implication is to market specific-use products close to the usage date for the product. For example, the sale of canned pumpkin should be promoted very close to the Canadian and U.S. Thanksgiving holidays. In addition, marketing communications about product usage should be timely and frequent.[30] For example, Campbell's soup web page and advertisements provide reminders and helpful usage ideas that decrease the likelihood that the product will be stockpiled.

Despite the merits of promotional activities that emphasize proper use of products, advertising ordinarily emphasizes the immediate purchase of products

---

[28] Blackwell, Roger D., Paul W. Miniard, and James F. Engel (2006), *Consumer Behavior*, Mason, OH: Thomson Higher Education.

[29] Wansink, Brian, S. Adam Brasel, and Steven Amjad (2000), "The Mystery of the Cabinet Castaway: Why We Buy Products We Never Use," *Journal of Family and Consumer Sciences*, 92 (1), 104–107.

[30] Wansink, Brian, and Rohit Deshpandé (1994), "'Out of Sight, Out of Mind': Pantry Stockpiling and Brand Usage Frequency," *Marketing Letters*, 5 (1), 91–100.

rather than usage. Since consumer education regarding proper use of a product reduces the consumer's carbon footprint and enhances customer satisfaction, marketers should consider dedicating some portion of advertising to product usage. In addition, many of these food products that will never be consumed can be recycled by donations to community action groups. Public service announcements that promote this form of recycling aid the underprivileged and lower the carbon footprint of the community.

Location (Place). The place chosen to consume products can have a marked influence on the sustainability of the product. In the restaurant industry, for example, consumers have purchased more takeout food than on-premise meals since 1988.[31] Restaurants like these off-premise meals because they increase revenue without raising costs associated with dining facilities. Nevertheless, the amount and form of materials used for carry-out items typically exceed the costs for on-premises meals.

This trend toward carryout sales has typically been associated with the quick service portion of the business, but increasingly casual dining restaurants are offering takeout food in the form of home meal replacement. Meals taken away from the casual dining restaurants often are designed to be reheated in a microwave. In many cases, the restaurateur must weigh the additional cost of sustainably developed packaging versus the lower costs of alternative packaging (e.g., Styrofoam).

Manner of Consumption. The manner of consumption refers to how and how much of product consumers use. Consistent with the reduce-reuse-recycle perspective, this action should ensure reductions in the amount of product used. Consumption of many energy-consuming products can be enhanced via sustainable marketing efforts. Although there is a wealth of information available regarding energy consumption, consumers in many cases are either unaware that this information exists, or they do not act based on this information. Consider first how consumption of energy to heat homes could be done more efficiently.

Efforts to enhance space heating must address both the amount of energy consumed and the related factor of how the energy is consumed. Although there have been strides in the fuel efficiency of heaters, the average U.S. home wastes 30 to 50 percent of the energy it uses. Heating and ventilation firms offer contracts that ensure low energy costs, prolonged equipment life, and heightened safety. It is fruitful for them to inform consumers that their energy bills and carbon footprints are lowest when their homes are properly sealed and insulated.[32] Duct systems should be periodically inspected for leakage, as porous duct systems waste substantial amounts of energy. Similarly, ducts located in unheated parts of the home (e.g., attic) should be insulated to reduce heat loss in the system. Air filters should be changed in accordance with manufacturer requirements, as the clean filters remove debris that reduces the efficiency of heating systems. Where possible, consumers should also use ceiling fans rather than air conditioners. Ceiling fans are substantially less expensive to operate than room and central

---

[31] Nation's Restaurant News (2007), "The Ten-Minute Manager's Guide to Improving Carryout Sales," *Nation's Restaurant News* (July 15), 20–21.

[32] economics.ag.utk.edu/extension/pubs/sp508h.pdf (September 29, 2008).

air units.[33] The homeowner should also recognize that older heating systems are less efficient than systems of today. If the central heating unit is 15 years old, then it is likely that a new system will lower the consumer's energy cost. Consumers should also consider adjusting thermostats to relatively low temperature in the winter and high temperatures in the summer. Home energy managers that use digital controls provide the ability to control multiple appliances, maintain the utility of the appliances, and conserve energy.[34]

The manner of consumption also influences the fuel efficiency of water heaters and, therefore, their carbon emissions. After a purchase, it is paramount for marketers to inform consumers about the financial and ecological merits of proper operations. Lowe's, for instance, outlines proper maintenance on its website (see Figure 5-8). First, consumers should recognize that every minute saved in the shower can conserve more than 4 gallons of water. Shorter showers use less water and require less energy to heat warm water. Similarly, low-flow plumbing devices reduce consumption of energy and water. Showers account for about 20 percent of total indoor water use. By replacing standard 4.5-gallon-per-minute showerheads with 2.5-gallon-per-minute heads, a family of four can save approximately 20,000 gallons of water per year.[35] Energy use can also be curtailed by insulating the water heater and hot water pipes. Water heater insulation jackets can save 4 to 9 percent of water heating bills, and insulation of pipes also reduces energy costs. In addition, maintaining the water heater at lower temperatures saves energy as a 10°F. reduction in water temperature generally saves 3 to 5 percent on water heating costs.[36]

The cost and carbon emissions associated with appliances and lighting can also be enhanced by effective consumption. Many appliances use batteries that account for a disproportionate amount of the toxic heavy metals contained in

FIGURE 5-8

Lowe's Guidelines for Water Heater Maintenance.[37]

[33] Rogers, Elizabeth, and Thomas M. Kostigen (2007), *The Little Green Book*, New York: Three Rivers Press.

[34] Inoue, Masahiro, Toshiyasu Higuma, Yoshiaki Ito, Noriyuki Kushiro, and Hitoshi Kubota (2003) Network Architecture for Home Energy Management System," *IEEE Transactions on Consumer Electronics*, Vol. 49 (3), 606–613.

[35] TN www.epa.gov/owow/nps/nps-conserve.html (September 29, 2008).

[36] www.aceee.org/consumerguide/waterheating.htm (September 29, 2008).

[37] www.lowes.com/projects/repair-and-maintain/water-heater-maintenance/project (October 2, 2015).

municipal solid waste, yet they make up less than 1 percent of that waste.[38] Single-use alkaline batteries contain fewer toxic chemicals than rechargeable batteries, but there are many more of them in the waste stream. Nickel-cadmium and lead-acid batteries have been targeted for elimination under an anticipated European Union directive and are banned from solid waste disposal facilities in several states. A single rechargeable nickel-metal hydride or nickel cadmium battery can replace up to 1000 single-use alkaline batteries over its lifetime.[39] Although the toxins in rechargeable batteries warrant their recycling, all rechargeable batteries except alkaline can be recycled. Fuel consumption for appliances and lighting can also be reduced by turning off these electronic devices when they are not in use. Ten percent of the energy consumed in the home is burned by communications devices and appliances that are turned off. If U.S. citizens turned off their computers and cell phone chargers when they were not being used, the country would save over $100 million.[40]

The manner in which food is consumed influences the environmental costs of consumption. Consumers can generate fewer emissions by efforts to reuse and reduce food-related products. Thus, consumers who reuse drinking receptacles limit the amount of solid waste. The water bottles that are sold in stores can be reused repeatedly to limit solid waste. The water that comes from the tap is more highly regulated than bottled water and is less expensive. Similarly, consumers who repeatedly use ceramic coffee mugs rather than Styrofoam cups limit environmental costs for product preparation and disposal. In addition, consumers can reduce consumption by using fewer napkins in restaurants and at home.

Another area of consumption that benefits from conservation is the use of paper. Conservation efforts that use less paper mean that less energy is consumed for production, and less waste is generated after consumption. A simple way to reduce costs is to use both sides of paper when writing or making copies. In addition, one can save paper costs by printing multiple pages on each side of a page. Moreover, the consumer should now question whether it is necessary to use paper when they communicate. Many messages can now be delivered via email without loss of content to message equality. Consumers should also consider whether they need paper copies of financial data such as pay stubs, ATM receipts, and bank statements. Every time the consumer opts exclusively for the digital version of these items, carbon emissions are lowered.

SUSTAINABLE MARKETING ACTION DESIGNED TO INFLUENCE POSTPURCHASE DECISIONS

The final stage of the consumer decision process occurs after some consumption of the product has begun. *Postconsumption evaluation* refers to the evaluation of a product after consumption has occurred. The buyer evaluates whether the level of satisfaction with the product meets or exceeds performance expectations before the purchase. When the performance of the product meets or exceeds

---

[38] www.epa.gov/epr/products/batteries.html (September 29, 2008).

[39] www.informinc.org/fact_CWPbattery.php#note4 (September 29, 2008).

[40] Rogers, Elizabeth, and Thomas M. Kostigen (2007), *The Little Green Book*, New York: Three Rivers Press.

expectations, the level of satisfaction reported by the consumer is greater than when the product does not perform as expected.[41] Higher levels of satisfaction increase the likelihood of repeat purchases, mollify price sensitivities, and influence word-of-mouth communication about a product.[42] In addition, as the level of satisfaction decreases, the consumer is more likely to sense a difference between ideal conditions and current conditions. Low levels of satisfaction increase the likelihood of need recognition occurring that prompts the consumer to engage in the decision-making process. When this process leads to the purchase of new products, the consumer no longer has a need for the older products.

The recognition that a product no longer offers sufficient utility should prompt consideration about what to with the product. *Divestment* refers to the disposal of products after consumers deem that the products no longer offer utility. The decision about how to deal with products that no longer offer utility is an important issue.

Before disposal occurs, the consumer must evaluate whether the product offers value to the owner or some other consumer. Thus, the consumer should decide whether the product can be *reused* in some way. For example, packaging and shopping bags are often reused for storage purposes. Consumers have always engaged in some forms of this activity, but increasingly they recognize value in the reuse of products in novel ways. For example, yard and food waste account for about 25 percent of consumer waste in the United States. The disposal of these items in landfills is not the environmentally effective means of divestment. Yard waste breaks down slowly in landfills and produces methane gas and acidic leachate as it decays.[43] Composting of this waste has the potential to reduce municipal solid waste by almost one-fourth, and it contributes to improved soil structure, texture, aeration, and water retention. Another means for facilitating reuse is to donate products. Computers, cell phones, and other equipment may no longer have value to a user, but these products can offer utility to other consumers.

The likelihood of recycling is associated with the individual's identity either to the self or to groups to which a person belongs as well as the type of appeal.[44] To varying degrees, consumers either focus on themselves as individuals or as part of groups, and the different contexts consumers may have either orientation. When the individual self is prominent, the consumer focuses on personal goals and is more likely to recycle when the marketer's appeal focuses on the benefit derived from recycling. By contrast, consumers with strong identities to a group are more likely to recycle when the appeal focuses on belonging to groups or fulfilling social obligations. The implication is that the marketer needs to consider the likely personal identity of the consumer and match it to the appeal.

When the product is no longer useful or capable of being reused buy the consumer, then one must consider whether the product offers utility to other consumers. Several classes of products offer examples of ways to make products

[41] Oliver, Richard L. (1980), "A Cognitive Model of the Antecedents and Consequences of Satisfaction Decisions," *Journal of Marketing Research*, 17(4), 460–469.

[42] Hawkins, Del I., and David L. Mothersbaugh (2013), *Consumer Behavior: Building Marketing Strategy*, New York: McGraw Hill.

[43] www.howtocompost.org/info/info_composting.asp (August 4, 2015).

[44] White, Katherine, and Bonnie Simpson (2013), "When do (and don't) normative appeals influence sustainable consumer behaviors?" *Journal of Marketing* 77 (2), 78–95.

available to other consumers. In the auto industry, for instance, consumers often sell used cars or trade cars in when making a new purchase. One of the motivations to establish franchised channels in the auto industry was to facilitate resale of cars when they no longer offered utility to the consumer.[45] In conjunction with government, bottlers of soft drinks and malt beverages also work in some markets to enable reuse. In Norway, for example, more than 95 percent of all soft drink and beer containers are returned, reused, or recycled.[46]

The most prominent means for making products available to other consumers for use is the Internet. For example, eBay facilitated over $60 billion in transactions in 2007, and the vast majority of these transactions involved making existing products available to other consumers.[47] eBay and other Internet provide online markets for the resale of virtually every type of product.

When reuse or resale are infeasible, then the consumer must find some other means to discard of the product. *Recycling* of products can take many forms depending on the product class and consumer needs (see Figure 5-9). Unwanted Appliances, for example, specializes in the removal of household appliances, exercise equipment, electronics, air conditioners, and water heaters. Most of the products that it buys are sold for scrap, but some products are resold to other consumers. Some industries that operate seemingly in unison have a remarkable

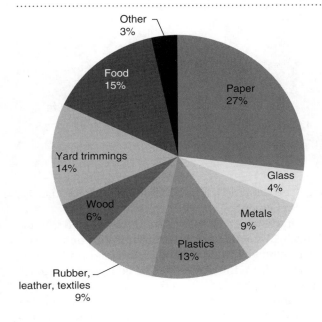

FIGURE 5-9

2013 Total MSW Generation - 254 Million Tons (Before Recycling).[48]

[45] Vaughn, Charles L. (1979), *Franchising: Its Nature, Scope, Advantages and Development*, 2nd edition. Lexington, MA.: Lexington Books.

[46] Hanssen, Ole Jørgen, et al. (2007), "The Environmental Effectiveness of the Beverage Sector in Norway in a Factor 10 Perspective," *The International Journal of Life Cycle Assessment*, 12 (4) 257–265.

[47] eBay (2007), *Annual Report*, San Jose, CA: eBay.

[48] www.epa.gov/solidwaste/nonhaz/municipal/pubs/2013_advncng_smm_fs.pdf (August 4, 2015).

TABLE 5-1
Generation and Recovery of
Materials in MSW, 2013
(In Millions of Tons and
Percent of Generation of
Each Material). [49]

Material	Weight Generated	Weight Recovered	Recovery as Percent of Generation	Weight Discarded
Paper and paperboard	68.60	43.40	63.3%	25.20
Glass	11.54	3.15	27.3%	8.39
Metals				
Steel	17.55	5.80	33.0%	11.75
Aluminum	3.50	0.70	20.0%	2.80
Other nonferrous metals	2.01	1.37	68.2%	0.64
Total metals	**23.06**	**7.87**	**34.1%**	**15.19**
Plastics	32.52	3.0	9.2%	29.52
Rubber and leather	7.72	1.24	16.1%	6.48
Textiles	15.13	2.30	15.2%	12.83
Wood	15.77	2.47	15.7%	13.30
Other materials	4.58	1.31	28.6%	3.27
Total materials in products	178.92	64.74	36.2%	114.18
Other wastes				
Food, other	37.06	1.84	5.0%	35.22
Yard trimmings	34.20	20.6	60.2%	13.60
Miscellaneous inorganic wastes	3.93	Negligible	Negligible	3.93
Total other wastes	**75.19**	**22.44**	**29.8%**	**52.75**
Total municipal solid waste	254.11	87.18	34.3%	166.93

job of recycling used products (see Table 5-1). The EU and U.S. auto industries, for instance, recycle more than 95 percent of auto batteries sold.[50]

In the consumer electronics industry, consumers have the combined interest in recycling and ensuring that sensitive data are not compromised or accessed after recycling. Dell provides free recycling of old computers and peripherals when a new computer is purchased from the company. The company evaluates whether a product can be resold, and proceeds from this resale are returned to the customer. If the product cannot be resold, then Dell recycles in a manner consistent with local, state, and federal requirements.[51] Importantly, such services enable the consumer to recoup some part of the investment in the computer, securely dispose of the computer, and contribute positively to the environment.

[49] www.epa.gov/solidwaste/nonhaz/municipal/pubs/2013_advncng_smm_fs.pdf (August 4, 2015).

[50] Gerrard, Jason, and Milind Kandlikar (2007), "Is European End-of-life Vehicle Legislation Living up to Expectations? Assessing the Impact of the ELV Directive on 'Green' Innovation and Vehicle Recovery," *Journal of Cleaner Production*, 15(1), 17–27. 50

[51] www2.epa.gov/sites/production/files/2013-08/documents/recycling.pdf (August 4, 2015).

Increasingly, there are community and corporate efforts that encourage the recycling of products that pose threats to persons exposed to products after consumption. Americans, for example, generate 1.6 million tons of household hazardous waste per year, and the average home can accumulate as much as 100 pounds of this waste stored in closets, basements, and garages.[52] Community action plans enable consumers to dispose of paints, cleaners, oils, batteries, and pesticides that require special care during disposal.

Although our treatment of recycling has focused on post consumption, it is also meaningful to recognize that recycling today begins in the new product development process. Savvy marketers are designing products in such a way that much of the product can be recouped after consumption. In the auto industry, approximately 15 million cars and trucks reach the end of their useful life each year, and more than 75 percent of the materials from end-of-life vehicles are profitably recovered and recycled.[53] Planning for post consumption enhances the value of products to consumers and limits the influence of the products on the environment.

SUMMARY

Recognizing the Central Importance of Influence on Consumption and Decision Making

This chapter underscores the role of marketing throughout the consumption process. Marketers seek to frame decision making prior to a purchase, and they employ sales promotions to influence consumers at the point of purchase. Marketers further influence the manner by which consumers use products and the decisions made when a product ceases to be useful.

Sustainable Marketing Action Designed to Influence Pre-purchase Decisions

Need recognition occurs when the consumer recognizes a discrepancy between current and desired conditions. Marketers often stimulate demand by altering consumer perceptions of currently owned products. They also may influence need recognition to increase the perceived value of alternative products. When a firm elects to stimulate need recognition, it may employ a generic need recognition strategy or employ a brand-specific need recognition designed to stimulate demand for a specific branded product.

Sustainable Marketing Action Designed to Influence Purchases

The second stage of the decision-making process is the point at which the consumer decides to make a purchase. This decision has many components that

[52] www.epa.gov/osw/conserve/materials/hhw.htm (October 3, 2008).

[53] Daniels, Edward J., et al. (2004), Sustainable End-of-life Vehicle Recycling: R&D Collaboration Between Industry and the U.S. DOE JOM *Journal of the Minerals, Metals and Materials Society*, 56 (8), 28–32.

can be influenced by sustainable marketing strategy. Marketers use a variety of sale promotions designed to influence purchases. These include price-based promotions, product-based promotions, relationship-building promotions, and onsite promotions. The efficacy of these promotions varies with the type of consumer.

Sustainable Marketing Action Designed to Influence Consumption

The consumption process continues as the consumer makes the transition from purchase to usage. The consumer who buys the product must decide the time, place, and manner by which to consume.

Sustainable Marketing Action Designed to Influence Postpurchase Decisions

The final stage of the consumer decision-making process occurs after some consumption of the product has begun. The buyer evaluates whether the level of satisfaction with the product meets or exceeds performance expectations before the purchase. When the performance of the product meets or exceeds expectations, the level of satisfaction reported by the consumer is greater than when the product does not perform as expected. Low levels of satisfaction increase the likelihood of need recognition occurring that prompts the consumer to engage in the decision-making process. When this process leads to the purchase of new products, the consumer no longer has a need for the older products.

KEY TERMS

need recognition	internal search	sweepstakes
promotion	external search	relationship-building
promotional mix	sales promotion	promotions
advertising	price reduction promotions	loyalty marketing programs
personal selling	coupon	frequent buyer programs
public relations	rebate	onsite promotions
sales promotion	product-based promotions	point of purchase
direct marketing	premium	postconsumption evaluation
generic need recognition strategy	sampling	divestment
brand-specific need recognition	contests	recycling

1. How does Levi's enable consumers to reduce their carbon footprint while also lowering their clothing costs?
2. What benefits accrue to people in the fashion industry that market their products in a sustainable manner?
3. What forms of promotion are likely emphasized in the need recognition stage?
4. Why would a firm elect to adopt a generic need recognition strategy?
5. Why do firms often treat sustainability as a second or third benefit of their products?
6. Describe three types of sales promotions that can enhance sustainability while increasing sales.
7. How does a firm's knowledge about the timing of purchases, location, and manner of consumption enable it to market sustainable product offerings more effectively?
8. What forms of promotion are likely emphasized in the consumption and post-consumption stages?
9. Under what conditions would a firm likely prefer to use product-based promotions over price-based promotions?
10. How has the advent of the Internet influenced product reuse and recycling?

6

Discovering Value via Market Analysis

INTRODUCTION

Green Weddings

A wedding day is one of the most important days in a couple's life. Given the importance of the day and the associated costs, many couples now consider how they can make the day appreciably green and sustainable. Couples can do many things to help ensure that their weddings are ecofriendly.[1] While a large wedding may be necessary with large families, smaller events mean less travel, food and drink, and waste. Couples can also lower their carbon footprints by using local sources of food and drinks and selecting venues that are as close as possible to guests. In addition, they can recommend the use of relatively sustainable sources of transportation such as trains, buses, bicycles, and carpools. They can also use recycled or handmade materials for invitations and other printed items.[2]

In their efforts to target this group of consumers, wedding planners like Green Carpet have made interesting strides to change the kinds of consumption associated with weddings.[3] These firms provide suggestions about making the wedding more ecologically friendly by making changes in the purchase of wedding rings, gifts, and floral arrangements. They also outline ways for couples to buy local products that lower wedding costs, and they recommend sustainable locations for the wedding rite.

FIGURE 6-1

Wedding Snap helps couples plan weddings that support conservation.[2]

---

[1] www.treehugger.com/htgg/how-to-go-green-weddings.html (February 1, 2016).

[2] blog.eversnapapp.com/5-fabulous-eco-friendly-wedding-favor-ideas-2/ (February 1, 2016).

[3] www.greencarpetevent.com/ (February 1, 2016).

Is the green wedding for everybody? Of course not, but there is a growing international target market that places great emphasis on the sustainability of their purchases. Weddings are an important part of life, and they often have substantial carbon footprints. One type of consumer that we will read about in this chapter is focused on trying to limit carbon usage, and this usage is not forgotten on one's wedding day. These lifestyle of health and sustainability (LOHAS) consumers are focused on health, the environment, and personal development and spend over $290 billion in the United States, and the LOHAS market segment is also gaining interest in Japan, Southeast Asia, and Europe.[4] This consumer group expresses concerns about the health of their families, the sustainability of the planet, their personal development, and the future of society. Consumers in the LOHAS segment are also inclined to offset the carbon dioxide emissions associated with the wedding by donating to programs that plant trees or preserve rain forests.[5]

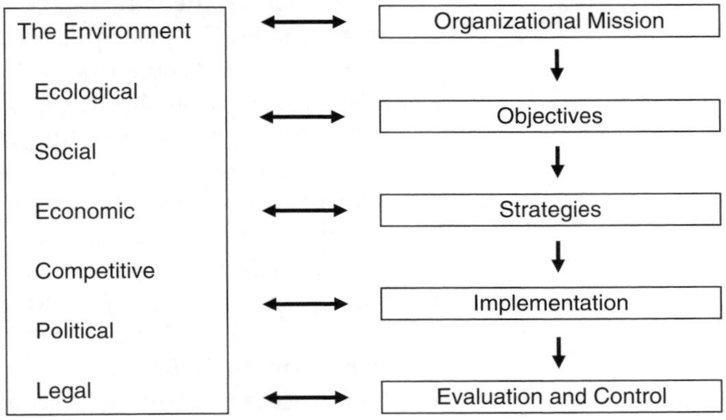

FIGURE 6-2
The strategic planning process

The sustainable wedding example illustrates how companies are using market analyses to help them discover sustainable green strategies. Recall that the strategic planning process (see Figure 6-2) underscores the interaction between environmental factors and business strategy. The central factor in the pursuit of sustainability is the *value* that market offerings provide to consumers. Sustainable value emerges from analysis of the economic, relational, and ecological returns sought in a market.

The successful organization must discover and identify the value sought by consumers within a market. A *market* consists of all organizations or people with a need or a want and the ability and the willingness to make purchases to address these needs and wants.[6] If any of these facets of the market are not present, then the market is also not present. Initial analysis of the market requires the marketer to gain an appreciation of each of these market components. The needs and the wants associated with products and services reflect the economic, social, and ecological value derived from a purchase. For example, the commuter who buys a bicycle incurs economic costs that yield financial savings over time. This consumer may also enjoy the camaraderie of other cyclists and will likely acknowledge the environmental benefits of cycling. Note that all three facets of value may not be understood or expressed by the consumer. In many cases, products are marketed to accentuate economic, social, or ecological merits without consideration of the returns associated with each facet of sustainability. The firm that adopts a sustainable orientation, however, has greater capacity to address the breadth of returns sought from purchases.

[4] www.lohas.com/about (May 13, 2017).

[5] Navarro, Mireya (2007), "How Green Was My Wedding," *The New York Times*, (February 11).

[6] Lamb, Charles W., Joseph F. Hair, and Carl McDaniel (2009), *Marketing*, Mason, OH: Cengage Publishing.

The firm must also assess the ability and the willingness of buyers to make a purchase. Many green marketing propositions fail because the organization does not recognize the consumers' abilities and willingness to invest in sustainable technologies. For example, for many American consumers, hybrid automobiles may not be desirable due to the inability to pay the premium associated with this ecofriendly technology.[7] These consumers may express an interest in the technology, but they do not have the ability to purchase the car at a premium. By contrast, some American consumers of diesel automobiles may not have an interest in the cars because of their previous experience with diesel engines.[8] These consumers may have the ability to buy the car, but their experience makes them unwilling to invest in a diesel car. The consumer must have both the ability and the willingness to buy to be part of the market.

After the market has been established, the firm can begin to investigate the extent to which there are subsets of the market with unique value statements. The process of moving from market analysis to marketing mix positioning is outlined in Figure 6-3. After the firm has identified the market, it engages in a series of activities referred to as *STP marketing,* characterized by efforts to segment, target, and position.[9] *Market segmentation* refers to the process of dividing a market into distinct segments or subsets of customers who have similar needs or behave in the same way.[10] Every segment of the market has the potential to be reached via a distinct marketing strategy. After the firm has identified the segments in a market, it engages in target marketing. *Target marketing* refers to the organization's efforts to serve a selected segment within the marketplace.[11] The prioritization and selection of various target markets is performed in conjunction with consideration of the competitive and environmental conditions associated with the market. After the firm has selected a target market, it then establishes a positioning strategy. *Positioning* refers to the development of the marketing mix to yield a distinctive appeal to the target segment. The positioning approach should reflect the values sought by consumers in the target market.

In the remainder of this chapter, we outline the procedures for identifying market segments and target markets. The positioning strategies are developed in the following chapter. For instructional purposes, we present this logic as a step-by-step process. In reality, the analysis of market segments and the development of the marketing mix are dynamic processes that the organization must continue to assess. Consumer preferences shift over time, and these changes in preferences demand the firm to review the market segmentation process and the

---

[7] Sangkapichai, Mana, and Jean-Daniel Saphores (2009), "Why are Californians Interested in Hybrid Cars?" *Journal of Environmental Planning and Management*, 52 (1), 79–96. Page, Tom (2009). Key Factors That Need Development In Order To Make Electric Cars Desirable To The Mass Market. i-Manager's Journal on Electrical Engineering, 2(3), 36–50.

[8] Turrentine, Thomas S., and Kenneth S. Kurani (2006), "Car Buyers and Fuel Economy?" *Energy Policy*, 35 (2), 1213–1223

[9] O'Guinn, Thomas C., Chris T. Allen, and Richard J. Semenik (2014), *Advertising and Integrated Brand Promotion*, Mason, OH: Thompson Higher Education.

[10] www.marketingpower.com/_layouts/Dictionary.aspx (March 28, 2016).

[11] Bennett, Peter D. (1988), *Dictionary of Marketing Terms*, Chicago, IL: American Marketing Association.

Segmentation, Target Markets, and Positioning

Market
All organizations or people with a need or want and the ability and willingness to make purchases to address these needs and wants

Market Segments
Groups of consumers that behave in the same way or have similar needs.

Target Market
A market segment which a marketing organization proposes to serve.

Positioning
Developing the marketing mix to yield a distinctive appeal to the target segment.

FIGURE 6-3
Segmentation, target markets, and positioning [12]

marketing mix. The positioning theme established as the product is introduced is likely to change over time in response to the needs of the market.

MARKET SEGMENTATION DECISION-MAKING FRAMEWORK

Segmentation of the market plays a critical role in the development of business strategies that yield desired value for firms, their suppliers, and their customers.[13] Segmentation enables companies to identify groups of consumers with similar needs and enables companies to analyze characteristics and buying behaviors of members of these groups. When the unique needs of a group are identified, the segmentation process also enables the firm to design a marketing mix that reflects the unique requirements of the group. Consequently, segmentation enables companies to address the value sought by consumers while simultaneously achieving the firm's needs.[12]

The segmentation process begins by identifying specific factors that reflect differences in customers' responsiveness to marketing variables or requirements. These differences in levels of responsiveness may be attributed to many factors such as purchase behavior, usage, benefits sought, or loyalty. After the segments are identified, segment descriptors are chosen based on the ability to suggest competitive strategies, account for variance in the basis for segmentation, or identify segments.

The process of market segmentation and the design of the marketing mix are not only activities that the firm performs on a regular basis, but these activities are

---

[12] O'Guinn, Thomas C., Chris T. Allen, and Richard J. Semenik (2014), *Advertising and Integrated Brand Promotion*, Mason, OH: Thompson Higher Education.

[13] Lamb, Charles W., Joseph F. Hair, and Carl McDaniel (2009), *Marketing*, Mason, OH: Cengage Publishing

costly to the organization. The segmentation process can be logically extended to the point at which each consumer in the marketplace is treated as an individual segment of the market. Although this process will identify the unique needs of each consumer, the analysis of the market and the design of the marketing mix would be cost prohibitive in most cases. Segmentation strategies should recognize that proposed segments should be:

Substantial. Substantiality is the criterion that emphasizes the need for the segment to be large enough to warrant attention. For example, prior to 2000, most grocers did not view the market for organic goods as substantial enough to warrant their attention.[14] Organic food sales have increased by 20 percent annually since 1990. As the demand for these products has increased, conventional grocers' interest in the group also increased. The size of the market segment is a particularly salient issue given that the interest in sustainability factors is increasing in many markets.[15] As the size of a segment interested in ecological performance increases, there is likely an increase in the amount of competition for the segment.

Identifiable and Measurable. The identifiable and measurable requirements reflect the need to be able categorize persons within and outside of the market segments. If we cannot identify who is and who is not in a group, then we cannot assess the size of the group, nor can we develop a marketing plan to serve the group. Although personal factors such as demographics (e.g., age or gender) are simple to measure, they are unlikely to be informative in the analysis of the degree to which consumers in a market are interested in sustainability issues. Consequently, many efforts to examine consumer predispositions toward sustainable marketing initiatives rely on personality and motives.

Accessible. In many cases, an organization may be able to quantify the size of market segments, but they cannot reach the segment via a customized marketing mix.[16] For example, millennial consumers have proven to be inaccessible to many forms of traditional advertising.[17]

Responsive. The responsiveness criterion considers whether the consumers in a market segment are more likely to respond to a marketing mix in manner that is different from other consumers. If the basis for distinguishing among market segments does not reveal differences in preferences with respect to some factor, then there is no need to treat a segment separately from other groups. Thus, if sustainability is a not a salient issue for a market segment, there is little value in emphasizing the ecological benefits of a product. For example, in 2005 Nike initially promoted the "Considered" walking boot as

---

[14] Philip, Robertson G., and Scott M. Swinton (2005) "Reconciling Agricultural Productivity and Environmental Integrity: A Grand Challenge for Agriculture," *Frontiers in Ecology and the Environment*, 3 (1), 38–46.

[15] Makower, Joel (2009), *Strategies for the Green Economy*, New York: McGraw Hill.

[16] Kotler, Philip, and Gary Armstrong (2010), *Principles of Marketing*, Upper Saddle River, NJ: Pearson Prentice-Hall.

[17] www.forbes.com/sites/danielnewman/2015/04/28/research-shows-millennials-dont-respond-to-ads/#7b93e4705dcb (March 5, 2017).

an environmentally friendly product. Since consumers were not responsive to this environmental appeal, the promotion shifted to other performance attributes of the footwear.[18]

If these criteria are not met, there is limited justification for market segmentation. When these criteria are met, however, firms benefit from looking at groups within the market.

....

CONSUMER MARKET SEGMENTATION

The process of market segmentation is an attempt to simplify the process of selecting potential buyers for a product. The segmentation for consumer marketing varies somewhat from the strategy for business-to-business marketing. Good segmentation strategies separate potential buyers from people who do not have the needs of the members of a buying group. In consumer markets, firms often use *demographics* to separate potential buyers based on age, gender, income, or occupation. For example, cities that are trying to attract Generation Y adults increasingly emphasize the ecological merits of their [18]communities.[19] Because a high percentage of consumers in this age bracket favor environmental causes, the cities recognize that marketing campaigns to this group must emphasize ecology.

Firms also separate groups of consumers based on *geography*. For example, California is a lead market for green building construction in the United States. The state has aggressively pursued efficiency measures since the oil price escalation era of the 1970s. The state's per capita electricity usage has remained virtually stable over the past 30 years even as per capita consumption has grown across the country. Experts credit state policies that have included establishing state-level appliance efficiency requirements, enacting strict building codes, and giving utilities the incentive to help their customers save electricity.[20]

Our analysis of consumer market segmentation reviews three perspectives on sustainable target markets. These include the research conducted by Roper Starch, Natural Marketing Institute, and the Futures Company.

Roper Starch Worldwide Sustainable Market Segmentation

Several analysts of green marketing in the consumer sector have used *psychographic segmentation* to distinguish among consumer groups. Psychographics refers to the use of attitudes, opinions, motives, values, lifestyles, interests, or personality to distinguish among consuming groups.[21] Roper Starch Worldwide is a marketing research firm that has pioneered analysis of the consumer's orientation

---

[18] *Business Week* (2009), "Nike Goes Green Quietly," *Business Week* (June 22), 56.

[19] Turok, Ivan (2009), "The Distinctive City: Pitfalls in the Pursuit of Differential Advantage," *Environment and Planning A*, 41(1), 13–30.

[20] Galbraith, Kate (2009), "Governments Can Promote Energy Efficiency," *The New York Times*, (August 2), www.nytimes.com/2009/08/03/business/energy-environment/03iht -green03.html?scp=23&sq=green%20buidlings&st=cse.

[21] Ferrell, O. C., and Michael D. Hartline (2014), *Marketing Strategy*, Mason, OH: Thompson Higher Education.

to the sustainability in North America. Similar efforts have been conducted in northern European markets.[22] Their research has uncovered the following five market segments (see Figure 6-4):[23]

True Blues. True Blues refer to those consumers with strong environmental values who seek to bring about positive change. Individuals who identify with this segment are also inclined to be politically active in their pursuit of sustainability. These individuals are four times more likely to avoid products marketed by companies that are not environmentally conscious. Roper Starch research indicates that 31 percent of consumers fit this category.

Greenback Greens. The Greenback Greens are also interested in sustainability concerns, but they are not inclined to be politically active. Importantly, these consumers are more willing to purchase environmentally friendly products than average consumers. Prior research suggests that this group represents 10 percent of the population.

Sprouts. This group of consumers appreciates the merits of environmental causes, but they do not take this appreciation with them to the marketplace. Although these consumers will be unlikely to spend more for green products, they can be persuaded to do so given the appropriate appeal. Research suggests that Sprouts account for approximately 26 percent of consumers.[24]

FIGURE 6-4

Roper Starch North American market segments concerning attitudes toward sustainability [24]

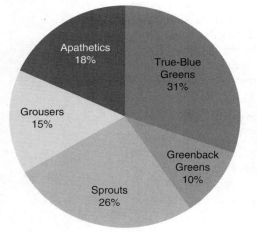

Grousers. This group of consumers tends to be cynical about their ability to bring about change, and they are relatively uneducated about ecological concerns. Research suggests that these consumers believe that green products are too expensive and do not perform as effectively as their non-green counterparts. Approximately 15 percent of consumers fit the Grouser category.

Apathetics. Formerly labeled "basic browns," the Apathetics do not concern themselves with sustainability or green marketing practices. The Apathetics represent about 18 percent of the population.

The Roper Starch analysis of green market segmentation has been tracking consumers since 1990. It is interesting to note that the preferences of consumers in the U.S. population have shifted over time. Although the number of Greenback Greens and Sprouts has remained relatively constant, the percentage of True

[22] Lorek, Agnieszka (2015), "Current Trends in the Consumer Behaviour towards Eco-friendly Products," *Economic and Environmental Studies* 15(2), 115–129.

[23] Ottman, Jacquelyn A. (2003), "Know Thy Target," *In Business,* (September-October) 30–31. Ginsberg, Jill M. and Paul N. Bloom (2004), "Choosing the Right Green Marketing Strategy," *MIT Sloan Management Review,* (Fall) 79–84.

[24] Makower, Joel (2009), *Strategies for the Green Economy*, New York: McGraw Hill.

Blue greens has escalated from 11 percent to 31 percent of the market. The percentage of grousers has moved from 24 percent in 1990 to 15 percent. Similarly, the percentage of Apathetics has shifted from 35 percent in 1995 to 18 percent in 2007. These shifts in the attitudes of consumers reflect a general change in the attitudes and understanding of sustainability. As the number of consumers touting a True Blue or Greenback perspective increases, the need for sustainable marketing strategies also escalates.

The Roper Starch study of consumer green marketing preferences addresses the attitudes that consumers have towards sustainability. Although attitudes provide insight into the likely action of consumers, behavior provides a stronger insight into market segments. *Behavioral segmentation* refers to the use of consumer behavior or product use to distinguish among market segments.[25] The market analyses provided by the Natural Marketing Institute (NMI) and Yankelovich, Inc. incorporate attitudes and behaviors toward environmentalism and consumption.[26] Both of these analyses provide insight into segmentation strategies. Consider first the research conducted by Natural Marketing Institute.

Natural Marketing Institute Sustainable Market Segmentation

The Natural Marketing Institute research identifies five market segments (see Figure 6-5):

The LOHAS Consumer. LOHAS refers to lifestyles of health and sustainability. This term describes an estimated $209 billion U.S. marketplace for goods and services. These consumers are focused on health, the environment, social justice, personal development and sustainable living.[27] This consumer group's attitudes, behaviors, and usage of goods and services are affected by their concern for health. They express concerns about the health of their families, the sustainability of the planet, their personal development, and the future of society. Approximately 17 percent (38 million) of the adults in the United States are considered LOHAS consumers. This group is not limited to the United States given that LOHAS is gaining interest in Japan, Southeast Asia, and Europe.

The LOHAS group is based on the Cultural Creatives label developed by sociologist Paul Ray to describe individuals on the cutting edge of social change.[28] He described Cultural Creatives as slightly more likely than average to live on the West Coast, but he noted that they are found in all regions of the country.

FIGURE 6-5

Green marketing segments from the Natural Marketing Institute[29]

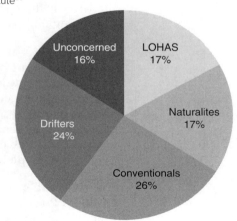

[25] Ferrell, O. C., and Michael D. Hartline (2014), *Marketing Strategy*, Mason, OH: Thompson Higher Education.

[26] www.lohas.com/about.html (August 4, 2009).

[27] www.lohas.com/about.html (August 4, 2009).

[28] Ray, Paul H. (1997), "The Emerging Culture," *American Demographics*, 19 (2), 29–35.

[29] *www.nmisolutions.com/lohasd_segment.html*.

These consumers are altruistic and often less concerned with success or making a lot of money, yet most live comfortably with middle to upper-middle incomes. Cognitive style is a key to understanding the Cultural Creatives. While these consumers take in a lot of information from a variety of sources, they are good at synthesizing it into a "big picture." The environment is central to the LOHAS consumers' belief system. The environment is interconnected with everything, from the way food is grown to the way the workers are treated. It is a holistic world view that recognizes the interconnection between political systems and ecocultures.[30]

LOHAS consumers provide insight into the future of progressive social, environmental, and economic change in multiple markets worldwide. Seventy-three percent buy recycled-paper goods, and 71 percent buy natural or organic personal care products.[31] They pay more to get food produced without pesticides and want their cars fuel-efficient. Although the cultural creatives label describes this group as countercultural, their buying preferences reflect many of the most popular consumer brands. A 2006 LOHAS analysis indicated that these consumers felt that Microsoft, Whole Foods, Kellogg's, McDonalds's, Home Depot, Disney, United Parcel Service, Coca-Cola, Starbucks, and PepsiCo ranked highest in their sustainability and environmental efforts. Thus, these consumers recognize the sustainable marketing efforts of some of the largest consumer brands. Furthermore, the listing of these brands illustrates that these firms have done a good job of incorporating and communicating sustainability efforts to consumers.[32]

NMI further separates this group into two segments.[33] The LOHAS *leaders* are early adopters and opinion leaders for products and concepts that emphasize healthy or green initiatives. They are the first candidates in a market to purchase new and innovative sustainable products. By contrast, LOHAS *followers* are more moderate in their preferences for green products. Like the leaders, however, they are cutting-edge consumers for most purchasing situations.

Naturalites. This second market segment refers to consumers primarily concerned about personal health and wellness. Their preference for foods and beverage products is motivated primarily by strong health focus, not an environmental focus. Although these consumers appreciate that companies should be environmentally conscious, they are not politically committed to the environmental movement, and they are not generally driven to buy ecofriendly durable goods. Naturalites represent 17 percent of U.S. households (38 million people).

Conventionals. The largest segment in the NMI analysis includes 58 million adults or 26 percent of the adult population. Because these individuals are practical and enjoy seeing the results of their action, they are likely to recycle

---

[30] Everage, Laura (2002), "Understanding the LOHAS Lifestyle," *Gourmet Retailer*, 23 (10), 82–86.

[31] Waldman, Steven (2006), "Lohasians," *Newsweek*, 147 (23), 10.

[32] Makower, Joel (2009), *Strategies for the Green Economy*, New York: McGraw Hill.

[33] www.nmisolutions.com/lohasd_segment.html (August 4, 2009).

and conserve energy.[34] They recognize the value in buying products that save money in the end, but the ecological merits of consumption are not paramount in their decision making.

Drifters. The drifter category refers to consumers who are not highly concerned about the environment and believe that the problems will eventually be resolved. Their concerns about the environment focus on things that affect them directly. Because they view sustainability as a trend, they want to be seen in places viewed as environmentally conscious even though they do not make substantial purchases of green products. They are somewhat price sensitive and offer many reasons why they do not make environmentally friendly choices. Drifters include 54 million people or 24 percent of the U.S. adult market.

Unconcerned. The final group in the NMI analysis is a group that has priorities other than the environment and society. They are not aware of green product choices and are generally unwilling to find out such information. These consumers buy based on convenience, price, quality, and value with little regard for the action of companies marketing the products. A total of 36 million U.S. adults representing 16 percent of the population are in the unconcerned market segment.

Greenprint Sustainable Market Segmentation

The Greenprint sustainability segmentation describes seven market segments and offers guidelines for connecting with consumers in each market segment.[35] The market segments are identified based on *consumer engagement, motivations,* and *barriers*. Consumer engagement refers to the degree of participation in sustainable consumption practices. The level of engagement includes engaged, conflicted, and disengaged consumers. Engaged consumers are buying sustainable products because they want to or they feel obliged to do so. Conflicted consumers have some motivation to buy sustainable products, but they recognize barriers to purchases of sustainable products. Disengaged consumers do not buy sustainable products because they feel constrained from doing so, or they do not see any benefits from purchasing sustainable products.

The second dimension of the Greenprint segmentation is the motivation to lead a more environmentally conscious lifestyle. Five motives associated with sustainable consumption decisions include:

General Motivation. This motive is embodied by consumers who have made a more environmentally conscious lifestyles a priority in their lives.

Greater Good. This motive refers to a desire to make a positive difference in the world or a desire to preserve the world for future generations. For example, the United Nations ad in Figure 6-6 depicts a desire to preserve the world for the future.

---

[34] Makower, Joel (2009), *Strategies for the Green Economy*, New York: McGraw Hill.

[35] Singer, Michelle, and Chris Hloros (2016), *Greenprint Sustainability Segmentation*, Global MONITOR – The Futures Company.

Societal Expectations. The recognition that society or government requires compliance is reflected in the societal expectations motive. For example, consumers are likely to comply with the San Francisco legislation outlawing the use of nonbiodegradable plastics.[36]

Personal Welfare. Consumers with this motivation feel that they are directly affected by environmental problems. People living on the cost of Florida, for instance, may engage in sustainable consumption as a result observing changes in shorelines.[37]

Saving Money. This motive refers to the recognition that sustainable products and services can save consumers money. For example, consumers may buy a new printer because it uses less ink and energy than an older model.

The third dimension of Greenprint segmentation addresses barriers that preclude consumer from making sustainable purchases. Five barriers to consumption include:

FIGURE 6-6
United Nations promotion advocating the greater good[38]

[36] Chanprateep, Suchada (2010), "Current Trends in Biodegradable Polyhydroxyalkanoates," *Journal of Bioscience and Bioengineering*, 1106 (6), 621–632.

[37] Lovelace, Susan, et al. (2013), "Selecting Human Dimensions Indicators for South Florida's Coastal Marine Ecosystem–Noneconomic Indicators," MARES Whitepaper (April 1, 2016).

[38] unfoundationblog.org/4-quotes-for-earth-day/ (March30, 2016).

Apathy. Consumers who either do not want to be bothered or do not believe that environmental issues are strong enough to warrant attention are apathetic towards sustainable consumption.

Reluctance to Compromise. Consumers who feel sustainable products are inferior to other products are reluctant to purchase such products due to product uncertainty or inconvenience. For example, consumers may be reluctant to buy cars that employ hydrogen fuel cell technology due to uncertainty about refueling stations.[39]

Transferred Responsibility. Some consumers believe that they should not do more because they believe industry and government are more responsible for environmental problems. For example, research indicates that consumers believe that oil companies should take more action to address climate issues.[40]

Confusion. Consumers who feel that environmental issues are complicated to the point that they do not know what the appropriate course of action should be are bound by confusion. For example, consumer misunderstandings about carbon costs complicate consumer decisions concerning air travel.[41]

Limited Resources. When consumers feel that they do not have sufficient money or time to buy sustainable products, they are constrained by personal resources. For example, the lower purchase price of incandescent light bulbs influences consumer decisions about lighting purchases.[42]

The collective consideration of engagement, motivation, and barriers reveals seven market segments (see Figure 6-7).

Engaged Consumers

Green Enthusiasts. These consumers feel that climate change is a major issue that directly affects them. They are most likely to take action such as recycling, using fewer resources, and buying from companies with environmental policies. These consumers can be reached via messages that have a deep emotional context associated with community, self-improvement, and personal integrity. Ads that feature beautiful landscapes and scenery evoke emotional appeals to sustainable consumption.

---

[39] Melaina, Marc W. (2003), "Initiating Hydrogen Infrastructures: Preliminary Analysis of a Sufficient Number of Initial Hydrogen Stations in the U.S.," *International Journal of Hydrogen Energy*, 28 (7), 743–755.

[40] Bonini, Sheila M. J., Greg Hintz, and Lenny T. Mendonca (2008), "Addressing Consumer Concerns about Climate Change," *McKinsey Quarterly* (2), 52–61.

[41] Hares, Andrew, Janet Dickinson, and Keith Wilkes (2010), "Climate Change and the Air Travel Decisions of U.K. Tourists," *Journal of Transport Geography* 18 (3), 466–473.

[42] Min, Jihoon, Inês L. Azevedo, Jeremy Michalek, and Wändi Bruine de Bruin (2014), "Labeling Energy Cost on Light Bulbs Lowers Implicit Discount Rates," *Ecological Economics* 97, 42–50.

FIGURE 6-7

Greenprint market segments[43]

Engagement Level	Market Segment
Engaged	Green Enthusiasts Following the rules
Conflicted	Doing my best In two minds What's in it for me?
Disengaged	Constrained by circumstances Not really bothered

Following the Rules. Engaged consumers with the strongest external motives from government and society are inclined to follow the rules of these entities. In contrast to green enthusiasts, they are reluctant to sacrifice quality for the sake of sustainability. These consumers can be reached by developing promotions that emphasize how sustainability supports product quality. Promotions targeting this group should associate environmental initiatives with innovation and quality using rational appeals. For example, the Air-O-Lator ad in Figure 6-8 offers a rational appeal.

FIGURE 6-8

Air-O-Lator ad emphasizing a rational appeal[44]

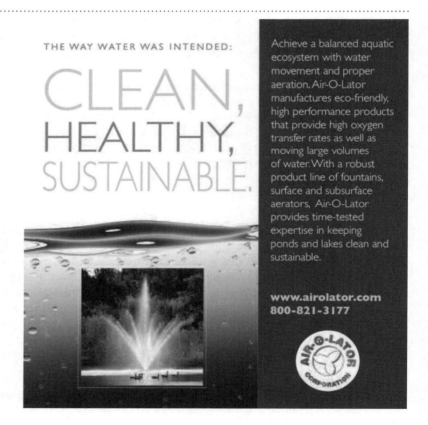

---

[43] Singer, Michelle, and Chris Hloros (2016), *Greenprint Sustainability Segmentation*, Global MONITOR – The Futures Company.

[44] virtualtradeshow.igin.com/places/view/427/air_o_lator_.html (March 31, 2016).

FIGURE 6-9
Promoting vegetarian diet as a conscious decision to help the environment[45]

Conflicted Consumers

Doing My Best. These consumers are second only to Green Enthusiasts in concerns about the greater good, climate change, and personal welfare. They are constrained by limited resources and availability of green options. These consumers can be reached through promotions that educate consumers about how sustainable action is associated with a resourceful, responsible, and secure lifestyle. For example, the ad depicted in Figure 6-9 indicates that a vegetarian diet is beneficial to the environment.

Of Two Minds. Consumers in this segment incur internal conflict. While they have strong recognition of environmental causes and the greater good, they are reluctant to compromise and feel that government and business should be more proactive. These consumers appreciate strong leadership that emphasizes the company's sustainability-related efforts. Sustainability should be positioned as a way to achieve healthy lifestyles, conservation, and national pride. For example, many large consumer and business-to-business firms publish ads emphasizing the sustainable action undertaken by the firm.[46]

What's In It for Me? The motivations and barriers of this segment focus on self-interest. These consumers are highly motivated to comply with government. They engage in sustainable consumption for health or financial reasons. Since these consumers are heavily brand aware, they prefer promotions that build a brand story based on the sustainable efforts of the firm. For example, the Toms of Maine website outlines the sustainable development of this brand.[47]

---

[45] www.thisdishisvegetarian.com/2012/04/vegetarian-actress-lisa-edelstein-bares.html (March 30, 2016).

[46] Schrettle, Stefan, Andreas Hinz, Maike Scherrer-Rathje, and Thomas Friedli (2014), "Turning sustainability into action: Explaining firms' sustainability efforts and their impact on firm performance," *International Journal of Production Economics* 147 (1), 73–84.

[47] www.tomsofmaine.com/home (April 1, 2016).

FIGURE 6-10
The Capital District
Physicians' Health Plan
(CDPHP) promotes the health
benefits of biking in New
York City.[48]

Disengaged Consumers

Constrained by Circumstances Consumers in this segment have low levels of engagement but are motivated by health concerns. They have the highest level of several barriers, including limited personal resources, confusion, and reluctance to compromise. Appeals to these consumers should emphasize how sustainable practices are healthy, cost-effective, or convenient. The ad in Figure 6-10, for instance, emphasizes the health benefits of biking.

Not Really Bothered. Consumers within this segment are the least likely to feel affected by climate concerns. Expectations of government and society are the only prominent motivations to engage in sustainable practices. They are apathetic and reluctant to compromise. Appeals to these consumers should emphasize value or convenience. For example, Tide laundry detergent ads emphasize the energy savings from washing clothes in cold water.

BUSINESS MARKET SEGMENTATION

Business marketing segmentation varies somewhat from the strategies available in the consumer realm. Although geography may be used as a basis for distinguishing among groups,[48] psychographics and lifestyle analysis do not translate well to business marketing.[49] One form of segmentation used frequently in business

---

[48] blog.cdphp.com/health-living/health-benefits-of-biking-in-new-york/ (March 30, 2016).

markets is *benefit segmentation*. Benefit segmentation refers to the delineation of segments based on the benefits that buyers hope to derive from a purchase. Thus, delivery truck requirements for florists and dry cleaners may be similar, despite differences in their respective clientele.

A related basis for developing business market segments is the type of industry. In general, the benefits sought by buyers in the same industry can be very similar. In North America, the North American Industrial Classification System (NAICS) employs a six-digit hierarchical coding system to classify all economic activity into 20 industry sectors. The NAICS is the standard used by federal statistical agencies to classify business establishments for the purpose of collecting, analyzing, and publishing statistical data related to the U.S. business economy.[50] NAICS was developed by the U.S. Economic Classification Policy Committee (ECPC), Statistics Canada, and Mexico's Instituto Nacional de Estadistica, Geografia e Informatica, as a means to facilitate comparison of business statistics among these three North American countries.[51] Every effort is made to make NAICS compatible with the Standard Industrial Classification of All Economic Activities of the United Nations.[52]

NAICS is developed based on grouping of producing units using the same or similar production processes. Five sectors are mainly goods-producing sectors, and 15 are entirely services-producing sectors. This six-digit hierarchical structure allows for the identification of 1170 industries compared to the 1004 found in the SIC. In developing NAICS, the governments in the United States, Canada, and Mexico agreed that the five-digit codes would represent the level at which the system is comparable among the countries. The sixth digit allows for each of the countries to have additional detail (i.e., subdivisions of a five-digit category).[53] For example, here is the NAICS for U.S. new car dealerships:

NAICS	Description
44	Retail sector
441	Retail: Motor vehicles and parts
4411	Retail: Auto dealers
44111	Retail: New auto dealers
441110	Retail: U.S. new auto dealers

Within sectors of the NAICS, industrial-level analysis is being developed to identify best practices, and many of these best practices include sustainability considerations. These industry-level analyses are being developed for many industries outlined in the appendices addressing manufacturing, services, and transportation. For example, the healthcare industry has been very active in its

---

[49] O'Guinn, Thomas C., Chris T. Allen, and Richard J. Semenik (2006), *Advertising and Integrated Brand Promotion*, Mason, OH: Thompson Higher Education.

[50] www.osha.gov/oshstats/ (April 8, 2016).

[51] www.census.gov/eos/www/naics/ (April 8, 2016).

[52] www.census.gov/eos/www/naics/history/docs/cm_3.pdf/ (April 11, 2016).

[53] www.naics.com/naics-code-description/?code=441110 (April 11, 2016).

pursuit of sustainability. The industry has developed a *Green Guide to Health Care* that identifies sustainable and green procedures that enable hospitals to enhance financial performance, improve patient satisfaction, protect health, attract and retain staff, and reduce fossil fuel emissions.[54] Organizations that understand these multiple facets of sustainability can develop strategies tailored to each set of demands associated with sustainable marketing.

The understanding of the various facets of sustainability within an industry can be coupled with the **buygrid framework** to isolate market segments. The buygrid framework describes the organizational buying process based on the type of purchase and the stage of the buying process.[55] The type of purchase may be a new task, a modified rebuy of a former purchase, or straight rebuy of a product bought previously. Companies or healthcare facilities that are making their initial investment in sustainable technologies will vary markedly in their preferences from firms that have repeatedly bought such technologies. The stages of the buying process include recognition of need; need definition and description; seller identification; proposal solicitation, evaluation, and selection; ordering procedures; and review. Firms that are just beginning to identify sustainability issues are substantially different from firms that have already placed orders for sustainable technologies.

One facet of the business marketing setting that stands in contrast to consumer marketing is *reverse marketing*. Reverse marketing refers to the proactive efforts within the firm to identify potential product providers or vendors.[56] In contrast to consumer markets in which the needs of the buyer can be difficult to establish, in a reverse marketing context, the needs of the buyer are clarified. Thus, sellers can use this information to categorize a buyer into a market segment.

Table 6-1 provides Wal-Mart's 2009 vendor sustainability criteria used to assess potential sellers to this retail giant. The sustainability criteria can be used initially to classify Wal-Mart as a firm with substantial interest in sustainable marketing activity. Given the firm's size, however, the sustainability criteria also provide the opportunity to classify vendors based on their energy and climate, material efficiency, natural resource utilization, and community involvement.

The market segments identified by Roper Starch and NMI in the consumer setting and the criteria characterized in the business marketing context provide starting points for individuals seeking to increase purchases of sustainable products. These studies underscore an observation made frequently in the marketing of sustainable products: Although many consumers will recognize the merits of ecofriendly products, this recognition is not incorporated into many purchase decisions. Thus, it is incumbent on the marketer to understand the motivations underlying consumer decision making. It is essential to identify the market niches and estimate their size. When the firm has identified these segments, it can then begin to prioritize potential target markets.

---

[54] gghc.org/ (April 11, 2016).

[55] www.marketingpower.com/_layouts/Dictionary.asp (March 28, 2016).

[56] Leenders, Michiel R., and David L. Blenkhorn (1988), *Reverse Marketing; The New Buyer-Supplier Relationship,*" New York: The Free Press.

Table 6-1
Wal-Mart Sustainability
Criteria[57]

Energy and Climate

1. Have you measured your corporate greenhouse gas emissions?

2. Have you opted to report your greenhouse gas emissions to the Carbon Disclosure Project?

3. What is your total annual greenhouse gas emissions reported in the most recent year measured?

4. Have you set publicly available greenhouse gas reduction targets? If yes, what are those targets?

Material Efficiency

1. If measured, please report the total amount of solid waste generated from the facilities that produce your product(s) for Wal-Mart for the most recent year measured.

2. Have you set publicly available solid waste reduction targets? If yes, what are those targets?

3. If measured, please report total water use from facilities that produce your product(s) for Wal-Mart for the most recent year measured.

4. Have you set publicly available water use reduction targets? If yes, what are those targets?

Natural Resources

1. Have you established publicly available sustainability purchasing guidelines for your direct suppliers that address issues such as environmental compliance, employment practices, and product/ingredient safety?

2. Have you obtained third-party certifications for any of the products that you sell to Wal-Mart?

People and Community

1. Do you know the location of 100 percent of the facilities that produce your product(s)?

2. Before beginning a business relationship with a manufacturing facility, do you evaluate the quality of, and capacity for, production?

3. Do you have a process for managing social compliance at the manufacturing level?

4. Do you work with your supply base to resolve issues found during social compliance evaluations and also document specific corrections and improvements?

5. Do you invest in community development activities in the markets you source from and/or operate within?

TARGET MARKETING

After the initial analysis of market segments, it is essential for the firm to select some subset of the market. A *target market* refers to a subgroup of the total market selected as the focal point for[57] the marketing mix.[58] Regardless of how the segmentation was established, the firm must select one or more targets as the basis for a marketing campaign.

One of the primary considerations for selecting a target market is the consideration of the firm's ability to satisfy the needs of the segment. Serving a market demands that the firm make sizeable investments that are often specific to the needs of the market segment. If the firm possesses the resources to satisfy

[57] *Material Handling Management* (2009), "Wal-Mart's 15 Questions," *Material Handling Management*, (August), 8.

[58] O'Guinn, Thomas C., Chris T. Allen, and Richard J. Semenik (2014), *Advertising and Integrated Brand Promotion*, Mason, OH: Thompson Higher Education.

the needs of market segment, it is logical for the firm to consider this group as a potential target. For example, Patagonia's recurring investment in organic cotton has enabled it to satisfy the needs of consumers with strong preferences for garments that contain ecofriendly components. In some cases, however, organizations cannot justify the investment needed to satisfy the needs of the market segment. Thus, an airliner may recognize that NMI's LOHAS' consumers may respond favorably to jets operated on vegetable oil, but the airliner may not have the capacity to modify its fleet to accommodate the desires of this market segment.

A second consideration in the selection of a target market is the size of a market segment. In general, a large group can be more easily justified as a target due to the sheer amount of consumption. When groups get too large, however, the market segmentation does not offer much insight. Thus, efforts to market to the restaurant industry are likely to be unsuccessful due to the failure to consider the multiple buying and consumption patterns across the group. The size of the group must be assessed relative to the amount of consumption within the group.

It is not surprising that the growth potential in market segment is also a consideration when selecting target markets. The recurring research by Roper Starch indicates that the number of true blue consumers has increased dramatically over the past few years. Firms such as Stonyfield that anticipated this market growth are well-positioned to meet the current needs of this target market. Similarly, developers of alternative auto fuels pursue the auto market primarily for the growth potential rather than current demand. As the volatility in oil prices increases, the consumer interest in alternatives also increases.[59]

In addition to the firm's capabilities, market size, and growth potential, firms must also direct substantial attention to competition. As the number of competitors pursuing a market increases, the potential to serve the market becomes compromised. Large competitors may be able to dedicate sizeable resources to the market that preclude a firm from competing effectively. For example, some question whether Tesla can compete favorably given the market capitalization of its competition.[60] Small firms, however, may be able to engage in *niche marketing strategies* whereby they serve a selected market better than their competition. For example, many local farmers are taking advantage of the ability to serve local markets with fresh foods that their multinational competitors cannot provide.[61]

When one considers both the market size and the competitive landscape, one can identify several contrasting opportunities to serve a target market. The **Lean Green** strategy refers to a situation in which the size of the green market is modest and the firm has limited ability to differentiate based on the greenness of product offerings. Firms in this category are likely to engage in corporate social responsibility, but they do not publicize this action.

---

[59] Friedman, Thomas (2008), *Hot, Flat, and Crowded*, New York: Farrar, Straus and Giroux.

[60] Welch, David (2009), "Can Tesla Become a Real Automaker?" *Business Week*, (June 24).

[61] Halweil, Brian, and Thomas Prugh (2002), *Home Grown*, Danvers, MA: World Watch Institute.

For example, 2 percent of the cotton used by Levi Strauss is organic.[62] Since few consumers in the jean market value green products, and this commitment to sustainability could be replicated, the strategy has to limit the emphasis on green products. This competitive position leads to a lean green marketing strategy. In addition, the publicizing of Levi's effort to go green could generate substantial criticism that at 2 percent of its sourcing, the firm has not done enough to promote sustainability. It is likely that firms that face this competitive environment will not be able to engage in a pricing strategy that asks consumers to pay more for products that are sustainable.

The **Defensive Green** strategy reflects a situation under which the market for green products is large, but the ability to differentiate based on the ecological merits of the product are low. For example, in the bottled water industry, many of the brands focus on health-conscious, environmentally aware consumers.[63] The products in this industry have been singled out due to the carbon footprint of moving water across continents and due to the number of water bottles in landfills. Consequently, many of the marketers of these products have aligned themselves with environmental causes.[64] Thus, this market is highly sensitive to the environment, but it is very difficult to establish one product offering as ecologically superior to other products. Relative to their Pepsi Aquafina and Coca-Cola Dasani competitors, Nestlé's uses a low-price strategy to make the Pure Life brand competitive in the U.S. market.[65]

The **Shaded Green** strategy refers to a market in which the demand for ecologically sensitive products is low, but there is a substantial opportunity to differentiate based on ecological viability of a product. For example, the hybrid automobile market represents about 3 percent of new car sales in the United States. Since demand is relatively soft, marketers often elect to focus on other merits of their product rather than environmentally benefits. Thus, the strategy *shades over* the green merits of the product in deference to other benefits that consumers derive from consumption. It is essential for the marketer of these products to have a refined understanding of the complete value sought by the consumer. For example, Toyota's Prius automobile offer is relatively environmentally friendly, but the marketing of this product focuses on the fuel efficiency of the auto relative to the competition. Promotional strategies used by firms in this competitive setting do not always emphasize the ecological merits of the product but also focus on efficiency considerations. In addition, pricing strategies emphasize the total cost of operations rather than solely the cost of purchasing the product. Value in use over the course of the life of the product is germane to the marketing strategy. Thus, the marketing of products with the Energy Star label emphasizes the cost savings over time rather than at the moment of purchase.

Extreme Green refers to a competitive context in which the demand for green products is large, and the ability to differentiate based on product greenness is substantial. The brands in this category often are initiated with a strong

[62] Makower, Joel (2009), *Strategies for the Green Economy*, New York: McGraw Hill.

[63] Behar, Hank (2004), "Let's Drink to Bottled Water," *Beverage Aisle*, 13 (4), 46.

[64] *Drug Store News* (2008), "Bottled Water Companies Adopt Eco-Friendly Causes," *Drug Store News*, 30 (6), 33.

[65] Zmuda, Natalie (2008), "Why Bottled Water Is Not All Washed Up," *Advertising Age*, 79(45), 16.

desire to promote and foster sustainability.[66] Firms that face this competitive landscape offer products with premium prices, but the value over the course of the product life is emphasized in marketing campaigns. For example, organic products from Patagonia, the marketer of outdoor gear and clothing, often have higher price points than alternative products.[67] Pricing strategies emphasize how the firm invests in enhancing the natural environment. The founder of Patagonia, for instance, cofounded the 1 percent for the planet program. Participants in this program pledge to provide 1 percent of net sales to environmental causes.[68] Firms such as Patagonia can rely on these pricing strategies because the market for environmentally sensitive products is large, and their opportunities to distinguish themselves from the competition are appreciable.

SUMMARY

Introduction

The purpose of this chapter has been to outline the facets of the market segmentation process. We initially outlined the elements of the segmentation-target-positioning framework. The segmentation process involves dividing a market into distinct segments or subsets of customers who have similar needs or behave in the same way. After the firm has identified the segments in a market, it engages in target marketing characterized by efforts to serve a selected segment within the marketplace. After the firm has selected a target market, it then establishes a positioning strategy in which the marketing mix is crafted to yield a distinctive appeal to the target segment. The positioning approach is designed to reflect the values sought by consumers in the target market.

Market Segmentation

Segmentation enables companies to identify groups of consumers with similar needs and enables companies to analyze characteristics and buying behaviors of members of these groups. The segments identified in the market must be substantial, identifiable, and measurable, as well as accessible and responsive to the marketer. Two common methods of segmentation include classification based on geography and demographics. Sustainable marketing analysts have also classified consumers based on psychographics and consumer behavior.

Target Marketing

Target marketing refers to the selection of a subgroup of the total market as the focal point for the marketing mix. Identification of a target market demands consideration of the firm's ability to satisfy the market as well as the size of the

---

[66] Ginsberg, Jill M., and Paul N. Bloom (2004), "Choosing the Right Green Marketing Strategy," *MIT Sloan Management Review,* (Fall) 79–84.

[67] Speer, Jordan K., (2006), "Patagonia: Shearing the Edge of Innovation," *Apparel Magazine,* 47 (9), 44–47.

[68] www.onepercentfortheplanet.org/en/aboutus/history.php (March 11, 2009).

target and the level of competition. Simultaneous analysis of size and competition yields defensive green, shaded green, extreme green, and lean green potential approaches to the target market.

KEY TERMS

market	Conventionals	North American Industrial
STP marketing	consumer	Classification System
market segmentation	engagement	(NAICS)
target marketing	motivations	buygrid framework to
positioning	barriers	reverse marketing
demographic segmentation	Green Enthusiasts	niche marketing strategies
geographic segmentation	Following the rules	Lean Green
psychographic segmentation	Doing my best	Defensive Green
True Blues	In two minds	Shaded Green
Greenback Greens	What's in it for me?	Extreme Green
Grousers	Constrained by circumstances	Benefit positioning
Apathetics	Not really bothered	User positioning
LOHAS	Drifters	competitive positioning
Naturalites	Unconcerned	value proposition

DISCUSSION QUESTIONS

1. Why is it necessary for the firm to analyze the market for segments and targets?

2. What are the elements of STP marketing?

3. What are the criteria for determining market segments?

4. Describe four types of market segmentation used by sustainable marketing firms.

5. What insight does the Roper Starch Worldwide research provide?

6. What is LOHAS? Contrast LOHAS with other market segments identified by the Natural Marketing Institute.

7. What criteria are used to select target markets?

8. How do market segment size and the level of competition influence target market selection?

9. What are the similarities and differences between the market segments established by the Natural Marketing Institute and Greenprint?

10. How does target marketing of sustainable business-to-business products differ from target marketing for sustainable consumer products?

7

Communicating Value via Integrated Marketing Programs

INTRODUCTION

The Body Shop

Since the opening of the first store in 1976, the Body Shop has identified itself as a revolutionary firm.[1] They have specific goals for enriching people, products, and the planet by 2020. It enriches lives by more than doubling its community trade program, by helping over 40,000 economically vulnerable people, and by investing over 250,000 hours to enrich biodiversity in local communities. It enhances products by protecting thousands of hectares of forest and other habitat, reducing its carbon footprint, and deriving cosmetic ingredients from biodiversity hotspots. It enriches the planet by ensuring that 70 percent of packaging does not contain fossil fuels and by powering stores with renewable or carbon-balanced energy sources.

Although the Body Shop has made appreciable efforts to become more sustainable, it is essential for them to continue to remind consumers of their efforts. In support of this desire to increase market share and broaden awareness of its sustainability efforts, the Body Shop has developed a series of promotions associate with Mother's Day (see Figure 7-1). The Body Shop uses integrated marketing communication to ensure consistency in the message

FIGURE 7-1
Body Shop Promotions associate the brand with Mother's Day.[2]

[1] www.thebodyshop-usa.com/commitment/manifesto.aspx (February 16, 2016).

[2] www.thebodyshop-usa.com/another-for-a-mother/index.aspx (February 16, 2016).

and its format. Thus, all forms of promotions, including advertising and sales promotions, use the same distinctive colors, graphics, and styles. Consumers who view promotions on any media see the same message about family life and sustainability.

In this chapter, we will examine alternative forms of promotion, and we will examine a variety of creative strategies. The Body Shop example illustrates how companies communicate the value associated with their products and brands. Companies seeking to promote a sustainable message use a variety of promotional messages and media. Since many companies have different objectives in promotion and have different means to distribute their products, companies in the same industry may develop very different promotional strategies.

Recall that in the last chapter we described the segmentation, target markets, and position (STP) framework as a process for the development of a value proposition designed to serve the needs of a target market. In this chapter, we examine a series of strategies that marketers employ to position products that *communicate* value to the consumer. We begin by characterizing integrated marketing communication as a series of processes that add continuity to the promotional strategy. We then describe the positioning process and the generic positioning themes, and we subsequently identify a number of message strategies used to achieve alternative objectives in promotion. We illustrate that the effectiveness of these strategies is related to the target market, product, and environmental considerations.

INTEGRATED MARKETING COMMUNICATION

Think about the number of advertisements a person witnesses on a daily basis. Because consumers are confronted with many messages from many companies, it is essential that marketers offer a consistent message. Thus, companies such as The Body Shop that want to associate their brands with the sustainability should offer a consistent message in advertising online, in print, and on television. Similarly, sales promotion and personal selling should also reflect the same message. *Promotion* refers to all communication from the marketer designed to persuade, inform, or remind potential buyers of a product in order to elicit a response of influence an opinion.[3]

The *promotional mix* includes advertising, personal selling, public relations, sales promotion, and direct marketing. Figure 7-1 offers an example of advertising developed for The Body Shop. *Advertising* refers to one-way, impersonal mass communication about a product or organization that is paid for by a marketing organization. By contrast, *personal selling* refers to personal, face-to-face interaction with a potential customer. The effort of Merrell's sales force to gain shelf space at Bass Pro Shops exemplifies personal selling. *Public relations* involves the use of publicity and other nonpaid forms of promotion and information to influence attitudes about a company, its products, or about the values of the

---

[3] Lamb, Charles, W., Joseph F. Hair, and Carl McDaniel (2011), *Marketing*, Mason, OH: Cengage.

organization. The Body Shop's press releases and publicity about Mother's Day campaigns provide an example of public relations. *Sales promotion* includes all marketing communication action other than advertising, personal selling, public relations, and direct marketing designed to influence consumer purchases and relationships with intermediaries in distribution channels.

Direct marketing refers to direct efforts to target an audience through the Internet, direct mail, telemarketing, direct-action advertising, and catalog selling.[4] Companies such as The Body Shop engage in direct marketing when they use email to invite consumers to enter a sweepstakes. Note that direct marketing serves as both a form of promotion and a means of retailing. As we will see in Chapter 11, retailing refers to all activities directly related to the sale of goods and services to the ultimate consumer. Direct marketing used to inform customers about an upcoming sale is a form of promotion, since it provides information to potential buyers about an opportunity to buy. By contrast, mail received by consumers that asks them to purchase a product or service warranty is a retailing activity because it asks the consumer to make a purchase. Since marketers can combine these objectives in a single communiqué to consumers, we include direct marketing as both a means of promotion and retailing.

When marketers deliberate about the degree to which promotional expenditures will be dedicated to various forms of promotion, it is in their best interests to examine the goals of the promotion as well as the costs and returns associated with each form of promotion. The company must determine the promotional objectives. Some companies use promotions to raise brand awareness and inform consumers, yet other companies use the promotional mix to generate sales. In the evaluation of the promotional mix, it is germane to identify the stage of the purchasing process and the goals of the promotion. Because one can modify the presentation made by a sales representative, there is a greater opportunity to change the presentation to focus on the specific needs of the consumer at the time they are making purchases. By contrast, advertising is an impersonal medium in which the marketer ordinarily cannot make changes to the presentation. Although the effectiveness advertising may be somewhat lower than that of personal selling when the sale is about to be made, advertising is more effective at gaining broad consumer awareness of a company's products and brands. In general, personal selling and sales promotion are most effective at the moment of a purchase decision, whereas other forms of promotion tend to be more effective before and after the purchase.

In addition to considering the consumer's stage in the purchasing process, marketers also examine the relationship between the returns and the costs of alternative forms of promotion. The average cost of a personal sales call for an industrial marketing firm has more than tripled since 1980.[5] Not only has this cost increased over time, but the consideration of cost has been broadened to include ecological costs. Personal selling is not only labor intensive, it often demands that sales representatives use substantial amounts of energy to get a message to the consumer. Advertising often is associated with substantially lower costs to reach the consumer, and it may require relatively little energy to deliver the message

---

[4] www.marketingpower.com/_layouts/Dictionary.aspx? (February 16, 2016).

[5] Nickels, William, James McHugh, and Susan McHugh (2008), Understanding Business, McGraw-Hill.

to the consumer. As marketer concerns about the environmental cost of communication increase, there will undoubtedly be increased evaluation of the ratio between the costs of promotion and the revenue generated from the promotion.

Although companies must make tough decisions about the allocation of resources across advertising, personal selling, public relations, direct marketing, and sales promotion, most companies value having a common message across components of the promotional mix. Since consumers are exposed to multiple promotions on a daily basis, companies find that consumer response to promotions is heightened when the promotional mix provides a consistent message.

Integrated marketing communication refers to coordination among the elements of the promotional mix to ensure the consistency of the message delivered at every contact point between the consumer and the company. For example, The Body Shop uses an integrated marketing communication approach in the days prior to Mother's Day. Print ads in magazines and banner ads on the Internet featured The Body Shop brand as well as reminders about the upcoming Mother's Day. Point-of-sale placards, provided via sales and distribution channels, used the same design. Press releases by public relations offered the same message about The Body Shop's Mother's Day promotions.

Integrated brand promotion is a related term used to describe efforts to bring consistency to the presentation of the *brand* to consumers. *Integrated brand promotion* refers to the use of the promotional mix to build brand awareness, identity, and preference.[6] Merrell, for instance, strives to have a consistent message about the brand's efforts to market outdoor products in an environmentally friendly manner. Whereas integrated marketing communication refers to coordination in the communication effort of a firm, integrated brand promotion addresses coordination in order to build brand awareness, identity, and preference for a specific brand. In a world in which firms rely heavily on brands, integrated brand promotion is essential to building the value of the brand in the marketplace. Firms today strive to achieve consistency in the messages sent as well as the brands associated with these advertisements and other promotions

MARKET POSITIONING

In the last chapter, we presented the STP strategy for the development of promotional campaigns. After a firm describes segments of the market and identifies a target segment, it develops a positioning strategy (see Figure 7-2). The *positioning strategy* refers to the development of the marketing mix to yield a distinctive appeal to the target segment. When the firm has effectively identified the market and its segments, the market position should flow naturally. Thus, the Body Shop positions itself as a firm that supports self-esteem, fair trade, ecology, human rights, and humane product testing.[7] Effective positioning strategies should contain several elements.[8] First, the organization must be committed to creating

---

[6] O'Guinn, Thomas C., Chris T. Allen, and Richard J. Semenik (2014), *Advertising and Integrated Brand Promotion*, Mason, OH: Thompson Higher Education.

[7] www.thebodyshop-usa.com/ (February 16, 2016).

[8] O'Guinn, Thomas C., Chris T. Allen, and Richard J. Semenik (2014), *Advertising and Integrated Brand Promotion*, Mason, OH: Thompson Higher Education.

FIGURE 7-2

Segmentation, Target
Markets, and Positioning.[9]

Market
All organizations or people with a need or want and the ability and willingness to make purchases to address these needs and wants

Market Segments
Groups of consumers that behave in the same way or have similar needs.

Target Market
A market segment which a marketing organization proposes to serve.

Positioning
Developing the marketing mix to yield a distinctive appeal to the target segment.

substantive value for the consumer. The Body Shop has developed a line of cosmetics that do not rely on animal testing, and the firm has gone to great lengths to develop products in a humane fashion. Consumers in the lifestyles of health and sustainability (LOHAS) group are inclined to favor such products, and they are willing to pay more to acquire them. Importantly, the shopping experience should reflect this commitment to humane product testing. Note that this position stands in contrast to the product testing strategies traditionally employed by major competitors in this industry.

A vital facet of the positioning strategy is that the value offered to the consumer must be meaningful to that target market. For example, the Segway two-wheeled transportation device offered marked ecological benefits to consumers, but the operations of the device and the initial price did not yield a value proposition that was meaningful to many consumers.[10] By contrast, ultra-mobile computers such as the MacBook Air have been introduced. The MacBook Air offers simplicity and mobility along with an ecofriendly design that enables Apple to increase its market share in the personal computer business.[11]

The positioning strategy that a firm selects must be consistent over time and be internally consistent. Internal consistency is achieved when every member of the organization and every associated message reflect the distinct position that the brand occupies in the eyes of the target market. Starbucks emphasizes the climate of the coffee purchase experience throughout its shops and promotions. Employees are trained to appreciate the issues of fair trade and organic products

[9] O'Guinn, Thomas C., Chris T. Allen, and Richard J. Semenik (2014), *Advertising and Integrated Brand Promotion*, Mason, OH: Thompson Higher Education.

[10] Horn, John T., Dan P. Lovallo, and S. Patrick Viguerie (2003), "Beating the Odds in Market Entry," *The McKinsey Quarterly*, (2), 26–39.

[11] cybernetnews.com/apple-computer-market-share-progress-report/ (February 16, 2016).

that are essential elements of the value that the firm offers to consumers[12]. A related factor is that the firm must be consistent with its message over time. For example, Volvo has built a reputation for safe automobiles through a prolonged commitment to research and development and communication strategies that emphasize safety. Brands such as Starbucks that hope to emphasize the organic, healthy nature of their products must offer a prolonged commitment to a product market.

The positioning strategy must also be simple and distinctive. Although a firm's product offerings may rest on highly sophisticated technologies, consumers and industrial buyers make purchases to satisfy needs. The firm that can effectively distill its product message into a simple idea is poised to capture a substantial share of the target market. In 2008, Clorox introduced the Clorox Green Works line of cleaning products that included Green Works natural laundry detergent, Green Works natural cleaning wipes, Green Works laundry stain remover, Green Works natural dishwashing liquid, and other household cleaning products. These products were recognized by the Environmental Protection Agency Design for Environment (DfE) program for their use of environmentally preferable chemical ingredients.[13] The simple logic linking these environmentally friendly products to cleaning resulted in the brand being rated as a top U.S. green brand in a survey completed by advertising agency WPP and consortium of other marketing and consulting firms.[14] The Clorox Green brand has been able to capture market share because the sustainability message is easily communicated to consumers. Moreover, the product stands out as a distinctively ecologically friendly product in a household chemical market not known for its environmental appeals.

The Value Proposition

At the end of the positioning process, the firm is in a position to announce the value proposition of a brand. The *value proposition* is a statement of the emotional, function, and self-expressive benefits delivered by a brand that provides value to consumers in a target market.[15] The value proposition is critical to the ongoing success of the firm given that this proposition is the basis for brand choice and consumer brand loyalty. For example, Whole Foods' value proposition emphasizes that it sells organic, natural, and healthy foods to consumers who are passionate about food and the environment.

In order for the firm to develop a value proposition that resonates in the market, it is important to proceed through STP marketing to arrive at a value proposition. Note that STP marketing occurs over time. The participants in the strategy development process are likely to change along with the needs of the consuming market. A carefully selected value proposition gives the firm direction that leads to strategic decision making. Importantly, if the benefits derived from

---

[12] Argenti, Paul A., (2004), "Collaborating with Activists: How Starbucks Works with NGOS," California Management Review, 47(1), 91–116.

[13] www.epa.gov/saferchoice/products#type=All-Purpose Cleaners (February 16, 2016).

[14] Defotis, Dimitra (2009), "Clorox Isn't Recession-Proof, but it May Be Close Enough," *Wall Street Journal* (May 10), online.wsj.com/article/SB124190163049204003.html.

[15] Frow, Pennie, and Adrian Payne (2011), "A Stakeholder Perspective of the Value Proposition Concept," *European Journal of Marketing*, 45 (1/2), 223–240.

the product exceed the price relative to other brands, there is potential for success. If the relative price exceeds the benefits realized from the brand, the potential for a successful brand is limited. Importantly, the developer of the value proposition must consider the extent to which consumers weigh ecological, relational, and economic returns relative to the cost of the product. When each facet of sustainability is incorporated into the development of the value proposition, there is greater potential to serve the needs of the target market successfully.

Effective Positioning Themes

When the positioning strategy is simple and distinctive, it helps the organization make internal decisions that yield value for consumers, and it further enables the firm to develop a focused communication strategy.[16] The STP marketing approach thus enables the firm to generate positioning themes that are viable in the marketplace. It is essential for the organization to settle on a single idea for the positioning theme. For example, Clorox Green Works drives home the notion that these products are clean and environmentally safe. The selection of this single premise must be made in conjunction with the needs of the target market. If the focal segment is LOHAS consumers, they are inclined to buy based on the premise that a product offers environmental benefits. In such cases, the strategy of firms such as Ben & Jerry's—who regularly invest in carbon reduction and alternative energy products—is salient and meaningful to the consumer. By contrast, Nike continues to market the *Considered* brand of footwear, but the emphasis on marketing is athletic rather than environmental performance. Thus, the determination of the single idea to be featured in communication must consider the target market.

Three general strategies for a positioning theme include benefit, user, and competitive positioning. ***Benefit positioning*** refers to an emphasis on a functional, emotional, or self-expressive return realized from product consumption. Since benefits are the basis for most purchases, it is valuable in many markets to focus on the returns derived from consumption. For example, the functional benefit of the energy-efficient appliances is the reduced fuel consumption and lower fuel costs realized over the life of the product (see Figure 7-3). Many green products may be purchased not for the functions but for emotional benefits. Just as airline passengers can invest in flight insurance to alleviate concerns about air travel safety, they can also balance the environmental influence of their travel by buying carbon reduction services. In many cases, the purchase of the carbon reduction credits provides an emotional benefit to consumers. The self-expressive benefit addresses how the product influences the presentation of the individual to relevant others. For example, the *drifter* category of consumers represents a segment that is generally unconcerned about the environment. Because they see sustainability as a trend, they want to be seen in places viewed as environmentally conscious, even though they do not make substantial purchases of green products. Thus, green grocers such as Trader Joe's can attract interest from these consumers because they want to be associated with current trends.

---

[16] O'Guinn, Thomas C., Chris T. Allen, and Richard J. Semenik (2014), *Advertising and Integrated Brand Promotion*, Mason, OH: Thompson Higher Education.

FIGURE 7-3
South Mississippi Electric Power Association ad Exemplifying Benefit Positioning.[17]

FIGURE 7-4
Chipotle ad Exemplifying User Positioning.[18]

User positioning is a second basis for the positioning theme. In this positioning theme, the marketer develops a profile of a specific target user as the focus of the positioning strategy. For example, Chipotle restaurant ads that show a family posing in a natural setting highlights the lifestyle of the target market (see Figure 7-4). Such ads seek to make the use of Chipotle restaurants consistent with the lifestyle of the target market.

---

[17] www.smepa.coop/images/ad_green_power_700.jpg (February 16, 2016).

[18] Olson, Elizabeth (2012), "An Animated Ad with a Plot Line and a Moral," *The New York Times*. February 9, p.2.

The third fundamental positioning theme is *competitive positioning*. Competitive positioning refers to the direct reference to the competition in order to illuminate the benefits of a firm's brand. In many cases, firms that have developed relatively environmentally friendly products compare the green features of their offerings to the competition. For example, Figure 7-5 reproduces a Honda motorcycle ad that emphasizes the fuel advantages of the Honda Metropolitan over the Smart car.

MESSAGE STRATEGY

Promotion strategies are developed to obtain a consumer response or influence a consumer opinion. One of the essential responses that the firm seeks is a product purchase. For example, Pizza Fusion encouraged customers to purchase a

---

[19] www.autospies.com/images/users/tryme/honda-smart-ad.jpg (February 16, 2016).

pizza on Earth Day by committing to plant a tree on their behalf for each pizza purchased (Figure 7-6). In addition, Pizza Fusion created a recycling rewards program that gave discounts to customers who brought their pizza boxes back to the restaurant for recycling.[20]

Although increased consumption is often the motivation underlying promotion and advertising, select groups are now also presenting promotional campaigns that emphasize reduced consumption. For instance, Patagonia place a full-page advertisement in *The New York Times* on Black Friday asking consumers to buy less of everything, even its own products (see Figure 7-7).[21] These advertisements often focus on the environmental or economic returns associated with conservation of resources.

The second objective of promotion involves influencing the opinion that a consumer has about a brand, product, product attribute, or behavior. In many cases, promotional strategies designed to influence a consumer are in place well before a potential buyer is able or ready to buy. The promotional or advertising manager seeks to develop some association with the brand so that the association with the brand becomes relevant at the time of purchase. For example, Coca-Cola's advertisements that focus on its sustainable packaging and recycling efforts are trying to foster an opinion about the firm rather than influence an immediate purchase (see Figure 7-8).

The ***promotional strategy*** refers to a plan for the optimal use of advertising, sales promotion, public relations, direct marketing, and personal selling. To varying degrees, firms use each of these elements to communicate the value of their brands and products to the target audience. The strategy that underlies each of these forms of promotion should be focused on a particular target market and the associated value proposition developed by the firm. The ***message strategy*** refers to the what the ad attempts to say about the brand, and the creative strategy refers

FIGURE 7-6
Pizza Fusion Plant-a-Tree Promotion.

[20] aaronallen.com/blog/restaurant-promotions/honor-earth-day-with-these-green-themed-restaurant-promotions (February 16, 2016).

[21] Nudd, Tim (2011), "Ad of the Day: Patagonia," Retrieved from: www.adweek.com/news/advertising-branding/ad-day-patagonia-136745 (February 16, 2016).

FIGURE 7-7

Patagonia ad Calling for
Reductions in Excess
Consumption.[22]

DON'T BUY THIS JACKET

It's Black Friday, the day in the year retail turns from red to black and starts to make real money. But Black Friday, and the culture of consumption it reflects, puts the economy of natural systems that support all life firmly in the red. We're now using the resources of one-and-a-half planets on our one and only planet.

Because Patagonia wants to be in business for a good long time – and leave a world inhabitable for our kids – we want to do the opposite of every other business today. We ask you to buy less and to reflect before you spend a dime on this jacket or anything else.

Environmental bankruptcy, as with corporate bank-ruptcy, can happen very slowly, then all of a sudden. This is what we face unless we slow down, then reverse the damage. We're running short on fresh water, topsoil, fisheries, wetlands – all our planet's natural systems and resources that support business, and life, including our own.

The environmental cost of everything we make is astonishing. Consider the R2® Jacket shown, one of our best sellers. To make it required 135 liters of

COMMON THREADS INITIATIVE

REDUCE
WE make useful gear that lasts a long time
YOU don't buy what you don't need

REPAIR
WE help you repair your Patagonia gear
YOU pledge to fix what's broken

REUSE
WE help find a home for Patagonia gear
you no longer need
YOU sell or pass it on*

RECYCLE
WE will take back your Patagonia gear
that is worn out
YOU pledge to keep your stuff out of
the landfill and incinerator

REIMAGINE
TOGETHER we reimagine a world where we take
only what nature can replace

water, enough to meet the daily needs (three glasses a day) of 45 people. Its journey from its origin as 60% recycled polyester to our Reno warehouse generated nearly 20 pounds of carbon dioxide, 24 times the weight of the finished product. This jacket left behind, on its way to Reno, two-thirds its weight in waste.

And this is a 60% recycled polyester jacket, knit and sewn to a high standard; it is exceptionally durable, so you won't have to replace it as often. And when it comes to the end of its useful life we'll take it back to recycle into a product of equal value. But, as is true of all the things we can make and you can buy, this jacket comes with an environmental cost higher than its price.

There is much to be done and plenty for us all to do. Don't buy what you don't need. Think twice before you buy anything. Go to patagonia.com/CommonThreads or scan the QR code below. Take the Common Threads Initiative pledge, and join us in the fifth "R," to reimagine a world where we take only what nature can replace.

patagonia®
patagonia.com

TAKE THE PLEDGE

*If you sell your used Patagonia product on eBay® and take the Common Threads Initiative pledge, we will co-list your product on patagonia.com for no additional charge.

[22] Nudd, Tim (2011), "Ad of the Day: Patagonia," Retrieved from: www.adweek.com /news/advertising-branding/ad-day-patagonia-136745 (February 16, 2016).

FIGURE 7-8
Coca-Cola ad Illustrating
Commitment to the
Environment.[23]

to how the ad expresses the ad claims.[24] Messages have verbal, nonverbal, and technical components that are employed to enhance the communication process and gain consumer acceptance.

In their analysis of advertising message strategies, O'Guinn, Allen, and Semenik identify 10 objectives associated with advertising and promotion, and they identify several different procedures employed to achieve these objectives.[25] The 10 objectives and the techniques ordinarily employed to achieve these objectives include:

Promote Brand Recall. The initial objective employed by many firms involves getting consumers to remember the service or brand name. If consumers can remember the brand or some attribute, they are more inclined to buy the brand or engage in an activity associated with the message. The seemingly ubiquitous "reduce, reuse,

---

[23] www.coca-colacompany.com/.

[24] Keller, Kevin Lane (2013) *Strategic Brand Management*, Prentice Hall: Upper Saddle River, NJ.

[25] O'Guinn, Thomas C., Chris T. Allen, Richard J. Semenik, and Angeline Close (2015), *Advertising and Integrated Brand Promotion*, 7th edition. Stanford, CT: Cengage Learning.

and recycle" motto exemplifies an attempt to get the consumer to remember this activity (see Figure 7-9). If consumers are unaware of these practices, they are unlikely to engage in them. Recurring use of a message builds retention, which increases the likelihood that the consumers will reduce, reuse, and recycle.

Firms and organizations also promote their ideas and brand names via jingles and slogans. These communications to the consumer attempt to increase the likelihood that a consumer will remember the idea, product, or service. For example, Nike's *Better World* campaign highlights the company's commitment to preserving the environment. This brand association is supported by the company's efforts to reduce waste through innovative design (e.g., Flyknit), sustainable processes (e.g., waterless dying) and recycling (e.g., Reuse a Shoe), and its efforts to use environmentally preferred materials.[27] Nike recently launched its *Making* app, which is intended to help "designers and product creators make informed decisions about the environmental impacts of the materials they choose"[28] (see Figure 7-10).

Link a key attribute to the brand name. In some cases, the firm seeks to associate particular attributes of a brand with the consumption decision. A properly developed value proposition identifies self-expressive, emotional, or

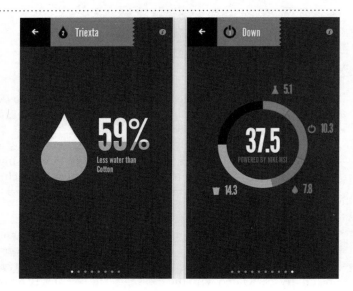

---

[26] www.flickr.com/photos/re3org/2324092769/ (February 16, 2016).

[27] news.nike.com/news/through-the-years-nike-s-history-of-sustainable-innovation--2 (March 26, 2015).

[28] news.nike.com/news/through-the-years-nike-s-history-of-sustainable-innovation--2 (March 26, 2015).

[29] www.wired.com/2013/07/what-are-the-most-sustainable-materials-nikes-new-app-shows-you/.

functional benefits delivered by a brand that provides value to consumers in a target market.[30] The ability to achieve these benefits should be, in some way, superior to the competition. The firm must, therefore, develop advertisements that emphasize the unique selling proposition of the brand. For example, consumers have many alternatives with respect to the purchase of shoes. The ads for TOMS emphasize that the company has made substantial commitments to improving the lives of people in need around the world. TOMS has donated over 35 million pairs of shoes in over 70 countries worldwide.[31] In contrast to brand recall ads, such ads require the consumer to learn somewhat more about the brand and the product class. A single viewing of TOMS ads will not likely project the message of the firm's commitment to improving the lives of those in need, but viewing multiple ads with this same message provides greater insight into the efforts of this company (see Figure 7-11).

In many cases, firms seeking to link a key attribute to a brand name will focus on a single attribute to the product. For example, Ford consistently promotes its EcoBoost technology, which improves fuel efficiency without sacrificing

FIGURE 7-11
TOMS One for One Program Donates One Pair of Shoes to a Child in Need for Every Pair of Shoes Purchased.[32]

---

[30] Aaker, David (1996), *Building Stronger Brands*, New York: Free Press.

[31] www.finehomesandliving.com/Shoes-with-a-Heart-The-Toms-Story-with-Founder-Blake-Mycoskie/ (February 16, 2016).

[32] www.finehomesandliving.com/Shoes-with-a-Heart-The-Toms-Story-with-Founder-Blake-Mycoskie/ (February 16, 2016).

power.[33] When the firm has made a long-term commitment to this single brand attribute (e.g., EcoBoost technology), they often find the strategy to be superior to a series of ads addressing multiple brand attributes. In addition, being the first to link an attribute to a brand makes it difficult for the competition to link the attribute to their products and/or use the attribute as a point of differentiation. Thus, competitors to Ford will have some challenge differentiating their brands with technologies similar to EcoBoost.

Persuade the consumer. In many cases, the marketer seeks to influence the buyer to make a purchase. Whereas the earlier discussed strategies offered one or two reasons to buy, efforts to convince the consumer to make a purchase involve several logical arguments. Marketers use this approach when they feel the consumer is highly involved in the purchase. These consumers are willing to listen to cogent arguments about branded products. For ads and other promotional vehicles of this nature to work, the consumer must understand the logic presented in the ad, and the consumer must also agree with the logic. Advertisements that explicitly offer reasons to buy a product embody this strategy. For example, Proctor & Gamble has developed print and television ads that inform consumers that they can save energy and money by washing their laundry with Tide Coldwater (see Figure 7-12).[34]

The success of the strategies to persuade or convince consumers is contingent on the consumer's involvement in the purchase process. On some occasions, companies draw attention to the relative advantage of their products. By illustrating the superior performance of a product, the marketer hopes to convince the consumer to buy. This method has been found to be effective for brands with low market share when compared with high market share brands, and it has been shown to be effective when consumers have not illustrated a brand preference.[35] Thus, many consumers faced with purchasing a new faucet are likely to have no brand preference. The Delta ad for the $Temp_2O$ faucet draws attention to the safety benefits of this faucet (see Figure 7-13).

Another means that marketers use to convince the consumer to buy is through ads that express a sense of urgency. For example, sellers of solar panels for homes may post a newspaper ad that indicates a "limited time offer" of a reduction in the price of goods. This form of ad is particularly effective when the consumer is comfortable with the benefits of a product but is looking for additional motivation to buy now.

Develop positive feelings toward the brand. In many cases, the goal of communication is not to influence an immediate purchase but to nurture preferences for the brand. These ads and promotions often emphasize the development of positive feelings toward the brand rather than rational thoughts about the salience of a product. One means of fostering these feelings is through ads

---

[33] www.ford.com/green/fuel-efficiency/ (February 16, 2016).

[34] www.tide.com/en-US/product/tide-coldwater-clean.jspx (March 26, 2015).

[35] O'Guinn, Thomas C., Chris T. Allen, and Richard J. Semenik (2014), *Advertising and Integrated Brand Promotion*, Mason, OH: Thompson Higher Education.

FIGURE 7-12
Tide Coldwater ad Highlighting the Energy Savings Benefits of Washing Laundry in Cold Water[36]

that attempt to make the consumer *feel good* about the brand. The logic rests on the presumption that consumers who like a brand will prefer the brand to alternatives. For example, Timberland attempts to foster positive feelings for the brand prior to purchase by showing its products in scenic outdoor settings (see Figure 7-14).

Two of the most common methods used to foster positive feelings toward a brand are through the use of humor and sex appeals. Humorous ads ordinarily attempt to create a memorable and pleasurable association with a product or brand. Humor is particularly effective when the punch line or payoff from the humor is directly associated with the product or brand. For instance, ads for the Chevy Volt telling "parents" that it is electric.[39] (see Figure 7-15).

---

[36] www.tide.com/en-US/product/tide-coldwater-clean.jspx (March 26, 2015).

FIGURE 7-13
Delta's ad for Temp$_2$O
Faucet.[37]

FIGURE 7-14
Timberland ad with
"Feel-Good" Quality.[38]

[37] www.deltafaucet.com/company/advertising/content/print/ads/Temp2O_Muddy KidAd.pdf (February 16, 2016).

[38] www.coloribus.com/adsarchive/prints/timberland-altitude-3160255/ (February 16, 2016).

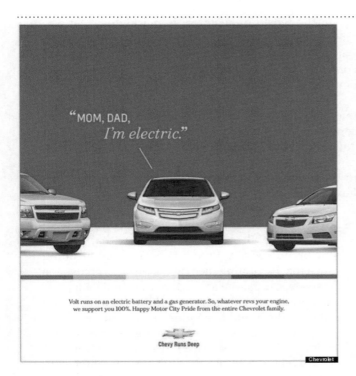

FIGURE 7-15
Chevy Volt Using Humor to
Appeal to Consumers.

Sexy ads similarly draw attention to the product with the hope that this attention will lead to brand preference. American Apparel, for example, uses racy advertisements with attractive models to draw attention to the firm's apparel line (see Figure 7-16). Although the advertisements are sometimes controversial, American Apparel engages in several charitable and environmental initiatives, including the use of more sustainable fabrics and a subsidized public transit for employees.[40] In fact, one of the company's billboard advertisements states, "We're not politically correct—But we have good ethics."[41]

Change behavior by inducing fear or anxiety. Marketers operating in some situations have found that they can get a consumer to act—or convince the consumer *not to act* by instilling fear or anxiety in the consumer. Fear apparently is most effective when consumers have engaged in some thought about the issue, and under such circumstances, fear can be an effective way to induce consumer action. Seventh Generation ads invoke fear in parents about the safety and well-being of their children. For example, one ad states that children's early exposure to toxic chemicals may lead to cancer and/or Alzheimer's disease (see Figure 7-17). This ad is designed to prompt consumers to keep their children safe by using Seventh Generation's toxin-free products.

---

[39] www.huffingtonpost.com/2012/06/05/chevrolet-volt-comes-out-gay-ad-motor-city-pride_n_1571084.html? (February 16, 2016).

[40] www.americanapparel.net/aboutus/corpresp/environment/.

[41] www.apparelnews.net/news/2014/aug/06/american-apparel-we-have-good-ethics/.

FIGURE 7-16
American Apparel ad Using Sex Appeal.[42]

In the world of sustainable marketing, fear is often used in public service announcements. World Wildlife Foundation ads, for example, are designed to instill the consumer to act in an environmentally responsible manner (see Figure 7-18).

The use of anxiety is related to the use of fear given that both methods attempt to call attention to the negative consequences of certain activities or consumption practices. Anxiety is not as strong an emotion as outright fear, and it can last longer. For example, Toyota invokes anxiety related to the range restrictions of electric cars in its ads for the Lexus Hybrid Drive (see Figure 7-19).

Situate the brand socially. The social nature of humans is at the core of this strategy that situates the brand socially. Products have social meaning such that by putting them in the proper context, the marketer can gain awareness and, hopefully, adoption of a product. Many ads use a *slice of life* appeal that situates the brand in an ideal usage setting. While this method is used extensively in television and print media, it is also used when marketers engage in ***product placement***. Product placement refers to efforts on the part of brand owners to feature their products in films, movies, plays, or other performances. By linking the brand to a seemingly real activity, the marketer hopes to foster awareness of the brand. Green Product Placement, a company specializing in environmentally friendly product placement, has placed products such as Applegate Farms and Pirate's Booty in numerous television shows and big-budget movies (e.g., *Blue Bloods*, *Gossip Girl*).[43] Figure 7-20 illustrates one product placed by Green Product Placement – the use of Repurpose compostable coffee cups on the television show *House of Cards*. Repurpose gains increased awareness of its products, and the television show receives revenue from the product placement.

Transform the consumption experience. Ads that transform the consumption experience seek to operate in a manner quite different from the strategies outlined previously. In most ads, the goal is to provide information about the product or enhance perceptions of the brand. When the firm elects to transform consumption, it is trying to make the consumption experience better. The marketer tries to make

[42] mariathrasher.wordpress.com/2014/07/07/week-1-effective-design-ads/ (March 26, 2015).

[43] www.mnn.com/leaderboard/stories/how-eco-friendly-brands-get-hollywood-exposure.

FIGURE 7-17
Seventh Generation ad Using Fear Appeal.[44]

FIGURE 7-18
World Wildlife ad Using Fear Appeal.[45]

expectations about the experience or memories of the experience better. For instance, Starbucks has attempted to transform the mundane experience of buying coffee and transform it into something else. The claim that it is *Starbucks or nothing* reflects the idea that it is trying to frame the experience of its coffee as different and superior to alternatives (see Figure 7-21).

---

[44] newlywedsurvival.com/fighttoxins-seventh-generation/ (February 16, 2016).

[45] www.treehugger.com/natural-sciences/surreal-fish-head-wwf-climate-change-ad.html (February 16, 2016).

FIGURE 7-19
Toyota Invokes Anxiety
Related to the Range
Restrictions of Electric Cars.[46]

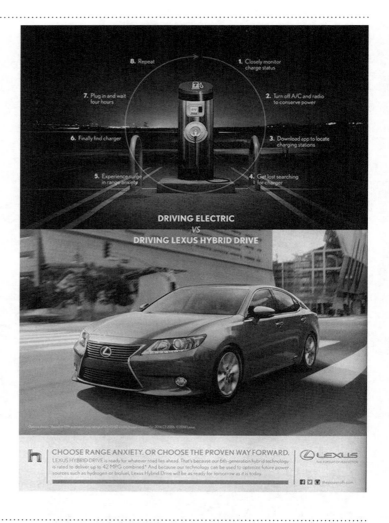

FIGURE 7-20
Product Placement of
Repurpose Compostable
Cups in the Television Show
House of Cards, Featuring
Kevin Spacey.[47]

---

[46] www.ibtimes.com/lexus-advertisement-hybrid-cars-has-infuriated-electric-car-fans
-who-accuse-toyota-stoking-1678790 (March 26, 2015).

[47] www.mnn.com/leaderboard/stories/how-eco-friendly-brands-get-hollywood-exposure
(March 27, 2015).

FIGURE 7-21
Starbucks ad Exemplifying
Transformation of the
Consumption Experience.[48]

FIGURE 7-22
Patagonia ad that Helps to
Define the Brand Image.[49]

Link the Brand to a Social/cultural Movement. Another strategy is to position the brand in a way that embraces a cultural or social movement. For example, Playtex Gloves collaborates with Susan G. Komen in the support of breast cancer awareness and research.[50]

Define the Brand Image. The final strategy refers to action taken by the marketing organization to define the brand. In this type of advertising, the goal is to project an image of what the marketer hopes the consumer will associate with the brand. Regardless of whether the ad relies solely on visual images or lengthy copy, the objective is to link specific attributes to the brand. The Patagonia ad (Figure 7-22) defines the brand image as consisting of environmentally conscious, quality clothing made from organic cotton, recycled materials, chlorine-free wool, hemp, and Tencel.

The strategies outlined in this section are representative of most advertisements and promotions, but they certainly do not include all strategies employed by firms. The selection of these various strategies is driven by the goals of the firm as well as the corporate and environmental context faced by the organization. In addition, it is not uncommon for firms to use multiple appeals in the same ad. Many humorous ads, for example, also are competitive promotions

[48] theinspirationroom.com/daily/print/2009/5/starbucks-no-compromise.jpg (February 16, 2016).

[49] www.stylepinner.com/red-clay-soul-patagonia/cmVkLWNsYXktc291bC1wYXRhZ29uaWE/ (February 17, 2016).

[50] www.komen.org/Playtex/ (March 7, 2017).

that link product to specific attributes. The competitive position of the firm also influences the strategy employed. Well-established firms are likely, for instance, to place less emphasis on achieving brand awareness, but they are more inclined to invest in promotional strategies that promote a brand image.

SUMMARY

Introduction

The purpose of this chapter is to illustrate how marketers communicate value through the promotional mix. We used logic based on the marketing efforts of The Body Shop to illustrate an integrated marketing communication strategy developed to promote a relatively sustainable brand and its related products.

Integrated Marketing Communication

Integrated marketing communication is concerned with coordination among the elements of the promotional mix to ensure the consistency of the message delivered at every contact point between the consumer and the company. The promotional mix includes advertising, sales promotion, personal selling, public relations, and direct marketing. Integrated brand promotion is a related term that refers to the use of the promotional mix to build brand awareness, identity, and preference. Many firms today that seek to promote the sustainability of their brands engage in integrated marketing communication along with integrated brand promotion.

Market Positioning

The positioning strategy refers to the development of the marketing mix to yield a distinctive appeal to the target segment. Three general strategies for a positioning theme include benefit, user, and competitive positioning. Benefit positioning refers to an emphasis on a functional, emotional, or self-expressive return realized from product consumption. User positioning is a positioning theme in which the marketer develops a profile of a specific target user as the focus of the positioning strategy. Competitive positioning refers to the direct reference to the competition in order to illuminate the benefits of a firm's brand. At the end of the positioning process, the firm is in a position to announce the value proposition of a brand. The value proposition is a statement of the emotional, function, and self-expressive benefits delivered by a brand that provides value to consumers in a target market.

Message Strategy

Since there are multiple communication objectives associated with a promotional campaign, marketers have developed a series of strategies designed to help realize these objectives. Firms use jingles and slogans to increase brand recall, and they develop unique selling propositions to link a key attribute to a brand. When consumers are more involved in the purchase process, marketers use cogent logic or positive sentiment to stimulate brand interest. Positive feelings toward the brand are also generated through promotions and advertisements that use humor or sex appeal. Anxiety and fear have also been found to be effective strategies to induce consumption. Advertisements that situate the brand socially attempt to shape the meaning of the brand, whereas promotions that transform the consumption seek to make the consumption experience better. Promotional campaigns that attempt to define the brand image link certain attributes of the product class to the brand.

KEY TERMS

promotion
promotional mix
advertising
personal selling
public relations
sales promotion

direct marketing
integrated marketing
  communication
integrated brand promotion
positioning strategy
value proposition

benefit positioning
user positioning
competitive positioning
promotional strategy
message strategy
product placement

DISCUSSION QUESTIONS

1. The introduction of this chapter characterizes The Body Shop as a company that engages in integrated marketing communication to present its brands and products. Describe the marketing mix of another firm that uses integrated marketing communication to stimulate sustainability.

2. Is direct marketing a component of the promotional mix? Under what circumstances would direct marketing be classified as either promotion or retailing?

3. What are the benefits that companies realize when they elect to develop integrated brand promotions?

4. Describe two currently running campaigns in which one competitor uses user positioning and another uses competitive positioning.

5. One of the purposes of promotion is to generate consumer responses in the form of immediate purchases. Describe an ad or point-of-sale display that has been used to get immediate consumer purchases of relatively environmentally friendly products.

6. The Green Works ad campaign uses a feel-good strategy to foster preferences for the brand. Describe another ad for an environmentally friendly product that is marketed using this strategy.

7. It is relatively easy these days to instill consumer anxiety about the environment. Under what conditions do you believe that such a strategy will either be effective or ineffective?

8. Describe a promotional campaign that uses humor. To what extent is the humor associated with the brand?

9. How could an ad for your college define the brand image? What would such an ad look like?

10. Describe three social movements that have been embraced by consumer brands.

8

Proclaiming Value via Branding and Labeling

In this chapter you will learn about:

Branding and Labeling

Sustainable Branding

Greenwashing

Certification Labeling

Demarketing

INTRODUCTION

The promotion of the sustainability of a brand is no longer solely a matter of corporate social responsibility or public relations. Just as more firms are finding it necessary to elaborate on the sustainability of their brands, consumers are becoming more informed about factors that influence the sustainability of a brand.

Chipotle is a quick, casual dining chain that illustrates many of the ways that a firm can nurture consumer preferences for sustainable brands and products. Chipotle is an industry leader concerning the quality of ingredients used in its burritos and other dishes. Recognizing that more than 2 million Americans contract antibiotic-resistant infections every year, and over 23,000 die as a result, the company no longer uses ingredients that are treated with antibiotics.[1] Similarly, it pledged in 2015 to sell food that is free of genetically engineered ingredients (see Figure 8-1). This announcement does not mean that the restaurant will be entirely genetically modified organism (GMO) free. The soft drinks it sells may contain corn-based GMO sweeteners made from GMO corn, and some meat and dairy supplies come from animals fed GMO grains. Nevertheless, this strategy illustrates the firm's commitment to food quality. Chipotle also provides complete information concerning the ingredients in its menu items, and it indicates where GMOs are used. This strategy is designed to illustrate that fast food does not need to be made with preservatives, artificial colors and flavors, and cheap raw ingredients. In the process, Chipotle has established a reputation as a purveyor of healthy food choices.

The Chipotle core mission is to sell "food with integrity.[2]" This strategy centers around having respect for all participants in the supply chain, including animals, farmers, and the environment. Strict standards for the raising of livestock, for instance, influence the ability of this firm to provide all the ingredients necessary for all menu

FIGURE 8-1

Chipotle strives to eliminate GMO ingredients.

[1] www.cnn.com/2015/09/15/health/fast-food-meat-antibiotics-grades/ (October 11, 2015).

[2] www.washingtonpost.com/news/wonkblog/wp/2015/01/14/why-chipotles-pork-problem-is-a-bad-sign-for-its-future/ (October 11, 2015).

items. When a recent audit uncovered that a supplier failed to meet standards for raising pigs, the company announced that it would temporarily stop offering carnitas as a protein option.[3] While animals in the Chipotle supply chain must be free-range, farms must operate in ways that ensure the health of the soil. Together these supply chain initiatives enhance the influence of Chipotle on the ecological environment.

Chipotle also makes sizeable financial commitments to sustainability. In 2011, it established the Chipotle Cultivate Foundation as a way to extend its commitment to creating a more sustainable food future. This foundation provides resources and promotes good stewardship for farmers, encourages regenerative agriculture practices, promotes enhanced livestock husbandry, and fosters food literacy and nutritious eating. Over its short existence, Chipotle Cultivate Foundation has contributed over $3 million to organizations committed to cultivating a better world through food.[4]

Chipotle incorporates sustainability into its relationships with customers and other members of the value chain, and in the process, it enhances its triple bottom-line performance. These supply chain activities and promotional efforts help to generate brand equity that frames Chipotle as a highly sustainable brand. In this chapter, we examine factors that influence consumer evaluations of brands. We initially illustrate how promotional strategies enable firms to establish consumer perceptions of the sustainability of brands. We then describe conditions under which firms engage in greenwashing that overstates their sustainable efforts. We subsequently examine the role of certification labels as a means of supporting sustainability and quality considerations. We close by describing the conservation of resources and energy via demarketing.

SUSTAINABLE BRANDING

The Chipotle strategy identified in the previous section addressed the development of a brand image. We define a **brand** as a name, term, design, or symbol that identifies a seller's products and differentiates them from competitors' products.[5] Firms are heavily focused on branding because at the product-market level, brand equity increases channel effectiveness and communications and decreases price sensitivity associated with the brand.[6] In some cases, firms are aggressively developing reputations for products that outperform the competition with respect to environmental concerns.[7] For example, Chipotle emphasizes natural ingredients designed to promote personal well-being while striving to achieve sustainability.[8] By contrast, other brands may pursue sustainability

[3] www.nytimes.com/2015/04/27/business/chipotle-to-stop-serving-genetically-altered-food.html?_r=0 (October 11, 2015).

[4] www.cultivatefoundation.org/?_ga=1.185023918.689218780.1444607618 (October 11, 2015).

[5] Keller, Kevin Lane (2013), *Strategic Brand Management, 4/E,* , NJ: Prentice Hall.

[6] Keller, Kevin Lane, and Donald Lehmann (2006), "Brands and Branding: Research Findings and Future Priorities, *Marketing Science*, 25(6), 740–759.

[7] Ginsberg, Jill M., and Paul N. Bloom (2004), "Choosing the Right Green Marketing Strategy," *MIT Sloan Management Review,* (Fall) 79–84.

[8] www.tomsofmaine.com/company/overlay/Stewardship-Model (July 9, 2015).

efforts within the firm, but this message is not integral to the manner in which they present the brand to consumers. Nike, for instance, has made noble commitments to reduce the firm's carbon footprint, but this message is not central to many of the promotions of its brands.[9]

In this section, we consider ways in which a brand can be differentiated from the competition based on appeals to sustainability or the environment. Firms that establish well-defined brand identity are substantially more likely to yield brand value.[10] The value of a brand expressed as brand equity has been examined from a *customer*, *corporate*, and *financial* basis.[11] Customer-based brand equity considers the attraction to a particular product from a particular company generated by factors other than the product attributes. Company-based brand equity refers to the additional value that accrues to a firm because of the presence of the brand name that would not accrue to the equivalent, unbranded product. Financially based brand equity is the price the brand brings in the financial market.

The level of company-based and financially based equity is driven by customer-based brand equity. Customer-level brand equity can be captured by five factors that form a hierarchy from the lowest to highest levels. This hierarchy is consistent with the awareness-interest-desire-action framework developed to describe and influence consumption.[12] These factors include:

Awareness. The initial step for a brand often involves positioning the brand and its promotion to increase the likelihood that consumers will remember the brand. Awareness of the brand fosters interest that prompts desire and, ultimately, action. Consumer awareness of the brand can be evaluated based on **brand recall**, the ability to retrieve the brand when given the product category, the needs fulfilled by the category, or some other type of cue. For example, Chipotle is likely to monitor the extent to which consumers recall its brand name when prompted with the Mexican food product category. **Brand recognition** refers to the consumer's ability to confirm exposure to the brand when given the brand as a cue. Thus, Chipotle could show consumers the product or the brand logo and assess recognition.

Associations. Firms that establish brand associations in the minds of customers differentiate the brand and have the potential to establish competitive superiority.[13] The tangible components of products are obvious ways to instill associations with the firm. Thus, Patagonia's use of organic cotton in its clothing products provides an association between this brand and environmental sustainability.

[9] www.nikeresponsibility.com/report/uploads/files/FY12-13_NIKE_Inc_CR_Report.pdf (March 23, 2016).

[10] Aaker, David A., and Joachimsthaler, Erich (2000), *Brand Leadership*, The Free Press, New York, NY.

[11] Keller, Kevin Lane, and Donald Lehmann (2006), "Brands and Branding: Research Findings and Future Priorities, *Marketing Science*, 25(6), 740–759.

[12] Strong, Edward K. (1925), Theories of selling. *Journal of Applied Psychology,* 9(1): 75–86.

[13] Keller, Kevin Lane, Brian Sternthal, and Alice Tybout (2002), "Three Questions You Need to Ask About Your Brand," *Harvard Business Review,* 80(9), 80–89.

Tangibles include product features, price, service reliability, style, design, and other factors incorporated into a product offering that provide superior performance relative to competition.

Intangibles are also germane to the development of associations with the brand. Intangibles develop **brand imagery** that influences how consumers think about a brand rather than their objective assessment of product attributes.[14] One source of imagery involves user profiles that describe the type of organization or person that uses a brand. The Whole Foods ad in Figure 8-2, for example, paints a picture about the types of consumers who shop at its stores. Imagery can also inform the consumer about the appropriate usage situation for a sustainable product. For example, advertisements for LED light bulbs illustrate the utility of these lights. Imagery can also be derived from personality and values associated with the brand. Research identifies five dimensions of brand personality that include sincerity, excitement, competence, sophistication, and ruggedness.[15] Burt's Bees ads, for instance, espouse the wholesome, sincere nature of the company's products. Finally, the history and the heritage associated with a brand fosters imagery about the firm. Eddie Bauer's trademark, for instance, indicates the long-term dedication of the firm to the environment.

A third means for developing associations with the brand lies in the reputation and the image of a brand. In a world in which greenwashing is rampant, it is essential that the firm establish credibility in the eyes of the consumer.

FIGURE 8-2
Whole foods
advertisement.[16]

[14] Keller, Kevin Lane (2001), "Building Customer-Based Brand Equity: A Blueprint for Creating Strong Brands," *Marketing Science Institute*, working paper 1–107.

[15] Aaker, Jennifer L. (1997), "Dimensions of Brand Personality," *Journal of Marketing Research*, 34 (3), 347–356.

[16] partnersandspade.com/studio/ (March 28, 2016).

Corporate credibility refers to the degree to which consumers believe that a company is willing and able to provide products and services that satisfy the needs and wants of consumers.[17] Credibility can be developed in a number of ways. For example, Seventh Generation launched a campaign to gather 100,000 signatures to support an overhaul of the dated Toxic Substances Control Act (enacted in 1976).[18]

Attitude. *Brand attitude* refers to the consumer's overall assessment of the brand. Attitudes are important because they form the basis for brand choice. Research indicates that attitudes toward brands are associated with beliefs a consumer has about a product and the evaluative judgment about those beliefs.[19] In their efforts to market its smartwatch, Apple may seek to assess consumer beliefs and assessments of this technology.

Attachment. The emotional bond that may exist between a consumer and a brand embodies ***brand attachment***.[20] The attachment that consumers have toward a brand is embodied in the affective, warm feeling for a brand, the passionate intense feelings toward the brand, and the consumers' feelings of being connected with the brand.[21]

Attachment is important because it can lead to brand loyalty and a willingness to spend more for a brand. For example, Starbuck's has developed many loyal customers by fostering an affiliation with the company through a unique, retail dining experience (see Figure 8-3).

Activity. The *activity* associated with the brand addresses the purchase and the consumption frequency of a brand as well as the consumer's involvement with the marketing program. In general, higher levels of activity should foster stronger consumer brand equity. Frequent buyer programs, for instance, enable consumers to take active parts in the marketing programs of the firm. For example, Staples ink cartridge recycling program is an activity that bolsters the environmental reputation of the brand while simultaneously stimulating brand loyalty and store traffic.

These five factors reflect ways in which firms have increasingly nurtured brand equity among consumers. Each level implies increasing interaction and involvement with the brand, thereby yielding higher levels of brand equity. *Sustainable*

---

[17] Keller, Kevin Lane, and David A. Aaker (1998). "Corporate-level Marketing: The Impact of Credibility on a Company's Brand Extensions," *Corporate Reputation Review* 1(August), 356–378.

[18] adage.com/article/cmo-strategy/seventh-generation-seeks-tougher-toxin-regulations/292266/ (March 28, 2016).

[19] Fishbein, Martin, and Icek Ajzen (1975), *Belief, Attitude, Intention, Behavior: An Introduction to Theory and Research*, Reading, MA: Addison-Wesley Publishing Company.

[20] Bowlby, John (1979), *The Making and Breaking of Affectional Bonds.* London: Tavistock.

[21] Thomson, Matthew, Deborah J. MacInnis, and C. Whan Park (2005), "The Ties That Bind: Measuring the Strength of Consumers' Emotional Attachments to Brands," *Journal of Consumer Psychology*, 15(1), 77–91.

[22] pixabay.com/en/coffee-shop-starbucks-coffee-729347/ (March 23, 2016).

FIGURE 8-3
Starbucks images on coffee sleeves.[22]

brand identity refers to a specific set of brand attributes and benefits associated with reduced environmental influence of a brand and the perception of being environmentally sound.[23] Positioning a brand as green or sustainable involves communication and differentiation of the brand through its environmental attributes. Companies specifically interested in enhancing their affiliations with green practices and sustainability have focused on the functional and the emotional benefits derived from the brands. Similar to the tangible brand associations addressed earlier, *functional benefits* are based on the relevant environmental advantages of the product compared to competing products. For example, Brita markets the functional benefits of lower costs and reduced landfills of its water purifiers over conventional bottled water.

As many analysts indicate, the functional, ecological benefits alone of a product can have a limited influence on consumption. In many cases, the environmental benefit is not realized by the consumer, and these benefits can be easily replicated by competitors.[24] The benefit of smaller landfills may not resonate with many consumers, and other marketers could make the same claims about landfills.

Emotional brand benefits can serve as an alternative complementary strategy to nurture green brand identity in three ways.[25] First, a brand can enhance its equity by engaging in altruistic acts that contribute to the environment. Burt's Bees, for example, in collaboration with Pollinator Partnership, created the Honeybee Health Improvement Project, which provides grants to scientists who are researching ways to improve honeybee health.[26] Similarly, Celestial Seasonings has partnered with Trees for the Future to plant one tree in a developing country

---

[23] Hartmann, Patrick, Vanessa Apaolaza Ibáñez, and F. Javier Forcada Sainz (2005), "Green Branding Effects on Attitude: Functional Versus Emotional Positioning Strategies," *Marketing Intelligence and Planning*, 23 (1), 9–29.

[24] Aaker, David A. (1996), *Building Strong Brands*, The Free Press, New York, NY.

[25] Hartmann, Patrick, Vanessa Apaolaza Ibáñez, and F. Javier Forcada Sainz (2005), "Green Branding Effects on Attitude: Functional Versus Emotional Positioning Strategies," *Marketing Intelligence and Planning*, 23 (1), 9–29.

[26] www.burtsbees.com/Burt's-for-Bees/wild-burtsforbees,default,pg.html (March 28, 2016).

for every box of Celestial purchased.[27] These benevolent activities enrich sentiments toward the brand. Second, consumers can express sustainable benefits through socially visible consumption of sustainable brands. The purchase of Tom's shoes, for instance, sends a message to other consumers that one is acting in an environmentally conscious manner.[28] Third, a brand can espouse a sustainable identity when it enables consumers to get in contact with natural environments. Thus, the Mitsubishi ad in Figure 8-4 associates the company's geothermal and wind power products with a pastoral setting.

FIGURE 8-4
Mitsubishi promotion of geothermal technology and wind power.[29]

[27] www.celestialseasonings.com/press-releases/297 (March 28, 2016).

[28] Gabler, Colin B., Timothy D. Butler, and Frank G. Adams (2013), "The Environmental Belief-Behaviour Gap: Exploring Barriers to Green Consumerism," *Journal of Customer Behaviour* 12 (2-3), 159–176.

[29] www.mhi-global.com/discover/advertisement/newspaper/pdf/advertisement_20101110.pdf (October 13, 2015).

GREENWASHING

The increasing consumer interest in purchasing environmentally friendly brands has stimulated increased interest in marketing products as safe for consumers and the environment. In some cases, however, firms may be inclined to market environmental performance even when the company's offerings are not sensitive to the ecological concerns.[30] *Greenwashing* refers to activity designed to mislead consumers regarding the environmental practices of a firm or the environmental benefits of a product or service. Importantly, this practice may refer to either a company or its products. Environmentalists accuse oil firms of greenwashing when their investments in renewable energy are small compared with the money that goes on their oil and gas divisions.[31]

Greenwashing can be understood in part by considering the activities undertaken by the firm and the firms' efforts to communicate about this action.[32] In the simplest form, firms may be categorized as either good (i.e., *green*) or poor (i.e., *brown*) performers. Similarly, they may offer positive communication about their performance or limited communication about their environmental performance. Together these two dimensions provide the basis for a typology of environmental performance and communication (see Figure 8-5). Firms that communicate about their good environmental performance are referred to as *vocal green firms*, whereas companies that communicate little about their positive environmental action are referred to as *silent green firms*. Firms that do not communicate about their poor environmental performance are referred to *silent brown firms*. By contrast, brown performers that offer positive communication about their action are referred to as *greenwashing firms*.

This typology reveals how firms can move toward the vocal green quadrant. While firms may need to change the action and the communication, the action must necessarily change prior to making any announcements about behavior. Brown firms, both greenwashing and silent, initially must change their action to become more environmentally friendly. When greenwashing firms make this transition, they can begin to espouse the positive ecological merits of their action. When silent brown firms make this transition, they effectively become

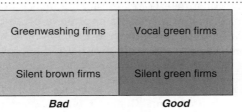

Communication about environmental performance	**Positive Communication**	Greenwashing firms	Vocal green firms
	No Communication	Silent brown firms	Silent green firms
		Bad	**Good**
		Environmental Performance	

FIGURE 8-5

A typology of environmental communication and performance.[33]

[30] sinsofgreenwashing.com/index35c6.pdf (March 23, 2016).

[31] *Economist* (2005), "Consider the Alternatives," April 30, 375 (8424), 21–24.

[32] Delmas, Magali A., and Vanessa Cuerel Burbano (2011), "The Drivers of Greenwashing," *California Management Review* 54 (1), 64–87.

[33] Delmas, Magali A., and Vanessa Cuerel Burbano (2011), "The Drivers of Greenwashing," *California Management Review* 54 (1), 64–87.

silent green firms. Silent green firms need to identify an ecological message that is relevant and important to the purchasing process.

Product greenwashing has received more scrutiny than corporate greenwashing. Product greenwashing can be manifest in several claims, including:[34]

1. **Hidden Trade-off Claims**: A hidden trade-off claim refers to a setting in which the benefits of a claim (e.g., recycled paper) do not exceed the additional environmental cost (e.g., energy costs associated with recycled paper). For example, a 2004 Ford ad in *National Geographic* touted "Green Vehicles, Cleaner Factories. It's the right road for our company, and we're well underway."[35] In the same year, Ford filed suit to block a California law limiting greenhouse gas emissions. Although the factories were more efficient, the products they made were not particularly environmentally friendly.

2. **No-proof Claims**: This form of greenwashing occurs when an environmental claim of a product cannot be substantiated via accessible information. For example, J.C. Penney's "Simply Green" program apparently has ecological merits, but they are not known to the consumer.[36]

3. **Vague Claims**: Vague claims refer to terminology that is poorly defined such as "all natural" or "green." This type of claim is prevalent in health and beauty products, but it is not limited to such products. For instance, Clorox Green Works ads claim to use "natural" ingredients but do not specify the ingredients. While most ingredients are safe, the synthetically produced dyes in some of these products are known skin irritants.[37]

4. **Irrelevant Claims**: When firms use truthful claims that are immaterial to the product class, they make irrelevant claims. "Gluten-free" water may be accurate, but it does not inform consumer decision making. Ford Motor Company, for instance, emphasizes the ethanol capabilities of its product. It sells few ethanol vehicles, however, and marketing of this feature is restricted to parts of the United States. The merits of ethanol use are largely irrelevant to new vehicle purchases.

5. **Categorical Claims**: These claims, also known as lesser of two evil claims, add a green attribute to a product category of substantial risk to the consumer. For example, organic cigars may offer lower health risk to consumers, but consumption of products in the category is inherently dangerous. Similarly, hybrid SUVs offer better mileage than conventional engines, but they still offer limited energy efficiency.[38]

[34] TerraChoice Environmental Marketing (2007), "The 'Six Sins of Greenwashing™": A Study of Environmental Claims in North American Consumer Markets," TerraChoice Environmental Marketing, Inc.

[35] Gibson, David (2008), "Awash in green: A critical perspective on environmental advertising," *Tulane Environmental Law Journal* 22, 423–440.

[36] Alves, Igor (2009), "Green Spin Everywhere: How Greenwashing Reveals the Limits of the CSR Paradigm," *Journal of Global Change and Governance* 2 (2), 1–26.

[37] Budinsky, Jennifer, and Susan Bryant (2013), "It's Not Easy Being Green": The Greenwashing of Environmental Discourses in Advertising," *Canadian Journal of Communication* 38 (2), 207–226.

[38] Alves, Igor (2009), "Green Spin Everywhere: How Greenwashing Reveals the Limits of the CSR Paradigm," *Journal of Global Change and Governance* 2 (2), 1–26.

6. **Misrepresented Claims**: Misrepresented claims rely on false information. For example, a firm may claim a product meets Energy Star criteria when it does not.[39] Clear Choice Housewares similarly markets products that it claims are biodegradable, yet the FTC alleges that the company makes unsubstantiated and false claims concerning product biodegradability.[40]

7. **False Labels**: This form of greenwashing refers to offering an impression of a third-party endorsement where no such endorsement exists. For example, S.C. Johnson placed the *Greenlist* trademark on Windex glass cleaner. This label is not owned by a third-party regulator but is owned by S.C. Johnson.

In order to reduce the potential accusations about greenwashing, firms should recognize that public statements about efforts to become sustainable subject the firm to greater scrutiny. In a global enterprise, these statements open up the firm to criticism from consumers, government, organizations, and individuals.[41] For example, Coke and Nestlé are two global consumer products companies that each developed commitments to sustainability.[42] These firms and their affiliated bottlers necessarily have to account for the manner in which water is treated in the production process. Each firm's expressed commitment to sustainability has been accompanied by critiques in some markets about water filtration and handling. The announced commitment to sustainability not only inspires employees and customers, but it also increases the amount of scrutiny the firm incurs.

Greenwashing is increasing as more companies attempt to boast about the ecological merits of their products. Firms can reduce the likelihood that they will encounter accusation of greenwashing by considering the following filter:[43]

Central: Is the claim central to the product and purchasing? For example, Trader Joe's labels for organic eggs (see Figure 8-6) indicate that chickens did not receive antibiotics. When the claims associated with a product are central to its usage, there is less likelihood of hidden trade-off claims and categorical claims.

Relevant: Are the ecological claims of the product relevant to consumption? The Trader Joe's label discussion of free-range, antibiotic-free chicken addresses criteria relevant to consumption. Relevant claims reduce the possibility of no proof and relevance claims.

---

[39] Fliegelman, Jessica E. (2010), "The Next Generation of Greenwash: Diminishing Consumer Confusion through a National Eco-Labeling Program," *Fordham Urban Law Journal* 37 (4), 1001–1056.

[40] www.ftc.gov/news-events/press-releases/2013/10/ftc-cracks-down-misleading-unsubstantiated-environmental (March 23, 2016).

[41] Delmas, Magali A., and Vanessa Cuerel Burbano (2011), "The Drivers of Greenwashing," *California Management Review* 54 (1), 64–87.

[42] Jones, Peter, David Hillier, and Daphne Comfort (2015), "Water Stewardship and Corporate Sustainability: A Case Study of Reputation Management in the Food and Drinks Industry," *Journal of Public Affairs* 15 (1), 116–126.

[43] www.greenbiz.com/blog/2009/04/15/seven-sins-greenwashing-everybody-lying (March 23, 2016).

FIGURE 8-6

Trader Joe's packaging addresses central concerns of consumers.[44]

External Verification: Have the claims been subjected to ongoing assessment by a third party? Trader Joe's inclusion of the Oregon Tilth Certified Organic (OTCO) logo indicates that the product is certified by the Oregon Tilth, a nonprofit organic product certifier (see Figure 8-6). Third-party verification by an objective source greatly reduces accusations of false labeling.

Specific: To what extent are the product claims specific and meaningful? The Trader Joe's label uses the specific term "organic" to qualify the growth and production process. Specific statements about brands avoid terms such as "natural" and "healthy" and thus reduce the likelihood of vague claims.

Truthful: Are the product claims truthful? Claims that are honest may not receive less scrutiny, but the claims are easier to support upon accusation.

CERTIFICATION LABELING

Businesses and consumers who want to act in environmentally responsible are looking for ways to do so when they go to market. Consequently, many certification labels have been developed in a variety of industries and contexts. For example, the Energy Star label is a joint program of the U.S. Environmental Protection Agency and the U.S. Department of Energy. This certification is designed to save money and protect the environment through energy efficient products and practices.[45] Certification labels include *ecolabels*, which reflect adherence to some standard associated with food safety and environmental performance, and *social labels*, which concern human rights and labor standards.[46] Although traditional labels focus on a single aspect of the useable life cycle of a product, increasingly these labels incorporate multiple criteria. For example, Food Alliance certification ensures that U.S. farms, ranches, and food handlers engage in both sustainable agricultural and facility management practices.[47]

---

[44] www.traderjoesreviews.com/product/trader-joes-organic-free-range-eggs-reviews/ (March 28, 2016).

[45] Boyd, Gale, Elizabeth Dutrow, and Walt Tunnessen (2008), "The Evolution of the ENERGY STAR® Energy Performance Indicator for Benchmarking Industrial Plant Manufacturing Energy Use," *Journal of Cleaner Production* 16 (6), 709–715.

[46] Grote, Ulrike, Arnab Basu, and Nancy Chau (2007), *New Frontiers in Environmental and Social Labeling*, Heidelberg, Germany: Springer-Verlag.

[47] ecolabelling.org/ecolabel/food-alliance-certified (March 28, 2016).

Retail Product Terminology

In the retail sector, consumers are increasingly interested in purchasing healthy and sustainable products.[48] Research suggests that 60 percent of consumers in the U.S. market select foods for health purposes, regardless of age or gender.[49] The challenge for many consumers, however, is to determine the meaning associated with high-quality products. Three terms are used to varying degrees to describe and classify products. Although these terms may be viewed as interchangeable by the consumer, they have different meanings, cost structures, and marketing implications. The terms include:

Natural

Few terms employed in consumer marketing are as confusing as the term *natural*. Since essentially all products derive from nature, every competitor can claim to have natural products. Although the definition of this term varies based on the type of product under consideration, there remains a lack of agreement on the meaning of this term. Since products are produced in a variety of ways that include new technologies such as genetic modification, the ability to label a product as natural continues to be problematic and confusing to consumers. Moreover, the natural term alone is likely to offer little competitive advantage in comparison to organic or other healthy claims.

Organic

Organic food sales tripled between 2003 and 2013 in the United States, reaching $32.3 billion in sales.[50] Due to the different interpretations of the term organic, many standards have been developed in different markets and states. In 1990, passage of the Organic Foods Production Act (OFPA) required that the U.S. Department of Agriculture (USDA) establish national standards for U.S. organic products. The USDA definition uses the term *organic* to refer to food that is generally free of synthetic substances, contains no hormones or antibiotics, has not been irradiated or fertilized with sewage sludge, was raised without the use of most conventional pesticides, and contains no genetically modified ingredients.[51] The USDA legislation (1) established standards for marketing organically produced products, (2) assured that organic products met a consistent standard, and (3) facilitated interstate commerce. The legislation targeted environmental quality by requiring that organic producers address soil fertility and regulate manure application to prevent water contamination. The act also included environmental and human health criteria to evaluate materials used in organic production. The USDA organic logo and the USDA National Organic Standards (NOS) were implemented in 2002, replacing the patchwork system of organic standards in various U.S. states.[52] Organic certification

---

[48] Makower, Joel (2009), *Strategies for the Green Economy*, New York: McGraw Hill.

[49] Milner, J. A. (2009), "Functional Foods and Health: A U.S. Perspective," *British Journal of Nutrition*, (2002), 88 (Supplement 2), S151–S158.

[50] www.wsj.com/articles/organic-food-firms-tackle-supply-constraints-1428081170 (March 28, 2016)

[51] Pittman, Mark (2009), "Eating Food That's Better for You, Organic or Not," *The New York Times*, (March 22).

[52] www.ers.usda.gov/Amberwaves/February06/Features/Feature1.htm.

is performed via state-run or accredited private agencies that see whether farms conform to the standards of the National Organic Program (NOP). Farmers who meet these requirements can market their products as "USDA Certified Organic" and display the USDA organic seal on their packaging.[53]

It is important to recognize the merits and limitations of organic farming. Note that research performed over several decades indicates that organic farming is usually associated with reduced soil erosion, lower fossil fuel consumption, less leaching of nitrate, greater carbon sequestration, and marked reductions in pesticide use.[54] Despite these merits of organic farms, the organic label, per se, does not mean food is necessarily healthier than nonorganic food. The label applies to the manner of production, yet it says nothing about the nutritional value.[55] There remains some debate as to whether food produced in an organic manner is necessarily *better* for the consumer.[56] While some studies indicate added nutritional value and flavor for organic products, the results vary somewhat from product to product. Making organic junk food does not alleviate any of the health problems associated with a regular diet of such food. In addition, some farmers are wary of future potential of organic farming. For example, Stonyfield Farm has faced challenge in their efforts to keep their product line organic. Because production of organic ingredients has not kept pace with the demand, companies such as Stonyfield are increasingly finding it difficult to find enough organic feed, organic cows, and organic fruit to make genuinely organic yogurt.[57] Other companies, such as Nature's Path Foods Inc., purchase farmland to gain control of the supply of organic ingredients (e.g., wheat and oats).[58] Other efforts to tackle supply constraints include providing financial assistance and technical training to organic farmers.[59]

Biodynamic

As the rapid commercialization of organic products has developed, there has been a complementary interest in developing and marketing products that exceed the organic criteria. Biodynamics is a farming orientation based on the teachings of Austrian philosopher Rudolph Steiner. *Biodynamics* refers to a specific form of organic farming that augments organic processes with consideration of the time of year, location, soil type, existing flora and fauna, and other factors.[60] Biodynamic farms are virtually complete ecosystems such that livestock create manure to fertilize fields, and natural predators, such as insects, provide pest

---

[53] attra.ncat.org/attra-pub/PDF/organiccrop.pdf (March 28, 2016).

[54] attra.ncat.org/attra-pub/PDF/organiccrop.pdf (March 28, 2016).

[55] McLaughlin, Katy (2005), "Is Your Tofu Biodynamic? Making Sense of the Latest Organic Food Terminology," *Wall Street Journal* (April 19), D1.

[56] Pittman, Mark (2009), "Eating Food That's Better for You, Organic or Not," *New York Times*, (March 22).

[57] Brady, Diane (2006), "The Organic Myth," *BusinessWeek*, (October 16), 50–56.

[58] www.wsj.com/articles/organic-food-firms-tackle-supply-constraints-1428081170 (March 28, 2016).

[59] www.wsj.com/articles/organic-food-firms-tackle-supply-constraints-1428081170 (March 28, 2016).

[60] Shadix, Kyle (2007), "Biodynamic Agriculture May Slowly Gain Fans among Chefs," *Nation's Restaurant News* (September 24), 26.

control. Since biodynamics does not use artificial settings such as greenhouse, seasonality becomes a major issue. For example, the U.S. vintners using biodynamic techniques must plant grapes at the seasonally appropriate time rather than use hothouses.

Demeter International is a Brussels-based nonprofit organization that oversees use of the term *biodynamics*. In order to be gain eligibility, a farm must first meet the National Organic Program standards for organic farms for at least three years. Given the variation among farms, a single threshold is not employed. On the contrary, certification is based on existing environmental and social conditions, with the goal that each farm evolves toward its maximum potential.

Certification labels help reduce the asymmetry of information between producers and consumers by allowing communication of credible characteristics of products.[61] Consequently, these labels are employed to inform consumers of product quality issues and the environmental processes used in production. The premise behind using these labels is that this information will be used in consumer decision making. The consumer must know what the label means, and the issues associated with the label must be meaningful to the consumer. Consider, for example, the purchase of a microwave oven. If the Energy Star label is to be instrumental to the purchase, consumers need to know that Energy Star is awarded to the most efficient products in this product class, and efficiency must be important to consumers. Indeed, 85 percent of U.S. consumers recognize the blue Energy Star label, and 75 percent of U.S. consumers purchasing a certified Energy Star product indicated that the label was an important factor in their purchase decision.[62] Increasingly, certification labels are not only used to indicate multiple diverse, criteria, but they are further associated with complete life cycle usage assessment. *Life cycle assessment* refers to accounting for production and processing as well as resource energy usage, emissions, and waste. Because of life cycle assessment, labeling criteria increasingly require firms to track products throughout the entire supply chain. The *life cycle inventory assessment* identifies the sum amount of resources and emissions associated with a product or service over its life.[63] The Eco Leaf label used in Japan uses life cycle assessment that quantitatively evaluates environmental information for all stages of the product's life.

Given that there are more than 450 ecolabels in use, it is meaningful to distinguish among the types of certification.[64] One can distinguish initially between labels that are mandatory versus voluntary.[65] The Energy Guide label, for example, is a required label for appliance sales in the United States. It provides the average yearly operating cost of an appliance as well as the average operating cost for all

[61] McEachern, Morven G. (2008), "Guest Editorial: The Consumer and Values-based Labels," *International Journal of Consumer Studies*, 32 (5), 405–406.

[62] www.energystar.gov/about (March 23, 2016).

[63] Rebitzer, G., et al. (2004), "Life Cycle Assessment: Part 1: Framework, Goal and Scope Definition, Inventory Analysis, and Applications, *Environment International* 30 (5), 701–720.

[64] www.ecolabelindex.com/ (March 28, 2016).

[65] Horne, Ralph E. (2009), "Limits to Labels: The Role of Eco-labels in the Assessment of Product Sustainability and Routes to Sustainable Consumption," *International Journal of Consumer Studies*; 33(2), 175–182.

other products in the class. Not only are these types of labels required in many markets, but the credibility of these governmental labels is higher than the level of credibility for labels developed by retailers.[66]

Among voluntary labels, one can distinguish between standards affiliated with the International Standards Organization (ISO). ISO 14000 certification is the international management standard associated with environmental management, and ISO 14020–29 address labeling (see Appendix A7). There are three types of labels associated with ISO 14000. First, labels can be based on *self-declarations* made by producers and suppliers without the direct authorization of a third party. For example, the "recycled content" label is featured on many supermarket products. Since corporately developed labels may lower levels of credibility than other labels,[67] it is germane for the marketer to consider whether these labels will lead to product associations that generate revenue. The credibility of these labels is likely to be associated with the overall credibility of the firm. These labels are used on the product and are featured in advertisements and other promotions.

It is noteworthy there are many standards not directly associated with the International Standards Organization. For example, the Energy Star label used in the United States is not, per se, based on ISO criteria. In many cases, these standards are focused on a single industry. There are standards and associated labels designed for assessment of buildings, carbon, electronics, energy, food, forest products, retail goods, textiles, tourism, and other industries.[68] For example, leadership in energy and environmental design (LEED) certification is focused on the construction and building industry. To use the fair trade label in the coffee industry, a company must buy coffee directly from certified small coffee producers, and it must offer long-term contracts beyond one annual harvest. They must agree to pay a price premium per pound of coffee, and they must offer producers pre-financing covering at least 60 percent of the annual contract.[69]

A second type of label is awarded by agencies external to the firm. For example, *The Blue Angel* is awarded to products and services that are of considerable benefit to the environment that further meet high standards of serviceability (see Figure 8-7). They must also achieve high ratings for health and occupational protection. Economical use of raw materials during production and use, a long service life, and a sustainable disposal are also factors of great importance in making this award.[70] The Blue Angel is awarded in Germany by government after a review by an independent decision making body.[71]

---

[66] Gertz, Renate (2005), "Eco-labelling—A Case for Deregulation?" *Law, Probability and Risk*, 2005 4(3), 127–141.

[67] Gertz, Renate (2005), "Eco-labelling—A Case for Deregulation?" *Law, Probability and Risk*, 2005 4(3), 127–141.

[68] ecolabelling.org/ (March 23, 2016).

[69] Lyon, Sarah (2006), "Evaluating Fair Trade Consumption: Politics, Defetishization and Producer Participation," *International Journal of Consumer Studies*, 30 (5), 452–464.

[70] www.blauer-engel.de/en/blauer_engel/whats_behind_it/index.php (March 23, 2016).

[71] www.blauer-engel.de/en/blauer_engel/who_is_behind_it/index.php (March 23, 2016).

A third type of label is awarded based on quantitative life cycle environmental data provided in an extensive report format.[73] In this case, an organization external to the firm provides extensive reporting and assessment of the sustainability efforts by a company. For example, the Environmental Product Declaration has developed integrated systems that enable companies to help communicate the environmental performance of their products in a credible and understandable way. Upon verification, companies qualify to use the EPD trademark label on products as well as in advertisements and packaging materials.

Since there are many types of labels, it can be overwhelming to decipher which labels are most informative in a particular context. The development of a certification label involves many challenges and trade-offs. At one extreme, the label must be simple and distinctive to enhance consumer awareness. At the same time, however, the certification must also be supported by significant investment in sustainable business practices. The label must, therefore, convey complex efforts in an uncomplicated way. The Blue Angel, for instance, offers an efficient way to communicate sustainable practices associated with responsible management of health, climate, water, and resources.[74]

There are several criteria that should be accessible regarding any label associated with an environmental claim or standard.[75] First, it is germane to consider the *coverage* of the standard. The developer of the standard needs to establish the breadth and the extent of the environmental coverage associated with the standard. Over its life, a product uses resources and influences water, air, land, and energy. The degree to which a label is associated with concern for each of these factors should be addressed.

In addition to the coverage of a standard, it is also important to know how the achievement of the standard is verified. The basis for *verification* should be available as well as the length of the time during which a company may use the

[72] www.blauer-engel.de/en/blue-angel/what-is-behind-it/the-logo (March 28, 2016).

[73] Horne, Ralph E. (2009), "Limits to Labels: The Role of Eco-labels in the Assessment of Product Sustainability and Routes to Sustainable Consumption," *International Journal of Consumer Studies*; 33(2), 175–182.

[74] www.blauer-engel.de/en/blauer_engel/whats_behind_it/protection-goals.php.

[75] Horne, Ralph E. (2009), "Limits to Labels: The Role of Eco-labels in the Assessment of Product Sustainability and Routes to Sustainable Consumption," *International Journal of Consumer Studies*; 33(2), 175–182.

label.[76] In addition, it is germane to report how often companies are audited with respect to the criteria associated with the award. For example, the Nordic Swan label is granted in 66 product categories based on environmental, quality, and health factors. The label is usually valid for three years, after which the criteria are revised, and the company must reapply for a license.[77] Information on environmental coverage and verification for a multitude of labels is provided at ecolabelling.org.[78]

In addition to the coverage of the label, it is also relevant to examine who is involved in developing and managing the standard. There is tremendous variation in the extent to which groups are included in the development and maintenance of standards and related labels. Government, producers and processors, nongovernmental organizations (NGOs), and consumers are included in the development of standards and labels to varying degrees. The extent to which these groups are involved in the labeling process is related to the credibility of the label. Research suggests that consumers have greater trust in labels developed by consumer and environmental groups than those developed by other third-party groups, government, or retailers.[79]

To this point, our review of labels has examined how the label is developed and the extent of environmental coverage associated with the standard. The logic of standards suggests that they inform the consumer, and the consumer thereby makes purchases of products developed in sustainable ways. The ultimate question of the label, then, is its effectiveness in gaining consumption and thereby increased revenues to the firm. If the label is effective, then revenue should increase after it is in place. For example, research has illustrated that under some conditions the use of the organic and free trade labels can be associated with increased willingness to pay for related products.[80]

Although we value measuring the effectiveness of a label in driving consumers toward sustainable products, results do not illustrate a strong relationship between labeling and consumption.[81] Consequently, few labels can illustrate a direct link between their application and performance. Although people want to act in an environmentally friendly way, in many cases, the environment is not a top priority in making a purchase.[82] The purchase process may also be driven by habit or heuristics such that the consumer gives little thought to the purchasing process.[83] In addition, the information overload can be overwhelming

[76] Stroud, Sara (2009), "The Great Eco-Label Shakedown," *Sustainable Industries* (August), 29–33.

[77] www.svanen.se/en/Criteria/EU-Ecolabel-criteria/ (March 28, 2016).

[78] ecolabelling.org/ (March 23, 2016).

[79] Gertz, Renate (2005), "Eco-labelling—A Case for Deregulation?" *Law, Probability and Risk*, 2005 4(3), 127–141.

[80] Tagbata, Didier, and Sirieix Lucie (2008), "Measuring Consumer's Willingness to Pay for Organic and Fair Trade Products," *International Journal of Consumer Studies*, 32 (2008) 479–490.

[81] McEachern, Morven G. (2008), "Guest Editorial: The Consumer and Values-based Labels," *International Journal of Consumer Studies*, 32 (5), 405–406.

[82] Esty, Daniel C., and Andrew S. Winston (2006), *Green to Gold*, New Haven, CT: Yale University Press.

[83] Kahneman, Daniel, and Amos Tversky (1973), "On the Psychology of Prediction," *Psychological Review,* 1973, 80, 237–257.

to the consumers. As the amount of information increases, it becomes increasingly more difficult to process the information.[84] When this information is not processed, it is unlikely that behavior will change. Lastly, there may also be a "sustainability liability," wherein some product labeled as ecofriendly may be perceived as inferior.[85]

DEMARKETING

The role of certification labels, like most marketing efforts, is to increase the amount of product consumed. By contrast, *demarketing* refers to action undertaken by marketers to discourage consumption.[86] Consumers may be asked to refrain from consumption on a permanent or temporary basis. For example, water is an increasingly more scarce resource, and industry, consumers, and government benefit from water conservation. Some consumers, however, are less receptive to demarketing efforts than others. Research investigating the response to government efforts to reduce water consumption indicates that minority groups are less responsive than the majority population in reducing water consumption.[87]

The firm can demarket in three contrasting ways:

General demarketing occurs when companies try to shrink the level of total demand. For example, the CEO of Levi's encouraged consumers to wash their jeans less often in an effort to conserve water.[88] A single pair of 501 jeans consumes nearly 3,800 liters of water over its lifetime. Washing jeans after every 10 wears, compared to washing after two wears, would decrease their energy and climate change impact by 80 percent over the jean's lifetime. Similarly, the advertisement listed in Figure 8-8 illustrates efforts by IKEA to limit consumption by asking consumers to use energy efficient LED lighting.

Selective demarketing occurs when an organization discourages demand from certain classes of consumers. Urban governments in some countries seek to fight congestion by raising toll prices at selective times of the day. For example, Stockholm sought to reduce road traffic by 10 to 15 percent. A congestion fee was differentially employed depending on the time one choose to enter the zone where the congestion fee was being

[84] Hemp, Paul (2009), "Death by Information Overload," *Harvard Business Review,* 87 (9), 82–89.

[85] Luchs, Michael G., Rebecca Walker Naylor, Julie R. Irwin, and Rajagopal Raghunathan (2010), "The Sustainability Liability: Potential Negative Effects of Ethicality on Product Preference," *Journal of Marketing* 74, (5), 18–31.

[86] Kotler, Philip, and Sidney Levy (1971), "Demarketing, Yes, Demarketing," *Harvard Business Review,* 49 (November–December), 74–80.

[87]

[88] fortune.com/2015/03/19/levis-ceo-do-the-world-a-favor-n-wash-your-jeans-once-every-10-wears/ (March 23, 2016).

FIGURE 8-8
IKEA demarketing[89]

charged. The highest fees were set from 7:30 until 7:59 in the morning and from 4:00 to 4:30 in the evening. The fee was reduced from 9:00 to 3:29, no fee was charged on weekends, and the maximum fee per car per day was established. Environmentally friendly vehicles, vehicles owned by disabled drivers, motorcycles, taxis, buses, and other essential vehicles (e.g., police and military) were exempt from congestion fees. This selective demarketing effort in Stockholm yielded a 10 percent total travel reduction and a 17 percent reduction in travel for shopping purposes.[90]

---

[89] www.google.com/search?biw=1361&bih=799&tbm=isch&sa=1&q=use+less+energy+ads&oq=use+less+energy+ads&gs_l=img.3...21896.22247.0.22656.0.0.0.0.0.0.0.0.0....0 ...1c.1.64.img..0.0.0.5H_lisCwmNs#imgrc=1VRNUdEJiMrAxM: (March 7, 2017).

[90] Daunfeldt, Sven-Olov, Niklas Rudholm, and Ulf Rämme (2009), "Congestion Charges and Retail Revenues: Results from the Stockholm Road Pricing Trial," *Transportation Research Part A: Policy and Practice*, 43 (3), 306–309.

Ostensible demarketing refers to a strategy that involves limiting consumption for the purpose of increasing sales. Note that in contrast to general and selective demarketing, the goal of this strategy is to stimulate additional demand. Companies sometimes use ostensible demarketing to increase brand awareness and attractiveness by claiming overwhelming demand for a product. Limited availability of a good is often used to stimulate consumers to act immediately to ensure product ownership. For example, the rising gas prices in the summer of 2008 led new car dealers to offer to pay for a buyer's petroleum for a year.

In many situations, marketers use the logic of ostensible demarketing to stimulate increased consumption of new, energy efficient technologies and products. These ostensible demarketing campaigns emphasize that investments in new technologies can yield less consumption, lower costs, and greater benefits to the community. The Lexmark Corporation, for instance, engages consumers in sustainability by encouraging them to print less. This developer of printers and related computer technologies has developed document scanning technologies, duplex and multipage printing capabilities, print preview, as well as draft print and quick print modes. Each of these technologies enables consumers to print less and, consequently, use less paper, energy, toner, and ink.[91] Higher levels of sustainability accrue due to greater financial performance, better working relationships with consumers, and relatively lower influences on the environment.

Demarketing practices are related to sustainability and green marketing practice because they are employed to influence the financial, relational, and ecological returns associated with consumption. For example, Eco Haus markets its low-flow showerheads as providing more than $100 in savings per year over earlier technologies.[92] Many of the promotions that emphasize demarketing are focused on the long-term health and relational benefits of reduced consumption. The American Lung Association, for instance, runs multiple programs and promotions designed to limit the amount of tobacco consumption. The ecological returns associated with limited consumption are also featured in promotions. The Peace River Water Authority in Florida, for example, has developed promotions designed to stimulate water conservation.

A recurring theme in promotions that feature calls for environmental responsibility is that the consumer is often more interested in other issues associated with product consumption and use.[93] Marketers who recognize this fact use multiple motivations to encourage reduced consumption. For example, Brita uses all three forms of demarketing in their ads for water filters. They emphasize the cost savings from reusing a single bottle, the health and relational merits of filtering water, and the environmental savings associated with limiting the number of water bottles.

---

[91] csr.lexmark.com/pdfs/Lexmark%202014%20CSR-HiRez-FINAL-rev8.26.15.pdf (March 23, 2016).

[92] www.ecooptions.homedepot.com/water-conservation/showerheads/ (March 23, 2016).

[93] Esty, Daniel C., and Andrew S. Winston (2006), *Green to Gold*, New Haven, CT: Yale University Press.

Introduction

The purpose of this chapter is to illustrate how marketers communicate value through the promotional mix. We used logic based on the marketing efforts of Chipotle to illustrate the marketing strategy associated with the promotion of a sustainable brand.

Sustainable Branding

Sustainable branding addresses the degree to which firms associate their brands with social, economic, and ecological merits. The value of the brand can be expressed on a customer, corporate, or financial basis, yet many assessments of corporate or financial brand equity are derived from customer-based brand equity. The customer-based value of the brand is based on consumer brand awareness, associations made with the brand, attitudes and attachments toward the brand, and consumer involvement with the brand.

Greenwashing

Greenwashing refers to activity designed to mislead consumers regarding the environmental practices of a firm or the environmental benefits of a product or service. While greenwashing can manifest itself in many ways, it typically is associated with environmental claims that are not supported by the firm's action.

Certification Labeling

Labels are used by marketers to increase consumer awareness of the product and brand attributes. They help reduce the asymmetry of information between producers and consumers by allowing communication of credible characteristics of products. Certification labels include ecolabels that reflect adherence to some standard associated with food safety and environmental performance and social labels that concern human rights and labor standards. The labels may be based on self-proclamation by a firm, or they may involve evaluation by a third party. Certification labeling is used to account for production and processing as well as resource energy usage, emissions, and waste.

Demarketing

Demarketing refers to action undertaken by marketers to discourage consumption. General demarketing refers to efforts by organizations such as power companies that seek to reduce the overall amount of energy usage. Selective demarketing is employed when a company seeks to limit the amount of consumption by target markets within a community. Ostensible demarketing refers to strategies that use limited consumption as a means for increasing revenue.

KEY TERMS

brand
brand recall
brand recognition
brand imagery
corporate credibility
brand attitude
brand attachment
(brand) activity
sustainable brand identity
functional benefits
emotional benefits
greenwashing

vocal green firms
silent green firms
silent brown firms
greenwashing firms
hidden trade-off claims
no-proof claims
vague claims
irrelevant claims
categorical claims
misrepresented claims
false labels
ecolabels

social labels
natural
organic
biodynamic
life cycle assessment
life cycle inventory assessment
demarketing
general demarketing
selective demarketing
ostensible demarketing

DISCUSSION QUESTIONS

1. The introduction of this chapter characterizes Chipotle as a company that employs a marketing strategy designed to promote the sustainability of their brand. Describe another branding strategy designed to promote the sustainability of a brand.

2. What are the benefits associated with developing brands at the product-market level?

3. Identify a brand marketed as sustainable and comment on the degree to which the brand-related ads address functional and emotional benefits.

4. How can silent brown firms become vocal green firms?

5. Describe five types of greenwashing and provide an example of a consumer product promoted using the greenwashing approach.

6. What steps can a firm take to limit greenwashing?

7. Compare and contrast organic and biodynamic products.

8. What is the difference between ecolabels and social labels? Describe a certification label that incorporates both ecological and relational components.

9. The logic of labels suggests that the presence of a certification label should lead to increased awareness and ultimately increased sales. How successful have labels been in stimulating sales of sustainable products?

10. Why would a company use a demarketing strategy when this strategy is designed to reduce consumption? Will this strategy necessarily mean lower revenues for the firm?

part three

Sustainability Throughout the Supply Chain

9

Proclaiming Value via Sustainable Pricing Strategies

INTRODUCTION

Sustainable Travel International

The flight from Los Angeles to New York is a long, five-hour, red-eye evening flight that can cost the traveler well over $1000. The financial and physical costs of this flight are tremendous, but many people forget about the substantial carbon cost of such an excursion. Clever marketers, however, are now enabling consumers to offset the cost of their travel. A recent review of the emerging industry examined 11 different firms that enable consumers to make some type of payment to offset the carbon cost of travel.[1] While these companies use different methods to determine offset prices and offer contrasting ways to offset carbon, the development of these firms is in response to a consumer need to reduce the environmental burden of travel.

Although the number of passengers willing to make this commitment is small, there is a growing number of *Green Enthusiasts* and *lifestyles of health and sustainability (LOHAS)* consumers who are willing to pay to offset the environmental cost of travel. Furthermore, there is also a growing breed of environmental entrepreneurs in the travel and hospitality industry. Hoteliers with conservation programs, taxi companies with hybrid automobiles, restaurateurs with large-scale recycling plans, and other eco-entrepreneurs use new technologies to limit the toll that travel and tourism take on the environment.[2]

Sustainable Travel International (STI) is among this group of environmental entrepreneurs committed to enabling consumers to lower the carbon cost of travel (see Figure 9-1). Founded in 2002, STI is not-for-profit organization created to reduce the toll that travel and tourism take on the environment and local cultures. Founding sponsors include Continental Airlines, United Airlines, Enterprise Car Rental, and several other firms. This firm estimates that the carbon cost of the Los Angeles to New York trip at 1.78 tons of carbon dioxide per person, and the cost to offset this price is around $45. This pricing strategy enables passengers to offset the carbon cost of this flight by making contributions to sustainable forests in the United States, China, Ghana, India, Madagascar, or Turkey. The company also provides a host of travel tools and tips designed to reduce the environmental cost incurred whenever anyone travels.

The Sustainable Travel International example underscores the role of pricing in the firm's efforts to deliver sustainable product offerings to consumers. Although the components of the marketing mix are often presented independently, these

FIGURE 9-1
Sustainable Travel
International.[3]

---

[1] Murray, Joy, and Christopher Dey (2009) "The Carbon Neutral Free for All," *International Journal of Greenhouse Gas Control*, 3, 237–248.

[2] Knight, Rebecca (2008), "Green Entrepreneurs with the Drive to Transform Travel," *Financial Times* (September 26).

[3] www.sustainabletravelinternational.org/images/stilogo_lg.gif (April 6, 2016).

marketing decisions must flow from organizational objectives and work together to yield desired outcomes for the firm. The proper pricing of an organization's product offerings enables the firm to achieve its objectives, and the development of the pricing strategy must be derived from the overall strategy of the organization.

In the remainder of this chapter, we examine how value is proclaimed through effective pricing strategies. We begin by describing the assessment of a product's costs over its life. This information is instrumental in determining the true cost of product ownership and identifying internal constraints on prices. We subsequently describe the price planning process, including pricing constraints, objectives, and strategy.

VALUE, BENEFITS, AND COSTS

An understating of value is necessary if one is to understand how sustainable marketing benefits can be incorporated into product offerings. *Value* may be defined in the following manner:[4]

$$\text{Value} = \text{Desired benefits}/\text{relative costs}$$

The expression of value in this equation illuminates several important facets of consumption. Value inherently is associated with trade-offs. Purchase decisions ask the consumer to forego something of value (e.g., money) for something of superior value (product). Desired benefits refer to things that matter to the consumers. They are willing to pay for these things that they genuinely want. The benefits of a product speak to what the product does for the consumer rather than the product components. The hybrid engine is a feature offered by many automobile companies, but the benefits of this component are the fuel savings of the product.

Effective marketing campaigns move beyond the mere proclamation of product attributes and focus on the aspects of the product that are meaningful to the consumer. The sustainable product proposition often fails to recognize that the promotion of sustainable benefits alone will not stimulate consumption. The Ford plant on the Rouge River in Dearborn, Michigan, offers one example of the promotion of sustainable benefits that do not resonate with consumers. This 90-year-old plant was rebuilt to sustainability specifications at a cost of $2 billion.[5] Although Ford's investment in sustainability is admirable, improvements to the plant do not address the primary environmental issue in the industry, the burning of fossil fuels. More importantly, this benefit does not address issues at the heart of auto purchase and consumption decisions.

The analysis of benefits derived via purchasing must consider the breadth of motivations related to the purchase. Many consumers are concerned about the environment, yet they are also concerned about other matters at the point of purchase. The Tesla automobile, for example, may offer substantial ecological benefits, but the base price makes the car infeasible for most consumers. The sustainable

---

[4] DeBonis, J. Nicholas, Eric Balinski, and Phil Allen (2002), *Value-Based Marketing for Bottom-Line Success*, New York: McGraw-Hill.

[5] McDonough, William, and Michael Braungart (2002), "Design for the Triple Top Line: New Tools for Sustainable Commerce," *Corporate Environmental Strategy* 9(3), 251–258.

benefits of products do not stand on their own but are incorporated into the value assessment made by the potential consumer. Marketers must understand the reasons behind consumption and present sustainable benefits as they relate to these motivations for purchase.

Understanding of the purchase criteria enables the marketer to develop a sustainable competitive advantage that focuses on purchase, usage, and sustainability. A *sustainable competitive advantage* refers to a company's performance relative to competition and the ability to outperform competition along one or more aspects. The development of competitive advantage requires the firm to take stock of its product offerings and those of the competition. Importantly, this assessment should focus on aspects most relevant to the consumption. The firm will realize that certain aspects of its product offerings will be superior to competition, yet the competitive landscape usually presents alternatives that outperform the firm's product along some dimension.

Importantly, the relative cost of a product is substantially more important than the price. To determine the value proposition, one must examine the acquisition, possession, usage, and opportunity costs.[6] *Acquisition cost* refers to the energy expended to make the purchase as well as the *purchase price*. This cost component includes the time dedicated to learning about the salient criteria associated with a purchase as well as the time dedicated to evaluating alternatives. Brands that have established themselves within a product class require less time for evaluation,[7] and these reductions in cost are associated with increased revenue. If a new, fuel efficient technology is presented to the consumer at the point of sale, the consumer will ordinarily need to develop an understanding of the technology prior to purchase. Effective advertising campaigns that make the consumer aware of the merits of the technology prior to purchase should lower acquisition costs and increase revenues.

Possession costs include all expenditures associated with gaining possession of the product after the purchase decision has been made. These include taxes, insurance, and transportation. Consider, for example, a consumer's possession cost for a water heater. After the consumer realizes that the current heater is not working, there is an immediate desire to get a replacement as soon as possible. The transition from an electric device to more fuel-efficient alternatives may not be relevant to many consumers when the installation is prolonged. Although solar water heaters are highly efficient, the installation is likely to take more time and require more space on the consumer's property. The consumer faced with making this purchase will be reluctant to consider alternative fuel sources or technologies.

Usage cost is the third facet of cost and includes the cost of operations as well as the disposal cost. In many cases, new technologies provide energy efficiency that yield lower costs in usage relative to alternatives. The marketers of such new technologies should present their products to illustrate the trade-off between acquisition costs and usage costs. The marketing of this product should prompt the consumer to consider the cost in use of the product over its life rather than the initial purchase price. Promotion online and at the point of sale can illustrate

---

[6] DeBonis, J. Nicholas, Eric Balinski, and Phil Allen (2002), *Value-Based Marketing for Bottom-Line Success*, New York: McGraw-Hill.

[7] Keller, Kevin Lane (2008), *Strategic Brand Management*, Upper Saddle River, NJ: Pearson /Prentice Hall.

to the consumer that an Energy Star appliance will be a less expensive alternative in the end.

The disposal facet of cost is an increasingly important factor in many industries. The European Union and the United States have implemented regulations requiring electronics manufacturers to reclaim products.[8] Because these products may still contain valuable components, policy makers in many countries have implemented policies requiring the end-of-life take-back of these products.[9]

Many industries understand that they must either establish industry standards for waste or face regulatory action by government. The *Product Stewardship Institute* (PSI) is a U.S.-based NGO that seeks to reduce the health and environmental impacts of consumer products.[10] PSI takes a unique product stewardship approach to solving waste management problems by encouraging product design changes and mediating stakeholder dialogues. PSI is supporting product end-of-life legislation in the several U.S. states. One initiative associated with this legislation concerns the proper disposal of paint. In the United States alone, approximately 10 percent of the amount sold or 64 million gallons of used paint is leftover annually. The disposal cost associated with the proper handling of this product is $8 per can.[11] PSI has similar initiatives addressing reclamation of medical waste, pharmaceuticals, fluorescent lamps, thermostat manufacturers, and phonebooks.

The final element of cost is the *opportunity* cost associated with one product over alternatives. Opportunity costs are forfeited by the consumer that incurs a cost. The purchaser of a gas appliance forfeits the chance to invest and learn about efficient solar water heaters. Since the average automobile lasts 17 years, the purchase of a new internal combustion engine commits to older technology and forfeits the opportunity to use more fuel-efficient transportation alternatives.

When the firm has properly identified the desired benefits and relative costs of a product, then the value assessment can be determined. For a product offering to be successful, it must be real, superior, and profitable.[12] For the product to offer real value, it must have relevance to an identifiable market that has specific customers and segments. The desired benefits of a product offering must exceed the perceived costs of ownership. Note that although the ratio of benefits to costs must exceed one, different consumers have different value ratios. Research of the market should provide insight into the various market segments associated with different benefits and relative costs. The buyers of a Toyota Prius, for example, may be distinguished based on the perceived importance of the ecological performance of the vehicle as a benefit that augments the fuel efficiency merits of the automobile.

[8] Stephenson, John B. (2008), "Electronic Waste: EPA Needs to Better Control Harmful U.S. Exports through Stronger Enforcement and More Comprehensive Regulation," *GAO Reports*, 1–62

[9] Linton, Jonathan (1999), "Electronic Products at Their End-of-Life: Options and Obstacles," *Journal of Electronics Manufacturing*, 9 (1), 29–40

[10] www.productstewardship.us/ (March 7, 2017).

[11] Truini, Joe (2009), "Recycling burden shifting toward manufacturers," *Waste News*, 14(18), 13.

[12] DeBonis, J. Nicholas, Eric Balinski, and Phil Allen (2002), *Value-Based Marketing for Bottom-Line Success*, New York: McGraw-Hill.

Although a product may reflect the desired benefits sought by the consumer, the value offered by a product must also be superior to the value of competitive products. For example, the traveler between New York and Boston may consider alternative forms of mass transportation. Although the cost of the airline flight may be less than the rail transportation, the consumer may elect to take the train because it is more convenient and has a lower carbon footprint. The advocate of sustainability that understands the breadth of benefits and the costs of alternative product offerings is more likely to influence consumers to choose one product offering over another.

When the value of a product offering is real and superior to the competition, the marketer must also examine whether the value proposition is profitable. A value proposition that is profitable is consistent with the firm's mission and objectives. The for-profit organization has a responsibility to earn a financial profit for the ownership. If the value of an offering does not help the firm realize its mission and objectives, the firm needs to re-examine the offering.

An important facet of the value proposition is the recognition that different consumers have different value ratios. It is, therefore, salient to consider devising multiple products with multiple value offerings and target different market segments. Greenprint sustainable market segmentation provides a starting point for analysis of the relevant segments in a market[13].

LIFE CYCLE SUSTAINABILITY ASSESSMENT

FIGURE 9-2

Components of life cycle sustainability assessment.

Environmental life cycle assessment

Economic life cycle costing

Societal life cycle assessment

Firms in many industries are increasingly examining the total costs associated with a product over its life. This logic requires firms to augment financial cost analysis with consideration of the social and ecological influences of products, production, and supply chains. This *life cycle sustainability assessment* parallels triple bottom-line performance given that the firm assesses its ecological, economic, and social costs[14] (see Figure 9-2). At this juncture, we address the sustainability of the products and their supply chains. Chapter 14 broadens this discussion by considering the sustainability of the corporation.

Environmental Life Cycle Assessment

Environmental life cycle assessment (ELCA) provides an opportunity to examine the environmental influences of products and processes over their lives.[15]

[13] Ottman, Jacqueline A. (2003), "Know Thy Target," *In Business*, (September-October) 30–31; Ginsberg, Jill M., and Paul N. Bloom (2004), "Choosing the Right Green Marketing Strategy," *MIT Sloan Management Review*, (Fall) 79–84; and Singer, Michelle, and Chris Hloros (2016), *Greenprint Sustainability Segmentation*, Global MONITOR – The Futures Company.

[14] International Organization for Standardization. (2008), *Environmental Management: Life Cycle Assessment: Principles and Framework*. Vol. 14040; and Kloepffer, Walter. (2008), "Life Cycle Sustainability Assessment of Products," *The International Journal of Life Cycle Assessment* 13(2), 89–95.

[15] Swarr, Thomas E., et al. (2011), "Environmental Life-Cycle Costing: A Code of Practice," *The International Journal of Life Cycle Assessment* 16 (5), 389–391.

ISO 14040 is an international standard that provides guidelines for the assessment of interaction with the environment.[16] This framework helps organizations identify opportunities to enhance environmental performance, inform decision makers in government and industry, and select pertinent indicators of environmental performance. The framework assists marketers in their efforts to make environmental claims and devise ecolabels. The four phases of ELCA include:

Definition of Goals and Scope. The goals define the reasons for carrying out the study and identify the intended audience for the assessment. The scope quantifies the product system under evaluation along with its functions and boundaries. The boundaries of the system become particularly important since they clarify the firm's expectations concerning its responsibilities. For example, in 2007 Mattel recalled toys coated in toxic paint. The most serious environmental problems were caused by subsuppliers rather than direct suppliers.[17] When a firm delineates lines of responsibility, it is instrumental for them to recognize environmental factors associated with subsuppliers.

The Inventory Analysis Phase. This stage refers to the data collection and calculation procedures used to quantify inputs and outputs of a system. Inputs include energy and raw materials, whereas outputs include products, waste, and emissions to air, water, and soil.

Life Cycle Impact Assessment. At this stage, the firm evaluates the potential environmental influence of a product based on the inventory analysis. The firm considers the environmental consequences of the procurement process for inputs and examines the ecological consequences of all outputs.

Life Cycle Interpretation. In this final stage, the firm summarizes the life cycle inventory and the impact assessment and provides recommendations relative to the goals and the scope of the assessment.

Economic Life Cycle Costing

Economic life cycle costing refers to a series of procedures designed to express all future costs and benefits in present day values.[18] The firm initially identifies all cash flows that occur during the life of an asset from initial expenditure to end of life.[19] These include the purchase price, the operating costs, the disposal

---

[16] International Organization for Standardization. (2008), *Environmental Management: Life Cycle Assessment: Principles and Framework*. Vol. 14040.

[17] Wilhelm, Miriam M., Constantin Blome, Vikram Bhakoo, and Antony Paulraj (2016), "Sustainability in Multi-Tier Supply Chains: Understanding the Double Agency Role of the First-Tier Supplier," *Journal of Operations Management* 41, 42–60.

[18] Taylor, Winston B. (1981), "The Use of Life Cycle Costing in Acquiring Physical Assets," *Long Range Planning* 14(6), 32–43.

[19] Woodward, David G. (1997), "Life Cycle Costing—Theory, Information Acquisition and Application," *International Journal of Project Management*, 15 (6), 335–344.

costs, and other concerns. The firm subsequently groups costs into categories such as engineering, production, and implementation. This process enables them to identify trade-offs and pursue optimal levels of life cycle costing. The firm then examines the costs of an item based on one or more independent variables. For example, firms could estimate computing costs based on the kilowatt hours of energy used per month. This process enables companies to examine costs and compare expenditures associated with alternative production strategies.[20]

Once this cost information is established, the firm takes the following steps to estimate life cycle costs[21] (See Figure 9.3):

Step 1: Operating profile. The operating profile refers to the periodic cycle of product operations that identifies the start-up, operating, and shut down.

Step 2: Utilization. Utilization identifies how the equipment will be functioning in each mode of operation. Operating characteristics of equipment may vary considerably in their use energy and other resources.

Step 3: Identify every cost element. The firm attempts to identify every cost, including acquisition, operating (including energy, water, and air), and maintenance costs. The firm also considers others costs, notably possession costs and opportunity costs.

Step 4: Identify critical cost parameters. In this step, the firm identifies factors that control the degree of costs incurred over the life of an asset. These include repair costs, failure rates, and energy usage rates.

Step 5: Calculate costs. The firm calculates costs at current prices and then adjusts the costs based on rates of inflation and discount rates. The sum of all costs becomes the life cycle cost.

FIGURE 9-3
Life cycle costing
procedures.

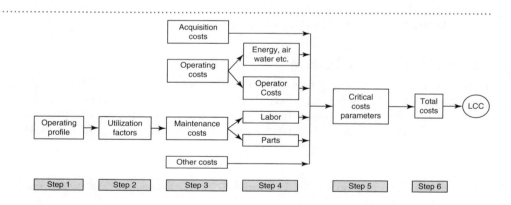

---

[20] Cole, Raymond J., and Eva Sterner (2000), "Reconciling theory and practice of life-cycle costing," *Building Research and Information* 28 (5-6), 368–375.

[21] Woodward, David G. (1997), "Life Cycle Costing—Theory, Information Acquisition and Application," *International Journal of Project Management*, 15 (6), 335–344.

Life cycle costing provides a great opportunity to assess the long-term benefits of relatively sustainable products and their alternatives. First, the marketer should invest the time to gain an understanding of the operating profile and product utilization. Marketers of sustainable products should identify how products will be used and examine the energy, water, and other resources associated with product usage. When the marketer has a strong grasp of product operations and resources, she can be more specific about the benefits of a product offering. The savvy marketer then examines the costs associated with the product and the costs of alternative products. In many cases, the initial product costs of a sustainable option are greater than those for a less-sustainable alternative, but the overall costs of operations is lower. For example, Figure 9-4 uses life cycle costing to illustrate how sustainable products can have lower operating costs than alternative products. In the example, a California manufacturer needs to replace lighting on the shop floor. The firm may need hundreds of lights, but focusing the analysis on a single bulb offers insight into total life cycle costs.

The operating profile indicates that the lights will be used every day of the year for eight hours per day (2920 hours per year). The light bulb has just two modes, on and off. The alternatives under consideration are incandescent and LED lights. Incandescent lights are less expensive ($1.19) than LEDs ($2.49), but the incandescent lights need to be changed three times during the year. The acquisition price is therefore greater ($3.57 for three lights at $1.19). If the installation of

		Incandescent light life = 1000 hours light wattage = 60 watts.	LED light life = 10,000 hours light wattage = 12 watts.
Step 3: Identify every cost element.	Acquisition cost	$3.57 The bulbs are $1.19 per bulb. With a with a productive life of 1000 hours, the buyer needs three bulbs to meet needs for one year (2920 hours).	$2.49 Since this bulb will last for 10,000 hours, only one bulb is needed.
	Operating costs	Kilowatt hours = light wattage x total hours of operation/1000 = 60 watts x 2920 hours/1000 = 175.2 kilowatt hours. At $0.12 per kilowatt hour, the operating cost is $0.12/kilowatt x 175.2 = $21.02.	Kilowatt hours = light wattage x total hours of operation/1000 = 12 watts x 2920 hours/1000 = 35.04 kilowatt hours. At $0.12 per kilowatt hour, the operating cost is $0.12/kilowatt x 35.04 = $4.28.
Step 4: Identify critical cost parameters.		The operating costs are substantially greater than the purchase price.	The operating cost is greater than the purchase price.
Step 5: Calculate costs.	Total cost = acquisition cost + operating cost.	$24.59 = $3.57 acquisition cost + $21.02 operating cost.	$6.77 = $2.49 acquisition cost + $4.28 operating cost.

FIGURE 9-4

Using life cycle costing to illustrate financial benefits of sustainable products.

this lighting is complicated (e.g., fixtures located in high ceilings), then the LED has an additional benefit associated lower maintenance costs.

The operating costs are more difficult for consumers to determine given that many people do not know prevailing electricity rates and how they influence costs. If a bulb operates at 60 watts for 2920 hours per year, then it requires 175,200 watts or 175.2 kilowatts. If electricity can be purchased at $0.12 per kilowatt hour, then the operating costs for the bulb are $21.04 (175.2 kilowatts x $0.12). The LED bulb uses 12 watts, and over 2920 hours, it will need 35.04kilowatts. At $0.12 per kilowatt hour, the operating costs are $4.28.

The data from this simple example illustrate how a sustainable marketer can use pricing information to her advantage. The initial LED price is higher, but over a year, both the acquisition and the operating costs are lower than the costs associated with the incandescent alternative.

The total costs for the incandescent lighting are $24.59, whereas the LED costs are $6.77. Each LED purchase saves the buyer $17.82 per year. When marketers illustrates the financial savings of the sustainable product, they are much more likely to close sales and generate revenue.

Societal Life Cycle Assessment

The goal of the societal life cycle assessment is to examine the social implications of products and systems over time.[22] Just as the boundaries of the systems are essential to the evaluation of ecological and economic costs, firms must similarly determine the relevant boundaries of a supply chain and its influences on society. In effort to concentrate on relationships a firm can influence, many analyses focus on relationships a firm has with its closest buyers and sellers.[23] Four classes of social indicators include:

Human Rights. Proper assessment of social costs should include a discussion of the diversity of employees at all levels of the organization. The firm should also report on the level of collective bargaining and indicate whether the supply chain relies on child labor or compulsory labor.

Labor Practices and Work Conditions. Labor practices include wages and consideration of equal remuneration in diverse groups. Firms also indicate (physical and psychological) working conditions as well as employee training.

Society. Societal indicators address the extent of contributions through job creation, support of local suppliers, investments in research and development, and infrastructure. In addition, companies explain the extent of local community acceptance of their operations, and they indicate how they ensure commitment to sustainability issues from business partners.

---

[22] Jørgensen, Andreas, Agathe Le Bocq, Liudmila Nazarkina, and Michael Hauschild (2008), "Methodologies for Social Life Cycle Assessment," *The International Journal of Life Cycle Assessment* 13 (2), 96–103.

[23] Benoît, Catherine, et al. (2010), "The Guidelines for Social Life Cycle Assessment of Products: Just in Time!" *The International Journal of Life Cycle Assessment* 15, (2), 156–163.

Product Responsibility. Product responsibility addresses product ingredients/components, product labeling, and marketing communications. Product reporting must address the threats and the benefits associated with ingredients.

Together, the environmental life cycle assessment, economic life cycle costing, and societal life cycle assessment provides the life cycle sustainability assessment. This assessment is instrumental to determining internal pricing constraints that frame corporate pricing decisions.

PRICING CONSTRAINTS

The development of the pricing strategy can be viewed as the multistage process,[24] outlined in Figure 9-4. The result of this process is the proclamation of value. The organization begins this process by determining the corporate mission and the objectives. Once the objectives are established, then the organization develops a series of pricing objectives that complement the overall goals of the firm. These objectives are then converted to specific action that the firm will take to achieve the pricing goals and the overall objectives of the firm. Before this conversion occurs, however, the firm must consider the internal and external constraints on this process. The pricing strategy must consider the internal constraints on price such as the costs of production, sales, and delivery. The life cycle sustainability assessment discussed previously in this chapter identifies important pricing contingencies related to economic, ecological, and social conditions. The firm must also recognize that customer demand, legal considerations, and competition influence are external constraints that influence pricing strategies. When all of these factors have been considered, the firm is in the position to proclaim the

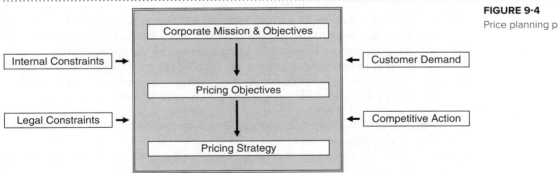

FIGURE 9-4
Price planning process.[25]

---

[24] Morris, Michael, and George A. Siragusa (1994), "Strategic Pricing," in *The Dartnell Marketing Manager's Handbook*, S. J. Levy, G. R. Frereichs, and H. L. Gordon, Eds., Chicago, IL: The Dartnell Corporation, 835-854.

[25] Morris, Michael, and George A. Siragusa (1994), "Strategic Pricing," in *The Dartnell Marketing Manager's Handbook*, S. J. Levy, G. R. Frereichs, and H. L. Gordon, Eds., Chicago, IL: The Dartnell Corporation, 835–854.

value of its product offerings in the form of pricing strategies. As a preface to our development of the pricing objectives and strategy, we outline these internal and external constraints on the price planning process.

Internal Pricing Constraints. The constraints within the firm reflect the costs incurred to produce, sell, and deliver a product. Many firms use cost as the basis for determining price, and costs must be covered if the firm is to generate a profit. Thus, it is essential to understand the components of cost. One can distinguish between fixed and variable costs associated with a product. *Fixed costs* refer to cost factors that do not change in the short run, whereas *variable costs* refer to costs that fluctuate with the amount product sold. Fixed costs are exemplified by investments in real estate, plant, and equipment. By contrast, the electricity consumed on an auto assembly line is a variable cost that fluctuates with the number of cars produced. Efforts to enhance the sustainability of product offerings must consider both cost elements.

In addition to the fixed-variable cost dichotomy, it is also relevant to consider how costs are allocated among the products manufactured at a specific location. Ford's efforts to enhance the sustainability of its operations and products exemplifies these allocation considerations. In the Rouge River plant, for example, Ford has invested over $2 billion to raise the sustainability of this facility.[26] These investments accommodate the concerns of many interest groups related to manufacturer such as employees, communities, and NGOs. The costs associated with the Rouge River plant are allocated across products that leave this assembly line. Regardless of their sentiments toward sustainable marketing and production, buyers of cars from this facility must pay some portion of the cost of raising the sustainability. By contrast, Ford has also invested €332 million in a joint agreement with Peugeot to develop diesel engines.[27] The investment in diesel engines is not carried to a large degree by all products coming off the assembly line but is allocated to the diesel vehicles. The investment in diesel engines can be allocated among a variety of users motivated to purchase fuel-efficient cars that produce relatively few carbon emissions. Given the breadth of consumer preferences in the auto industry, Ford faces a much tougher challenge to assess the consumer response to enhanced production sustainability in the Rouge River facility. By contrast, the consumer response to adding sustainable components to products enables the firm to estimate returns from specific segments of the auto market. Although the assembly line challenge is more daunting, in both cases, the firm must consider customer demand in their allocation and pricing decisions.

Customer Demand. Grocery stores offer consumers a variety of products that offer differential levels of value. Most large retailers offer competitively priced private-label products that deliver the same ingredients as the nationally advertised brands. Private-label products such as Wal-Mart's Equate brand

[26] McDonough, William, and Michael Braungart (2002), "Design for the Triple Top Line: New Tools for Sustainable Commerce," *Corporate Environmental Strategy* 9(3), 251–258.

[27] *Automotive Engineer* (2005), "Joint Investment in Diesel," 30 (10), 4–5.

[28] Hoch, Stephen J., and Shumeet Banerji, (1993), "When Do Private Labels Succeed? *Sloan Management Review;* 34, (4), 57–67.

are sold at lower cost to the consumer, yet these products have higher gross margins than the advertised brand counterparts.[28] The variety at the retail level enables the consumer to select among products with different levels of value, and this diversity enables the retailer to serve multiple segments of the market. Grocers recognize that they can increase their revenues by offering multiple products directed at different market niches that desire different levels of value.

In order to assess the potential of a market or a market segment, it is necessary to understand what is valued by the customer. Note that this call for understanding the value derived from consumption *does not* necessarily include sustainability considerations. The marketer of ecologically friendly products must recognize that consumers *rarely* cite sustainable marketing issues as the primary motivation for consumption. Traditional selling considerations such as price, quality, and performance are often central motivations that are expressed prior to sustainability concerns.[29] For example, Brita water filtration products offer consumers clean water that offers health, fitness, and vitality benefits to the body. In addition, the combined costs of tap water and these filtration products are frequently lower than the cost of bottled water. These biological and economic benefits are likely to prompt consumers to invest in Brita filtration devices. One primary sustainability benefit is the reduction in the size of landfills associated with fewer purchases (and disposal) of bottled water. While it is likely that consumers would have a strong interest in the stamina-related and biological benefits of the product without the sustainability benefit, it is unlikely that the reduction in landfills alone would prompt substantial purchases. The sustainability benefit does not stand alone and requires consideration of the broader value assessment.

Legal Constraints. The legal constraints refer to the regulatory requirements associated with the marketing of products. To varying degrees, industries face regulations concerning sourcing of component parts, promotions, and post-consumption product disposal. The need to adhere to these regulations can result in higher costs of sourcing, production, distribution, promotion, and disposal. These constraints are established and regulated at the international, federal/regional, state, and local levels. The Kyoto Protocol of 1997 and the Doha Amendment of 2012 illustrate the influence of international environmental agreements.[30] Adherence to standards has resulted in new regulation in participating countries, and new standards for greenhouse gas emissions have been incorporated into municipal planning in over 600 cities worldwide.

The U.S. Environmental Protection Agency (EPA) provides an illustration of national environmental regulation. The EPA creates and enforces regulations concerning environmental issues. The enforcement of environmental concerns is derived from the Clean Air Act (CAA) of 1970 and the Clean Water Act of

---

[29] Esty, Daniel C., and Andrew S. Winston (2006), *Green to Gold*, New Haven, CT: Yale University Press.

[30] Grunewald, Nicole, and Inmaculada Martinez-Zarzoso (2016), "Did the Kyoto Protocol Fail? An Evaluation of the Effect of the Kyoto Protocol on CO2 Emissions," *Environment and Development Economics* 21 (1), 1–22.

1972. The Clean Air Act placed control of air pollution and enforcement of air pollution regulations in the hands of the EPA.[31] The CAA regulates stationary and mobile sources of air emissions. Thus, the pollution control associated with auto assembly and auto operations are regulated as a result of the CAA. In 2007, the Supreme Court ruled that the CAA gives the EPA the authority to regulate carbon dioxide as a pollutant.[32] The EPA also regulates vehicle emissions for hydrocarbons, carbon monoxide, and nitrogen oxides.

The Clean Water Act (CWA) provides standards, technical tools, and financial assistance to limit water pollution and enhance poor water quality. The CWA requires major industries and municipalities to meet and adhere to standards for water quality and pollution control. It sets state-level specific water quality criteria and provides funding to states and communities to help them meet their clean water infrastructure needs. In addition, it employs permit systems designed to facilitate development while simultaneously protecting wetlands and other aquatic ecosystems.[33]

Organizations must also monitor and adhere to the regulations established at the state and local levels. For example, the state of California enacted the California Global Warming Solutions Act in 2006.[34] This act strives to achieve gas emissions levels of 1990 throughout the economy by 2020. This goal represents approximately an 11 percent reduction from current emissions levels and nearly a 30 percent reduction from projected business-as-usual levels for 2020.[35] The act also requires annual monitoring and reporting of greenhouse gases as well the accounting for greenhouse gas emissions from all electricity consumed in the state. The pursuit of these goals and requirements demands that firms operating in every sector of the California economy invest in energy efficient technologies. These organizations must also attend to the regulations at the municipal level. San Francisco, for example, has implemented a green building ordinance that requires new buildings meet or exceed the requirements established by Build It Green in the GreenPoint Rated (GPR) system or the U.S. Green Building Council's leadership in engineering and environmental design (LEED) building rating system.[36]

These regulatory conditions—from the Kyoto Protocol to the San Francisco green building ordinance—underscore the influence of legal requirements on

---

[31] Winters, Nicholle (2004), "Carbon Dioxide: A Pollutant in the Air, but is the EPA Correct that It Is not an "Air Pollutant"?" *Columbia Law Review* 104 (7), 1996–2031.

[32] Hecht, Alan D. (2007), "Exploring How Today's Development Affects Future Generations around the Globe: In This Issue: Sustainable Directions in U.S. Environmental Law: The Next Level of Environmental Protection: Business Strategies and Government Policies Converging on Sustainability," *American University/Sustainable Development Law & Policy*, 8 (Fall).

[33] Grooms, Katherine K. (2015), "Enforcing the Clean Water Act: The Effect of State-level Corruption on Compliance," *Journal of Environmental Economics and Management* 73, 50–78.

[34] Duane, Timothy P., and Joanna D. Malaczynski (2009), "Reducing Greenhouse Gas Emissions from Vehicle Miles Traveled: Integrating the California Environmental Quality Act (CEQA) with the California Global Warming Solutions Act," *Ecology Law Quarterly* 36 (1), 9–27.

[35] www.energy.ca.gov/commission/index.html (April 6, 2016).

[36] Cardno, Catherine A. (2009), "California Energy Commission Approves San Francisco 'Green' Ordinance," *Civil Engineering*, 79 (2), 19–22.

pricing decisions. It is incumbent upon the firm to recognize current sustainability standards for operations in each geographic market it serves. In addition, organizations that monitor or participate in developing regulations have a greater opportunity to anticipate changes in environmental law.

Competitive Action. Our pricing model (see Figure 9-4) recognizes that pricing decisions must take into environment in which the firm operates. Decisions about the pricing strategy must consider the nature of the market as well as the nature of the competition.[37] The organization should evaluate the size of the sustainable consumer segments in the marketplace. Some markets are characterized by a strong preference for sustainable products. For example, Starbucks recognizes that a strong portion of the retail coffee consumers have a preference for fair trade, sustainably produced coffee.[38] Because many of these consumers are willing to pay more for these coffees, Starbucks can retain a premium price for fair trade coffee. By contrast, some markets are characterized by negative predisposition toward sustainability concerns.

The competitive landscape should be considered in conjunction with the consumer's attitude towards sustainable products. Thus, the organization must examine differentiability based on greenness. To varying degrees, companies have resources that enable them to compete favorably based on the ecological sensitivity of the strategy. The competition to the firm also has resources that could be (or are already) committed to achieving sustainability. Thus, the Body Shop's commitment to sustainability makes it difficult to compete with this firm based on green marketing and production practices.

Analysis of the competitive landscape should incorporate consideration of the market factors outlined in Chapter 6. These factors include the ability to differentiate based on sustainability and the size of the green market segments. *Lean green* and *defensive green* marketing strategies are appropriate where the ability to distinguish market offerings based on ecological considerations is modest. For example, consumers in the heavy-duty pickup truck market are not favorably disposed to hybrid technology. Although there may be many consumers with strong (favorable or unfavorable) attitudes toward sustainability, consumers are indifferent to green marketing concerns when making purchases. In such cases, the firm is likely to benefit from a pricing strategy that does not ask the consumer to invest more for sustainable technology. Similarly, Nike introduced the *Considered* brand of footwear in 2005. This environmentally friendly shoe made from brown hemp fibers was marketed at $110 per pair. Ecological concerns were not salient to consumers in this marketplace. The consumers in the market purchased shoes to make them feel slick, fast, and hip. Nike learned from this product launch that most consumers do not use sustainability criteria when they purchase footwear. Nike continues to enhance the sustainability of its product offerings, but new products do not emphasize sustainable factors.[39]

---

[37] Ginsberg, Jill M., and Paul N. Bloom (2004), "Choosing the Right Green Marketing Strategy," *MIT Sloan Management Review*, (Fall) 79–84.

[38] Makower, Joel (2009), *Strategies for the Green Economy*, New York: McGraw Hill.

[39] Jana, Reena (2009), "Nike Goes Green, Very Quietly," *Business Week*, 4136 (June 22, 2009).

In markets characterized by marked opportunity to distinguish product offerings based on sustainability, the firm must also consider the size of the green market. The *extreme green* strategy reflects a competitive situation in which there is a substantial demand for green products and the firm has the appreciable ability to differentiate based on the green qualities of its products.

Consider, for example, Stonyfield Farms, the New Hampshire producer of dairy products. This firm has the fourth-largest market share in the yogurt industry, trailing only Yoplait, Dannon, and private-label products.[40] Stonyfield recognizes that one segment of the yogurt market is highly cognizant of the merits of organic food, and it has crafted its product line to address the demand in this segment. The organic label is a form of sustainable differentiation that enables the firm to offer products at a price premium.[41] The average price of its products is greater than twice the price of the market leader. Stonyfield's price premium must exceed the cost incurred to differentiate based on the organic quality of the products. It is, therefore, essential for a firm using this pricing strategy to monitor its cost position. The firm using this strategy attempts to achieve price parity by reducing costs in areas other than the source of the differential competitive advantage. Firms such as Stonyfield can shore down promotional and supply chain costs relative to their competition. Companies that are able to control these costs and maintain their competitive advantages can be strong performers in the industry.

The *shaded green* strategy refers to a market in which the demand for ecologically sensitive products is low, yet there is a substantial opportunity to differentiate based on the environmental merits of a product. For example, in the clothing market, roughly 0.1 percent of the cotton products sold are organic. Organic products tend to be more expensive than competitive products that use inorganic fertilizers.[42] Nonorganic cotton farming has substantial implications for the environment. The nonorganic industry covers 2.4 percent of the world's farmland, but it uses 25 percent of the world's pesticides and 10 percent of the world's synthetic fertilizers. Large quantities of defoliants, fungicides, and herbicides are sprayed into fields, causing harm to other crops, farm workers, and neighbors.

Patagonia serves this niche market by marketing jeans, hats, shirts, and undergarments made exclusively from organic cotton.[43] The firm's products command prices roughly 20 percent higher than those of other outdoor wear specialists. Patagonia customers tend to be better educated and have higher incomes than most consumers in the markets served by the firm. Patagonia donates 1 percent of its net profit to nonprofit charitable organizations that promote environmental conservation and sustainability.[44] It also tries to reduce the environmental impacts of its processes and products and processes. Most Patagonia's costs of goods sold are attributable to the garments' raw materials. Fabric accounts for about 80 percent of the total costs of raw materials, and the firm estimates that its fabric costs can

---

[40] Phillips, David (2008), "Yogurt Still the Bright Spot," *Dairy Foods*, 109 (11), 66–73.

[41] Porter, Michael E. (1985), *Competitive Advantage*, New York: Free Press.

[42] *Economist* (2006), "How green is your wardrobe?" 381 (8506), 67–68.

[43] Casadesus-Masanell, Ramon, Michael Crooke, Forest Reinhardt, and Vishal Vasishth (2009), "Households' Willingness to Pay for "Green" Goods: Evidence from Patagonia's Introduction of Organic Cotton Sportswear," *Journal of Economics & Management Strategy*, 18 (1), 203–233.

[44] www.patagonia.com/pdf/en_US/bcorp_annual_report_2014.pdf (April 6, 2016).

be as much as 20 to 30 percent higher than those of its competitors. Patagonia's primary marketing vehicle is a series of catalogs that display men and women using the products in spectacular settings. The catalogs also offer essays about environmentalism and cultural values. In contrast to competition that uses less than 10 percent of catalog space for nonselling activities, Patagonia dedicates roughly 50 percent of the catalog space to nonselling activities.

In 1996, Patagonia made the decision to convert to organic cotton. This decision demanded attention to consumer attitudes, retail prices, and costs of goods sold. The spring 1996 catalog featured an opening article from Patagonia's founder concerning the switch to organic cotton, and the description of such organic products offered repeated references to organic components. The firm recognized that its consumers were sensitive to organic products, but it also modified prices. Patagonia reduced margins on most cotton sportswear products so that the retail price on an organic product would not be more than 20 percent over the price of the conventional product. Products that could not meet the goal were eliminated, resulting in organic cotton garments selling for not more than 8 percent above comparable garments made from conventional cotton. Although the cost of goods sold increased, the additional average willingness to pay for the organic cotton exceeded the costs incurred.

The Patagonia example underscores a situation in which the market for sustainable products is modest, yet the firm has the ability to offer a product with sustainable competitive advantage to the market. By understanding the needs of the consumer base and its responsiveness to price and quality modifications, firms can successfully implement strategies to accommodate shaded green markets.

CORPORATE MISSION AND PRICING OBJECTIVES

It is vital to recognize that the outcome of the marketing mix embodies the only manner by which the firm can achieve objectives. If each element of the mix, and notably price, does not reflect the mission and objectives of the firm, then there is little likelihood these goals of the firm will be obtained. When the firm establishes a clear mission and objectives, the pricing strategy must be designed to complement these goals. For example, Procter & Gamble places a heavy emphasis on the desire for the firm to grow via innovation.[45] Across the multiple brands of this firm, the goal is increased revenues by a steady flow of innovative ideas with respect to products, their delivery, and their consumption. In many markets, price is an important means for differentiation among branded products and retailers' private-label brands. The constant pursuit of innovation enables Procter & Gamble to compete with premium and midtier-priced products. Thus, the pricing strategy can be implemented because it is consistent with the innovation goals of the firm.

The pricing strategy should be consistent with the overall objectives of the firm. The specific pricing strategy may focus on multiple objectives and varying levels of these potentially inconsistent objectives.[46] Organizations that

---

[45] www.annualreport.pg.com/ (April 6, 2016).

[46] Lanzillotti, Robert F. (1958), "Pricing Objectives in Large Companies," American Economic Review, 48 (5)., 921–940.

have corporate objectives that revolve around the targeted return on investment or targeted profit levels are likely to adopt pricing objectives consistent with these corporate objectives. One objective of the pricing strategy concerns the extent to which the firm seeks a targeted *return on investment*. Firms that focus on this objective determine their costs and then establish prices based on a desired rate of return. Similarly, some firms rely on targeted *level of profitability*. These firms estimate costs and then add a margin designed to yield a level of profit.

The organizational goal to achieve some level of the market share may not be compatible with targeted ROI or profits. Firms with a market share objective will have pricing strategies that ensure they attain or maintain a presence in the market. Companies with a targeted market share are likely to charge lower prices than firms that are focused on the return on investment. Note that firms can either engage in these strategies to maintain a position in the market, increase market share, or prevent competition from gaining a foothold in the market.

In addition to targeted returns and market share, an organization also seeks to convey an image about the firm and its products. Thus, pricing objectives are developed that focus on the image the firm seeks to convey.[47] Some firms such as Gucci are inclined to price products to convey the luxury associated with the company's offerings. In contrast, firms such as Costco seek to convey that they are the low-price leader in a market.

Firms are increasingly incorporating sustainability goals into their objectives, and this enhancement strategy has strong implications on the pricing objectives of the firm. For example, Timberlands mission is to equip people to make a difference in the world, and it seeks to approach this mission by becoming carbon neutral.[48] Firms with the objective to achieve higher levels of sustainability can engage in multiple strategies and must take into consideration other aspects of the competitive marketplace and consumer preferences.

PRICING STRATEGIES

Because different market segments have different value ratios, one needs to a wide arsenal of strategies for approaching a market. In this section, we address several strategies that enable firms to increase revenues and simultaneously address the firm's sustainability objectives.

We distinguish among three pricing strategies. First, we discuss the use of carbon offset pricing. We then outline pricing strategies associated with the competitive position and product line pricing.[49]

---

[47] Wilson, Dominic (2005), "Pricing Objectives," *Blackwell Encyclopedic Dictionary of Marketing*, 1–264, 264p.

[48] www.greenbiz.com/news/2011/04/13/timberland-cuts-ghgs-38-percent-falls-short-aggressive-goal (April 6, 2016).

[49] Tellis, Gerard J. (1986), "Beyond the Many Faces of Price: An Integration of Pricing Strategies," *Journal of Marketing*, 50 (4), 146–160.

Carbon Offset Pricing

Carbon offset pricing refers to situations under which the marketer of a product enables the purchaser to compensate for the greenhouse emissions associated with consumption. This pricing strategy places the cost of sustainability directly in the hands of the consumer.[50] Two parameters associated with determining the offset price are the determination of the carbon-related cost of a product and the determination of the cost of the offset investment. For example, several airlines have joined Sustainable Travel International (STI) and offer passengers the opportunity to carbon offset air travel. On short-distance domestic flights, approximately 0.54 metric tons are discharged per passenger, whereas 3.68 metric tons of carbon dioxide (CO_2) are emitted per passenger on international, long-distance flights.[51] The second consideration is the cost of the offset. STI offers different offset programs that vary based on the location of the offset and the form of service. The Conservation Carbon offset supports reforestation projects in Asia that are distinct from the offset projects in North and South America.

Competitive Pricing

In many cases, the specific strategies the firm will use are based on the firm's position in the market. Consider how these pricing strategies have been used in conjunction with products that offer sustainability advantages:

Break-even Pricing. The *break-even pricing* strategy attempts to establish a price that covers all costs of operations. To use this pricing strategy, the firm must determine its fixed and variable costs. The organization then estimates demand for the product. The price is then determined as the sum of the fixed and variable costs divided by the number of units sold. This strategy is essential to the success of many pricing decisions regardless of whether the consumer base is favorably disposed to sustainable products. The strategy forces the firm to determine its costs, and sustainable technologies that lower the cost of operations are implemented. For example, propane is a variable cost that poultry farmers face in the operations of their facilities. These farmers are switching to biofuels to lower their costs of operations and reap the ecological benefits of renewable fuel.[52]

Cost-based Pricing. A *cost-based pricing* program adds a markup to the cost of the product to establish the price. This strategy is used by many firms to establish pricing structures. For example, utility companies use their cost structures as a basis for determining the cost of water within the municipalities they serve.[53] The marketer of sustainable technology can influence purchasing by illustrating how the investment in sustainable technology can lower their

---

[50] Gogoi, Pallavi (2008), "Carbon Offsets Take Flight," *Business Week Online* (March 25), 26.

[51] cotap.org/carbon-footprint-calculator/ (April 6, 2016).

[52] Uptagraff, Donna (2008), "Co-op Development Action: Poultry Industry Explores Ecological Options to Save Energy," *Rural Cooperatives*, 75 (6), 14–15.

[53] Moorhouse, John C. (1995), "Competitive Markets for Electricity Generation," *CATO Journal*, 14 (3), 412–423.

overall cost of operations. Because price is directly linked to cost, lower costs translate to lower prices for consumers. For example, Staples is committed to lowering its energy to 7 percent below 2001 levels. They are retrofitting lighting systems, and they are using biogas, wind, solar, and biomass for over 14 percent of their energy needs. Their integrated strategy for energy conservation has enabled them to reduced net greenhouse gas emissions by nearly 5 percent compared to 2001. These costs reductions help Staples remain competitive in a volatile retail market.[54]

Value-based Pricing. This pricing strategy uses the consumers' perceived value of a good to establish price. In contrast to the preceding strategies that focus on cost to determine price, this *value-based pricing* addresses the relative value of the product to the consumer. The firm begins by identifying the desired benefits and the relative costs of a product, and the value assessment can be determined. Thus, the various facets of benefits and the multiple facets of cost are used to determine the price. Products that feature the Energy Star label offer one example of value-based pricing. Energy Star-qualified refrigerators, for instance, are 20 percent more efficient than other products, but the *initial* costs of the Energy Star product is typically higher than the cost of other models.[55] Consumers evaluating Energy Star products weigh initial cost and value in use over the productive life of the appliance versus the alternative, non-Energy Star appliances.

Status Quo. The *status quo* price refers to charging a price that is consistent with the competition. Firms can effectively use this strategy to offer a product that is superior in terms of sustainable marketing, yet the product sells at the same price point as the alternative. For example, Starbuck's has made a corporate commitment to sustainability throughout its supply chain. The company has also employed a status quo pricing strategy in which it charges $1 for an eight-ounce cup of coffee.[56] This pricing strategy enables the firm to remain price competitive while still pursuing the company's sustainability objectives.

Skimming Pricing. A *skimming pricing* strategy refers to setting a price to reach consumers willing to pay a higher price for a product prior to marketing the product to more price-sensitive consumers.[57] For example, Seventh Generation is committed to becoming the world's most trusted brand of authentic, environmentally responsible products for the home.[58] The household cleaners offered for sale by this company tend to be higher priced than the products sold by competitors such as Procter & Gamble.[59] The skimming strategy would seem to work best when there is a sizeable group of consumers in the *Green Enthusiasts*

[54] Wilson, Marianne (2006), "Staples Aims for a Greener Planet," *Chain Store Age*, 82 (13), 60–66.

[55] *Agency Group 05* (2007), Energy *Department Announces More Stringent Criteria For* Energy Star *Refrigerators FDCH Regulatory Intelligence Database.*

[56] Adamy, Janet (2008**), "**Starbucks Tests $1 Cup, Free Refills in Seattle," *Wall Street Journal* January 23, B4.

[57] www.marketingpower.com/_layouts/Dictionary.aspx (April 6, 2016).

[58] www.seventhgeneration.com (April 6, 2016).

[59] Wasserman, Todd (2008), "Will Green Product Sales Wither?" *Adweek*, 49 (36).

market segment. In contrast to the skimming strategy, P&G has adopted a status quo strategy whereby they offer Bounty Select-A-Size paper towels. These paper towel sheets are 45 percent smaller than regular towels and enable the consumer to use a smaller amount of paper with every cleaning task. The innovations in product design and logistics enable P&G to market a relatively ecofriendly product at a competitive price.

Penetration Pricing. A *penetration pricing* policy sets a low initial price in an attempt to increase market share rapidly.[60] This policy is effective if demand is perceived to be fairly elastic. For example, the three largest utilities in California were instructed in 2007 to reduce the amount of energy consumed or face strong financial penalties. Pacific Gas and Electric and other utilities elected to pour millions of dollars into subsidizing the cost of compact fluorescent light (CFL) bulbs. As a result, bulbs that sold for $5 to $10 in 1999 could be purchased for 25 cents to 50 cents.[61] This strategy resulted in sales of more than 7.6 million CFL bulbs in 2007 in California alone.

Product Line Pricing

In some cases, the specific strategies the firm will use are not based on the firm's position in the market, but they primarily focus on relationship among products in the product line. Consider how these product line strategies have been used to market products with ecological benefits:

Price lining. *Price lining* refers to the offering of merchandise at a number of specific predetermined prices. By offering ecological benefits at several price points, the marketer grants the consumer the flexibility to engage in sustainable consumption that is consistent with the consumer's budget. For example, the carbon offset programs offered by Sustainable Travel enable consumers to select from among several plans. These plans vary in price based on the level and the location of the offset carbon activity.[62]

Bundling. Bundling is the practice of offering two or more products or services for sale at one price. *Bundling* can be used across contexts to lower consumer overall costs and enhance sustainability. For example, retailers that market personal electronic devices such as cameras can market product bundles that include rechargeable batteries. By bundling the batteries to the electronics, consumer satisfaction is raised, and the product yields a lower carbon footprint due to the rechargeable devices. This strategy is also used in the construction industry to bundle sustainable products within a new building. Construction certified by the U.S. Green Building Council receives leadership in energy and environmental design (LEED) certification.[63] The certification ensures that the all products (e.g., lighting, windows, and heating/air conditioning) are sustainable.

[60] www.marketingpower.com/_layouts/Dictionary.aspx (April 6, 2016).

[61] Smith, Rebecca (2008), "Utilities Amp Up Push to Slash Energy Use," *Wall Street Journal*, 251 (7), A1–A12.

[62] www.sustainabletravelinternational.org/ (April 6, 2016).

[63] www.usgbc.org/DisplayPage.aspx?CategoryID=19 (April 6, 2016).

SUMMARY

Introduction

The purpose of this chapter has been to outline the relationship between pricing strategies and sustainable marketing. Because the pursuit of sustainable marketing may not be paramount to the consumer, the sustainable pricing strategy must be incorporated into the overall strategy and the planning process. We, therefore, outlined the influences of internal constraints, customer demand, legal constraints, and competitive action on the price planning process. We then outlined the relationship between corporate strategy and pricing objectives. The internal and external constraints and the corporate strategy provided a basis for development of the pricing objectives and the pricing strategy. We finished our treatment of pricing by outlining specific carbon offset, competitive, and product line pricing tactics.

Value, Benefits, and Costs

The value associated with a product refers to the ratio of benefits to costs. Firms assess the acquisition, possession, usages, and opportunity costs of product ownership.

Life Cycle Sustainability Assessment

Life cycle assessment examines the total costs associated with products and product systems over their lives. Life cycle sustainability assessment incorporates environmental life cycle assessment, economic life cycle costing, and societal life cycle assessment.

Pricing Constraints

The constraints faced by the firm include internal constraints, customer demand, legal constraints, and competitive action. Internal constraints refer to the costs incurred to produce, sell, and deliver a product. Fixed costs refer to cost factors that do not change in the short run, whereas variable costs refer to costs that fluctuate with the amount product sold. It is also relevant to consider how costs are allocated among the products manufactured at a specific location. Firms that invest in technology and infrastructure to enhance sustainability should recognize that this cost burden is carried by all products leaving a facility or location.

In order to understand the role of consumers, it is essential to frame value as the relationship between desired benefits in relation to the relative cost. Desired benefits refer to things that consumers are willing to pay for these things and that they genuinely want. These benefits must be weighed against the acquisition, possession, usage, and opportunity cost associated with a product. The value offered by a product offering must also be superior to the value of competitive products, and the marketer must ensure that the value proposition generates a profit.

Legal constraints refer to regulatory requirements associated with the marketing of products. Industries face regulations concerning sourcing of component parts, promotions, and post-consumption product disposal. The need to adhere to these regulations can result in higher costs of sourcing, production, distribution, promotion, and disposal. These constraints are established and regulated at the international, federal/regional, state, and local levels.

The role of competition should be considered in conjunction with the consumer's attitude towards sustainable products. The organization must examine the differentiability based on greenness. Companies have resources that enable them to compete favorably based on the ecological sensitivity of the strategy. The competition to the firm also has resources that could be (or are already) committed to achieving sustainability. By understanding the needs of the consumer base and the influence of competition, firms can successfully developed strategies that lead to increased market share.

Corporate Mission and Pricing Objectives

The pricing strategy should be consistent with the overall objectives of the firm. The specific pricing strategy may focus on multiple objectives and varying levels of these potentially inconsistent objectives. Firms that have objectives that emphasize market share or a level of profitability will price their product with these goals in mind. Similarly, firms that seek to raise perceptions of sustainability will similarly adjust price to achieve these objectives.

Pricing Strategies

Three types of pricing strategies include carbon offset pricing, competitive pricing, and product line pricing. Carbon offset pricing refers to situations under which the marketer of a product enables the purchaser to compensate for the greenhouse emissions associated with consumption.
Competitive pricing is a pricing strategy based on the firm's position in the market. These strategies include break-even pricing, cost-based pricing, value-based pricing, status quo pricing, skimming, and penetration pricing. Product line pricing includes price lining and bundling techniques that use the relationship among products in the product line to establish prices.

KEY TERMS

life cycle sustainability assessment
environmental life cycle assessment
economic life cycle costing
societal life cycle assessment
fixed cost
variable cost

value
acquisition cost
possession cost
usage cost
opportunity cost
carbon offset pricing
break-even pricing
cost-based pricing

value-based pricing
status quo
skimming pricing
penetration pricing
price lining
bundling

DISCUSSION QUESTIONS

1. How does Sustainable Travel International enable consumers to reduce the environmental cost of air travel? What does such action do to the overall cost to the consumer?

2. Why is it necessary for companies to incorporate product, promotion, and distribution considerations into pricing decisions?

3. How can a company determine the desired benefits and costs inherent to a pricing decision?

4. Distinguish among four costs that factor into value decisions.

5. Name and describe an international, national, and local sustainability-based regulation that influences a firm's pricing strategy.

6. How does the level and the form of competition influence pricing decisions?

7. How do the objectives and the mission of the firm influence the pricing strategy?

8. Describe the two parameters associated with determining the offset prices, and explain why different firms come up with different estimates for these parameters.

9. Describe a skimming strategy and a penetration strategy used by a company to help it increase sales of sustainable products.

10. How do firms use price lining and price bundling to increase the market share of sustainable products?

chapter

10

Providing Value in Sustainable Supply Chains

INTRODUCTION

Starbucks

Consumers can buy coffee anywhere, but there is no mistaking the ambiance and the aroma that surrounds a Starbucks. The company that revolutionized the way we buy coffee has also been working behind the scenes to ensure that its rich coffee will continue to be available in more than 40 countries across the globe for a long time. The company is committed to minimizing its impact on the planet, and it is passionate about sharing this commitment with its partners throughout the supply chain.

Starbucks' Shared Planet program is an environmental commitment which recognizes that conservation needs to occur throughout the supply chain, from coffee growers in Guatemala to recyclers in Seattle (see Figure 10-1). On the supply side, Starbucks has worked in conjunction with *Conservation International* for 10 years to develop coffee and farmer equity (CAFE) practices. CAFE consists of 24 comprehensive, measurable standards designed to enable suppliers and farmers to become sustainable sources of coffee. Growers are required to meet criteria for product quality, ethical accounting, social responsibility, and environmental leadership. The program has paid huge dividends for growers as it enables them to strengthen their marketplace positions and exercise some control over their organizations and operations.[1]

In 2014, 95 percent of the coffee Starbuck bought was purchased from suppliers verified and approved under CAFE practices guidelines.[2] The average cost per pound is 5 percent above the average price for C-grade Arabica. This price enables producers to increase their quality of life in terms of improved housing, enhanced education, and increased investments in their farms. In addition, the stability realized through stable incomes reduces the need to migrate for employment.[3]

The premium price on the supply side has enabled the company to refund some portion of the price back to suppliers. In contrast to many performance standards, growers are rewarded rather than penalized for meeting sustainability standards. Growers must have third-party verification of their performance, and this performance is reviewed annually.[4] Starbucks ecological commitment has enabled the company to establish sustainable sources of supply to meet its rapidly growing demand while simultaneously providing a systematic response to consumer concerns about social and environmental facets of production.[5] The environmental commitment is carried throughout its distribution channels.

---

[1] McDonald, Kate (2007), "Globalising Justice within Coffee Supply Chains? Fair Trade, Starbucks and the Transformation of Supply Chain Governance," *Third World Quarterly*, 28 (4), 793–812.

[2] globalassets.starbucks.com/assets/ea2441eb7cf647bb8ce8bb40f75e267e.pdf (April 14, 2016).

[3] McDonald, Kate (2007), "Globalising Justice within Coffee Supply Chains? Fair Trade, Starbucks and the Transformation of Supply Chain Governance," *Third World Quarterly*, 28 (4), 793–812.

[4] www.starbucks.com/responsibility/sourcing/coffee (April 15, 2016).

[5] McDonald, Kate (2007), "Globalising Justice within Coffee Supply Chains? Fair Trade, Starbucks and the Transformation of Supply Chain Governance," *Third World Quarterly*, 28 (4), 793–812.

FIGURE 10-1
Starbucks Shared Planet
program

The company takes stock of its greenhouse gas emissions and recognizes that 75 percent of its footprint is associated with electricity for stores, offices, and roasting plants; 24 percent is associated with store operations roasting; and has less than 1 percent is related to corporate jets and vehicles. It is also aggressive about post-consumer waste and significantly increased the amount of purchases that use reusable tumblers rather than paper products.[6]

The Starbucks example illustrates how companies can take command of their supply chains to deliver value to consumers. In this chapter, we examine the role of distribution as a central facet of efforts to achieve sustainability. Consistent with our focus on marketing as the means by which firms offer value to consumers, we focus in this chapter on the distribution function as the way by which the firm delivers value to consumers. We begin by defining supply chain management and discussing the value creating activities of firms in the supply chain. We then discuss sustainable supply chain management and design. We subsequently discuss the benefits and the challenges that firms face when they attempt to raise the sustainability of their distribution efforts.

SUPPLY CHAIN ESSENTIALS

Supply chains support virtually every marketing product delivery across industries. The supply chain for textbooks, for example, includes the timber industry, soybean farmers (who supply raw materials for ink), paper producers, ink manufacturers, printers, bookbinders, wholesalers, retailers, teachers, students, and recycling centers. An understanding of supply chains requires that one appreciate both the *organizations* involved in making a product available for sale as well as the *functions* performed by these organizations. An understanding of the functions performed within the chain is highly germane to efforts to raise sustainability. In efficient supply chains, these functions offer benefits to some member of the supply chain. As discussed in Chapter 1 in the treatment of the *triple bottom line*, these benefits may be associated with heightened economic, social, and financial performance. The sustainability of the organization, however, derives from the simultaneous pursuit of these alternative facets of performance in the triple bottom line. When one has an understanding of the benefits derived from each function, then one can work towards developing environmentally friendly supply channels that offer heightened benefits throughout the value chain.

In many industries, the functions performed within the channel are ascribed to specific organizations. For example, the auditing function to some degree is

---

[6] globalassets.starbucks.com/assets/ea2441eb7cf647bb8ce8bb40f75e267e.pdf (April 14, 2016).

FIGURE 10-2

Simplified supply chain for a bicycle.

Iron ore producer → Steel Manufacturer → Bicycle Manufacturer → Wholesaler → Retailer → Consumer

associated with accounting firms. Although in many cases one can eliminate an organization from the supply chain, one cannot eliminate the value derived from the activities performed by an organization. Thus, a textbook manufacturer may elect not to use retailers, but then the sale of books to students must be achieved via the Internet or other means. In the following section, we outline a series of activities performed in a supply chain, and we treat these entities as separate organizations. We present these activities as separate but recognize that in many cases one organization will elect to perform multiple functions in the supply chain. For example, Starbucks is a retailer that owns most of the supply chain from coffee bean processing to retail operations.[7]

Products and services pass through several organizations (suppliers, manufacturers, wholesalers, and retailers) before a consumer can purchase the product. For example, raw materials pass through six to 10 suppliers before reaching Ford Motor Company's manufacturing facilities.[8] The set of organizations linked directly to the flow of products from a source to the consumer is referred to as a *supply chain*.[9] Figure 10-2 displays a simplified supply chain for bicycles. Each member of the supply chain adds value. Raw material suppliers and components part manufacturers provide value by supplying materials and parts to the bicycle manufacturer. The bicycle manufacturer turns the raw materials and component parts into a product. A transportation intermediary takes the bicycle to wholesalers and retailers.

The retailer provides several value-added functions, including: 1) providing a wide selection of bicycles for consumers in one location, 2) breaking down bulk shipments from the manufacturers and offering bicycles in quantities that match consumers' purchasing patterns, 3) holding the bicycle until consumers are ready to purchase, and 4) other value-added services such as assembling the bicycle, providing credit, and having salespeople on hand to answer questions about the bicycles offered. The bicycle becomes more costly in each stage of the supply chain.

Supply chain management refers to a set of approaches that firms use to integrate their suppliers, manufacturers, warehouses, stores, and transportation intermediaries efficiently to ensure that the right product is at the right place in the right quantity when the consumer is ready to make a purchase.[10] Firms in a supply chain often work together to minimize system-level costs while still meeting the needs and the wants of the consumers. Traditionally, *efficiency* focused on cost savings, but more recently firms' supply chain management

---

[7] Macdonald, Kate (2007), "Globalising Justice within Coffee Supply Chains? Fair Trade, Starbucks and the Transformation of Supply Chain Governance," *Third World Quarterly*, 28 (4), 793–812.

[8] corporate.ford.com/microsites/sustainability-report-2013-14/supply-materials.html (April 15, 2016).

[9] Monczka, Robert, Robert Trent, and Robert Hadfield (2005), *Purchasing and Supply Chain Management*, Mason, OH: Thompson-Southwestern.

[10] Grewal, Dhruv, and Michael Levy (2014), *M: Marketing* (4th ed.). New York: McGraw-Hill.

efforts have shifted toward the triple bottom-line people, planet, and profits. Ford, for example, seeks to identify and work with suppliers who align with its policies concerning human rights and basic working conditions.[11] Furthermore, Ford encourages its suppliers to adopt and enforce similar policies with their suppliers and subcontractors.[12] In addition to the focus on people and basic human rights, there is an increased emphasis on environmental outcomes.[13]

SUSTAINABLE SUPPLY CHAIN MANAGEMENT

Sustainable supply chain management (SSCM) is "the strategic, transparent integration and achievement of an organization's social, environmental, and economic goals in the systemic coordination of key interorganizational business processes for improving the long-term economic performance of the individual company and its supply chains."[14] SSCM extends the traditional concept of supply chain management by integrating environmental and social concerns into the planning, development, and operations of the supply chain.[15] The goal of SSCM is to reduce materials flow and the negative, unintended consequences of production and consumption processes.[16]

Supply chain managers are in a key position to influence not only the financial performance of a firm but also the environmental and social performance. They do so through their decisions related to supplier selection, modal and carrier selection, vehicle routing, location decisions, and packaging choices.[17] The ISO 14000 standards outlined in Appendix 7 describe a firm's policies and approaches to achievement of sustainable triple bottom-line performance. They underscore the need to consider each facet of performance. Focusing solely on financial outcomes (e.g., lower costs or higher profitability) may lead to decisions that adversely affect environmental and social performance. Pharmaceutical companies, for example, are increasingly sourcing active and inactive ingredients

---

[11] corporate.ford.com/microsites/sustainability-report-2013-14/supply-materials.html (April 15, 2016).

[12] corporate.ford.com/microsites/sustainability-report-2013-14/blueprint-governance-sustainability-policy.html (April 15, 2016).

[13] knowledge.wharton.upenn.edu/special-report/greening-the-supply-chain-best-practices-and-future-trends/ (April 15, 2016).

[14] www.sustainable-supplychain.com/sscm.php (April 15, 2016).

[15] Wittstruck, David, and Frank Teuteberg (2011), "Development and simulation of a balanced scorecard for sustainable supply chain management–a system dynamics approach," 10th International Conference on Wirtschaftsinformatik; and Ahi, Payman, and Cory Searcy (2013), "A Comparative Literature Analysis of Definitions for Green and Sustainable Supply Chain Management." *Journal of Cleaner Production*, (52), 329–341.

[16] Genovese, Andrea, Adolf A. Acquaye, Alejandro Figueroa, and S. C. Lenny Koh (2015), "Sustainable Supply Chain Management and the Transition Towards a Circular Economy: Evidence and Some Applications," *Omega* (2015).

[17] Carter and Rogers (2011), "Sustainable Supply Chain Management: Evolution and Future Directions." *International Journal of Physical & Logistics Management*, 41(1), 46–62.

from emerging economies where costs are lower, particularly for generic drugs.[18] Global sourcing of these ingredients bolsters financial performance, but the long supply chain negatively affects environment performance.

Lax regulations in emerging countries may also result in a high level of pharmaceutical pollution during the production process.[19] This pollution has a negative social impact; the release of antibiotics into the environment through mismanagement in factories is cited as one of the main reasons for antimicrobial resistance (i.e., antibiotic medications become less effective with more exposure to them).[20] A long supply chain, with sourcing, manufacturing, packaging, and distribution in different locations, globally increases the risks of product contamination.[21] In 2008, a contaminated blood thinner from China, which resulted in 81 deaths in the United States, was discovered in drug supplies in 11 different countries.[22] Given the implications of their decisions, the triple bottom line is guiding more and more supply chain manager decisions.

As this pharmaceutical example illustrates, supply chain managers should consider financial, environmental, and social performance in evaluating their supply chain decisions. Two related and prominent strategies used in sustainable supply chains are reducing material inputs and deployment of innovative technologies.

Reducing Material Inputs

Dematerialization, also referred to as *source reduction*, refers to the reduction of substance and material weight at the product or firm level.[23] The weight of an average automobile, for example, decreased by about 408 kilos (900 pounds) between 1975 and 1989.[24] The average weight of cell phones decreased from 298 grams (10.5 ounces) in the early 1990s to 113 grams (4 ounces) in 2005.[25] In recent years, cell phones have increased in size to provide a larger screen size. Despite increasing in size, the newer model cell phones tend to weigh less. For example, the iPhone 6 is a larger phone in terms of height and width compared to the iPhone 1, yet the iPhone 6 weighs 5 percent less than the original model

---

[18] dspace.lib.cranfield.ac.uk/bitstream/1826/7690/1/Product_safety_and_security.pdf (April 15, 2016).

[19] noharm-europe.org/articles/blog/europe/new-report-links-major-pharmaceutical-companies-global-rise-antibiotic (April 15, 2016).

[20] s3.amazonaws.com/s3.sumofus.org/images/BAD_MEDICINE_final_report.pdf (April 15, 2016).

[21] dspace.lib.cranfield.ac.uk/bitstream/1826/7690/1/Product_safety_and_security.pdf (April 15, 2016).

[22] www.nytimes.com/2008/04/22/health/policy/22fda.html?_r=0 (April 15, 2016).

[23] van den Bergh, Jeroen C. J. M., and Marco A. Janssen (2004). "The Interface between Economics and Industrial Ecology: A Survey," In Jeroen C. J. M. van den Bergh and Marco A. Janssen (Eds.), *Economics of Industrial Ecology: Materials, Structural Change, and Spatial Scales* (p. 13–54). Cambridge, MA: MIT Press.

[24] Frosch, Robert A., and Nicholas E. Gallopoulos (1989), "Strategies for Manufacturing," *Scientific American*, 261 (3), 144–152.

[25] Sullivan, Daniel E. (2006), "Recycled Cell Phones-A Treasure Trove of Valuable Metals," No. 2006-3097. *Geological Survey* (US).

FIGURE 10-3
Size of the iPhone 1 (2008)
compared to the iPhone 6
and 6 Plus (2014).[26]

(see Figure 10-3)[27]. These product-level examples illustrate the historical trend of producing smaller and lighter products over time. At the firm level, dematerialization refers to more material-efficient production processes and/or a shift to other materials (e.g., from steel to aluminum).[28]

Reducing material inputs is considered the most attractive waste management strategy since using materials in production processes is generally more detrimental to the environment than waste processing after consumption.[29] Reduction of inputs is a proactive approach to minimizing waste before production, whereas reuse and recycle are means of closing the loop once after production.

Innovative Technology

Several innovative technologies provide enormous opportunity to manage sustainable supply chains. Four technologies that influence operations include *routing and tracking computer systems*, *inventory management software*, *RFID*, and *GPS*.

Routing and Tracking Computer Systems. Advanced computing technology enables firms to optimize the returns from their supply chains. In the global courier services and shipping industry, United Parcel Service (UPS) faces a

---

[26] www.gizmag.com/iphone-1-vs-iphone-6-vs-iphone-6-plus/35856/.

[27] www.gizmag.com/iphone-1-vs-iphone-6-vs-iphone-6-plus/35856/.

[28] van den Bergh, Jeroen C. J. M., and Marco A. Janssen (2004). "The Interface between Economics and Industrial Ecology: A Survey," In Jeroen C. J. M. van den Bergh and Marco A. Janssen (Eds.), *Economics of Industrial Ecology: Materials, Structural Change, and Spatial Scales* (p. 13–54). Cambridge, MA: MIT Press.

[29] van den Bergh, Jeroen C. J. M., and Marco A. Janssen (2004), "The Interface between Economics and Industrial Ecology: A Survey," In Jeroen C. J. M. van den Bergh and Marco A. Janssen (Eds.), *Economics of Industrial Ecology: Materials, Structural Change, and Spatial Scales* (p. 13–54). Cambridge, MA: MIT Press

marketplace characterized by increased need for time-definite services.[30] UPS has expanded its reputation as a leading package distribution company by developing an equally strong capability as a mover of electronic information. The company has developed an information processing system designed to provide a competitive advantage in this challenging market[31]. UPS delivery specialists capture the signature of every package and document recipient using hand-held, pen-based custom computers. The system collects electronic data on over 9.5 million packages each day. The system has been designed in such a way to allow simple introduction of future technologies into the network. In addition, reporting capabilities provide the opportunity to deliver customized reports to UPS customers about their products and customers. The *routing and tracking computer system* has improved the company's efficiency and price competitiveness while simultaneously offering improved information handling and customer service.

Inventory Management Software. *Inventory management software* is a second innovative technology that provides a source of competitive advantage. Inventory represents a sizeable investment to many organizations. Money invested in inventory does not provide the return that is realized when this money is invested in a financial institution. Organizations, therefore, prefer to minimize the inventory to levels that meet the service expectations of customers. The cosmetics industry exemplifies a market characterized by highly volatile demand along with potential risks of inventory obsolescence and, simultaneously, out-of-stock conditions. Procter & Gamble markets Olay skin, CoverGirl cosmetics, Aussie shampoo, and many other products in this setting. Several years ago, the firm began implementing *multiechelon inventory* (MEI) tools designed to optimize inventory throughout the supply chain.[32] This MEI software has been designed to accommodate increasingly global supply chains, contract manufacturing, dynamic product life cycles, and multichannel distributions systems. This software incorporates mathematical models that enable managers to plan around complex market scenarios. The software uses probabilistic optimization techniques that identify demand and supply variability to make better decisions about inventory policy and strategy. The software has enabled P&G to work with suppliers to cut materials inventories and has enabled it to collaborate with customers to reduce retail inventories. These reductions have been implemented while improving materials and production planning along with improved responsiveness of the firm's manufacturing and distribution systems. Importantly, this system primarily focuses on the optimization of inventory rather than the reduction in inventory. In the initial installation at P&G, the Beauty Care division trimmed total

---

[30] Souza, Gilvan C. (2014), "Supply chain analytics," *Business Horizons* 57, (5), 595–605; and Alghalith, Nabil (2005), "Competing with IT: The UPS Case," *Journal of American Academy of Business*, Cambridge, 7 (2), 7–15.

[31] Chesbrough, Henry W. (2011), "Bringing Open Innovation to Services," *MIT Sloan Management Review* 52 (2), 85.

[32] Kerr, John (2008), "P&G Takes Inventory Up a Notch," *Logistics Management*, 47 (2), 24–26.

inventory by 3 to 7 percent while maintaining service levels greater than 99 percent. Net earnings increased by 13 percent, sales increased by 7 percent, and the number of inventory days on hand dropped by eight days. These results prompted P&G to implement the inventory management software across all of the firm's strategic business units.

Radio Frequency Identification. *Radio frequency identification* (RFID) is an innovative technology that has significant applications in supply chains and retailing.[33] The RFID technology consists of a radio frequency tag with a printed antenna and a radio frequency emitter/reader.[34] The signal from the tag provides a unique 96-bit product identification code. In contrast to bar codes, the RFID tag can be read without line-of-sight reading.

Some of the most insightful initial research on RFID was performed at the Auto-ID Center at MIT[35] by a consortium that included the Uniform Product Code, P&G, Gillette, Coca-Cola, the Department of Defense, and Wal-Mart. In manufacturing, these readers offer a number of benefits. The presence of these tags ensures that all items associated with an assembly are, in fact, present. Similarly, RFID readers simplify the process of confirming the accuracy of plant deliveries by eliminating the need to corroborate physical delivery of product with a driver's bill of lading. These systems also enable management to determine the appropriate positioning of product in storage. For example, out-of-stock items that arrive at the loading dock can be immediately positioned on the assembly line to increase manufacturing throughput. Because the devices do not require line of sight to read the contents of a container, the warehousing of inventory can be performed with considerable flexibility. RFID devices also provide the ability to identify compatibility issues between two chemical reagents and, therefore, allow warehousing staff to store such products in separate locations. The tracking capability of RFID also reduces the potential for employee theft by identifying any item leaving a distribution facility.

The RFID readers also offer a number of important benefits to retailers, and the importance of these benefits is reflected in Wal-Mart's 2005 decision to require its top 100 vendors to implement RFID chips.[36] This technology enables retailers to allocate inventory accurately among various locations in the store and price products variably based on their location. Thus, refrigerated soft drinks could be priced higher than those located on normal shelves. In addition, because the products each possess information that links the date sold with the date of delivery, retailers can be more focused in their efforts to rotate stock in their stores.

[33] Rutner, Stephen, Matthew A. Waller, and John T. Mentzer (2004), "A Practical Look at RFID," *Supply Chain Management Review*, 8 (1), 36–41.

[34] Vandenbosch, Mark, and Niraj Dawar (2002), "Beyond Better Products: Capturing Value in Customer Interactions," *MIT Sloan Management Review*, 43 (4), 35–42.

[35] Schwartz, Ephraim (2003), "RFID About to Explode," *InfoWorld*, 25 (5), 28–29.

[36] Rutner, Stephen, Matthew A. Waller, and John T. Mentzer (2004), "A Practical Look at RFID," *Supply Chain Management Review*, 8 (1), 36–41.

The ability to track products also provides the opportunity to reduce shrinkage at the retail level.[37]

The implementation of RFID technology has strong implications for the supply chain.[38] The information enables firms to lower costs through process improvements. The retailer can use the RFID technology to develop its own category management system without the aid of manufacturers. The retailer can also use this information to negotiate higher compensation for obsolescence and spoilage, and it can be used to urge manufacturers to develop retail-ready displays. These displays fuel additional costs to manufacturers and lower the product stocking cost to retailers.

Global positioning systems. *Global positioning systems* (GPS) represent another technology that has the potential to transform logistics. GPS is a U.S. radio-navigation system that provides free positioning, navigation, and timing service on a continuous worldwide basis. GPS consists of satellites orbiting the Earth, control and monitoring stations on Earth, and GPS receivers owned by users. The satellites broadcast signals from space that are picked up and identified by GPS receivers. Each receiver provides the location (latitude, longitude, and altitude) plus the time.[39]

Two primary benefits of GPS in the supply chain involve the ability to monitor delivery drivers and their vehicles. GPS allows managers to track every vehicle in their fleet at any given moment. Managers can determine driver safety, location, and speed at any time during a route. In addition, GPS ensures that the most optimal routing is taken, resulting in more efficient use of gasoline and diesel. The tracking units also enable managers to assess vehicle performance. Management can determine whether the optimal speed, tire air pressure, and others factors are in place that affect fuel usage.[40]

SUSTAINABLE SUPPLY CHAIN DESIGN

Supply chains have traditionally been examined as linear models, starting with the extraction of raw materials and ending with the sale and distribution of goods to the end consumer (see Figure 10-2).[41] This linear take-make-dispose model relies on constant input of virgin natural resources and unlimited capacity for

[37] Howell, Sydney D., and Nathan C. Proudlove (2007), "A statistical Investigation of Inventory Shrinkage in a Large Retail Chain," *International Review of Retail, Distribution & Consumer Research*, 17 (2), 101–120.

[38] Miraldes, Tatiana, Susana Garrido Azevedo, Fernando Bigares Charrua-Santos, Luís António F. Mendes, and João Carlos Oliveira Matias (2015), "IT Applications in Logistics and Their Influence on the Competitiveness of Companies/Supply Chains," *Annals of the Alexandru Ioan Cuza University-Economics* 62 (1), 121–146.

[39] www.gps.gov/ (April 15, 2016).

[40] Colwell, Stephen (2008), "Go Green with GPS," *GPS World*, 19 (10), 30–31.

[41] Geyer, Roland, and Tim Jackson (2004), "Supply Loops and their Constraints: The Industrial Ecology of Recycling and Reuse," *California Management Review*, 46 (2): 55–73.

waste and emissions.[42] The resource flows into and out of such linear systems are large and impose large environmental costs.[43] The linear model leads to the deterioration of the environment in two ways. First, it removes natural capital from the environment. Second, it reduces the value of the natural capital due to pollution caused by the waste.[44] For example, pollution decreases soil fertility and soil yield. Furthermore, the nutritional levels of fruits and vegetables grown in the soil are lower.[45]

Although there are still opportunities to increase cost efficiency in the linear models, the gains are incremental and insufficient to gain a competitive advantage.[46] Moreover, the linear paradigm is facing increasing pressure as resource prices continue to increase.[47] Value creation becomes increasingly difficult under such conditions. As a result, firms have turned to reducing, reusing, and recycling to transform their supply chains and bolster value creation.

Reuse is a generic term for product recovery, whereas *recycling* is the reuse of materials derived from used products or components.[48] More specifically, recycling entails material recovery without conserving any product structures. Reuse is preferred over recycling in the waste hierarchy since it offers environmental benefits through displaced production; reusing a product replaces new products that would require more resources (e.g., water, energy, timber, petroleum, and other limited natural resources) to manufacture them.[49] Further, reuse generally requires less physical and chemical processing than recycling and thus uses less energy and creates fewer environmental burdens.[50]

[42] Geyer, Roland, and Tim Jackson (2004, p. 56), "Supply Loops and Their Constraints: The Industrial Ecology of Recycling and Reuse," *California Management Review*, 46 (2): 55–73.

[43] Graedel, T. E., and Braden R. Allenby (2010), *Industrial Ecology and Sustainable Engineering*. Upper Saddle River, NJ: Pearson Education.

[44] Murray, Alan, Keith Skene, and Kathryn Haynes (2015), "The Circular Economy: An Interdisciplinary Exploration of the Concept and Application in a Global Context," *Journal of Business Ethics*, 1–12.

[45] www.conserve-energy-future.com/causes-and-effects-of-soil-pollution.php (April 15, 2016).

[46] www.ellenmacarthurfoundation.org/publications/towards-a-circular-economy-business-rationale-for-an-accelerated-transition (April 15, 2016).

[47] Preston, Felix (2012), "A Global Redesign? Shaping the Circular Economy." *Energy, Environment and Resource Governance* (March 2012). Chatham House briefing paper.

[48] Geyer, Roland, and Vered Doctori Blass (2010), "The Economics of Cell Phone Reuse and Recycling," *The International Journal of Advanced Manufacturing Technology*, 47 (5-8), 515–525; and Thierry, Matijn, Marc Salomon, Jo Van Nunen, and Luk Van Wassenhove. (1995, p. 120). Strategic Issues in Product Recovery. California Management Review, 37 (2): 114–135.

[49] Thomas, Valerie M. (2003, p. 66). Demand and Dematerialization Impacts on Second-hand Markets. *Journal of Industrial Ecology*, 7 (2): 65–78.

[50] van den Bergh, Jeroen C. J. M., and Marco A. Janssen (2004), "The Interface between Economics and Industrial Ecology: A Survey," In Jeroen C. J. M. van den Bergh and Marco A. Janssen (Eds.), *Economics of Industrial Ecology: Materials, Structural Change, and Spatial Scales* (p. 13–54). Cambridge, MA: MIT Press.

FIGURE 10-4

The recycled content in the interior of select Ford models.[51]

Vehicle	Material	Partner	Benefits
2015 Mustang base series	Seat fabric bolster: 54 percent recycled content from post-consumer and post-industrial recycle yarns.	Sage Automotive Interiors, Unifi	• Reduces consumer and industrial waste. • Reduces depletion of natural resources. • Reduces energy consumption. • Uses closed-loop system for recycling manufacturing waste.
	Seat fabric insert: 38 percent recycled content from post-industrial recycled yarns.	Sage Automotive Interiors	• Reduces waste. • Reduces depletion of natural resources.
2015 Ford Mustang 14/GT series	Seat fabric insert and bolster: 54 percent recycled content from post-consumer and post-industrial recycled yarns.	Sage Automotive Interiors, Unifi	• Reduces consumer and industrial waste. • Reduces depletion of natural resources. • Reduces energy consumption. • Uses closed-loop system for recycling manufacturing waste.
2015 Ford F-150 XL series	Seat fabric insert bolster: 54 percent recycled content from post-consumer and post-industrial recycled yarns.	Sage Automotive Interiors, Unifi	• Reduces consumer and industrial waste. • Reduces depletion of natural resources. • Reduces energy consumption. • Uses closed-loop system for recycling manufacturing waste.
	Seat fabric insert: 25 percent recycled content from post-industrial recycled yarns.	Aunde	• Reduces waste. • Reduces depletion of natural resources.
2015 Ford F-150 XLT series	Seat fabric bolster: 33 percent recycled content from post-consumer and post-industrial recycled yarns.	Sage Automotive Interiors, Unifi	• Reduces consumer and industrial waste. • Reduces depletion of natural resources. • Reduces energy consumption. • Uses closed-loop system for recycling manufacturing waste.

---

[51] corporate.ford.com/microsites/sustainability-report-2013-14/environment-products-materials-choosing.html.

2012 Ford Focus electric	Seat fabric: 100 percent recycled content from post-consumer and post-industrial recycled yarns.	Unifi, Sage Automotive Interiors	• Uses material from approximately 22 recycled plastic bottles in each vehicle. • Reduces consumer waste to landfill. • Reduces depletion of natural resources.
2011-12 Ford Fiesta (North America)	Seat fabric: 25 percent post-consumer recycled yarns	Aunde	• Reduces consumer waste. • Reduces depletion of natural resources.
	Nonwoven headliner: 75 percent post-consumer recycled yarns.	Freudenberg	• Reduces consumer waste. • Reduces depletion of natural resources.
	Carpet: 100 percent recycled content from post-consumer and post-industrial recycled yarns.	Peltzer	• Reduces waste, energy consumption, and depletion of natural resources.

Many companies are creating value by incorporating reused and recycled materials into their supply chains. Ford, for example, uses a hybrid fiber made from recycled plastic bottles and post-industrial waste for seating fabric[52] in 15 vehicle lines.[53] It estimates that it saves $10 million annually (in North America) and diverts 2 million plastic bottles from going into landfills by using the recycled fabric. Figure 10-4 highlights some other benefits of using recycled material in Ford's vehicle lines.

A *closed-loop cycle or system* is one where waste is continually reused and recycled back into the system rather than dissipated into the environment.[54] Some waste can be recycled into new materials without losing any of its quality or purity (e.g., glass), but many recycled materials are of lower quality than the original material.[55] This reduction in product value is referred to as *downcycling*.[56] As a result of downcycling, these materials will eventually be discarded from the loop as waste. An *open-looped system* is one in which the waste cannot be continually recycled back into system as useable resources.[57]

[52] corporate.ford.com/microsites/sustainability-report-2013-14/environment-products-materials-choosing.html.

[53] www.thegreensupplychain.com/news/13-05-20-1.php?cid=7093.

[54] Frosch, Robert A., and Nicholas E. Gallopoulos (1989), "Strategies for Manufacturing," *Scientific American*, 261 (3), 144–152; and Garner, Andy, and Gregory A. Keoleian (1995). Industrial ecology: An introduction. Retrieved October 5, 2009, from: www.umich.edu/~nppcpub/resources/compendia/INDEpdfs/INDEintro.pdf.

[55] www.e-education.psu.edu/eme807/node/624.

[56] Braungart, M., McDonough, W., and Bollinger, A. (2007). "Cradle-to-cradle Design: Creating Healthy Emissions–A Strategy for Eco-Effective Product and System Design," *Journal of Cleaner Production*, 15(13), 1337–1348.

[57] www.e-education.psu.edu/eme807/node/624.

Waste is increasingly viewed as a potential new resource or by-product that our economy has not yet to learn to use efficiently.[58] Reusing and recycling not only reduces waste, but it also reduces natural resource depletion. A *closed-loop supply chain* is one in which the original manufacturer reclaims the product from customers for the recovery of added value by reusing some part or all of the product. An example of a closed-loop systems is Shaw Industries (see Figure 10-5). An *open-loop supply chain*, by contrast, involves materials recovered by parties other than the original manufacture who are capable of reusing or recycling these materials. Hence, the material is reclaimed and used in a different system (i.e., supply chain). Ford's use of recycled fabric (discussed above) is an example of an open-loop supply chain. Ford has four global suppliers of recycled fabric,[59] which is made from materials recovered from plastic bottled water.

Cradle-to-cradle logic takes the logic of closed-loop systems to a new level. As firms embrace triple bottom-line performance in their supply chains, their relationships with the environment becomes more central to managerial decision making. Firms replace a cradle-to-grave orientation with a cradle-to-cradle perspective driven by the synergistic pursuit of positive social, environmental, and economic goals.[60] Rather than merely closing the loop by reusing and recycling, cradle-to-cradle calls for the redesign of industrial processes altogether. Products that are not designed for reuse, for example, have lower material recovery rates since the product and/or its parts are often damaged during disassembly. When products are not designed for disassembly, remanufactures must use reverse engineering to generate disassembly sequences.[61] Reverse engineering is a time-consuming and costly process that does not achieve maximum yield due to parts damaged in the trial-and-error disassembly process.

The supply chains of Shaw Industries illustrate cradle-to-cradle logic. Shaw Industries reclaims and recycles approximately 100 million pounds of carpet each year. The company converts the materials back into carpet, into products for other industries, or into energy to power its own manufacturing operations.[62] In its marketing communications, Shaw Industries highlights its cradle-to-cradle process. It emphasizes that "Carpet produced today becomes more carpet tomorrow in an endless closed-loop cycle, without ever landing in a landfill."[63]

Cradle-to-cradle design enables firms to develop industrial process that turn materials into *nutrients* that flow within the biological and technical

[58] Huysman, Sofie, et al. (2010), "The Recyclability Benefit Rate of Closed-loop and Open-loop systems: A Case Study on Plastic Recycling in Flanders," *Resources, Conservation and Recycling* 101, 53–60; and Graedel, T. E., and Braden R. Allenby (2010), *Industrial Ecology and Sustainable Engineering.* Upper Saddle River, NJ: Pearson Education.

[59] www.thegreensupplychain.com/news/13-05-20-1.php?cid=7093.

[60] McDonough, William, and Michael Braungart (2010), *Cradle to Cradle: Remaking the Way We Make Things.* New York: North Point Press.

[61] Guide, V. Daniel R. Jr. (2000), "Production Planning and Control for Remanufacturing: Industry Practice and Research Needs," *Journal of Operations Management*, 18: 467–483.

[62] shawfloors.com/shaw-sustainability/post-consumer-carpet-recycling (April 15, 2016).

[63] www.shawcontractgroup.com/Html/MarketSegmentsWorkplace (April 15, 2016).

metabolism of a supply chain. *Biological nutrients* refer to natural or plant-based materials and their derivatives. The metabolism of these biological nutrients includes resource extraction, manufacturing, and customer use.[64] The metabolic process also includes procedures of returning these materials to natural systems where they can be transformed once again into resources for human activity. Products that are formed from biological nutrients are called *products of consumption*. Since these products are designed for living systems, they can be returned to the natural environment after use to become nutrients again for living systems. For example, The Saltwater Brewing Company uses beer by-products to make biodegradable beer rings that are environmentally safe and edible.[65]

Technical nutrients refer to material, frequently mineral or synthetic, that has the potential to remain safely in a closed-loop system of manufacture, recovery, and reuse. These nutrients can maintain their highest value through many product life cycles.[66] Since these nutrients render a service in the form of a durable good, they are referred to as *products of service*. For example, microchips used in mobile phones are products of service. The chips derived from used products can be reincorporated into new products. The manufacturer or commercial representative of the product also fosters long-term relationships with returning customers through many product life cycles.

In a cradle-to-cradle or circular economy, firms strive to maximize the life and utility of both products of consumption and products of service. The circular economy strives to create value through positive restoration and the design of self-sustaining production processes.[67] These supply and production processes should ideally have no net effect on the environment, meaning that they restore any damage done in resource acquisition and generate little to no waste.[68] The ultimate goal is to achieve growth through the circulation of resources so that the materials and energy are used over and over again in a closed-system, reducing the need for new raw material and energy inputs.[69]

---

[64] Braungart, Michael, William McDonough, and Andrew Bollinger (2007), "Cradle-to-cradle Design: Creating Healthy Emissions–A Strategy for Eco-effective Product and System Design," *Journal of Cleaner Production*, 15 (13), 1337–1348.

[65] www.huffingtonpost.com/entry/saltwater-brewery-edible-six-pack-rings-beer-plastic-marine-life_us_573b796ce4b0ef86171c5fe4 (June 7, 2016).

[66] Braungart, Michael, William McDonough, and Andrew Bollinger (2007), "Cradle-to-cradle Design: Creating Healthy Emissions–A Strategy for Eco-effective Product and System Design," *Journal of Cleaner Production*, 15 (13), 1337–1348.

[67] Genovese, A., A. A. Acquaye, A. Figueroa, and S. C. L. Koh (2015), "Sustainable supply chain management and the transition towards a circular economy: Evidence and some applications. *Omega*; and Murray, Alan, Keith Skene, and Kathryn Haynes (2015), "The Circular Economy: An Interdisciplinary Exploration of the Concept and Application in a Global Context." *Journal of Business Ethics*.

[68] Murray, Alan, Keith Skene, and Kathryn Haynes (2015), "The Circular Economy: An interdisciplinary exploration of the concept and application in a global context." *Journal of Business Ethics*.

[69] Genovese, A., A. A. Acquaye, A. Figueroa, and S. C. L. Koh (2015), "Sustainable Supply Chain Management and the Transition Towards a Circular Economy: Evidence and Some Applications. *Omega*.

A model circular economy is Kalundborg Symbiosis in Denmark. Kalundborg is an industrial ecosystem in which by-products or residual product of one firm are used as a resource by another enterprise, in a closed cycle.[70] This industrial ecosystem started over 40 years ago when Kalundborg's Statoil refinery agreed to provide excess butane gas to a neighboring gypsum wallboard manufacturer and exchange water with a power plant that was in close proximity. As new firms moved in, the sharing of resources and by-product exchange expanded, and over time, Kalundborg created a closed-loop system. In addition to reducing materials flow, Kalundborg reduced carbon dioxide emissions by 275,000 tons per year and saved 3 million cubic meters of water through reuse and recycling.[71]

The Kalundborg example illustrates consideration of the flows throughout a supply chain. Although logistics has traditionally been associated with the flow of goods toward consumption, *reverse logistics* that trace product back from the point of consumption have increasingly been addressed in supply chains.[72] The interest in reverse logistics has been prompted by concerns about returned goods, proper disposal of end-of-life products, production planning and inventory management, and supply chain management.[73] In 2005, the total cost of returns was estimated to be $100 billion, and roughly 70 percent of this merchandise was not defective but returned for some other reason (e.g., wrong color, size, minor package defect). Recognizing the high cost of returns, Wal-Mart set a goal to end defective product returns among its largest 1000 suppliers. The company uses onsite audits, enforcement of social and environmental standards, and the threat of lost business to support efforts to realize this goal.[74] Reverse logistics provides the opportunity to examine the influence of return goods, and it further provides the opportunity to determine the extent to which promotional campaigns, product life cycle issues, and retail inventory levels influence supply chain decisions.[75]

Given the magnitude of logistics and the effect of logistics management on the cost of operations, it is imperative that the firm view this function as a source of sustainable competitive advantage. Firms can achieve higher levels of efficiency by controlling the energy utilization at distribution and production centers. Enhanced efficiency is realized due to the use of advanced building materials. New construction that focuses on the design of air-tight facilities enables companies to limit waste associated with heat and cooling losses.[76] For example,

[70] www.symbiosis.dk/en (June 10, 2016).

[71] www.symbiosis.dk/en (June 10, 2016).

[72] Rogers, Dale, and Ronald S. Tibben-Lembke (1998), *Going Backwards: Reverse Logistics Trends and Practices*, 1998 (Reverse Logistics Executive Council: USA).

[73] Rubio, Sergio, Antonio Chamorro, and Francisco J. Miranda (2008), "Characteristics of the Research on Reverse Logistics (1995-2005)," *International Journal of Production Research*, 46 (4), 1099–1120.

[74] Hoffman, William (2008), "Reversing Returns," Traffic World, 272 (45), 16.

[75] Bernon, Michael, and John Cullen (2007), "An Integrated Approach to Managing Reverse Logistics," *International Journal of Logistics: Research and Applications*, 10 (1), 41–56.

[76] Trunick, Perry A. (2008), "Green is Good Business: In Logistics, Best Practice is Green," *Outsourced Logistics*, 1(6), 22–23. 77 Hoffman, William (2007), "The Greening of Logistics," *Traffic World*, 271 (25), 10–13.

in the United Kingdom, Prologis has developed a warehouse for Sainsbury, one of England's largest grocers. This facility features wall-mounted photovoltaic panels that generate electricity, solar walls that produce heat from sunlight, an on-site power plant that reuses the heat produced by air conditioning, an on-site recycling facility, energy efficient lighting, and air-tight construction that minimizes energy loss.

It is important to recognize that the ability of these third-party providers to raise sustainability is linked to the incentives and the monitoring practices implemented by retailers and manufacturers.[77] Firms increasingly will reward suppliers with additional business when they pursue these sustainability efforts. Former arms' length agreements are being replaced with joint process improvements whereby the manufacturer and the supplier collectively work to address the sustainability concerns in the supply chain. Manufacturers and retailers are asking suppliers to provide sustainability metrics and tracking this performance over time.

BENEFITS OF SUSTAINABLE SUPPLY CHAINS

There are several benefits associated with sustainable supply chain management,[78] including better working conditions, reduced turnover, improved product quality, improved efficiency and profitability, better management of risk, and enhanced brand reputation. Consider each in turn.

Better Working Conditions, Reduced Turnover, and Improved Product Quality

When an organization takes the time to investigate the firms and activities within its supply chain, it has the opportunity to identify the conditions under which raw materials are transformed into consumer products. For example, the Mayflower Vehicle System PLC is a Birmingham, England-based subcomponent assembler in the British auto industry.[79] In its analysis of the sustainability of operations, it addressed the waste associated with shop floor operations. Consideration of waste included defective parts, personal productivity, frequency of stock turns, delivery schedule achievement, equipment effectiveness, value added per person, and floor space utilization. Change agents realized that these waste reductions goals were more palatable to employees when the employees were endowed with a sense of ownership over processes and equipment associated with the jobs. Thus, the review of operations to achieve heightened levels of sustainability yielded better working conditions, a social facet of the triple bottom line.

---

[78] United Nations Environment Program (2008), *Unchaining Value: Innovative Approaches to Sustainable Supply*, Paris; United Nations Environmental Programme; and Willard, B. (2002) *The Sustainability Advantage: Seven Business Case Benefits of a Triple Bottom Line*, Gabriola Island, BC: New Society Publishers.

[79] Tilson, Barbara (2001), "Success and Sustainability in Automotive Supply Chain Improvement Programmes: A Case Study of Collaboration in the Mayflower Cluster," *International Journal of Innovation Management*, 5 (4), 427–456.

Better working conditions also produce economic returns in the forms of lower employees turnover and enhance product quality.[80]

Improved Efficiency and Profitability

The pursuit of sustainability in the delivery of value calls attention to the inputs and outputs associated with every level of the supply chain. By focusing on efforts to reduce inputs and maximize the productivity of outputs, the firm has tremendous opportunity to raise profitability. Packaging exemplifies several ways in which sustainability can influence profits. By employing efficient packaging, the firm reduces warehouse, distribution, and transportation costs. Efficiency can be achieved by lowering the amount of fiber in packaging via package designs that are lighter in weight and use less corrugated board. Efficiency can also be realized by using reusable packaging and through the automation of case forming and stretch-wrapping of pallets of materials. Another innovative example of packaging sustainability is in club stores such as Sam's Club. The packaging that is employed at such stores often functions as a shipping container and display package. Optimal packaging in these stores ensures defect-free delivery, enhanced shelf appeal, and lowered store waste. Together these benefits raise the productivity of retail space while simultaneously reducing overhead.

A critical look at the role of packaging must consider the overall supply chain rather than a single level of the distribution channel. The packaging needs of products vary based on whether rail or truck transportation are involved in moving product to its destination.[81] Truck-based transportation requires balanced, stackable pallets that maximize the use of trailer space. By contrast, secure and stable packaging is essential for the rigors of rail transportation. Stretch hoods that cover product on five sides provide a higher level of protection than the stretch wrap that secures only the sides of a pallet.

Supply chain managers recognize carton optimization and other freight packaging techniques limit packaging to minimal levels necessary to deliver product free of damage. Implementation of these strategies can yield savings of 10 to 50 percent of the total transportation and packaging cost. In addition, supply chain managers are increasingly re-using materials within the supply chain. For example, AmerisourceBergen, the medical supply company, saved thousands of dollars and cut 13,600 kilos (30,000 pounds) of paper boxes a year by reusing vendor supply boxes to ship orders.

The efficiency of the supply chain is also enhanced via fleet optimization. The costs associated with product transportation are extensive, and since most forms of transportation rely heavily on fossil fuels, this issue is highly germane to sustainability concerns. Organizations are making a host of efforts to curb this function carried out either within the firm or via third-party supplier. Importantly, optimization of the fleet cost is achieved by limiting the cost of transportation

---

[80] Griffeth, Rodger W., Peter W. Hom, and Stefan Gaertner (2000), "A Meta-Analysis of Antecedents and Correlates of Employee Turnover: Update, Moderator Tests, and Research Implications for the Next Millennium," *Journal of Management* 26 (3), 463–488; and Mas, Alexandre (2008), "Labour Unrest and the Quality of Production: Evidence from the Construction Equipment Resale Market," *Review of Economic Studies*, 75, 229–258.

[81] Bunker, Greg (2007), "Five Tips for Improving the Effectiveness and Efficiency of Your Logistics Operations," *Logistics Today*, 48 (9), 34-34.

travel as well as by limiting the amount of travel undertaken by these vehicles. For example, UPS implemented a system several years ago that trained drivers to map their routes to turn right whenever possible. This simple strategy saves fuel, reduces emissions, and yields safety advantages because drivers do not have to cross traffic. In addition, left turns require more idling time waiting for oncoming traffic, whereas right-on-red regulations help save fuel. UPS estimates that in 2007 the company saved 3.1 million gallons of fuel and eliminated 32,000 metric tons of emissions via the right turn policy.[82]

A second means by which to lower transportation costs is associated with the planning of the distribution function. When organizations take into consideration the relative location of the ultimate consumer and the firm's distribution centers, they can get aggressive about the costs to deliver product to consumers. For example, Procter & Gamble reassessed its staging and distribution costs and reduced the number of distribution centers by 200 locations.[83] In the process, the firm was able to deliver products to consumers in a more timely fashion.

Waste reductions also yield profitability. Prior to closing the loop, Wal-Mart spent $16 million a year to haul plastic waste from its stores to landfills. Wal-Mart now pelletizes the plastic waste and sells it back to its suppliers, adding $28 million a year to the firm's bottom line.[84] Given these numbers, it is not surprising that financial incentives is a major driver of greening the supply chain.[85]

Risk Management

Firms that understand their liabilities are better positioned to limit their exposure to risk. Risk refers to variations in possible outcomes and their likelihoods.[86] Assessment of liabilities includes analysis of supply chain disturbances and their negative consequences.[87] Lowered risk can be associated with cost avoidance, lower insurance premiums, reduced legal and regulatory costs, and preferred rates on loans.[88]

In the supply chain, risk emerges from value stream, asset considerations, interfirm networks, and macroenvironmental issues. Analysis of risk in the value stream takes into consideration the flow of materials, information, and money in the supply chain. Firms evaluate the sourcing and processing of products and by-products (including waste) by upstream partners in the value cycle. In addition, organizations also assess the consumption and post-consumption practices of consumers of their products. Asset considerations refer to conditions under which a firm invests in specific technologies that have limited use

[82] Long, Tom (2008), "Right Turns Make the Most Out of Gas," *Boston Globe* July 10.

[83] Hoffman, William (2007), "Logistics Redraws Efficiency," *Traffic World*, 271(51/52), 19–21.

[84] Plambeck, Erica, and Lyn Denend (2011), "The Greening of Wal-Marts' Supply Chain. . . Revisited" *Supply Chain Management Review* (Sept/Oct 2011).

[85] Chan, H. K., H. He, and W. Y. C. Wang (2012), "Green marketing and its impact on supply chain management in industrial markets," Industrial Marketing Management (41), 557–562.

[86] March, James G., and Shapira, Zur (1987), "Managerial Perspectives on Risk and Risk Taking," *Management Science*, 33, 1404–1418.

[87] Peck, H. (2006), "Reconciling Supply Chain Vulnerability, Risk and Supply Chain Management," *International Journal of Logistics: Research and Applications*, 9 (2), 127–142.

[88] Willard, B. (2002) *The Sustainability Advantage: Seven Business Case Benefits of a Triple Bottom Line*, Gabriola Island, BC: New Society Publishers.

outside of their intended purpose.[89] When organizations embrace global supply specialization of processes, they face greater risk associated with quality control and security of component supplies.[90] Interfirm networks call attention to the degree to which one is dependent on other organizations in the supply chain. When firms are highly dependent on other organizations, they face greater levels of risk that should be controlled via contracts or strong working relationships with stakeholders.

Enhanced Brand Reputation

Firms that invest in sustainable practices in the supply chain develop positive brand reputations that pay dividends in multiple relationships. For example, Cisco Systems has developed a strong reputation as an industry supply chain leader. In this firm's supply network, almost 90 percent of the production is delivered by someone other than a Cisco employee.[91] Its proactive approach to the supply chain fosters strong working relationships with a few suppliers. Its supply strategy also involves listening carefully to customer requests, monitoring technological advancements, and offering customers a range of options.

Stakeholder Returns Increased

Organizations that focus on the triple bottom line have the ability to anticipate and monitor risk associated with economic, social, and environmental returns. By engaging dialogue with both upstream partners and downstream consumers, Cisco has been able to establish strong interfirm relationships. In addition, it is able to maintain a very low level of turnover in volatile high technology markets.[92] Consequently, this firm (and firms that nurture strong supply chains) are more attractive to investors because they are better equipped to manage these multiple facets of risk better than their competitors.[93] Attention to supply chain sustainability also reduces the likelihood of a firm encountering criticism or other reprisals from NGOs and communities.

Enhanced Customer Service

Due to experience with a variety of users and applications, third-party logistics agents can optimize distribution networks and consolidate routes. Importantly, third-party vendors that approach the supply chain as a chain of events—rather than discrete processes—can provide synergy to distribution by focusing efforts on maximizing throughout to end users. Manufacturers enjoy lowered greater

---

[89] Williamson, Oliver E. (1985), *The Economic Institutions of Capitalism*, New York: The Free Press.

[90] de Man, Reinier, and Tom R. Burns (2006), "Sustainability: Supply chains, Partner Linkages, and New Forms of Self-regulation," *Human Systems Management*, 25 (1), 1–12.

[91] Corrales, Eugenia (2007), "Cisco Builds a Supply Chain," *World Trade*, 20 (3), 34–40.

[92] O'Reilly, Charles A., and Jeffrey Pfeffer (2000), "Cisco Systems: Acquiring and Retaining Talent in Hypercompetitive Markets," *Human Resource Planning*, 23(3), 38–52.

[93] Galea, Claire (2008), "Selling Sustainability," *Money Management*, 22 (24), 14–15; and Blanchard, David (2009), "Green is the New Black," Industry Week/IW, 258 (3), 46–47.

product availability rates, improved order accuracy, and fewer customer complaints. These activities enhance the level of customer service and preclude the firm from engaging in special deliveries and other accommodations associated with inefficiency. Collectively, this enhanced customer service lowers the environmental influence of the entire supply chain.[94]

CHALLENGES FACING SUSTAINABLE SUPPLY CHAIN MANAGEMENT

The pursuit of triple bottom-line performance has repercussion for members of the supply chain. Notable challenges that firms face include efficiency trade-offs (doing more for less) and the costs associated with closing the loop.

Doing More with Less Equals Less for Some

Of course, efforts to enhance the efficiency have repercussions for members of the supply chain. Firms have an incentive to reduce their material input, but they also have an incentive to increase their material output.[95] A systems approach (versus a linear approach) highlights the inherent problem in supply chains: a reduction in material input for one channel member will adversely affect the material output of another supply chain member. Furthermore, a reduction in material input resulting from a new production technology or product design will theoretically increase the supply of the material, which in turn, will put downward pressure on the price of the material.[96] The lower price charged by the material suppliers may increase the use of the material or stimulate new uses of the material. A reduction in material input can result in a counterproductive increase in demand for the material.[97] This *rebound effect* occurs when improvements in material efficiency are offset by increased demand and use of the material.[98] Research suggests that increased demand per capita overcompensates for efficiency gains in every case (e.g., steel, computer chips, or wood products) they have investigated.[99]

---

[94] Blanchard, David (2007), "Making Effective Use of 3PLs," *Industry Week*, (June), 78–80.

[95] Jackson, Tim, and Roland Clift (1998). "Where's the Profit in Industrial Ecology?" *Journal of Industrial Ecology*, 2 (1): 3–5.

[96] Greening, Lorna A., David L. Greene, and Carmen Difiglio (2000), "Energy Efficiency and Consumption—The Rebound Effect—A Survey," *Energy Policy*, 28: 389–401.

[97] Ayres, Robert U., Leslie W. Ayres, and Benjamin Warr (2004), "Is the U.S. Economy Dematerializing? Main Indicators and Drivers," In Jeroen C. J. M. van den Bergh and Marco A. Janssen (Eds.), *Economics of Industrial Ecology: Materials, Structural Change, and Spatial Scales* (p. 57–93). Cambridge, MA: MIT Press.

[98] van der Voet, Ester, Lauran van Oers, and Igor Nikolic (2005), "Dematerialization: Not Just a Matter of Weight," *Journal of Industrial Ecology*, 8 (4): 121–137.

[99] Ayres, Robert U., Leslie W. Ayres, and Benjamin Warr (2004), "Is the U.S. Economy Dematerializing? Main Indicators and Drivers," In Jeroen C. J. M. van den Bergh and Marco A. Janssen (Eds.), *Economics of Industrial Ecology: Materials, Structural Change, and Spatial Scales* (p. 57–93). Cambridge, MA: MIT Press.

Alternatively, the supplier may attempt to reduce its costs and thus preserve its profit margin by decreasing the quality of its materials or component parts. Quality shirking may lead to increased scrap or waste throughout the channel. A vinyl supplier facing decreasing demand, for example, may provide lower quality vinyl to automobile manufacturers. The lower quality vinyl may create more scrap material in the manufacturing process. As a result, a larger quantity of lower quality vinyl is needed to produce the same amount of output as a higher quality vinyl.

The High Costs of Closing the Loop

As mentioned, reuse and recycling (henceforth, referred to collectively as reuse) are means to close the loop once waste has been created. Some firms in a supply chain may be reluctant to close the loop for several reasons. First, it may be too costly to acquire products leaving the use phase. Access to end-of-use products requires *reverse channels of distribution*—channels in which the consumers become the producers and vice versa.[100] Reverse channels face a higher level of uncertainty than their forward counterparts.[101] Producers using reused products or materials face uncertainty from the supply side and the demand side.[102] The supply of used products and materials is limited by sales of the products in the previous periods and the timing of returns.[103] Uncertain supply, which is further exacerbated by the varying levels of quality of the returned or used products, may require companies to keep larger (and more expensive) inventories to guarantee availability when needed.[104]

To realize the benefits of reuse, companies must learn to manage the supply of used products.[105] Used products, therefore, often have to be collected from many widespread sources, making it costlier to accumulate and transport the products back to the manufacturer.[106] Sourced from individual consumers or

[100] Ginter, Peter M., and Jack M. Starling (1978), "Reverse Distribution Channels for Recycling," *California Management Review*, 20 (3): 72–82.

[101] Fleischmann, Mortiz, Hans Ronald Krikke, Rommert Dekker, and Simme Douwe P. Flapper (2000), A characterisation of logistics networks for product recovery. *OMEGA The International Journal of Management Science*, 28, 653–666.

[102] van der Laan, Erwin, Marc Salomon, Rommert Dekker, Luk Van Wassenhove (1999), "Inventory Control in Hybrid Systems with Remanufacturing," *Management Science*, 45 (5), 733–747.

[103] van der Laan, Erwin, Marc Salomon, Rommert Dekker, Luk Van Wassenhove (1999), "Inventory Control in Hybrid Systems with Remanufacturing," *Management Science*, 45 (5), 733–747; and Guide, V. Daniel R. Jr. (2000), "Production Planning and Control for Remanufacturing: Industry Practice and Research Needs," *Journal of Operations Management*, 18, 467–483.

[104] Guide, V. Daniel R. Jr. (2000), "Production Planning and Control for Remanufacturing: Industry Practice and Research Needs," *Journal of Operations Management*, 18, 467–483; and Thierry, Matijn, Marc Salomon, Jo Van Nunen, and Luk Van Wassenhove (1995), "Strategic Issues in Product Recovery," *California Management Review*, 37 (2), 114–135.

[105] Guide, V. Daniel R. Jr., Ruud H. Teunter, and Luk N. Van Wassenhove (2003), "Matching Demand and Supply to Maximize Profits from Remanufacturing," *Manufacturing & Service Operations Management*, 5 (4): 303–316.

[106] Fleischmann, Mortiz, Hans Ronald Krikke, Rommert Dekker, and Simme Douwe P. Flapper (2000), "A Characterisation of Logistics Networks for Product Recovery," *OMEGA The International Journal of Management Science*, 28: 653–666.

intermediaries, used products must be generated in sufficient quantities to be worthy of recovery.[107] In fact, identifying sources of sufficient quantities of used products is a major acquisition management problem.[108]

Second, it may be too costly to reprocess the product or extract its materials. Reuse may entail minor repairs to complete remanufacturing, with the latter requiring more disassembly and reassembly.[109] In many cases, it takes considerable time for a remanufacturer to reverse engineer the disassembly sequence, costing the company thousands of dollars per product. Products that are not designed for reuse have lower material recovery rates since the product and/or its parts are often damaged during disassembly.[110] Specialized investments may also be needed for extraction and/or reprocessing. Sand recycling and carpet reprocessing, for example, require substantial investments in advanced technological equipment.[111]

Third, there may be a limited market for the used product or materials. Finding markets for used products or materials can be very difficult. The acceptance of used products depends on the differences in perceived quality and costs between used and virgin products or materials.[112] Many reused materials lose quality in reprocessing (e.g., fiberglass, plastics, or paper)[113] and/or do not last as long as virgin materials.[114] Even when the quality is not compromised, perceived quality of the reprocessed products or materials may limit their use.[115] One copy machine manufacturer, for example, had to convince it customers that the machines with the recycled materials still met all requirements with respect to product quality.[116] Another company had to limit the amount of recycled corrugated boxes it used to ship component parts because of customer concerns about lower quality.[117]

---

[107] Barnes Jr., James (1982), "Recycling: A Problem in Reverse Logistics," *Journal of Macromarketing*, 2 (2), 31–37.

[108] Guide, V. Daniel R. Jr. (2000), "Production Planning and Control for Remanufacturing: Industry Practice and Research Needs," *Journal of Operations Management*, 18, 467–483.

[109] Thierry, Matijn, Marc Salomon, Jo Van Nunen, and Luk Van Wassenhove (1995), "Strategic Issues in Product Recovery," *California Management Review*, 37 (2): 114–135.

[110] Guide, V. Daniel R. Jr. (2000), "Production Planning and Control for Remanufacturing: Industry Practice and Research Needs," *Journal of Operations Management*, 18, 467–483.

[111] Fleischmann, Mortiz, Hans Ronald Krikke, Rommert Dekker, and Simme Douwe P. Flapper (2000), "A Characterisation of Logistics Networks for Product Recovery," *OMEGA The International Journal of Management Science*, 28, 653–666.

[112] Thierry, Matijn, Marc Salomon, Jo Van Nunen, and Luk Van Wassenhove (1995), "Strategic Issues in Product Recovery," *California Management Review*, 37 (2): 114–135.

[113] Geyer, Roland, and Tim Jackson (2004), "Supply Loops and Their Constraints: The Industrial Ecology of Recycling and Reuse," *California Management Review*, 46 (2): 55–73.

[114] Bloemhof-Ruwaard, J. M., L. N. Van Wassenhove, H. L. Gabel, and P. M. Weaver (1996), "An Environmental Life Cycle Optimization Model for the European Pulp and Paper Industry," *Omega, The International Journal of Management Science*, 24 (6): 615–629.

[115] Matthews, B. Scott. (2004). Thinking Outside 'The Box': Designing a Packaging Takeback System. *California Management Review*, 46 (2): 105–119.

[116] Thierry, Matijn, Marc Salomon, Jo Van Nunen, and Luk Van Wassenhove (1995), "Strategic Issues in Product Recovery," *California Management Review*, 37 (2): 114–135.

[117] Matthews, B. Scott. (2004). Thinking Outside 'The Box': Designing a Packaging Takeback System. *California Management Review*, 46 (2): 105–119.

Fourth, product displacement may also be a concern of some members of the supply chain. The environmental cost of continuing to use an old product is small compared to the net environmental impact of disposal of the old product and manufacture and use of a new model of the same product. As a result, the primary environmental benefit from reuse and recycling is the displacement of primary production.[118] The sale of used products may cannibalize sales of new products. Internet sales of used books, for example, decrease demand for new books.[119] Similarly, used clothing exports reduce sales for new clothing in the receiving countries.[120] In addition, second-hand markets can reduce profitability of a monopoly sellers and firms with substantial market power.[121] Because the price of used products on the second-hand market limits the price firms can charge for their new units, firms with market power have some incentive to build less durability into the product[122] and, in some cases, eliminate the second-hand market.[123] High displacement rates (actual or perceived) generate strong economic disincentives for manufacturers of new products and raw materials to support closed-loop systems.[124]

---

[118] Thomas, Valerie M. (2003), "Demand and Dematerialization Impacts on Second-hand Markets," *Journal of Industrial Ecology*, 7 (2): 65–78.

[119] Kirkpatrick, David D. (2002), "Online Sales of Used Books Draw Protest," *The New York Times*, April 10, Section C:1.

[120] Thomas, Valerie M. (2003), "Demand and Dematerialization Impacts on Second-hand Markets," *Journal of Industrial Ecology*, 7 (2): 65–78.

[121] Benjamin, Daniel K., and Roger C. Kormendi (1974), The interrelationship between the markets for new and used durable goods. *Journal of Law and Economics, 17* (October): 381–401; and Waldman, Michael (1996), Durable goods pricing when quality matters. *Journal of Business*, 69 (4): 489–510.

[122] Waldman, Michael (1996), "Durable Goods Pricing when Quality Matters," *Journal of Business*, 69 (4): 489–510.

[123] Rust, John. (1986), "When Is it Optimal to Kill off the Market for Used Durable Goods?" *Econometrica*, 54 (1), 65–86.

[124] Geyer, Roland, and Vered Doctori Blass (2009), The economics of cell phone reuse and recycling. Retrieved November 1, 2009, from: www.bren.ucsb.edu/academics/courses/289/Readings/Geyer%20&%20Doctori%20Blass%202009.pdf.

Introduction

The goal of this chapter has been to examine the role of supply chains in a firm's efforts to achieve sustainability. We begin by defining supply chain management and discussing the value creating activities of firms in the supply chain. We then discuss sustainable supply chain management and design. We subsequently discussion of benefits and challenges that firms face when they attempt to raise the sustainability of their distribution efforts.

Supply Chain Essentials

Our reporting of supply chain essential highlighted the number of entities involved in a supply chain and the functions they perform. Management of supply chains must assess how to design and implement manufacturing and distribution systems that maximize desired performance.

Sustainable Supply Chain Management

We presented supply chains as the entities associated with yielding environmental, social, and economic value from resource procurement through resource processing, consumption, and post-consumption. This approach calls for understanding of the input-output process at each stage of the supply chain as well as an understanding of the value chain. The input-output process presumes that at each level of the supply chain engages in some sort of processing that yields products and by-products.

Sustainable Supply Chain Design

Sustainable supply chain design moves the firm from a static, linear approach to the supply chain to one that focuses on resource flows throughout the system. As firms move from linear supply chains to cradle-to-cradle systems, they increase their efforts to achieve triple bottom-line performance.

Benefits of Sustainable Supply Chains

Sustainable supply cycles offer benefits that include better working conditions, reduced turnover, and improved product quality. In addition, these supply cycles yield improved efficiency and profitability, better management of risk, enhanced brand reputations, and increased stakeholder returns.

Challenges Facing Sustainable Supply Chain Management

The pursuit of triple bottom-line performance produces challenges for supply chain management. Firms throughout the supply chain must account for efficiency trade-offs that enable firms to do more for less. They also face several costs, including used product acquisition costs, product reprocessing costs, product utility assessment costs, and product cannibalization costs.

KEY TERMS

supply chain	radio frequency identification	cradle-to-cradle
supply chain management	global positioning systems	biological nutrients
sustainable supply chain management	reuse	products of consumption
	recycling	products of consumption
dematerialization	closed-loop cycle or system	products of service
routing and tracking computer system	downcycling	reverse logistics
	closed-loop supply chain	rebound effect
inventory management software	open-loop supply chain	reverse channels of distribution

DISCUSSION QUESTIONS

1. To what extent does the Starbucks' sourcing strategy enable it to secure long-term commitments from suppliers and consumers?

2. What is the ultimate source for resources entering a supply chain? How does this differ from the output of the supply chain?

3. Why is it necessary for firms to assess the by-products of their supply chains?

4. Why would a manufacturer take time to learn about Wal-Mart's supply chains even though it does not do business directly with the retailer?

5. What is downcycling, and why is it relevant to assessing sustainability in the supply cycle?

6. What benefits can a company realize from incorporating RFID technology into the supply chain?

7. How can GPS technology enable a firm to lower its distribution costs?

8. How do relationships with suppliers and customers benefit from sustainable supply chains?

9. What are the consequences of improvements in material efficiency in a supply chain?

10. Provide an example of a supply chain's biological and technical nutrients. What products do these nutrients provide?

Delivering Value in Retailing

INTRODUCTION

IKEA

In 2007, IKEA began offering premium parking for consumers who drive hybrids or other highly fuel efficient automobiles to one of its Canadian stores.[1] The company subsequently began providing premium parking at all 11 locations in Canada and later added this amenity to its stores in the United States.[2] The parking spots are located near handicapped and family parking areas at the entrance of IKEA stores. Green signage at ground and eye levels reminds drivers of the preferred spaces (see Figure 11-1).

FIGURE 11-1

Reserved parking for hybrid vehicles at IKEA.[3]

[1] CBCNEWS.CA (2007), "Ikea to introduce anti-idling program, hybrid preferential parking," *CBCNEWS.CA*, www.cbc.ca/consumer/story/2007/05/10/ikea-hybrid.html (September 15, 2009).

[2] Galbraith, Kate (2009), "Priority Parking for Hybrids?" http://greeninc.blogs.nytimes.com/2009/07/14/priority-parking-for-hybrids/ (February 9, 2017).

[3] www.greencarreports.com/news/1058561_attention-shoppers-infiniti-qx56s-diesels-are-not-hybrids (February 9, 2017).

The subtle incentive behind this simple parking plan is to reward consumers for acting in a sustainable manner. Founded by Ingvar Kamprad in Agunnaryd, Sweden, in 1943, IKEA's business philosophy is to offer a wide range of products of quality design and function at prices that enable the majority of people to afford them. Today IKEA is a leading home furnishings retailer with 389 stores in 46 countries worldwide. Each year, IKEA stores receive more than 915 million visitors.[4] IKEA has grown into a major retail experience with 183,000 co-workers and annual sales of more than 36.4 billion euros ($38.9 billion).

IKEA's decision to provide premium parking to hybrid vehicles is part of its environmental commitment to finding business solutions that have an overall positive influence on the people and the communities in which it operates.

Sustainable retailing is at the center of this company's mission and operations.[5] This commitment is reflected in the firm's management of transportation, supply chains, and product packaging. The fuel-efficient car parking arrangement is one facet of transportation. Since hybrid and fuel-efficient cars help the company realize its environmental objectives, IKEA rewards consumers for their commitments via preferred parking and more convenient shopping experiences. The firm also ensures that all stores are located close to public transit for co-workers and customers. In some markets, the firm even manages a bus system that routes consumers and employees to the store at no cost to the riders. IKEA has shuttle bus routes servicing stores in Richmond, British Columbia, as well as the North York and Etobicoke locations in Ontario. These services have been set up adjacent to central public transit hubs for the convenience of customers.

IKEA's commitment to efficient supply chains is reflected in its transportation and product shipping policies. It seeks to minimize the route from supplier to customer with as little effect on the environment as possible. The efficiency of product shipping is addressed via the product packaging and the containers. Most IKEA furniture is distributed in flat packs that enable larger quantities to be transported with less environmental impact.[6] Flat packaging reduces the amount of space required on a pallet, leading to optimized loads, lower transportation costs, and reduced emissions.[7] For example, when the Helmer chest of drawers is completely flat packed, the number of products that can be shipped on a single pallet jumps from six units to 39. Consequently, carbon dioxide emissions are reduced by 79 percent.[8]

Getting product and consumers to the store is not the end of this company's commitment to the environment. On the consumption side, the company has many initiatives that include waste minimization and post-purchase packaging. IKEA stores provide collection points for electrical and electronic equipment, discarded packaging, spent batteries, and low-energy bulbs. In some markets, customers can return unwanted furniture, enabling IKEA to work with charities

[4] franchisor.ikea.com/wp-content/uploads/2016/12/IKEA-Highlights-2016-Facts-and-Figures.pdf (February 9, 2017).

[5] www.ikea.com/ms/en_US/this-is-ikea/people-and-planet/index.html (February 9, 2017).

[6] Rosenhauer, Sven (2005), *Profit is a Wonderful Word: IKEA's Strategy Behind the Profit*, Norderstedt, Germany: Grin Verlag für Akademische Texte.

[7] www.ikea.com/us/en/ts_dynamic/dynamiclist/filt_nel_glob?filter=-1 February 9, 2017).

[8] www.ikea.com/ca/en/about_ikea/newsitem/2007_hybrid_parking (February 9, 2017).

to rehome the products.[9] In addition, the company has a bagging policy that charges consumers for bags as they check out of the store. Consumers quickly learn that they can purchase IKEA bags made of recycled material or bring their own bags with them on the shopping trip. Regardless of which strategy the consumer employs, the environment is served by this policy.

The action of IKEA underscores the sustainability efforts currently being undertaken in the retail sector. Our review of sustainability in retailing begins with a discussion of the central role of retailers in supply cycles. We subsequently examine the sustainability of the product lines offered by retailers, and we conclude by addressing the merits of marketing of sustainable consumption at the retail level.

THE CENTRAL ROLE OF RETAILING IN THE SUPPLY CYCLES

Several factors combine to make retailing the epicenter of the supply cycle in many industries. The first of these factors reflects the change in access to information within the industry. Historically, market research conducted for the retail sector was often completed by manufacturers.[10] Although the retailer is typically closer to the customer, retailers often lacked the financial and human resources needed to gather market information. The cost to collect data on more than just a small fraction of the products sold in a retail store was infeasible. The *universal product code* (UPC) changed the way business was conducted. In addition to reducing labor costs, the universal product codes provided retailers with access to market information on product movement, consumer purchasing behavior, and the use of marketing mix variables by manufacturers and retailers.[11] These data provide the foundation for assessing the efficacy of promotional strategies.[12] Consequently, retailers no longer rely on the market research provided by manufacturers to the same degree they once did.

The second factor that makes retailing central to the supply cycle reflects the increasing market power of selected retailers. The increase in access to information—in part due to the UPC—was accompanied by the development of larger retail outlets and the growing concentration of market share among a few retailers.[13] Wal-Mart's development of the superstore paralleled the trend toward larger retail outlets. The company's superstores, which are roughly 75 percent larger than its regular store counterparts, were introduced in 1988.

---

[9] www.ikea.com/ms/en_US/img/ad_content/IKEA_Group_Sustainability_Report_FY16 .pdf (February 9, 2017).

[10] Dolan, Robert J. (1987), "Note on the Marketing Information Industry," Harvard Business School Note, 9-588-027, Boston: Harvard Business School Publishing Division.

[11] Chu, Wujin, and Paul R. Messinger (1997), "Information and Channel Profits," *Journal of Retailing*, 73(4), 487–499.

[12] Kalyanam, Kirthi, Rajiv Lal, and Gerd Wolfram (2010), "Future Store Technologies and Their Impact on Grocery Retailing," in *Retailing in the 21st Century*, pp. 141–158. Springer Berlin Heidelberg.

[13] Wahl, Michael (1992), *In-Store Marketing: A New Dimension in the Share Wars*, New York: Sawyer Publishing Worldwide.

FIGURE 11-2
Wal-Mart Express is a new format designed to compete with convenience stores.[14]

Approximately four supercenters are opened each week in the United States.[15] The trend of larger retail outlets, however, has slowed as consumers are finding large store formats more inconvenient.[16] Figure 11-2 depicts a new format that Wal-Mart introduced to compete with convenience stores. Target and Ikea are also testing smaller store formats[17].

The retail market share is also edging toward fewer competitors. Wal-Mart is the largest competitor in the United States, Mexico, and Canada, and it controls a large and increasing share of the business done by most every major U.S. consumer-products company.[18] As the share of the market becomes more concentrated among fewer retailers, there is potential for the retailers to gain a lion's share of the profit at the expense of their suppliers. Research suggests, for instance, that Wal-Mart suppliers holding a small share of their respective markets do not perform relatively as well financially when Wal-Mart is one of their primary customers. Large-share suppliers to Wal-Mart, however, perform better than their large-share counterparts reporting other retailers as their primary customers. Thus, suppliers

---

[14] foodbeverage.about.com/od/Market_Updates/a/Walmart-Plans-To-Open-Its-First-Walmart-Express-Stores.htm (February 9, 2017).

[15] Levy, Michael, Barton A. Weitz, and Dhruv Grewal (2013), *Retailing Management*. New York: McGraw-Hill/Irwin.

[16] news.walmart.com/news-archive/2014/02/20/walmart-us-accelerates-small-store-growth (February 9, 2017).

[17] fortune.com/2015/02/02/target-express/ (February 9, 2017); and www.reuters.com/article/2015/06/24/ikea-stores-idUSL8N0ZA12X20150624 (February 9, 2017).

[18] www.thebalance.com/largest-north-american-retail-companies-2892270 (February 9, 2017); Bianco, Anthony et al. (2003), "Is Wal-Mart Too Powerful?" *Business Week* (October 6).

that seek Wal-Mart's broad market reach may derive benefits from using this association if it can be used to strengthen their market positions.[19]

As large companies with substantial visibility associated with large stores in many communities, retailers have become easy targets for concerns about sustainability. For example, Wal-Mart has been attacked for its international environmental record as well as for the treatment of workers and shoppers.[20] The visibility of large retailers makes them easy targets for criticism and results in them receiving a substantial amount of scrutiny in the media. In addition, the focus on these companies provides an opportunity to receive mammoth returns from getting these large retailers to reconsider their procurement, processing, and waste disposal systems. Despite the backlash associated with retailer size, retailers observe substantial merit from taking sustainable approaches to interaction with buyers and suppliers. Consumers are willing to accept higher indirect (i.e., taxes) and direct costs when they buy from retailers that take a proactive stance toward the environment and promote themselves as environmentally friendly.[21] Sustainable investments coincide with enhanced customer-oriented practices such as increased product assortment, competitive prices, and enhanced customer service. They also accrue from enhanced communication with suppliers.[22]

Over the past few years, retailers have begun to recognize that there are appreciable triple bottom-line rewards from embracing sustainability. Retailers with a green orientation achieve greater market share financial gains and customer satisfaction.[23] Wal-Mart management offers evidence that economic objectives and environmental goals can be reached in tandem. In the United States, over 80 percent of the materials that flow through its stores, clubs, and distribution centers is diverted from landfills.[24] The company further invested $500 million in sustainability projects, and it began developing more sustainability targets. The firm quickly became the world's biggest seller of organic milk and the biggest purchaser of organic cotton. More recently, Wal-Mart debuted its *Sustainable Leaders* shop, "an online shopping portal on Walmart.com that helps customers identify and purchase products from suppliers that are leading in sustainability."[25]

---

[19] Bloom, Paul N., and Vanessa G. Perry (2001), "Retailer Power and Supplier Welfare: The Case of Wal-Mart," *Journal of Retailing,* 77(3), 379–396.

[20] Fishman, Charles (2006), *The Wal-Mart Effect: How the World's Most Powerful Company Really Works—and How it is Transforming the American Economy*, New York: Penguin Press.

[21] Tsarenko, Yelena, Carla Ferraro, Sean Sands, and Colin McLeod (2013), "Environmentally Conscious Consumption: The Role of Retailers and Peers as External Influences," *Journal of Retailing and Consumer Services* 20, (3), 302–310.

[22] Claro, Danny Pimentel, Silvio Abrahão Laban Neto, and Priscila Borin de Oliveira Claro (2013), "Sustainability Drivers in Food Retail," *Journal of Retailing and Consumer Services,* 20 (3), 365–371.

[23] Menguc, Bulent, and Lucie K. Ozanne (2005), "Challenges of the 'Green Imperative': A Natural Resource-Based Approach to the Environmental Orientation–Business Performance Relationship," *Journal of Business Research* 58 (4), 430–438; and Luo, Xueming, and Chitra Bhanu Bhattacharya (2006), "Corporate Social Responsibility, Customer Satisfaction, and Market Value," *Journal of Marketing* 70 (4), 1–18.

[24] corporate.walmart.com/global-responsibility/sustainability/ (February 9, 2017).

[25] news.walmart.com/news-archive/2015/02/24/walmart-expands-online-sustainable -shopping-offering (February 10, 2017).

The Wal-Mart example illustrates how retailers have begun to recognize that they are accountable for the consumption associated with their entire supply chain from the procurement of raw materials to the post-consumer waste. Retailers are quantifying their supply chains' influences on the environment so that they can take action to reduce these influences. In addition, they are seeking third-party certification to ensure that the accuracy of the reporting. Retailers are actively assessing five areas of the supply chain that include:

Land and Soil

The treatment of land and soil throughout the retail supply chain is being assessed by most large retailers. Suppliers increasingly recognize that retailers require adherence to ISO 14000 land requirements or other environmental specifications.[26]

The retailer, rather than its predecessors in the supply chain, is the focus of many discussions about land use. Retailers receive criticism about their own land use and its relationship to urban sprawl.[27] *Urban sprawl* refers to the widespread movement of households and private firms from city centers and inner suburbs to very low-density suburbs.[28] Ten factors endemic to urban sprawl include:[29]

1. Seemingly unlimited extension of new development.
2. Low-density commercial and residential settlements, particularly in new-growth areas.
3. *Leapf*rog development that jumps out beyond established settlements.
4. Fragmented power over land use distributed among many small localities.
5. Private automobile dominance of transportation.
6. Absence of centralized planning or control of land uses.
7. Widespread strip center commercial development.
8. Large fiscal disparities among localities.
9. Segregation of types of land uses in different zones.
10. Reliance on filtering or trickle down processes to provide housing to low-income households.

Sprawl generates substantial environmental concerns that include increased traffic congestion, large-scale absorption of open space, extensive use of energy for movement, and air pollution.[30] Moreover, suburban sprawl concentrates poor households in certain high-poverty neighborhoods. These neighborhoods subsequently suffer from high crime rates, poor-quality public services and public schools, and fiscal resources that are inadequate for the services needed.

---

[26] González-Benito, Javier, and Oscar González-Benito (2005), "An Analysis of the Relationship between Environmental Motivations and ISO 14001 Certification," *British Journal of Management*, 16, 133–148.

[27] Hicks, Michael J. (2007), "Walmart's Impact on Local Revenue and Expenditure Instruments in Ohio, 1988–2003," *Atlantic Economic Journal*, 35, 77–95.

[28] Downs, Anthony (1997), "Suburban Ecosystem Inner-city," *Journal of Property Management*, 62 (6), 60–66.

[29] Downs, Anthony (1998), "The Big Picture," *Brookings Review*, 16 (4), 8–11.

[30] www.preservationist.net/sprawl/overview.htm (September 20, 2009).

Three strategies that have emerged as alternatives to urban sprawl involve regional development that selectively permits growth.[31] The first strategy involves the development of tightly bounded higher-density development typical of many Western European metropolitan areas. The second strategy involves a loosely drawn growth boundary that permits some development outside the boundary. This strategy raises population densities above sprawl levels and relies on increased use of public transit and carpooling. The third strategy is the development of new outlying communities and green spaces surrounded by tightly drawn urban growth boundaries. Regardless of the strategy, there are opportunities for retailers to work with state and local government that contribute to development while simultaneously increasing revenues and limiting urban sprawl. Retailers and other citizens who are active participants in the development process can actively work to realize the firm's objectives while reducing their influences on sprawl.[32] For example, Subway is a retail franchise that requires very little space and can therefore easily be implemented in existing manufacturing plants, hospitals, churches, schools, and appliance stores.[33]

Another criticism retailers encounter is storm water runoff from rain or snow melt that flows off streets, roofs, parking lots, sidewalks, and lawns into the soil or bodies of water.[34] Impervious surfaces, such as the streets and parking lots, prevent storm water from naturally soaking into the ground. If not managed properly, excess storm water runoff carries debris, dirt, chemicals, and other pollutants into storm sewers, ultimately pouring into waterways. Polluted storm water runoff can harm plants, fish, animals, and people. Sediment, for example, can cloud the water and make it difficult for plants to grow. Used motor oils and other car fluids that are transported into bodies of water by excess storm water runoff can poison aquatic life. Polluted storm water runoff also affects drinking water sources, adversely affecting human health and increasing drinking water treatment costs.[35]

The negative effects of storm water runoff can be managed with proper planning and development to control the flow and volume of runoff. First, land developers can minimize directly connected impervious areas (DCIAs) to reduce the volume of runoff. Second, using concrete grid or other porous materials for parking lots and streets allows the storm water to infiltrate the soil. Third, structural designs can be used to control the storm water runoff or to store the runoff on a site temporarily.[36] Grass swales, buffer strips, filter strips, storm water

---

[31] Downs, Anthony (1998), "The Big Picture," *Brookings Review*, 16 (4), 8–11. *Material Handling Management* (2009), "Walmart's 15 Questions," *Material.*

[32] Downs, Anthony (2005), "Break Down Those Barriers," *Planning*, 71 (9), 20–23.

[33] York, Emily Bryson (2008), "While Competitors Shut Doors, Subway is Still Growing," Advertising Age, 79 (28), 24–25; and www.chainstoreage.com/article/subway-opens-8000th-non-traditional-location (March 7, 2017).

[34] water.epa.gov/infrastructure/drinkingwater/sourcewater/protection/upload/storm-water.pdf (February 10, 2017).

[35] water.epa.gov/action/weatherchannel/stormwater.cfm (February 10, 2017).

[36] water.epa.gov/infrastructure/drinkingwater/sourcewater/protection/upload/storm-water.pdf (February 10, 2017).

Grassed swales can be used along roadsides and parking lots to collect and treat stormwater runoff

FIGURE 11-3

Grass swales are used to help manage store water runoff.

ponds, constructed wetlands, and detention basins are examples of structural designs that can help manage runoff. See Figure 11-3.

Energy and Climate

The energy and climate concerns refer to the amount greenhouse gas emissions associated with the supply chain. Given the amount of disparity in wages across the globe, there are some tremendous cost advantages from product processing in low economies. For example, cod caught off the coast of Norway is shipped to China where it is turned into filets and then shipped back to Norway.[37] Although the overall processing cost is lowered under such circumstances, greenhouse gas expenditures are magnified due to this strategy. Retailers that recognize these trade-offs have begun to ask suppliers to report the amount of greenhouse gases produced by suppliers. In addition, they have asked suppliers to set greenhouse gas reduction targets and make these targets available to the public. In some cases, retailers and their suppliers are reporting this information to the Carbon Disclosure Project (CDP). The CDP is a nonprofit organization that collects and distributes information designed to motivate investors, corporations, and governments to take action to prevent dangerous climate change. The data collected by CDP provide insight into the strategies used by many of the largest companies in the world to address climate change.[38] For example, Carrefour, the French

---

[37] Rosenthal, Elisabeth (2008), "Environmental Cost of Shipping Groceries Around the World," *The New York Times*, (April 26); and www.fco.cat/files/imatges/Butlleti%20135/NYT.pdf (September 16, 2009).

[38] www.cdp.net/en/info/about-us (February 10, 2017).

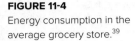

FIGURE 11-4

Energy consumption in the average grocery store.[39]

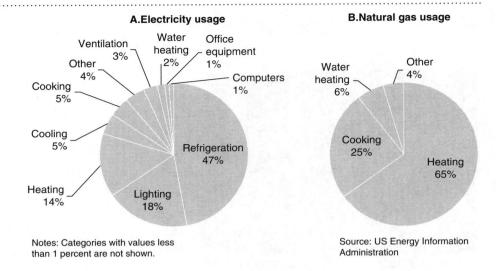

A. Electricity usage

Ventilation 3%
Water heating 2%
Office equipment 1%
Computers 1%
Other 4%
Cooking 5%
Cooling 5%
Refrigeration 47%
Heating 14%
Lighting 18%

Notes: Categories with values less than 1 percent are not shown.

B. Natural gas usage

Water heating 6%
Other 4%
Cooking 25%
Heating 65%

Source: US Energy Information Administration

retailer, used information generated by the CDP in the formulation of its policies to reduce greenhouse gas production throughout its retail network.[40]

At the retail level of the supply chain, the three greatest culprits for energy use are lighting, heating/cooling, and equipment.[41] In a typical grocery store, for example, refrigeration and lighting account for about 65 percent of total energy used.[42] See Figure 11-4. Increasingly, retailers are taking measures to reduce their energy expenditures. Kroger, for example, has reduced its overall energy consumption in its stores by over 34 percent since 2000.[43] In 2015, Kroger earned the *Energy Star Partner of the Year Award* for its efforts to reduce energy consumption.

To reduce energy consumption, firms are aggressively using alternative lighting sources that include light emitting diode (LED) technologies.[44] LEDs are very efficient and, unlike compact fluorescent lights, they do not contain mercury. In addition, modern stores are likely to use direct sunlight where possible on the shop floor. In general, 1 watt of power used in an electronic device creates 1 watt of heat.[45] Thus, for every watt used by a cash register, computer, or other device, 2 watts of energy are required. The installation of energy-efficient appliances

---

[39] bizenergyadvisor.com/grocery-stores.

[40] b8f65cb373b1b7b15feb-c70d8ead6ced550b4d987d7c03fcdd1d.ssl.cf3.rackcdn.com/ cms/reports/documents/000/001/228/original/CDP_Climate_Change_Report_2016 .pdf?1485276095 (February 10, 2017).

[41] Thompson, Bob (2007), "Green Retail: Retailer Strategies for Surviving the Sustainability Storm," *Journal of Retail and Leisure Property*, 6 (4), 281–286.

[42] bizenergyadvisor.com/grocery-stores.

[43] www.thekrogerco.com/.

[44] Kimura, Naoki, et al. (2007), "Extra-high Color Rendering White Light-emitting Diode Lamps Using Oxynitride and Nitride Phosphors Excited by Blue Light-emitting Diode," *Applied Physics Letters* 90, 051109–051109-3.

[45] Thompson, Bob (2007), "Green Retail: Retailer Strategies for Surviving the Sustainability Storm," *Journal of Retail & Leisure Property*, 6 (4), 281–286.

and climate-control products, however, enables retailers to lower their cost of operations at the store level.

Air

The influence of retailing on air quality is assessed at the retail and supply chain levels. At the retail level, a substantial portion of the influence on air quality is associated with the transportation costs associated with getting product to the stores and procuring products within the stores. It is not surprising that air pollution is also related to increases in retailing that accompany sprawl.[46] Consequently, retailers interested in enhancing air quality should benefit from working together with government-based planning organizations that seek to develop unified plans for development.

Water

The use of water in the supply chain is gaining increasing interest in several parts of the world. Processors of water within the supply chain are increasingly being asked to report on their efforts. ISO 14000 standards require firms to report their use of water in the supply chain, as water usage is an essential consideration in agriculture and production.

The sale of water at the retail level and the processing of this water is a highly contested issue in many markets. The U.S. market share leader at the retail level is private label products, yet branded products incur much of the scrutiny over water.[47] Facing water shortages and restrictions on water usage, Californian consumers are outraged that Nestlé is permitted to continue its bottling operations in California with no water restrictions. Each year, Nestlé uses 725 million gallons of water in its five water bottling plants in California.[48] Nestlé also faces environmental challenges for its use of spring water in Michigan. Pepsi (Aquafina water) and Coca-Cola (Dasani water), however, have already switched to processing of municipal water for the sale of water at the retail level.[49]

Community and People

Community and people considerations refer to the retailer's responsibility for fair treatment of employees within their organization and throughout the supply chain. Whole Foods, for example, recently stopped sourcing foods that were produced with prison labor.[50] Although the program is designed to help prisoners develop employment skills so they can obtain employment once release, these

---

[46] Kahn, Matthew E., and Joel Schwartz (2008), "Urban Air Pollution Progress Despite Sprawl: The "Greening" of the Vehicle Fleet," *Journal of Urban Economics* 63, 775–787.

[47] Beverage Industry (2009), "Bottled Water's Perfect Storm," *Beverage Industry*, 100 (7), SOI8.

[48] money.cnn.com/2015/05/26/news/companies/california-bottled-water-drought/ (February 10, 2017).

[49] Thottam, Jyoti, Paige Bowers, Stefanie Friedhoff, and Sean Scully (2005), "War on the Water Front," *Time*, 166 (25), 60.

[50] www.npr.org/sections/thesalt/2015/09/30/444797169/whole-foods-says-it-will-stop-selling-foods-made-by-prisoners (February 10, 2017).

[51] money.cnn.com/2015/09/30/news/whole-foods-prison-labor/

FIGURE 11-5

Fair Trade certified produce.

prison-work programs are not regulated by the federal government, and the prisoners are grossly underpaid for their work. Many Whole Foods shoppers questioned the justness of these programs and, therefore, were uncomfortable with Whole Foods sourcing foods made with prison labor.[51]

In the supply chain, many retailers have begun to engage in fair trade in their interaction with their trading partners. ***Fair trade*** refers to a family of principles that include guaranteed minimum floor price for products; safe working conditions and living wages; direct transactions between producer, retailers, community development; and environmentally sustainable farming methods.[52] Fair trade yields reduced debt, more economic options for producers, and increasingly sustainable agricultural practices.[53]

The Fair Trade Certified label started with coffee and now has expanded into "nearly every aisle of the grocery store and beyond" (e.g., apparel).[54] Sales of Fair Trade products are estimated to be around $2 billion annually in the United States, and this number should grow as demand for Fair Trade products continues to rise. Sixty percent of consumers says that they are willing to pay more for Fair Trade products.[55]

To varying degrees, retailers are working with their supply chains to enhance the sustainability of the distribution channel. Since 2006, Wal-Mart has substantially enhanced its commitment to sustainability, reducing its energy consumption, installing solar panels, reducing emissions from its fleet of trucks, and increasing recycling. In 2009, Wal-Mart turned its sustainability efforts

[52] www.fairtradeusa.org/what-is-fair-trade (February 10, 2017).

[53] Cameron, Katie (2008), "Brewing Justice: Fair Trade Coffee, Sustainability, and Survival," *Berkeley Journal of Employment and Labor Law*, 29(1), 267–268.

[54] fairtradeusa.org/press-room/press_release/fair-trade-rise-2015-brings-wave-new-fair-trade-certified-products (February 10, 2017).

[55] www.nytimes.com/aponline/2014/07/23/business/ap-us-smallbiz-small-talk.html

[56] www.greenbiz.com/blog/2013/04/15/game-why-walmart-ranking-suppliers-sustainability.

[57] mhlnews.com/global-supply-chain/wal-mart-s-green-mandate (February 10, 2017).

[58] Guzman, Doris De, and Joseph Chang (2009), "Responsible Retailing," *ICIS Chemical Business*, 276 (3), 16.

Energy and Climate

1. Have you measured your corporate greenhouse gas emissions?

2. Have you opted to report your greenhouse gas emissions to the Carbon Disclosure Project?

3. What is your total annual greenhouse gas emissions reported in the most recent year measured?

4. Have you set publicly available greenhouse gas reduction targets? If yes, what are those targets?

Material Efficiency

1. If measured, please report the total amount of solid waste generated from the facilities that produce your product(s) for Wal-Mart for the most recent year measured.

2. Have you set publicly available solid waste reduction targets? If yes, what are those targets?

3. If measured, please report total water use from facilities that produce your product(s) for Wal-Mart for the most recent year measured.

4. Have you set publicly available water use reduction targets? If yes, what are those targets?

Natural Resources

1. Have you established publicly available sustainability purchasing guidelines for your direct suppliers that address issues such as environmental compliance, employment practices and product/ingredient safety?

2. Have you obtained third-party certifications for any of the products that you sell to Wal-Mart?

People and Community

1. Do you know the location of 100% of the facilities that produce your product(s)?

2. Before beginning a business relationship with a manufacturing facility, do you evaluate the quality of, and capacity for, production?

3. Do you have a process for managing social compliance at the manufacturing level?

4. Do you work with your supply base to resolve issues found during social compliance evaluations and also document specific corrections and improvements?

5. Do you invest in community development activities in the markets you source from and/or operate within?

FIGURE 11-6

Wal-Mart sustainability criteria.[57]

toward its suppliers.[56] The company developed a supplier survey that focuses on energy and climate, material efficiency, natural resources, and people and community.[58] The questions are provided in Figure 11-6. In 2014, about 1300 suppliers answered these questions in Wal-Mart's supplier sustainability survey; approximately, 150 of those companies received the new Sustainability Leaders designation,[59] as displayed in Figure 11-7. Ultimately, the 100,000 worldwide suppliers to the firm will answer these questions, and the firms will be ranked from best to worst in each product category. Although these ranking will not be made public, they will be shared with Wal-Mart's retail buyers, who determine what products get onto Wal-Mart's store shelves.[60]

[59] www.greenbiz.com/article/inside-walmarts-new-plan-scale-supply-chain-transparency (February 10, 2017).

[60] www.greenbiz.com/blog/2013/04/15/game-why-walmart-ranking-suppliers-sustainability (February 10, 2017).

FIGURE 11-7
Wal-Mart sustainability
leaders suppliers.[61]

Wal-Mart also created a consortium of universities that collaborate with suppliers, retailers, nongovernmental organizations, and governments to develop a global database of information on the life cycle of products from raw materials to disposal.[62] These data are shared globally as a common database designed to prompt environmentally competitive efforts by suppliers. The index has potential to raise the product quality, lower products costs, and fuel innovation throughout the supply cycle. The final step of this initiative will involve transforming this sustainability information into a simple rating for consumers.

MARKETING SUSTAINABLE PRODUCT LINES

In the previous section, we examined efforts to enhance the sustainability of the upstream supply chain and retail operations. In this section, we examine several ways in which the marketer can make sustainable products available at the store level. Our discussion of sustainable product lines focuses on two issues: the incorporation of sustainable technology into the product mix and the appropriate distribution of products. Although retailers are beginning to grapple with these issues, very few empirical studies have been developed that provide insight into these decisions.

Sustainable Technology in the Product Mix

Consider first, the producer of a product that recognizes that some technologies can be incorporated into the product mix that markedly enhance product sustainability. For example, over the past 15 years, automobile manufacturers have developed alternative fuel technologies that significantly lower consumption. Firms can elect to market these technologies in existing brands, or they may develop new brands. In the small car market, for instance, Toyota introduced the Prius hybrid vehicle in 2000.[63] The third generation of the model is now being

---

[61] www.greenbiz.com/article/inside-walmarts-new-plan-scale-supply-chain-transparency.

[62] www.sustainabilityconsortium.org/walmart/ (February 10, 2017).

[63] Kranhold, Kathryn (2000), "Toyota Makes a Bet on New Hybrid Prius," *Wall Street Journal* (July 20), 18.

sold in North America, Europe, and Japan. Toyota also markets hybrid versions of its Highlander, Camry, and Lexus RX 400, yet each of these other models is available in conventional internal combustion engine and hybrid models. In 2014, alternative fuels accounted for 5 percent of vehicles in Europe and 0.5 percent of U.S. vehicles.[64] Although many factors contribute to these numbers, the model that is sold exclusively as a hybrid has sales that exceeds all other models. Recent research suggests that the consumers' desire to be seen doing something for the environment is an important motivator among some consumers.[65] While the purchase of any model illustrates to others that one is concerned about the environment, the clarity of this message is diluted among cars that are sold via internal combustion and hybrid models. Drivers, for instance, will notice that a fellow motorist is driving a Camry, but the fact that this car is a hybrid will likely go unnoticed. By contrast, motorists necessarily recognize the Prius as a hybrid. Since the commitment to the environment is more visible with the Prius, one might expect that consumers interested in gaining recognition for their purchases would buy a model sold exclusively as a hybrid.

Distribution of Sustainable Products

A second facet of establishing sustainable product lines at the retail levels concerns the distribution of products. Regardless of whether a product is sustainable, the level of competition on the grocery shelf is quite large. Retailers stock, on average, more than 39,000 unique products,[66] and they are approached with thousands of new products every year.[67] Retailers typically want to carry sufficient numbers of products that enable them to serve customers and generate a profit. Because shelf space is limited, introductions of new products often come at the expense of other products in the merchandise category. New products must be justified by the demand so that the cost of carrying inventory for the new brand is relatively low. To be successful in this setting, producers of new branded products need to illustrate that the demand for the new product is substantial. If the demand for the new product and its related profitability are not appreciable, the retailer will not be able to justify adding the new product to the retail product mix.

Consumer demand for products influences the form of distribution sought by producers of sustainable products lines. Consider, for example, a company such as Light of Day organic teas and tisanes of Traverse City, Michigan.[68] This entrepreneurial firm would like to increase the distribution of its products. The company is an organic, biodynamic producer that incorporates sustainability logic into its supply chain and operations (see Figure 11-8). It also engages in fair trade with its international suppliers of tea and related products. Firms of this

[64] www.eea.europa.eu/data-and-maps/indicators/proportion-of-vehicle-fleet-meeting-4/assessment-1 (February 10, 2017); and www.eesi.org/briefings/view/converting-vehicle-fleets-to-alternative-fuels (February 10, 2017).

[65] Ariely, Dan, Anat Bracha, and Stephan Meier (2009), "Doing Good or Doing Well? Image Motivation and Monetary Incentives in Behaving Prosocially," 99(1), 544–555.

[66] Chiang, Jeongwen, and Ronald T. Wilcox (1997), A Cross-Category Analysis of Shelf-Space Allocation, Product Variety, and Retail Margins, *Marketing Letters*, 8(2), 183–191.

[67] aginfo.psu.edu/PSA/ss96/aisles.html (September 28, 2009).

[68] www.lightofday organics.com/ (October 1, 2015).

FIGURE 11-8
Light of Day organic teas and
tisanes

type that seek to market their products through grocery stores can pursue one of three paths. They can either market their brand through grocers that market predominantly sustainable and organic brands. A second option is to market their branded precuts through full-line grocers that market products supported and developed with varying levels of sustainability. The third option is to focus on production technologies and serve as a private label brand for a retailer.

Although large firms may be able to support marketing through all three forms of distribution, young entrepreneurial companies may find it advantageous to market through one of these distribution channels. Several advantages accrue to the firm that elects to market its branded products through specialty grocery retailers such as Whole Foods and Trader Joe's. The first advantage to marketing through these retail chains is their size. These stores have grown rapidly in the past decade and now represent a significant portion of the retail grocery market. For example, Whole Foods has 427 stores in North America and the United Kingdom, and it has become the world's largest retailer of natural and organic food.[69] As the eighth largest food and drug store in the United States, Whole Foods employs over 90,000 people and ranks 218th on the Fortune 500 list.[70] As the size of these retail chains has increased, the visibility of brands marketed through these locations has also increased.

A second advantage associated with these retail locations is the credibility that affiliation with these retailers brings to the brand. Sustainable operations and natural products are at the heart of the marketing strategy for these retailers, and they prefer to work with producers that share these dispositions towards consumer marketing. For example, Whole Foods is the only multistore retailer in North America that markets the Hervé Mons brand of French cheese.[71] The relationship between these companies was established over a five-year period that preceded the decision to begin marketing Hervé Mons' products at Whole Foods. Since the

---

[69] www.wholefoodsmarket.com/company-info(October 1, 2015)

[70] media.wholefoodsmarket.com/fast-facts/.

[71] wholefoodsmarket.com/pressroom/blog/2009/05/06/whole-foods-markets-exclusive
-herve-mons-camember (September 28, 2009).

retailer has a core mission and values statement that emphasizes green marketing and sustainability, it goes to great lengths to ensure that its suppliers have the same philosophy. Whole Foods found Hervé Mons to be an attractive supplier because the company sells high-quality, traditional products that are sustainability developed by farmers in the Normandy region of France. Although the review process for Whole Food was prolonged, the wait was worth it. Consumers at Whole Foods understand the natural and organic emphasis throughout the product mix, and are likely to make purchases without engaging much effort to scrutinize the brand.

It is interesting to note the challenge associated with electing to market via the specialty retailers. Although the inclusion of a product in the Whole Foods or Trader Joe's product line immediately brings recognition as a product of some natural, organic, or sustainable character, the brand is surrounded by other products that have similar attributes. The competitive advantage of the product is unlikely to be sustainable, since virtually all the competition offers this benefit. The savvy marketer must illustrate the sustainability of the product, but it cannot rely on this attribute exclusively. In addition, the target market of these specialty stores is likely to be *lifestyles of health and sustainability* (LOHAS) [72] or *True-Blue* consumers.[73] Although these market segments are growing, a substantial portion of the consuming public may not frequent specialty grocery stores.

The branded alternative to marketing through specialty retailers is marketing via a general grocery merchandiser such as Wal-Mart or Kroger. General grocery merchandisers have always had a strong emphasis on product quality, and in recent years, these firms have made substantial investments in sustainable business practices and green marketing. Moreover, these retailers are capitalizing on the organic trend and expanding their organic offerings.[74] As a result, general grocery retailers are beginning to steal market share from Whole Foods. In fact, within two years, Kroger is expected to surpass Whole Foods as the top seller of organic and natural food in the United States.[75]

One of the advantages of working with these larger firms is the economies of scale in their operations. For example, Wal-Mart is the largest grower of organic cotton in the world.[76] Products that are welcomed to the product line of these general merchandise grocers have greater distribution that, in some cases, leads to greater sales and revenue.

Several issues complicate the sale of products through these grocers. Products of high sustainability may be placed either in a special part of the store or alongside products in the same category. For example, Kroger stores often feature a healthy foods section that stands outside of the regular offering for a product class. The product offerings from a company such as *Light of Day* teas could be sold in either location. Sale of the product in the healthy choice section of the store has some of the advantages and disadvantages of the specialty retail alternative.

---

[72] Everage, Laura (2002), "Understanding the LOHAS Lifestyle," *Gourmet Retailer*, 23 (10), 82–86.

[73] Makower, Joel (2009), *Strategies for the Green Economy*, New York: McGraw Hill.

[74] www.nytimes.com/2014/04/10/business/walmart-to-offer-organic-line-of-food-at-cut-rate-prices.html.

[75] www.businessinsider.com/krogers-strategy-to-take-over-grocery-stores-2015-3 (October 9, 2015).

[76] www.thebalance.com/organic-retailers-in-north-america-2011-2538129 (February 10, 2017).

The products may be seen primarily by *LOHAS* consumers, and the differential advantage of the product cannot solely reside in the sustainability of its production and distribution. Consequently, labeling should feature advantages associated with product quality, nutrition, or other potential competitive advantages.

If the sustainable product is marketed alongside all products in the class, there is greater potential for it to reach a broader audience. This broader audience includes "unconcerned" and "drifter" market segments, who may not appreciate the benefits associated with sustainable operations. Many consumers will also be unwilling to dedicate the time to understand the benefits of the sustainable product. The price-sensitive consumer will often select the product with the lowest sticker price regardless of the product's sustainability. To the extent that sustainable products are more expensive than their alternatives, price-sensitive consumers should be less willing to purchase the sustainable products. In addition, companies run the risk of cannibalizing sales of nonsustainable product offerings by offering sustainable products in the same location. For example, a company that sells organic, sustainably produced and conventionally produced strawberries may witness some cannibalization of sales by offering the products together. Although the increase in sales of the sustainable product is beneficial to the consumer, it could yield lower profits for the firm. The retailer that is interested in maximizing financial and ecological performance will be reluctant to sell these products at the same place in the store.

The third alternative for the entrepreneur is to market the brand as a private-label product. A ***private label*** refers to a product in which the brand is owned by the retailer or wholesaler rather than the producer. For example, Kroger offers over 10,000 private-label products sold in a multitier strategy that includes *Private Selection, Naturally Preferred,* H*ome Sense, Kroger brand, Comforts for Baby, Big K,* and others.[77] Kroger's fastest growing private-label brand, *Simple Truth,* was introduced in 2013 and reached $1 billion in sales in 2014, making Simple Truth one of the fastest brands to reach that benchmark.[78] The *Simple Truth* brand, which is free of over 100 different artificial preservative and ingredients, is offered in over 600 items in 50 different product categories.[79] Sales of private-label brands have been growing rapidly in recent years, and they represent over 17 percent of supermarket sales.[80] In some categories, private-label brands have higher unit market share than the top national brands.[81]

The private-label alternative also involves trade-offs for the producer and the retailer. Because companies such as Kroger and Whole Foods have hundreds of outlets, the sale of these products enables the producer to operate with economies of scale. Although the producer gains efficient access to a large distribution channel, the identity of the product is entirely associated with the retailer. Over time, retailers can establish specific production criteria that enable them to select the lowest-cost producer of the product. In the absence of a brand or other means by which to distinguish one's product, the producer is subject to greater price scrutiny.

---

[77] www.kroger.com/topic/our-brands (October 9, 2015).

[78] eproxymaterials.com/interactive/kr2014factbook/ (October 9, 2015).

[79] eproxymaterials.com/interactive/kr2014factbook/ (October 9, 2015).

[80] Levy, Michael, Barton Weitz, and Dhruv Grewal (2014). "Retail Management," 9th edition. New York: McGraw-Hill.

[81] Batra, Rajeev, and Indrajit Sinha (2000), "Consumer-level Factors Moderating the Success of Private Label Brands," *Journal of Retailing* 76 (2), 175–191.

MARKETING SUSTAINABLE CONSUMPTION

The need to promote and ensure sustainable use of products is extensive. Our analysis focuses on two facets of sustainability that are most prominent after a purchase at a retail store: post-retailing packaging and efforts to reclaim products and restrict component parts usage. In both cases, marketers have made tremendous strides to reduce the carbon footprint of the retail sector.

Post-retail Packaging. We use the term *post-retail packaging* to refer to the form of packaging used by the consumer to transport product away from a retail establishment. The amount of this material is substantial. In Massachusetts alone, more than 1.5 billion paper or plastic bags are thrown away every year.[82] The form of packaging used in retailing varies by the culture and by the form of retailing. In the U.S. grocery store, for example, consumers are accustomed to hearing "paper or plastic" at the cash register, and traditionally, consumers bear no direct cost for these bags as the merchandise is packed for them. By contrast, in many parts of Europe, consumers pack their own groceries at the register, and they pay a fee for each bag they purchase.

Post-retail packaging is changing is many markets. Consumers are beginning to recognize the substantial limits to using either paper or plastic bags. Paper is the traditional packaging material made from a renewable source. Paper, however, consumes more energy and water in its production and further yields higher levels of pollution and more greenhouse gases.[83] Plastic bags were introduced to the market 30 years ago as a low-cost alternative to paper. The lightweight nature of plastic means that it is less expensive to transport. Plastic is also longer lasting and less expensive. Nevertheless, plastic is rarely recycled, and it is a formidable trap for fish, birds, and other wildlife. For example, while filming a documentary on Midway Island in the Pacific Ocean, Rebecca Hoskins encountered hundreds of albatross carcasses with plastic bags lodged in their stomachs.[84] When she returned home, she convinced her hometown of Modbury and 80 other English towns to ban plastic bags. Her action led to a reduction in the 200 million bags that litter Britain's parks and beaches every year.[85]

There is a clear trade-off between plastic and paper. Plastic is lighter and less expensive, but it is rarely recycled and a threat to wildlife. By contrast, paper has a larger carbon footprint, yet it is heavier and more expensive to produce. Recognizing these trade-offs, consumers, government, and retailers have begun to explore other packaging options. Some consumers have taken this charge on themselves and have begun to use reusable bags. A study conducted by French retailer Carrefour in 2004 indicated that a reusable bag was better for the environment—regardless of the material—so long as the bag was used at least four times.[86]

In order to influence consumer behavior associated with post-retail packaging, government has also intervened. For example, the city of San Francisco

[82] Johnson, Jim (2009), "Paper or Plastic?" *Waste and Recycling News*, 14 (24), 1–2.

[83] Ball, Jeffrey (2009), "Currents—Power Shift: Paper or Plastic? A New Look at the Bag Scourge—Improved Recycling Options Lessen Plastic's Stigma, Even as Cities and States Consider Imposing Bans or Taxes," Wall Street Journal (June 12), A11.

[84] www.dailymail.co.uk/news/article-494758/How-womans-battle-save-dying-albatross-spawned-national-campaign-ban-plastic-bags.html (October 10, 2009).

[85] Adams, William Lee (2009), "Banning Plastic Bags," *Time*, 174(11).

became the first U.S. city to ban conventional plastic bags in grocery stores in 2007. Similarly, China banned the distribution of free grocery bags in 2008. In other markets, government has imposed a tax on plastic bags. Ireland, for instance, imposed a tax on plastic bags in 2002 as a means of maintaining the country's clean, green image. In 2009, the residents of Seattle, Washington, voted down a referendum that would have required grocers to charge 20 cents for each plastic bag provided at the check-out counter. Stores with annual revenues of less than $1 million would have kept the bag receipts to cover their costs, while those grossing more would have kept 25 percent and passed the remainder on to the city for recycling, environmental education, and reusable bags for low-income consumers. Many residents indicated that they opposed the bill as an unnecessary tax rather than a means to enhance levels of sustainability in the city.[87]

Government has also placed restrictions on the type of paper and plastic used in restaurants. This retail industry is entertaining the use of some novel forms of packaging made from sugar cane, corn, and other replenishable sources. The Federal Trade Commission has set guidelines for the claims manufacturers can make regarding their recycled products. *Biodegradable* materials refer to packaging that will break down and return to nature within a reasonably short time after the usual disposal. *Compostable items*, however, break down organically into humus-like material and return nutrients to the Earth.

Retailers have also made strong strides to reduce the amount of post-retail packaging. In 2007, IKEA began charging 5 cents for each plastic bag that was used at the checkout counter in North America. The store also enables shoppers to walk away with a reusable blue bag for 59 cents.[88] The response to this action has been a substantial reduction in the number of single-use bags sold. In 2009, the Canadian branch of the firm was able to phase out the single-use bag completely.[89] Similarly, the Kroger company offers incentives to customers who use reusable bags. Since inception of the program, over 1 billion plastic bags have been replaced with reusable bags.[90]

Restaurateurs are also employing new materials to reduce their carbon footprint of their packaging. The dining-in option has been revolutionized through plates and bowls made from plant-based materials that are compostable or biodegradable.[91] EATware International, for instance, produces a line of 100 percent biodegradable tableware made from bamboo, sugar cane pulp, water, and cellulose.[92] The company claims their microwave- and oven-safe plates will decompose in 180 days in a landfill. The Sugar Cane Paper Company combines the residue left over after sugar cane is crushed with bamboo to make paper products.[93] Solo similarly offers the Bare collection of hot cups lined with a plant-based polylactic

[86] Ball, Jeffrey (2009), "Currents—Power Shift: Paper or Plastic? A New Look at the Bag Scourge—Improved Recycling Options Lessen Plastic's Stigma, Even as Cities and States Consider Imposing Bans or Taxes," Wall Street Journal (June 12), A11.

[87] seattletimes.nwsource.com/html/politics/2009686467_elexseabagfee19m.html.

[88] www.grist.org/article/ikea/ (February 10, 2017).

[89] network.nationalpost.com/np/blogs/posted/archive/2009/04/14/ikea-canada-to-eliminate-plastic-bags.aspx (October 10, 2009).

[90] sustainability.kroger.com/environment-zero-waste.html (February 10, 2017).

[91] O'Brien, Tom (2009), *The greening of paper and plastic,* Restaurant Business, 108 (3), FSB13.

[92] www.eatware.com/Home/SiteContent?NavID=50&ContentID=24&SideID=63 (February 10, 2017).

acid resin.[94] The cups are compostable, made 100 percent from renewable resources, and range from 8 to 20 ounces. Even plastic silverware has been replaced with ECO Products cutlery made from cornstarch.[95]

Together these examples illustrate the measures that the retailing industry is taking to lower its cost of operations while simultaneously lowering the carbon footprint of its operations.

Reclamation and Component Restriction

Reclamation refers to the responsible collection of products once they no longer offer value to consumers. For example, the *Environmental Quality Company* provides retailers with the means for handling hazardous electronics (including lighting and batteries), pharmaceuticals, and medical waste.[96] Land and soil considerations also prompt retailers and their suppliers to develop programs that facilitate product reclamation. *Component restriction* refers to limits placed on the ingredients that can be incorporated into a product. For example, asbestos has been banned from most potential uses in the United States since 1990.[97] Since the regulations associated with reclamation and restriction often address the same materials (e.g., iron ore) and end products (e.g., personal computers), these issues are examined in tandem.

The historical perspective on reclamation is the *cradle-to-grave* logic used in the 1980s to ensure that manufacturers and users properly disposed of chemicals and other hazardous materials. This logic has been replaced with a *cradle-to-cradle* perspective that emphasizes recovery, recycling, and reuse.[98]

Some industries face legislation that compels companies to reclaim products and modify components. Automobiles, electronics, and appliances face regulations in several geographic markets, notably the European Union. Firms from the United States, Japan, and other non-EU countries must adhere to these directives if they wish to conduct business in the EU. Moreover, firms use the mandates of progressive regulation as pre-conditions that influence product design, manufacture, and reclamation. Four regulatory acts that influence reclamation and component restrictions include:

End-of-Life Directive

Established in 2000, the EU's *end-of-life directive* requires automotive manufacturers and component suppliers to reclaim auto products.[99] Specifically, this directive

---

[93] sugarmade.com/products/ (February 10, 2017).

[94] www.dartcontainer.com/products/foodservice-catalog/hot-coldcups/paper/bare -by-solo-eco-forward-single-sided-pla-sspla-paper-hot-cups/#filter= (February 10, 2017).

[95] www.ecoproducts.com/plantware_cutlery.html (February 10, 2017).

[96] www.usecology.com/Libraries/EQ_News/EQ_%E2%80%93_The_Environmental_Quality _Company_and_US_Ecology_Announce_Acquisition_Agreement.sflb.ashx (February 10, 2017).

[97] www.epa.gov/asbestos/us-federal-bans-asbestos#banned (February 10, 2017).

[98] Kumar, Sameer, and Valora Putnam (2008), "Cradle to Cradle: Reverse Logistics Strategies and Opportunities across Three Industries," *International Journal of Production Economics* 115, 305–315.

requires all manufacturers to take back and dismantle all motor vehicles for domestic use at the end of their useful lives. Component parts are then either reused or recycled. The goal is for all motor vehicle manufacturers to have a reuse or recyclable content of 85 percent at the end of their useful lives now and move toward 95 percent. Assessment of the effectiveness of this directive shows that progress has been made towards reducing vehicle-based hazardous substances, increasing reuse, recycling and recovery, and ensuring that End-of-life vehicles are treated in environmentally sound conditions.[100] This directive requires manufacturers and their component manufacturers to innovate and design for disassembly. This requirement can be at odds with the goal of trying to limit carbon emissions and enhance fuel efficiency. Nevertheless, it has also fostered stronger relationships among component producers, manufacturers, disassemblers, and recyclers.[101] Figure 11-11 illustrates how the various parts of an automobile are re-introduced into the supply chain. This directive has also opened up entrepreneurial opportunities for disassemblers.

Restriction of Hazardous Substances (RoHS)

Restriction of hazardous substances (RoHS) is an EU directive that severely restricts the use of lead, hexavalent chromium, mercury, cadmium, and some flame retardants. In order to address the increasing waste stream from electronics, RoHS was recast in 2011. The goal of this revision was to reduce administrative overhead and ensure coherency with newer policies and legislation.[102] The new directive requires substitutes for heavy metals such as lead, mercury, cadmium, and hexavalent chromium and flame retardants such as polybrominated biphenyls (PBB) or polybrominated diphenyl ethers (PBDE).[103] RoHS' regulations apply to large and small household appliances, information technology and telecommunications equipment, consumer equipment, electrical and electronic tools, toys, leisure equipment, and other devices.[104] Compliance with this directive is required for manufacturers, resellers marketing under their own brand names, and importers or exporters of electrical and electronic equipment. The primary implication of RoHS is the need to comply with the directive or face punitive charges. Producers and retailers must, therefore, request documentation from suppliers regarding supplies, components, subassemblies, and equipment to ensure compliance. Companies can be convicted and fined for failing to comply with the directive and for failing to submit technical documentation.

---

[99] Directive 2000/53/EC on End-of-Life Vehicles, 2000. *Official Journal of the European Communities* dkc3.digikey.com/ PDF/Marketing/ELVdirective_2000-53-EC.pdfS.

[100] ec.europa.eu/environment/waste/pdf/target_review/Final%20Report%20Ex-Post. pdf (February 10, 2017).

[101] Crotty, Jo, and Mark Smith (2008), "Strategic Responses to Environmental Regulation in the U.K. Automotive Sector: The European Union End-of-Life Vehicle Directive and the Porter Hypothesis," *Journal of Industrial Ecology*, 10 (4), 95–111.

[102] ec.europa.eu/environment/waste/rohs_eee/index_en.htm (February 10, 2017).

[103] ec.europa.eu/environment/waste/weee/index_en.htm (February 10, 2017).

[104] Wright, Robin, and Karen Elcock (2006), "The RoHS and WEEE Directives: Environmental Challenges for the Electrical and Electronic Products Sector," *Environmental Quality Management*, 15 (4), 9–24.

Waste Electrical and Electronic Equipment Directive (WEEE). *Waste electrical and electronic equipment directive (WEEE)* is a directive designed to reduce the amount of electronic waste in landfills. It addresses all the products in RoHS, and it further includes medical devices and monitoring and control instruments. WEEE began to take effect in 2005, and in light of growing e-waste, it was revised in 2012.[105] Adherence to WEEE requires the seller to demonstrate that it will cover the cost of disposal in an environmentally friendly manner.[106] The producer is also required to educate consumers regarding the recycling and recovery options available to them. Before a new product enters the market, producers are required to provide "do not landfill" labels on each package.

The retailer's role in WEEE administration is substantial given that consumer participation is crucial to the success of this directive. Although producers can set up recovery facilities anywhere, in many cases, these collection sites are at retail locations. For example, Best Buy and Staples enable consumers to return used equipment at their stores. In addition, retailers provide incentives to consumers to return used equipment. These incentives include store rebates, coupons, and other store credit. Upon receipt of product, the retailer sends it to the producer or its affiliate that determines whether recycling, reuse, or disposal are appropriate for the product.

Registration, Evaluation, Authorization and restriction of Chemical Substances (REACH)

Registration, evaluation, authorization, and restriction of chemical substances (REACH) was adopted by the EU in 2006 to provide information on chemicals that are used and to phase out chemicals that pose unacceptable risks.[107] The health-related issues of exposure to toxic chemicals is substantial. The incidence of cancer, for instance, is in part related to exposure to toxins. In the United States alone, the annual cost of treating cancer is over $210 billion, and this number is increasing at 7 percent annually.[108] Reductions in the number of toxic chemicals have the potential to enhance the environment and the quality of life.

REACH regulation is designed to protect human health and the environment while enhancing innovation and competitiveness. REACH approaches this goal by requiring businesses to register the substances in their products and make public any potential risks from the use of these chemicals. In order to manage REACH, a firm must assess its product portfolio. This assessment should identify products either sourced from, or imported into, the European Union

---

[105] ec.europa.eu/environment/waste/weee/index_en.htm (February 10, 2017).

[106] Wright, Robin, and Karen Elcock (2006), "The RoHS and WEEE Directives: Environmental Challenges for the Electrical and Electronic Products Sector," *Environmental Quality Management*, 15 (4), 9–24.

[107] Kumar, Sameer, and Valora Putnam (2008), "Cradle to Cradle: Reverse Logistics Strategies and Opportunities across Three Industries," *International Journal of Production Economics* 115, 305–315. http://ec.europa.eu/environment/chemicals/reach/reach_en.htm (February 10, 2017).

[108] Lockwood, Doug (2008), "The REACH Regulation: Challenges Ahead for Manufacturers of Articles," *Environmental Quality Management*, 18 (1), 15.

(EU). The substances contained in these products should then be inventoried. After the firm has inventoried the components of its products, it develops a plan to implement to achieve heightened sustainability by phasing out restricted substances.[109]

Although the legal requirements associated with reclamation and restriction are substantial, there are marketplace opportunities that arise from these requirements. Several benefits accrue to the firm that adopts this perspective toward reclamation and component restrictions.[110] First, there is substantial potential for cost reductions. Because component parts are reused and restored, production costs are lowered. For example, the cost of recycling aluminum is roughly 5 percent of the cost to refine it from raw materials. Second, constraining the firm's influence on the environment also enables the firm to manage risk effectively. Because the firm that adheres to regulations has a lower likelihood of facing litigation or marketplace criticism, the overall level of risk is reduced through copious attention to regulations.

A third benefit of reclamation and component restrictions is the brand differentiation that it affords to the firm. Since only brands that adhere to standards can compete, the brands that meet regulatory requirements open themselves to market opportunities unavailable to the competition. The adherence to environmental standards is viewed as favorable by many consumers, and this same track record for sustainability fosters an image that is preferred by some employees and stockholders. Retention of loyal consumers and employees can be achieved through adherence to regulation.

Another inherent benefit to sustainability regulation is that it fosters innovation in the supply chain and in product components. The institution of a new regulation requires the firm to review the complete supply chain for a product. In many cases, firms engage in a ***reverse logistics*** whereby a manufacturer accepts previously shipped products or parts from the point of consumption for recycling, reuse, or disposal.[111] Firms have developed ***close-looped systems*** in which manufacturers work with downstream channel partners to ensure the reclamation of products. For example, Ford Motor Company and Alcan established the first closed-loop system recycling system for auto aluminum in 2002.[112] Innovations also accrue in product design as a result of regulation. The firm that can no longer offer a toxic product must find a new solution that meets addresses the product need at a reasonable cost. Thus, regulations also foster innovations in product design.

The final benefit of regulation is that it enables firms to respond to the economic realities of supply and demand. Because the supply of landfills is limited, companies

[109] Borkhoff, Joyce (2008), "European Union's REACH Regulation," *Paint and Coatings Industry*, 24 (5), 88–89.

[110] Alston, Ken (2008), "Cradle-to-Cradle Design Initiatives: Lessons and Opportunities for Prevention through Design (PtD)," *Journal of Safety Research*, 39, 135–136.

[111] Dowlatshahi, Shad (2000), "Developing a Theory of Reverse Logistics," *Interfaces*, 30 (3), 143–155.

[112] Millbank, Paul (2004), "Aluminum Recycling Vital to Global Supply Chain," *Aluminum International Today*, 16 (5).

that reduce their need for landfills lower their costs of operations. Similarly, the demand for steel and aluminum are strong, yet the supply of raw materials (and costs of refining) provide ample opportunities to recycle these materials. Since the costs of mining and refining bauxite (for aluminum) and iron ore (for steel) are appreciable, there are substantial opportunities to reclaim these products after products have reached the end of their productive lives.

SUMMARY

Introduction

The purpose of this chapter has been to underscore the importance of the retailing sector to the sustainability. Since by definition retailing addresses the interface between producers and consumers, analysis of retailing offers substantial opportunities to limit the carbon footprint of manufacturers, distributors, retailers, and consumers.

The Central Role of Retailing in the Supply Cycles

Several factors place retailing at the heart of the supply cycle in many industries. The first of these factors reflects the change in access to information within the industry. The universal product code provides retailers with access to market information on product movement, consumer purchasing behavior, and the use of marketing mix variables by manufacturers and retailers. The increase in access to information has been accompanied by the development of larger retail outlets and the growing concentration of market share among a few retailers. As large companies with substantial visibility operate large stores in many communities, retailers have become easy targets for concerns about sustainability. Retailers are, therefore, developing solutions that limit their carbon footprints and enhance relationships with the communities where they source and sell products.

Marketing Sustainable Product Lines

The incorporation of sustainable and green technology into the product mix and the appropriate distribution of sustainable products are two of the most salient issues facing retailers. Firms can elect to market green technologies in existing brands, or they may develop new brands. When firms have developed new products that incorporate sustainable technologies, they can market these products through specialty retailers, general merchandise retailers, or through private-label arrangements.

Marketing Sustainable Consumption

Since a sizeable portion of the greenhouse gases associated with products occurs after their purchase, this chapter also examined sustainable post-purchase practices. The discussion of post-retail packaging illustrated limitations to paper and plastic bags and the sustainability-related benefits of reusable bags. In addition, retailers have adopted a cradle-to-cradle perspective in which they attempt to reclaim as many products as possible, and they refrain from using products that have substantial negative influences on the environment.

KEY TERMS

universal product code
urban sprawl
private label
post-retail packaging
biodegradable
compostable items

reclamation
component restriction
cradle-to-cradle
end-of-life directive
restriction of hazardous
    substances

waste electrical and electronic
    equipment directive
registration, evaluation,
    authorization and restriction
    of chemical substances

DISCUSSION QUESTIONS

1. How has the access to consumer purchasing information changed, and how has this changed the role of retailers?

2. Over the past decade, has retailing become more or less important to the supply chain? What factors support your conclusions?

3. To what extent is urban sprawl a retailing problem, and how does sprawl influence the carbon footprint of a community?

4. Name and describe four ways in which retailers are actively assessing sustainability in supply chains.

5. Is the revenue stream of a firm favorably enhanced by incorporating sustainable features into existing brands, or are firms better off incorporating these features into new brands?

6. What are the advantages and the disadvantages of promoting sustainable or organic brands in a specialty aisle of the store rather than with other items in a product class?

7. Why might a large consumer products company prefer marketing of its branded products to private-label products?

8. Regarding shopping bags, which is preferred—paper or plastic?

9. What steps can retailers take to increase product reclamation?

10. Why should retailers participate in discussions about the components and the ingredients in the products they market?

12

Producing Value via Innovation

INTRODUCTION

Landfills are increasing problem in parts of the world. Land set aside for this purpose has limited other value for considerable time. Landfills account for 20 percent of the methane produced globally.[1] Food consumption, or lack thereof, is an important contributor to landfills, and estimates suggest that 40 percent of all food purchased in the United States ends up in landfills.[2]

In 2017, the Whirlpool Corporation announced the first residential composting appliance, the Zera food recycler.[3] This indoor recycler can transform a weeks' worth of food scraps into homemade fertilizer in 24 hours. With dimensions of 11 x 22 x 33.75 inches (28 x 55.9 x 85.3 cm), the Zera is designed to be an integral part of the home kitchen. The Zera combines food scraps with a coconut husk-based material and baking soda. When combined with the proper aeration, heat, and moisture, decomposition occurs rapidly. Consequently, the product has great potential to redirect much of the 400 pounds (181.4 kg) of waste produced annually in a typical American home.

Whirlpool has teamed up with Indiegogo Enterprise Crowdfunding to enable early adopters to buy the product at an early bird discount. Initial

FIGURE 12-1

Whirlpool's Zera food recycler.[4]

---

[1] Yusuf, Rafiu O., Zainura Z. Noor, Ahmad H. Abba, Mohd Ariffin Abu Hassan, and Mohd Fadhil Mohd Din (2012), "Methane Emission by Sectors: A Comprehensive Review of Emission Sources and Mitigation Methods," *Renewable and Sustainable Energy Reviews* 16 (7), 5059–5070.

[2] Gunders, Dana (2012), "Wasted: How America is Losing up to 40 Percent of Its Food from Farm to Fork to Landfill," *Natural Resources Defense Council*, 1–26.

[3] www.engadget.com/2017/01/05/whirlpools-zera-food-recycler-easily-turns-food-scraps-into-com/ (February 17, 2017).

[4] www.indiegogo.com/projects/zera-food-recycler-recycling--2#/ (February 16, 2017).

availability will be online or at selected partners such as Williams-Sonoma, TreeHouse, and Abt.[5]

As the Whirlpool example illustrates, innovative companies are incorporating sustainability concerns into the design of new products. The purpose of this chapter is to identify strategies that enable firms to develop innovations that offer sustainable competitive advantage. We view *innovation* as the effort to create purposeful, focused change in an enterprise's economic, social, and ecological potential.[6] If organizations are to attain sustainability, it is essential for them to develop innovations that attend to each facet of the triple bottom line. It is essential for firms to recognize that focused change can occur to meet a variety of sustainability needs. Firms invest in new ideas in order to address growing populations, provide affordable products and services, serve growing unmet needs, and reduce environmental influences.[7]

As emerging markets mature and mature markets continue to develop, the need for sustainable innovations continues to escalate. Research suggests, for instance, that if per capita consumption rates in the developing economies mirror the rates in developed markets, it will take the equivalent of three Earths to support resource consumption.[8] Innovations are necessary that promote sustainability by finding new ways to perform old things as well as new ways to perform new things.[9]

We focus our analysis of innovation on practices associated with developing innovative, new products. It is essential, however, to recognize that firms innovate in a number ways that include new channel development, new business models, and novel product ideas.[10] We distinguish between product and **process innovation** as two components of development. *Product innovation* refers to new goods and service that offer improvements in technical abilities, functional characteristics, ease of use, and other dimensions.[11] By contrast, *process innovation* refers to novel techniques for producing goods and services. These production enhancements are often designed to yield higher levels of triple bottom-line effectiveness. Understanding of the innovation process demands consideration of both activities within the firm. In many cases, the process innovations developed by one firm become the product innovations of a second organization. For example, the innovations that United Parcel Service (UPS) has made in its package tracking technology has enabled the firm to market these capabilities to their clients.[12]

---

[5] www.whirlpoolcorp.com/whirlpool-corporation-debuts-new-zera-food-recycler-on -indiegogo/ (February 17, 2017).

[6] Drucker, Peter F. (1985), "The Discipline of Innovation," *Harvard Business Review* 63 (3), 67–72.

[7] Holliday, Chad, and John Pepper (2001), *Sustainability through the Market; Seven Keys to Success*, Geneva: World Business Council for Sustainability.

[8] Placet, Marylynn, Roger Anderson, and Kimberly Fowler (2005), "Strategies for Sustainability," *Research Technology Management*, 48(5), 32–41.

[9] Holliday, Chad, and John Pepper (2001), *Sustainability through the Market; Seven Keys to Success*, Geneva: World Business Council for Sustainability.

[10] Carr, Nicholas G. (1999), "Visualizing Innovation," *Harvard Business Review*, 77 (5), 16.

[11] Mohr, Jakki, Sanjit Sengupta, and Stanley Slater (2010), *Marketing of High-Technology Products and Innovations*, Upper Saddle River, NJ: Prentice-Hall.

[12] Soupata, Lea (2001), "Managing Culture for Competitive Advantage at United Parcel Service, *Journal of Organizational Excellence*; 20 (3), 19–26.

In the following text, we begin by outlining the new product development process. We subsequently address the preliminary assessment, business case analysis, product development, and marketability of innovative product offerings. Consider first a general framework for the development of new products.

PRODUCT INNOVATION FRAMEWORK

Firms engage in an interactive process in their efforts to develop new product and service offerings. The stage-gate process outlined in Figure 12-2 elucidates the series of activities involved in designing new products.[13] Stage-gate recognizes that firms engage in a number of activities between idea generation and the market launch of a product. These phases are multifunctional and require interaction among marketing, research and development (R&D), production, and other activities internal and external to the firm.[14] Despite rigorous product development processes, over 50 percent of consumer and industrial products fail.[15] Technical flaws account for about 20 percent of product failures, whereas marketing and management-related deficiencies account 75 percent of product. The various departments within the firm must work together to increase the likelihood of new product success.[16]

Each phase and stage of the development framework is accompanied by a complementary gate. *Gates* are the points in the development process at which the firm evaluates the potential for a product. The gates are pre-determined and specify *must meet* requirements of a project and *should meet* requirements of a product. At each stage in the process, firms deliberate whether to *kill* the project or allow it to *go* forward to the next stage. Firms make substantial investments in new product development, and the benefits of successful new products and the costs of failure are staggering. Estimates indicate that products released in the past five years account for 33 percent of a firm's revenue on average.[17] By contrast, failed product launches in the electronics industry are estimated at more than $20 billion per year.[18] For example, Sony incurred losses of $3.5 billion in in 2007 and 2008 before the PlayStation 3 became profitable until 2011.[19]

---

[13] Cooper, Robert G. (2009), "How Companies Are Reinventing Their Idea-to-Launch Methodologies," *Research Technology Management*, (March-April) 47–57.

[14] Ayers, Doug, Dahlstrom, Robert, and Skinner, Steven J. (1997), "An Exploratory Investigation of Organizational Antecedents to New Product Success," *Journal of Marketing Research*, 34 (1), 107–116.

[15] www.foodnavigator-usa.com/Markets/Why-do-85-of-new-CPG-products-fail-within-two-years (February 17, 2017); www.forbes.com/sites/mikecollins/2015/04/30/reducing-the-failure-rate-of-new-products/ (February 17, 2017); and Ogawa, Susumu, and Frank T. Piller (2006), "Reducing the Risks of New Product Development," *MIT Sloan Management Review* 47 (2), 65–72.

[16] Clugston, Christopher O. (1995), "Product Failures: Why Are We Implementing Wrong Solutions?" *Electronic News*, 41(2069), 50.

[17] Cooper, Robert G. (2001), *Winning at New Products: Accelerating the Process from Idea to Launch*. 3rd edition. New York: Basic Books.

[18] Clugston, Christopher O. (1995), "Product Failures: Why Are We Implementing Wrong Solutions?" *Electronic News*, 41(2069), 50.

[19] www.gamespot.com/articles/sony-not-expecting-ps3-like-losses-for-ps4/1100-6412760/ (February 17, 2017).

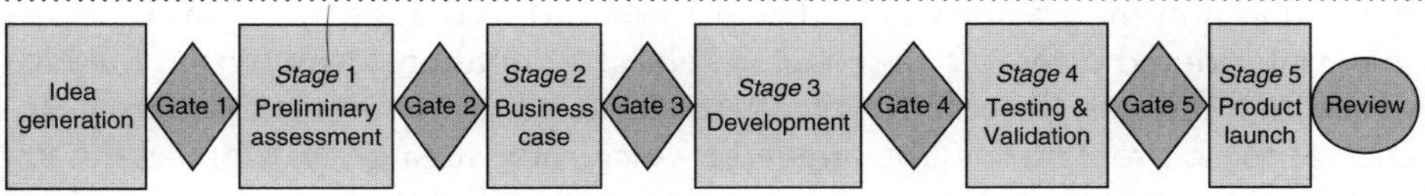

FIGURE 12-2
Product innovation
framework.[20]

By devising an appropriate series of gates or checkpoints, firms increase the likelihood of success and reduce the potential for failure. Figure 12-2 offers a typical product development process. As the product develops toward full market launch, the costs associated with the product increase. Consequently, each stage of the process demands more stringent gates that serves as barriers to advancement of the new product project. Decisions that are made to *kill* products should be made as early as possible in the development process. The early elimination of products destined for market failure prevents the firm from spending valuable resources needlessly. Nevertheless, the decision to eliminate a known unsuccessful project benefits the firm regardless of the stage at which the project is killed.

We next outline the various phases of the new product development process. We begin with a discussion of idea generation.

PRODUCT INNOVATION: IDEA GENERATION

The initial activity in the new product development process is the generation of an idea. The stakeholders associated with an organization are at the forefront of this phase of the new product development process, and it is essential to treat stakeholders as partners throughout product innovation. New ideas can emerge from virtually any aspect of the environment, and it is important to work with stakeholders to understand their vantage points for innovations. Participation product development should, therefore, include employees, consumers, vendors, government, nongovernment organizations, and the general public.

Employees are often valuable sources of information as they have the potential to understand the market as well as the production and strategic objectives of the firm. Note, however, that this understanding can also be delimiting to employees. The logic of "business as usual" may detract from the ability to offer ideas that genuinely challenge current operations. In many situations, organizations develop teams of employees involved in new product development. These individuals come from the marketing function as well as other technical areas of the firm.[21] If these teams are to generate ideas successfully, it is imperative to recognize some of the inherent challenges of group development. The group process may generate **production blocking** characterized by the inability to offer opinions simultaneously. When individuals cannot simultaneously express opinions, unexpressed opinions can be forgotten or dismissed by others involved

---

[20] Cooper, Robert G. (1990), "Stage-Gate System: A New Tool for Managing New Products," *Business Horizons*, (May-June), 44–54.

[21] Lilien, Gary L., Pamela D. Morrison, Kathleen Searls, Mary Sonnack, and Eric von Hippel (2002), "Performance Assessment of the Lead User Idea-Generation Process for New Product Development," *Management Science*, 48 (8), 1042–1059; and Hirunyawipada, Tanawat, and Audhesh K. Paswan (2013), "Effects of Team Cognition and Constraint on New Product Ideation," *Journal of Business Research* 66 (11), 2332–2337.

in the decision-making process.[22] The firm should recognize that group process may be hindered by employee concerns about evaluations drawn from the idea generation process. Research indicates that under some circumstances the influence of these problems can be quelled by electronic idea generation sessions.[23] Bayer, for example, implemented a program called "Triple-I: Inspiration, Ideas, Innovation," which uses an intranet portal to collect ideas from its employees across the globe. Over 9,000 ideas were submitted by employees within the first four years of implementing the program, and Bayer brought three of those ideas to market, with 32 more being developed and tested.[24]

The organization must also contend with the possibility that some team members free-ride in the development process by failing to offer ideas in the product development process. This failure to participate in idea generation can be lowered by offering employees incentives for their participation.[25] These incentives can be nonmonetary, such as public recognition for a creative idea, or monetary, such as a financial bonus for creative ideas. To encourage employees to think outside the box, some companies may even reward the "wackiest" ideas generated in the new product development process.[26]

Beyond the organization, it is also clearly essential to poll the activity of consumers of the firm's product. Although the typical process in the firm has been to survey the breadth of consumers in a market, research emphasizes the need to look at lead users. **Lead users** are consumers who expect attractive innovation-related benefits from a solution and experience needs for an innovation earlier than most participants in a target market.[27] A representative sample of the target market customers that is familiar with existing product uses may have difficulty conceiving of novel product uses and attributes. By contrast, future-oriented lead users are more inclined to face issues today than most users will face in the coming months.[28] These lead users tend to have more consumer product knowledge and experience than other consumers. Relative to other users, they more frequently commit to risky, innovative, and difficult tasks, and they are more likely to be predisposed to innovation.[29]

---

[22] Stroebe, Wolfgang, and Michael Diehl (1994), "Why Groups Are Less Effective than Their Members: On Productivity Losses in Idea-Generating Groups," *European Review of Social Psychology* 5 (1), 271–303.

[23] Gallupe, R. Brent, Lana M. Bastianutti, and William H. Cooper (1991), "Unblocking Brainstorms," *Journal of Applied Psychology*, 76 (1), 137–142.

[24] www.forbes.com/2010/03/15/bayer-employee-innovation-leadership-managing -engagement.html (February 17, 2017).

[25] Toubia, Olivier (2006), "Idea Generation, Creativity, and Incentives," *Marketing Science*, 25 (5), 411–425.

[26] Burroughs, James E., Darren W. Dahl, C. Page Moreau, Amitava Chattopadhyay, and Gerald J. Gorn (2011), "Facilitating and Rewarding Creativity during New Product Development," *Journal of Marketing*, 75 (4), 53–67.

[27] von Hippel, Eric (1986) "Lead Users: A Source of Novel Product Concepts," *Management Science* 32(7), 791–805.

[28] Lilien, Gary L., Pamela D. Morrison, Kathleen Searls, Mary Sonnack, and Eric von Hippel (2002), "Performance Assessment of the Lead User Idea-Generation Process for New Product Development," *Management Science*, 48 (8), 1042–1059.

[29] Schreier, Martin, and Reinhard Prügl (2008), "Extending Lead-User Theory: Antecedents and Consequences of Consumers' Lead Userness," *Journal of Product Innovation Management*, 25 (4) 331–346.

Firms may also benefit from examining the commonalities of noncustomers. Specifically, firms should identify their noncustomers and ask them, "Why aren't you using the product?" Answering this question may lead to new product ideas with substantial growth potential.[30] For example, Nintendo found that their noncustomers (e.g., older gamers, elderly consumers, parents with small children) did not play video games because the controllers were too difficult to master and playing games led to a more sedentary lifestyle.[31] Based on the noncustomers' feedback, Nintendo developed the Wii, a gaming console that captured the simplicity and interactivity the noncustomers desired. Nintendo stripped all the bells and whistles (e.g., no DVD player and no high-definition graphics), lowering its manufacturing costs and improving the operational efficiency of the console. The Wii not only had fewer component parts, but it was smaller and ran more efficiently than the competitor products at the time. In contrast to the Wii, which used less than 14 watts for one hour of play, competitive products used over 80 watts.[32]

Vendors, the organizations that market to one's firm, can also be a source of new product ideas. Competitive suppliers operating close to the firm provide shortened communication lines that facilitate the exchange of ideas that yield innovations.[33] Furthermore, sales organizations can take an innovative idea generated in one context and adopt this logic in a novel setting. Nevertheless, vendors operate in a mixed-motive model and may not have the best interests of the seller in mind. In some cases, firms have, therefore, elected to develop teams of personnel from the vendor as well as the user.[34] These interfirm teams can increase the quality of new product ideas by reducing the misunderstanding that arises from working across corporate boundaries. Similar to their intra-firm counterparts, cross-functional teams that share information early and throughout their operations can identify problem areas early in the development process.[35]

Government at all levels—from local operations to multinational alliances—is also a valuable source of new ideas. For example, the U.S. Department of Commerce supports efforts to bring new technology to markets via the National Institute of Standards and Technology (NIST). NIST promotes innovation in the United States through high-risk, high-reward research in areas of critical national need.[36] Scientists affiliated with NIST conduct breakthrough research that leads to the innovations, but the range of NIST effort does not extend to

---

[30] Kim, W. Chan, and Renee Mauborgne (2005), *Blue Ocean Strategy: How to Create Uncontested Market Space and Make Competition Irrelevant*, Boston, MA: Harvard Business Press.

[31] www.blueoceanstrategy.com/teaching-materials/nintendo-wii/ (July 30, 2015).

[32] www.greenbiz.com/news/2010/12/16/nintendo-wii-ranked-most-energy-efficient -game-system (February 17, 2017).

[33] Porter, Michael (1990), "The Competitive Advantage of Nations," *Harvard Business Review*, 68 (2), 73–93.

[34] Potter, Anthony, and Benn Lawson (2013), "Help or Hindrance: Causal Ambiguity and Supplier Involvement in New Product Development Teams," *Journal of Product and Innovation Management*, 30 (4), 794–808.

[35] Fu, Frank Q., Eli Jones, and Willy Bolander (2008), "Product Innovativeness, Customer Newness, and New Product Performance: A Time-Lagged Examination of the Impact of Salesperson Selling Intentions on New Product Performance," *Journal of Personal Selling & Sales Management*, 28 (4), 351–364.

[36] www.nist.gov/director/pao (February 17, 2017).

product development in any of its research areas. The work needed to exploit NIST technologies for commercial viability requires innovation on behalf of the private sector. Commercially promising patents are identified together with the technological gaps that impede their direct transition to the marketplace. For example, recently supported NIST research has fostered the development of flexible computer chip technology. Innovators who gain an understanding of this technology can develop marketable processor chips for a variety of applications[37].

Nongovernment organizations (NGOs) are similar to government in the sense that they serve as sources of information for the development of new ideas. GreenBlue, for example, is an NGO that encourages product and process innovation to achieve a more sustainable material economy.[38] Organizations such as McDonalds, IBM, and Wal-Mart have recognized that interaction with these organizations can provide a wealth of information that is relevant to the generation of new ideas.

While it is insightful to examine the source of an innovation, it is also illuminating to examine the events that serve as the impetus for developing an innovation. Prior research suggests seven possible sources of innovation that vary based on whether they are associated with events occurring within or outside of an industry.[39] Internal events the yield innovation include:

Unexpected occurrences. Unexpected occurrences refer to situations in which customers find novel unanticipated uses for a product. For example, backpackers who hike long distances are reluctant to carry many items in their backpacks as each item increases the burden of the journey. Many backpackers will, therefore, forego the use of a pillow when a makeshift one can be made from clothing and a nylon bag. When the utility of an item can broaden to include multiple functions, a new use for a product emerges. In addition, by enabling a single product to do the work of multiple items, the economic and ecological costs associated with the activity decline.

Incongruities. Incongruities arise when the assumptions under which an industry operates do not align with reality. Manufacturing incongruities are associated with incongruities in the logic or rhythm of the manufacturing process, whereas economic incongruities are associated with discrepancies between expectations and results. For example, Quick Beauty House in Japan recognized a discrepancy between the prevailing logic of the Asian barbershop industry and reality. Prior to Quick Beauty House, haircuts followed a ritual-like process where numerous hot towels are applied, the head and shoulders are massaged, green tea is served, and special hair and skin treatments are applied during the haircut.[40] The entire

---

[37] www.nist.gov/pml/engineering-physics-division/memory-twist-nist-develops-flexible-memristor-video-transcript (February 17, 2017).

[38] www.greenblue.org/about/ (February 17, 2017).

[39] Drucker, Peter R. (2002), "The Discipline of Innovation," *Harvard Business Review*, 80 (8), 95–103.

[40] Kim, W. Chan, and Renee Mauborgne (2005), *Blue Ocean Strategy: How to Create Uncontested Market Space and Make Competition Irrelevant*, Boston, MA: Harvard Business Press.

process lasts about an hour.[41] Realizing that working men did not have an hour to waste, Quick Beauty streamlined the haircutting process offered a basic cut in 10 minutes. Although Quick Beauty House had to install sinks due to a dated, postwar Barber Law, water is not used in the haircutting process, making it a more ecofriendly process.

Process Needs. Process needs refer to modifications in the operations of a product to enhance its performance. For instance, consumers' increasing need for connectivity has given rise to Bluetooth technology. This technology lets consumers send vital information, listen to music, and share videos and pictures amongst other things between paired devices. Billions of devices ranging from mobile phones and medical devices to forks and toothbrushes have Bluetooth technology. This technology was developed to replace the cables needed to connect devices while maintaining high levels of security.[42]

External events refer to factors happening outside of the industry that prompt innovation. These include:

Market Changes. Market changes refer to situations in which the nature of the industry or market changes. In the television industry, for instance, the basic operation of the product changed from an analog to digital device in 2009. This change in the product requirements occurred despite recognition that more than 3.5 million U.S. homes were not ready for digital broadcasting.[43]

Demographic Changes. Demographics refer to the study of vital statistics such as race, age, gender, and income. Changes in these factors within a population can have a dramatic effect on innovations. With the world's aging population, companies such as IBM and Apple are developing products and applications to ensure the elderly population maintains a good quality of life.[44] In Japan, which has the fastest growing aging population, new products are being developed used to ease "the social pain of aging."[45] Panasonic, for example, developed a robot programmed to gently wash the hair of those who have difficulty raising their arms, and Toyota is trying to develop robots to assist the elderly with household chores.

Changes in Perception. Changes in perception occur when consumers modify their opinions about some factor in the marketplace. For example, consumers' perceptions of food safety and the use of chemical pesticides has changed over the years, fueling a 3400 percent increase in sales of organic products since 1990.[46] Consumers perceive organic products as safer, healthier, and better tasting than

[41] www.ft.com/cms/s/0/8cded488-57d9-11e1-ae89-00144feabdc0.html#axzz3hp07KpLm (February 17, 2017).

[42] www.bluetooth.com/what-is-bluetooth-technology (February 17, 2017).

[43] Schatz, Amy (2009), "FCC to Hold National Digital-TV Test Before Switch," *Wall Street Journal*, (May 5).

[44] fortune.com/2015/04/30/apple-ibm-japan-post/ (February 17, 2017).

[45] www.industryweek.com/automation/robots-help-japans-aging-population (February 17, 2017).

[46] www.wholefoodsmarket.com/mission-values/organic/growth-organics-industry

their nonorganic counterparts. Sales of organic products hit a record in 2014, totaling $31.9 billion.[47] Now 8 of 10 U.S. families report purchasing organic products.[48]

New Knowledge. New knowledge refers to the use of new technical, scientific, or social information that can be instrumental in addressing a market problem. For example, the advent of hybrid automobile engines was prompted in part by new knowledge associated with fuel cell and electric motor technologies.[49]

After the initial generation of an idea, the firm implements its first assessment of the viability of the topic. Throughout the development process at each stage of the model, many firms use checklists or scorecards to determine the degree to which the idea fulfills "must meet" and "should meet" criteria. The product development evaluations are a *funnel rather a tunnel* used to assess products that move toward the market.[50] Thus, the initial screen of the product is less stringent than later gates in the process. Although there are must meet and should meet criteria at this stage, there are no financial criteria at this juncture. The evaluation focuses on project feasibility, strategic alignment, synergy, market attractiveness, and synergy with company's core resources and business. If the decision is made to move forward, the firm begins the preliminary assessment.[51]

PRODUCT INNOVATION: PRELIMINARY ASSESSMENT

The preliminary analysis is the first stage of the new product development process. At this stage, the firm performs an initial market assessment in which the organization determines the market potential and size. The firm will ordinarily perform an online and library search for related products and use focus groups and interaction with key users to assess the likelihood of marketplace acceptance of the product.[52] The market analysis is complemented by a preliminary technical analysis in which the firm assesses the manufacturing and development feasibility of a project. The organization will seek to quantify the time and costs associated with manufacturing the product.[53]

(February) 17, 2017); and www.foodsafetynews.com/2014/04/report-fast-growing-organics -industry-is-intentionally-deceptive/#.VcGWhflViko (February 17, 2017).

[47] ota.com/resources/organic-industry-survey (February 17, 2017).

[48] ota.com/resources/consumer-attitudes-and-beliefs-study (February 17, 2017).

[49] auto.howstuffworks.com/hybrid-car.htm (February 17, 2017).

[50] Cooper, Robert G. (2009), "How Companies are Reinventing their Idea-to-Launch Methodologies." *Research and Technology Management*, (March-April), 47–57.

[51] Cooper, Robert G. (1990), "Stage-Gate System: A New Tool for Managing New Products," *Business Horizons*, (May-June), 44–54.

[52] Cooper, Robert G., and Elko J. Kleinschmidt (1986), "An Investigation into the New Product Process: Steps, Deficiencies and Impact," *Journal of Product Innovation Management*, 3, 71–85.

[53] Fairlie-Clarke, Tony, and Mark Muller (2003), "An Activity Model of the Product Development Process," *Journal of Engineering Design*, 14 (3), 247–252.

Because the firm will move forward in multiple directions that may include marketing, procurement, logistics, manufacturing, and R&D, it is essential to build effective project teams at this beginning of the development process. Effective new product teams must have clear goals and unified commitment among the team members.[54] Team members should collectively possess the capabilities to achieve the project's objectives, and they should be supported by resources and psychological support needed to maintain a high level of motivation and focus. Furthermore, the team structure should emphasize a collaborative work environment that promotes effective communication. Team leaders should provide a consistent focused message that directs all team members to achieve high levels of performance.[55]

Gate 2 is the screen used to evaluate potential products at the end of the first stage. Although the *go/kill* will not be markedly different from the initial screen, the "should meet" criteria now incorporate considerations brought to the process by customers and sales representatives. Financial criteria at this point are not substantial, but they do address the potential break-even point for the venture. If the project adequately addresses the should meet and must meet criteria, the project moves forward to the business case preparation.[56]

PRODUCT INNOVATION: BUSINESS CASE PREPARATION

The business case preparation phase is the last stage in the process before substantial investment is made in product development. Consequently, it is essential for the firm to identify the attractiveness of the product associated with manufacturing, marketing, legal, and financial constraints.[57] The manufacturing assessment must address the investment required to engage in production as well as the costs of manufacturing. Since organizations that do not address sustainability concerns face increased social and economic liability, it is important for the manufacturing cost analysis to consider triple bottom-line costs associated with manufacturing and the supply chain.[58]

The marketing component of the business case requires the organization to assess consumer needs and wants to determine customer expectations for the ideal new product. In addition, the firm will propose new products to customers to determine their likely acceptance of a new product. Firms that engage in dialogue with potential consumers gain input that enables them to make product

[54] Larson, Carl, and Frank LaFasto (1989), *Teamwork: What Must Go Right/What Can Go Wrong*, Sage Publications (1989).

[55] Componation, Paul J., Alisha D. Youngblood, Dawn R. Utley, Phillip A. Farrington (2008), "A Preliminary Assessment of the Relationships Between Project Success, System Engineering, and Team Organization," *Engineering Management Journal*, 20 (4), 40–46.

[56] Cooper, Robert G. (1990), "Stage-Gate System: A New Tool for Managing New Products," *Business Horizons*, (May-June), 44–54.

[57] Cooper, Robert G., and Elko J. Kleinschmidt (1986), "An Investigation into the New Product Process: Steps, Deficiencies and Impact," *Journal of Product Innovation Management*, 3, 71–85.

[58] Bernon, Michael, and John Cullen (2007), "An Integrated Approach to Managing Reverse Logistics," *International Journal of Logistics: Research and Applications*, 10 (1), 41–56.

enhancements prior to the product development stage.[59] This dialogue enables the firm to identify the economic, social, and ecological merits of the product as they relate to potential consumers. The marketing analysis will also require a competitive analysis to determine the relative advantage of a new product. Similarly, the firm will assess the patentability of a new product as well as a review of legal and regulatory constraints. Increasingly, the legal requirements are embracing technologies that are more beneficial or less harmful to the environment. For example, prevailing EU law prevents firms from marketing electrical or electronic components made from mercury, lead, cadmium, and hexavalent chromium.[60]

The third gate in the new product development process is critical because it is the last chance to eliminate the idea prior to a sizeable investment. Research within the stage-gate model indicates the need to incorporate the following considerations before advancing to product development:[61]

Product Competitive Advantage. The value proposition for the new product must be compelling and superior with respect to some facet of the triple bottom line. This benefit should be recognized and viewed as favorable by the consumer. If the value proposition is based on ecological merits, then the trade-offs associated with this benefit should be greater than any associated limitations with respect to the social and economic benefits of the product.

Strategic Fit. It is essential that the new product be consistent with the firm's business strategy. Furthermore, the importance of the product to the business strategy must be recognized.

Market Attractiveness. The attractiveness of the market includes consideration of the market size and the growth potential. The margins realized by competitors in this market should be established, and the intensity of the competition in the market must be determined.

Core Competencies Relatedness. New projects should reflect the core strengths in the firm. The attractiveness of new products should increase when they enable a firm to leverage strengths in marketing, production, technology, and distribution.

Technical Feasibility. The feasibility of the technology is addressed by identifying the results to date of a technology and the complexity of the technology associated with a new product. The firm should also identify the degree to which it is familiar with the technology inherent to a new product.

---

[59] Seidel, Victor P. (2007), "Concept Shifting and the Radical Product Development Process," *Journal of Product Innovation Management*, 24 (6), 522–533.

[60] Ogunseitan, Oladele A. (2007), "Public Health and Environmental Benefits of Adopting Lead-Free Solders," *Journal of the Minerals, Metals and Materials Society*, 59 (7), 12–17.

[61] Cooper, Robert G. (2009), "How Companies Are Reinventing Their Idea-to-Launch Methodologies." *Research and Technology Management*, (March-April), 47–57.

Financial Risks and Rewards. The financial assessment should consider the level of risk associated with a product as well as the ability of the firm to address the risk. The organization should also examine the financial reward in terms of the net present value, the productivity index, and the size of the financial opportunity.

PRODUCT INNOVATION: PRODUCT DEVELOPMENT

When a product concept successfully passes through the third gate in the development process, it then it moves into product development.[62] Marketing and manufacturing activities move in parallel at this stage. The marketing function must continue to track the potential for the product and continue to obtain customer feedback concerning the ecological, social, and economic value associated with the new offering. It is essential to determine the extent to which consumers understand, recognize, and value the benefits derived from the product. On the manufacturing side, the firm develops a product prototype. In the process, the firm assesses the technical feasibility of the new product.

In the development of Tide Pods, for example, Proctor & Gamble faced many technical challenges.[63] Proctor & Gamble introduced a pod-like product in 2000, but it pulled the product from the market because it did not dissolve properly.

FIGURE 12-3

Proctor & Gamble faced many challenges in the development of Tide Pods.

---

[62] Miller, Lawrence, Ruth Miller, and John Dismukes (2005-2006), "The Critical Role of Information and Information Technology in Future Accelerated Radical Innovation," *Information Knowledge Systems Management*, 5 (2), 63–99.

[63] news.yahoo.com/making-product-takes-lots-time-money-142418488.html (February 17, 2017).

Designing a water-soluble film was a key step in determining the product's technical feasibility. Proctor & Gamble partnered with MonoSol, a company that makes water-soluble films. The film, which is designed to dissolve in water, had to withstand the detergent. Proctor & Gamble reformulated its detergent to contain only 10 percent water to prevent the premature dissolving of the film. The next challenge was getting the cleanser, fabric softener, and brightener into one product without them mixing before dissolving in the wash. After 450 product sketches, Proctor & Gamble developed a technology to separate the three components in the pod. Proctor & Gamble dedicated eight years and 75 technical employees to the development of Tide Pods,[64] one of the biggest innovation in laundry in the last 25 years.

At the close of this stage, the firm faces gate 4 in the development process. The criteria outlined in gate 3 are reviewed to evaluate the attractiveness of the product. Although the evaluative criteria do not change much from the previous gate, new information concerning the marketplace attractiveness and financial merits of the project are incorporated into the decision calculus. If the decision is made to go forward, the firm mobilizes to perform a market test.

PRODUCT INNOVATION: TEST MARKET AND VALIDATION

In the final stage before full market launch of the product, the firm examines whether the product can be manufactured and marketed in a profitable manner. The firm will engage in pilot production during which it will determine the production rates and costs.[65] Importantly, the triple bottom-line criteria identified previously must be observable in the test runs of the production process. The firm cannot determine the total number of by-products that emerge from production, but it will be able to observe which by-products are provided by manufacturing. The firm can determine whether these products can be used in alternative operations as well as the costs and the returns associated with the by-product. For example, steel manufacturers identify the amount of slag produced that can be marketed to the cement industry. The assessment of by-products should also examine the amount of greenhouse gases produced in the manufacturing process. Firms that identify greenhouse gas production can act to offset the cost of this operation by making carbon dioxide available to industry or via carbon offset trading.

The marketing activity at this stage focuses on the determining the level of interest and acceptance among consumers. If the firm can adequately determine demand, it can accurately determine the resources needed in production and marketing. Test marketing of the product is one activity that provides substantial insight into resource constraints. In a test market, the firm implements a complete market strategy in a single market over a short-term horizon. The test

---

[64] news.tide.com/press-release/detergents/tide-puts-spin-laundry-introduction-tide-pods (February 17, 2017).

[65] Cooper, Robert G. (1990), "Stage-Gate System: A New Tool for Managing New Products," *Business Horizons*, (May-June), 44–54.

FIGURE 12-4
Advertisement for Scott
Naturals Tube Free tissue
paper.[66]

market provides new information about consumer responses to products, and it provides an estimate of sales and profitability.[67] For example, in 2010 Kimberly-Clark began test marketing its Scotts Natural Tube Free bath tissue in a limited number of cities in northeastern United States.[68] After a successful test market, the company began distributing the product nationally in 2014. Estimates indicate that 17 billion toilet paper tubes are produced annually, enough to fill the Empire State building twice.[69] See Figure 12-4.

To further its sustainability efforts, a subsidiary of the company, Kimberly-Clark Professional, has test marketed tissue products in North America that contain 20 percent bamboo and marketed tissues in the U.K. that contain 10 percent bamboo and 90 percent recycled fiber.[70] These tests provide the opportunity to learn about consumer acceptance of the new sustainable products. The company subsequently introduced Green Harvest products made with 20 percent plant fiber.[71] Use of plant fiber enables the firm to reduce the amount of tree fiber in this product line. Furthermore, the company can determine the amount of sustainable materials used while maintaining the characteristics of the tissue products that consumers desire (e.g., softness and quality).

Gate 5 at the end of the test market is a crucial point at which to assess whether the product should go into full production. Given the overall costs of producing and selling the product, it is important to be frank in the evaluation

[66] www.sustainablebrands.com/news_and_views/products_design/hannah_ritchie/scott_brand_launches_tube-free_toilet_paper_invite_peo (February 17, 2017).

[67] www.ama.org/resources/Pages/Dictionary.aspx?dLetter=T (February 17, 2017).

[68] usatoday30.usatoday.com/money/industries/environment/2010-10-27-1Atube27_ST_N.htm (February 17, 2017).

[69] www.treehugger.com/sustainable-product-design/one-toilet-paper-company-decides-to-ditch-the-tube.html (February 17, 2017).

[70] www.environmentalleader.com/2012/06/19/kimberly-clark-to-use-50-alternative-wood-fiber-by-2025/

[71] www.kcprofessional.com/sustainability/greenharvest-products (February 17, 2017).

at this stage. Many organizations grapple with the desire to be objective at this stage given that many individuals have dedicated substantial effort to product development.[72] Projects that will not obtain profitable levels of sales that are eliminated at this stage save the firm sizeable investments. Financial projections are paramount at this stage, and the test market and the pilot production provide great insight into these projections. The test market illuminates the potential sales, whereas the test market and the pilot production inform the firm about the ecological, social, and economic costs of the product. Consequently, the firm is poised to offer a more precise prediction of the sales and profit potential of a product. This information is essential as it enables the firm to project human resource needs for production and marketing. This information further enables the firm to estimate its resource requirements as well as the by-products of production. If the profit potential of a product is sizable, then the firm begins full product production.

PRODUCT INNOVATION: FULL PRODUCTION AND FOLLOW-UP

When the product reaches the commercialization stage, the production staff commits resources to full-scale manufacturing. Similarly, marketing and sales must be fully committed to the product. Review of operations, regardless of the level of performance, is germane to this stage of operations. Despite the detailed analysis associated with the new product development process, upward of half of all new products still fail to achieve commercial success.[73] It is incumbent on the firm to review the product development process to reconcile marketplace and production realities against the projections. Sustainability assessments associated with the ecological and social returns of a project necessarily should augment that economic costs and benefit considerations.

Data associated with expenditures, revenues, profits, and timing should be compared to related projections so that the firm can identify opportunities to learn from the new product development process. Note this exercise should be performed regardless of the degree of success with the project. Recognizing individuals who made quality projections and evaluations likely reinforces their predisposition to continue to perform adequately. Critiques that identify potential areas for improvement similarly enable members of the new product development team to refine their evaluation and assessment of future projects.

---

[72] Mohr, Jakki, Sanjit Sengupta, and Stanley Slater (2010), *Marketing of High-Technology Products and Innovations*, Upper Saddle River, NJ: Prentice-Hall.

[73] Ogawa, Susumu, and Frank T. Piller (2006), "Reducing the Risks of New Product Development," *MIT Sloan Management Review*, 47 (Winter), 65–71.

Introduction

The goal of this chapter has been to develop strategies that enable firms to innovative product and product strategies. New products are important to success, yet many products fail to enhance the performance of the firm. We presented the stage-gate model of new product development as a framework for product development. We augmented the discussion of this framework by outlining a process by which firms can enhance process innovations.

Product Innovation Framework

The stage-gate process refers a series of activities involved in designing of new products. Stage-gate recognizes that firms engage in a number of activities between idea conception and the market launch of a product. These phases are multifunctional and require interaction among marketing, R&D, production, and other activities internal and external to the firm.

Product Innovation: Idea Generation

The initial activity in the new product development process is the generation of an idea. Since new ideas can emerge from virtually any aspect of the environment, it is important to work with stakeholders to understand their vantage points for innovations. Participation in product development should include employees, consumers, vendors, government, and other stakeholders.

Product Innovation: Preliminary Assessment

The preliminary analysis is the stage in which the firm performs an initial market assessment to determine the market potential and size. The firm will ordinarily perform an online and library search for related products and use focus groups and interaction with key users to assess the likelihood of marketplace acceptance of the product. The market analysis is complemented by a preliminary technical analysis in which the firm assesses the manufacturing and development feasibility of a project.

Product Innovation: Business Case Preparation

The business case preparation phase is the stage in which the firm evaluates the attractiveness of the product given manufacturing, marketing, legal, and financial constraints. The manufacturing assessment must address the investment required to engage in production as well as the costs of manufacturing. The marketing component of the business case requires the organization to assess consumer needs and wants to determine customer expectations for the ideal new product. The firm also assesses the patentability of a new product and reviews other regulatory constraints.

Product Innovation: Product Development

During this stage, marketing and manufacturing work in tandem to bring the product closer to market. The marketing function tracks the potential for the product and obtains customer feedback concerning the ecological, social, and economic benefits derived from the product. On the manufacturing side, the firm develops a prototype and assesses the technical feasibility of the new product.

Product Innovation: Test Market and Validation

In this final stage before full market launch of the product, the firm examines whether the product can be manufactured and marketed in a profitable manner. The firm will engage in pilot production during which it will determine the production rates and costs. The marketing activity at this stage focuses on determining the level of interest and the acceptance among consumers. When the firm adequately determines demand, it can accurately determine the resources needed for production and marketing.

Product Innovation: Full Production and Follow-up

At this stage, the production staff commits resources to full-scale manufacturing, and marketing similarly commits to the product. Review of operations, regardless of the level of performance, is germane to this stage of operations. It is essential for the firm to review the product development process to reconcile marketplace and production realities against the projections. Sustainability assessments associated with the ecological and social returns of a project necessarily should augment that economic costs and benefit considerations.

KEY TERMS

product innovation   production blocking
process innovation   lead users

DISCUSSION QUESTIONS

1. How is sustainability relevant to new product development?
2. Figure 12-2 outlines a series of processes that precede the development of new products. Why is it necessary for the firm to pass through each phase?
3. What are gates, and why are they important to the new product development?
4. Explain why the decisions made at each gate should involve sustainability considerations.
5. Who are the stakeholders who should be consulted during idea generation, and how does each inform the development process?
6. Describe a situation in which internal events lead to the development of an innovation.

7. What are the potential consequences to the firm that does not adequately engage in the business case preparation?

8. What critical decision is made after test marketing, and what information contributes to this decision?

9. How do the financial considerations of a new product development emerge over time?

10. Why is the third gate critical to new product development? What factors should be assessed before advancing to product development

13

Sustainable Services Marketing

INTRODUCTION

Kimpton Hotels

A woman walks into a hotel bar in San Francisco and asks whether any of the featured wines is organic. At the same time, a vacationer checking into a room in New York asks whether the hotel uses recycled paper and nontoxic cleaning supplies. In both cases, the hotel and the restaurant staff at Kimpton Hotels are able to provide a satisfying answer to the patrons. Founded in 1981, the Kimpton Hotel chain now includes more than 60 properties in the United States.[1] Guests consistently rank these hotels among the highest for customer satisfaction and emotional attachment.

Although many things contribute to the customer evaluations of a hotel, Kimpton has made a notable investment in sustainability for several years, and it has actively promoted this investment with its customers, vendors, and other stakeholders. One of the more noticeable features of these hotels is the practice of remodeling and refurbishing existing buildings in urban settings.[2] For example, Kimpton has transformed a Seattle building constructed in 1901 into the Alexis Hotel. These preservation activities nurture urban traditions while fostering increased sustainability.

FIGURE 13-1

A cable car passes the Sir Francis Drake, a Kimpton Hotel in San Francisco.[3]

---

[1] www.kimptonhotels.com/kimpton-experience (January 23, 2017).

[2] www.kimptonhotels.com/kimpton-history (January 23, 2017).

[3] www.travelpod.com/hotel_photo/Sir_Francis_Drake_Hotel_A_Kimpton_Hotel-San_Francisco_large.jpg (January 23, 2017).

In 2005, Kimpton initiated a campaign called *EarthCare* that examined eco-friendly practices performed daily at each hotel.[4] The program involved such practices as placing recycling bins in guest rooms for the disposal of organic mini-bar items.[5] This program was developed with a particular interest in the guest experience and financial performance. Kimpton recognized early on that this sustainability initiative would only be successful if it did not compromise the quality of the hotel experience or detract from the bottom line for shareholders.

As a complement to the EarthCare program, Kimpton also developed *EarthCare Champions* in every restaurant and hotel. Any associate can be a champion—from general managers to housekeepers. These champions meet twice a month to ensure compliance with standards, develop tools to train new employees, and keep the sustainability focus on the minds of all employees. These champions have also generated many of the new ideas for products and services that enable Kimpton to remain at the forefront of sustainability in the hotel industry.

The sustainability efforts of the firm are also incorporated into the product offerings in the restaurants. One of the means for pursuing sustainability in the food service industry is to buy food products grown locally. This practice increases food freshness while decreasing the restaurant's carbon footprint. In addition, this practice provides the opportunity for chefs to offer unique menu options not available in other parts of the country. Implementation of this strategy enables Kimpton chefs to serve unique menu choices made from fresh and organic ingredients.[6] Where healthy local alternatives are not available, the firm emphasizes sourcing of ecofriendly products produced in a sustainable, organic, or biodynamic fashion.

Kimpton has been able to incorporate sustainability into operations while simultaneously achieving milestones in financial, relational, and environmental performance. In the first year of EarthCare, Kimpton attributed over $500,000 in new revenue to the program. It also saved considerably from directives that examined room occupancy and energy usage.[7] The company has fostered closer relationships with employees via the EarthCare Champions program, and the ecofriendly requirements for food service products have nurtured relationships with local producers. Among the environmental benefits are reduced water usage and reduced use of toxins.

One of the ways that Kimpton Hotels make consumers aware of its commitments to sustainability is through its participation in the Green Key Global Program.[8] Green Key Global is an internationally recognized environmental certification body. The criteria for certification are based on the voluntary principles established by Global Sustainable Tourism Council[9] and are designed specifically for the lodging industry.

---

[4] Hurley, Lisa (2009), "The Green Room," *Association Meetings* (August), 35; and www.kimptonhotels.com/blog/down-to-earth-kimpton-celebrates-earth-day-every-day/ (January 23, 2017).

[5] Jenning, Lisa (2007), "Eco-friendly Ways Bring in Green," *Nation's Restaurant News*, (October 1), 90, 92.

[6] www.kimptonhotels.com/restaurants/restaurants.aspx (October 21, 2009).

[7] www.hospitalityupgrade.com/_magazine/magazine_Detail.asp?ID=307 (January 23, 2017).

[8] greenkeyglobal.com/news/kimpton-hotels-restaurants-group-secures-green-key-certification-portfolio/ (January 26, 2017).

[9] greenkeyglobal.com/about/ (January 26, 2017).

The Kimpton Hotels example underscores the work undertaken in the services sector to enhance sustainability. In order to contribute to these efforts, it is meaningful to characterize how services can be offered in sustainable manner. We also describe the sustainable delivery of services, and we describe the use of energy in education, health care, and lodging sectors of the economy.

SUSTAINABLE VALUE IN SERVICES

The term *services* refers to processes, deeds, and performances coproduced or provided by one entity for another entity.[10] The service sector includes service businesses (e.g., retail stores and hotels), educational institutions, correctional facilities, religious groups, and fraternal organizations. Even though services account for more than 50 percent of the gross domestic product (GDP) in most mature economies, few countries collect detailed information concerning energy consumption in this sector.[11] Japan, the United States, and Canada provide the greatest level of information concerning services and energy consumption. The service sector of an economy is an important source of employment and GDP. In the United States, for example, the services sector accounts for over 80 percent of the jobs in the economy as well as 80 percent of the GDP.

The delivery of most services is contingent on the action of people, and the personnel-based facet distinguishes these products from goods. These product offerings possess several traits that distinguish them from goods and other product offerings. Importantly, these traits have significant implications concerning the firm's efforts to enhance their sustainability efforts. Consider each in turn.

Intangibility

The *intangibility* of services recognizes that services are performance rather than objects that can be touched, felt, tasted, or seen. Services may be difficult to patent since they can be easily duplicated.[12] In addition, service quality can be hard to communicate to consumers. Consequently, sustainable marketers must offer, where possible, tangible evidence of the merits of service. For example, Waste Management promotes consumer recycling of plastic bottles by drawing attention to the fact that 88 percent less energy is consumed when producing plastic from existing plastic rather than manufacturing plastic from oil and gas.[13]

---

[10] Zeithaml, Valarie A., Mary Jo Bitner, and Dwayne D. Gremler (2006), *Services Marketing: Integrating Customer Focus across the Firm*, New York: McGraw-Hill.

[11] International Energy Agency (2008), *Tracking Industrial Energy Efficiency and CO2 Emissions*, Paris, France: OECD/IEA.

[12] Zeithaml, Valarie A., Mary Jo Bitner, and Dwayne D. Gremler (2006*), Services Marketing: Integrating Customer Focus across the Firm*, New York: McGraw-Hill.

[13] www.wm.com/location/california/ventura-county/thousand-oaks/recycle/facts.jsp (November 13, 2015).

Simultaneous Production and Consumption

Unlike many physical products, the delivery of a service is simultaneous to its production.[14] A surgeon may have decades of knowledge about an operation, but the actual provision of the service includes the production by the surgeon and the consumption by the patient. Because consumers are present during service provision, they may take an active role in the design and creation of the service. Consequently, the first implication for sustainable marketers is the need to have service offerings available that address the sustainability concerns of their clients. For example, the Domini Social Equity Fund provides the opportunity to invest in a fund dedicated to sustainable and responsible investment.[15] When customers make inquiries concerning the ecological or social merits of alternative investment opportunities, brokers that represent Domini can offer a sustainable solution. A second implication of *simultaneous production and consumption* is the necessary decentralization of operations in order to provide acceptable service at multiple outlets. Firms must determine how to establish and reinforce a culture of sustainability across multiple locations. Chipotle, for instance, primarily relies on corporately owned locations rather than franchises. Franchisees often face pressure regarding food prices and production, but by maintaining corporate ownership, Chipotle removes the possibility of cutting corners in food preparation. In addition, corporate ownership enables Chipotle to control the employee culture while maintaining control over employee wages, operations, and company structure.[16]

Heterogeneity

Heterogeneity refers to the recognition that no two service providers are completely alike, and their delivery of a service is not identical. Consequently, the mass production of services is infeasible, and marketers must consider how to deliver services efficiently. A firm can overcome some of the heterogeneity challenges through online services that feature standardized web presence and employ standardized communication protocols.[17] For example, auto mechanics can outline their commitment to sustainable oil changes. Drivers can have their oil changed knowing that heavy metal and greenhouse gas emissions are reduced.

In addition, the heterogeneity in service delivery can be reduced by ensuring that all employees are not only aware of the firm's sustainability efforts (both locally and globally), but they are also able to articulate this strategy to consumers. All personnel that interact with customers need to understand that they are involved in marketing. Firms, therefore, need to establish a sustainability-based culture that emphasizes how services are delivered with consideration of their influence on financial, social, and ecological performance of the firm and its customers. Kimpton Hotels, for instance, trains employees concerning the sustainability efforts at a specific property and throughout the chain. This training accentuates the sustainability efforts of the firm while offering greater standardization over the provision of the service.

---

[14] Zeithaml, Valarie A., Mary Jo Bitner, and Dwayne D. Gremler (2006), *Services Marketing: Integrating Customer Focus across the Firm*, New York: McGraw-Hill.

[15] www.kiplinger.com/article/investing/T041-C016-S001-5-mutual-funds-for-socially-responsible-investors.html (January 25, 2017).

[16] www.entrepreneur.com/article/237252 (November 12, 2015).

[17] Beamon, Benita M. (2008), "Sustainability and the future of supply chain management," *Operations and Supply Chain Management* 1 (1), 4–18.

Perishability

The provision of services largely involves people, and as a result, the "inventory" that comprises services cannot be resold, stored, saved, or returned. A dentist's office hours or the showing of a movie cannot be recouped or saved for a later time—once the time associated with these services has passed, the potential revenue cannot be realized. One implication for the sustainable marketer is the need to have accurate *demand forecasting* that ensures productive use of resources. For example, proper forecasting of demand for taxi cabs increases corporate and customer satisfaction.[18] By reducing the number of idle taxis, firms also lower their carbon footprint.[19] In this way, demand forecasting contributes to triple bottom-line performance.

ENSURING SUSTAINABLE DELIVERY OF SERVICES

The customer experience in the delivery of services is crucial to success of the firm. Firms can ensure the sustainable delivery of services by recognizing potential gaps between expectations of the service provider and the client. Proper service delivery enhances financial performance and customer satisfaction and lowers the ecological footprint of the firm. Firms that identify the potential gaps between the customer and the service provider can proactively enhance the consumer experience. The four types of service gaps include:[20]

Listening Gap. The *listening gap* refers to the separation between customer expectations of a service and the firm's perceptions of the customer expectations. Service providers need to understand the objectives of the buyer and incorporate sustainable features into service provisions. Companies can limit their carbon footprint by illustrating how some service provisions are sustainably superior to other offerings. For example, Cintas' Chemtron air conditioner coil cleaning service offers a professional cleaning system that enables hoteliers to lower their energy bills, improve indoor air quality, and extend the life of units. By listening to consumer needs and explaining how products meet financial and ecological criteria, the company provides exceptional customer service.

Service Design Gap. The *service design gap* refers the separation between customer driven service designs and standards and management's perceptions of these service designs and standards. Firms overcome this gap by developing services without oversimplification, subjectivity, bias, and incompleteness. Firms

[18] Mukai, Naoto, and Naoto Yoden (2012), "Taxi Demand Forecasting Based on Taxi Probe Data by Neural Network" in *Intelligent Interactive Multimedia: Systems And Services Smart Innovation, Systems and Technologies*, 14, 589–597

[19] Moreira-Matias, Luis, Joao Gama, Michel Ferreira, João Mendes-Moreira, and Luis Damas (2013), "Predicting Taxi–Passenger Demand Using Streaming Data," *Intelligent Transportation Systems, IEEE Transactions* 14 (3), 1393–1402.

[20] Zeithaml, Valarie A., Ananthanarayanan Parasuraman, and Leonard L. Berry (1990), *Delivering Quality Service: Balancing Customer Perceptions and Expectations*. New York: Simon and Schuster.

can develop *service blueprints* that portray a service so that people involved in providing it can understand it objectively.[21] This blueprint identifies the physical evidence of the service, customer action, visible and invisible contact by the service provider, and the support processes. Developing this blueprint and reviewing it with the customer enables the firm to minimize material use and emissions. For example, car-sharing services that use service blueprints yield sustainability by providing customers with the functionality of the vehicle without ownership.[22]

Service Performance Gap. The *service performance gap* refers to the separation between the customer service design and standards and the actual service delivery by the provider. This gap is overcome by communicating to the service provider and the customer concerning the delivery of the service and the customers' responsibilities associated with the service delivery. Both parties need to understand their roles in the provision of services and appreciate the influences of their action on the service quality. For example, over the life of an automobile, service technicians and customers need to appreciate how proper maintenance ensures better automobile performance, lower emissions, and higher customer satisfaction.[23]

The Communications Gap. The *communications gap* refers to the separation between the service delivery and the external communications to customers about the service. Sustainably-oriented marketers need to recognize that overstating or exaggerating the merits of a service can lead to accusations of greenwashing. Service providers risk accusations of greenwashing when they emphasize a narrow set of attributes without regard for important environmental issues. Hotels, for instance, that state they use solar panels for water heating but do not have water conservation programs risk accusations of greenwashing due to their depletion of a community's water table.[24]

A second source of a communication gap lies in the failure of a firm to educate the consumer about the proper use and benefits of a service. For example, smoking cessation programs often employ behavioral therapy, yet the effects of this therapy on patient coping skills is enhanced when they also use a transdermal patch.[25] When patients are properly informed about the combined benefits of therapy and the patch, patients report higher levels of satisfaction with cessation services.

---

[21] Zeithaml, Valarie A., Mary Jo Bitner, and Dwayne D. Gremler (2006), *Services Marketing: Integrating Customer Focus across the Firm*, New York: McGraw-Hill.

[22] Geum, Youngjung, and Yongtae Park (2011), "Designing the sustainable product-service integration: A product-service blueprint approach," *Journal of Cleaner Production*, 19 (14), 1601–1614.

[23] Sivak, Michael, and Brandon Schoettle (2011), "Eco-driving: Strategic, tactical, and operational decisions of the driver that improve vehicle fuel economy," (2011). University of Michigan Report No. UMTRI-2011-34.

[24] ecoopportunity.net/2011/05/greenwashing-in-the-travel-and-tourism-industry/ (November 13, 2015).

[25] Cinciripini, Paul M., Lynn G. Cinciripini, Annette Wallfisch, Waheedul Haque, and Helen Van Vunakis (1996), "Behavior Therapy and the Transdermal Nicotine Patch: Effects on Cessation Outcome, Affect, and Coping," *Journal of Consulting and Clinical Psychology* 64 (2), 314.

EDUCATIONAL INSTITUTIONS

The pursuit of sustainability within a number sectors of the service economy has been advanced via the efforts of trade organizations. These interorganizational groups identify crucial factors that influence the ability of firms to pursue sustainability. Recognition of these standards is important to firms that value greater sustainability efforts, and this recognition is equally important for companies that want to market to these firms. Knowing that a university annually reports on sustainability, for instance, provides rich incentives to companies that offer sustainable products and services. Education, health care, and lodging have notably identified criteria related to the sustainability of their operations. Consider first sustainability within education.

Education institutions refer to buildings used for academic or classroom instruction. These buildings include elementary, middle, or high schools, and classrooms on college or university campuses. Educational institutions account for 13 percent of energy consumption in the services sector. Space heating (41 percent), water heating (22 percent), and lighting (20 percent) represent over 80 percent of the power expenditures in education. Most educational facilities are part of a multibuilding campus, and schools in the Northeast and Midwest are generally larger than schools in the South and West. Almost two-thirds of the schools are government owned, and three-fourths of the government-owned buildings are owned by local government.

Although there are notable efforts to raise the sustainability of operations at the elementary and high school levels, the action undertaken at the collegiate level provides the opportunity to compare sustainable marketing action across campuses. Since 2010, the *sustainability tracking, assessment, and rating system* (STARS) has been publishing rankings of universities. Developed by the Association for the Advancement of Sustainability in Higher Education (AASHE), participants in this program pursue credits and may earn points in order to achieve a STARS bronze, silver, gold, or platinum rating or recognition as a STARS reporter. The credits included in STARS span the breadth of higher education sustainability and include performance indicators and criteria organized into four categories: academics, engagement, operations, planning and administration, and innovation.[26]

Academics. This category refers to the degree to which curriculum and research address sustainability. Institutions earn credit for courses, learning outcomes, and programs that examine sustainability, and they receive credit for academic research and support associated with sustainability.

Engagement. Colleges illustrate shareholder engagement by establishing committees of students, faculty, and alumni to advise the trustees regarding sustainability. Engagement refers to campus activities (e.g., student educators program, student orientation, student life, outreach materials and campaigns, staff professional development, and employee orientation) as well as public engagement (e.g., community partnerships, intercampus collaboration, and community service).

---

[26] stars.aashe.org/pages/about/stars-overview.html (January 23, 2017).

Operations. The assessment of operations examines air and climate, building efficiency, dining services, energy usage, grounds, purchasing, transportation, waste, and water. Conservation campaigns may encourage college community members to monitor their energy consumption, retrofit appliances or power plants with energy-efficient technology, conduct a carbon emissions inventory, and commit to emissions reductions. Schools also earn higher evaluations based on the quantity and the availability of locally grown food, as well as organic and sustainably produced food. The use of reusable dishware and ecofriendly to-go containers is also taken into consideration. In addition, this category also examines campus-wide and dining-specific programs for recycling and composting food and landscape waste.

Planning and Administration. This category addresses action regarding sustainability by colleges and universities at the administrative or trustee level. This action includes commitments to sustainability in the institution's mission statement or master plan and commitments to local, national, or international sustainability agreements. Institutions are monitored for coordination, planning and governance; diversity and affordability; health, wellbeing and work; and investment strategies. Investment priorities focus on prioritizing return on investment, investing in renewable energy funds, and investing in community-development loan funds. Access to endowment information fosters constructive dialogue about opportunities for clean energy investments and shareholder voting priorities.

Innovation. Innovation refers to extraordinary, new, ground-breaking, unique, or uncommon outcomes, policies, and practices that markedly exceed the highest criterion of an existing STARS credit or are not covered by an existing STARS credit.

STARS offers a number of benefits to institutes of higher education. The specific criteria provide the opportunity to make significant advances in aspects of a university's sustainability evaluation that fall below desired levels. By charting this activity over time, the university can illustrate to stakeholders the amount of progress achieved over time. The rankings provide insight to colleges, but they also provide insight to marketers who seek to make product offerings available to institutions of higher learning. By analyzing these criteria, firms can develop campaigns that illustrate how their product offerings help schools achieve sustainability goals. For example, firms that market sustainable lighting systems (i.e., LED) should take note of whether a school participates in STARS. Sales representatives marketing these products to universities can illustrate how retrofitting of these devices to existing fixtures can enable the firm to achieve sustainability goals while simultaneously lowering operating costs.

HEALTH CARE

Healthcare buildings are those used as diagnostic and treatment facilities for both inpatient and outpatient care. The healthcare sector has a set of unique conditions that influences the measures taken to conserve energy. The buildings used in health have energy intensities that are more than twice the average of all buildings in the sector. Healthcare facilities must cope with 24/7 operations accompanied by chemical use, infectious control requirements, and substantial regulatory requirements that challenge efforts to achieve higher levels of sustainability.

The healthcare industry has been working toward developing sustainability standards since the 2002 release of the Green Healthcare Construction Guidance statement by the American Society for Healthcare Engineering.[27] In the following year, the Green Guide for Healthcare initiative began when a team of geographically and professionally diverse industry leaders established a steering committee to direct development of the document. Importantly, the members of this committee include a wide range of stakeholders who do not have direct financial interests in certification processes or products addressed in the document. The guide has evolved from a pilot project to become a full-fledged registration and certification program. In its current form, the *Green Guide to Health Care* is intended to serve as a reference for best practices in the industry. The *Guide* provides the healthcare sector with a voluntary, self-certifying metric toolkit that designers, owners, and operators can use to guide and evaluate their progress towards high-performance healing environments. The detailed guide provides insight into the manner by which healthcare facilities can enhance the extent of sustainability in building construction and operations.

The guidelines for healthcare sustainability can be separated based on those associated with construction and those concerned with operations. When a hospital elects to add new construction either in the form of a new building or remodeled wing, they are increasingly basing their construction decisions on the Green Guide to Health Care. The construction-related issues for health care facilities include:[28]

Integrated Design. The healthcare facility must implement a collaborative multistakeholder goal setting and design process and establish human health as a criterion for design, construction, and operations.

Sustainable Sites. Site development must limit the environmental impact from the location of a building on a site. Developments in urban areas should protect green fields and preserve natural resources, and developments in rural areas should focus on previously developed sites. Facilities should also rehabilitate sites where development is complicated by environmental contamination. Sites should be regulated to limit pollution from automobiles as well as pollution from storm water run-off.

Water Efficiency. Healthcare facilities must eliminate the use of potable water for cooling of medical equipment of for landscape irrigation. At the same time, the healthcare facility should maximize drinkable water efficiency within facilities and monitor water consumption practices over time.

Energy and Atmosphere. The healthcare facility should establish minimum energy efficiency standards, encourage performance above these standards, and monitor this performance over time. The facility should also encourage the use of renewable and

[27] Guenther, Robin, and Gail Vittori (2008), *Sustainable Healthcare Architecture*. New York: John Wiley & Sons.

[28] www.gghc.org/documents/Version2.2/GGHC-v2-2-Construction.pdf (January 25, 2017).

self-supplied energy while simultaneously reducing energy consumption. In addition, the facility should illustrate compliance with the Montreal Protocol for ozone depletion.

Materials and Resources. Healthcare facilities should eliminate the use of mercury-containing building products and reduce the release of bioaccumulative toxic chemicals associated with building materials. Hospitals can redirect recyclable resources into manufacturing, redirect reusable materials to appropriate sites, and direct hazardous waste in compliance with governmental regulations.

Environmental Quality. Healthcare facilities should provide natural ventilation to enhance occupant comfort and minimize indoor air contaminants that are potentially harmful. They should also minimize the use of furnishings that release air contaminants and limit the amount of disruptive sound near the facility.

Innovation and Design Process. Healthcare firms should also establish programs that reward design teams and projects that achieve performance above the goals established by the Green Healthcare Guide.

The ongoing operations of the facility are also addressed in the Green Health Care Guide. Hospitals and other healthcare facilities are increasingly using the healthcare guide in operations. Consequently, marketers need to be prepared to illustrate how their product offerings enable healthcare facilities to enhance the following aspects of operations:[29]

Integrated Operations. Healthcare facilities should demonstrate a cross-disciplinary approach to operations that ensures safe and environmentally sensitive methods. This includes training and monitoring to ensure that buildings perform adequately over time.

Energy Efficiency. Hospitals should illustrate levels of energy performance and provide ongoing accountability of energy performance. They should support Montreal Protocol and support the use of renewable energy onsite as well as off-site.

Water Conservation. Healthcare providers should seek to reduce energy costs by using energy efficient equipment and maximize water efficiency to reduce the burden on potable water. They can also conserve water through elimination of the use of drinkable water for landscaping irrigation.

Chemical Management. The healthcare facility should minimize airborne effluents and hazardous spills while also reducing the potential for building occupant exposure to PCBs and PCB combustion by-products. They can also limit the amount of pharmaceutical waste in sanitary sewer discharge.

Waste Management. Waste reduction can be achieved through waste reduction and recycling programs. Facilities can reduce solid waste in landfills and incinerators by reuse, reductions, recycling, and composting. They can reduce medical waste through improved segregation and modified work practices.

[29] www.gghc.org/documents/Version2.2/GGHC-v2-2-Ops-08Rev.pdf (January 25, 2017).

Environmental Services. Healthcare facilities should develop grounds management practices that enhance the ecological integrity of the property. They can reduce exposure to physical and chemical hazards and limit land development and pollution effects by limiting the amount of vehicle transportation.

The merits of the Green Guide for Health Care are similar to those enjoyed by universities that use the sustainability tracking, assessment and rating system. The guidelines provide clear objectives for the hospitals, and they enable healthcare institutions to track their level of progress over time. Moreover, the *Green Guide* provides significant help to marketers seeking to make their product offerings available to hospitals. Marketers who can illustrate how their products augment construction and operations guidelines are well-positioned to increase market shares in the healthcare industry.

TOURISM AND TRAVEL

The tourism industry is forecast to reach over 1.56 billion people by the year 2020, and the hotel industry will need to accommodate the demand by providing more properties.[30] Industry participants recognize that new hotel construction must occur in a manner that incorporates sustainability concerns.[31] The industry recognizes the need to enhance sustainability, but many of the efforts in operations have occurred independently by various hoteliers.[32] The Global Sustainable Tourism Council (GSTC), however, was established to design and oversee the implementation of global sustainable standards for tourism and travel. The GSTC is independent and neutral, serving the important role of managing its global baseline standards for sustainability in travel and tourism. The sponsors of GSTC include InterContinental Hotels, TUI Group, and the United Nation's World Tourism Organization. InterContinental has over 4700 hotels that include InterContinental, Crown Plaza, and Holiday Inn. TUI serves the tourism industry and includes 1800 travel agencies, six airlines, and over 300 hotels. GSTC provides baseline sustainability standards for tourism and travel. These standards enable hotels and destinations with guidelines for enhancing sustainability. In addition, GSTC accreditation provides guidance to tourists seeking sustainable vacation locations.

Three sets of criteria addressing sustainable hotels, tour operators, and destinations provide minimal criteria to approach achieving cultural (social), economic, and ecological sustainability.[33] Firms seeking to achieve sustainability

[30] Brebbia, C. A. (2011), *The Sustainable World*, WIT Press: Ashurst, Southampton, U.K.

[31] Legrand, Willy, Philip Sloan, and Joseph S. Chen (2016), *Sustainability in the Hospitality Industry: Principles of Sustainable Operations*. Routledge.

[32] Houdré, Hervé (2008), "Sustainable Development in the Hotel Industry," *Cornell Industry Perspectives No. 2* (August).

[33] www.gstcouncil.org/en/gstc-criteria-hotels-tour-operators-destinations/criteria-for-destinations.html; www.gstcouncil.org/en/gstc-criteria-hotels-tour-operators-destinations/criteria-for-hotels-tour-operators-industry.html?id=1297:global-sustainable-tourism-criteria-tour-operator; and www.gstcouncil.org/en/gstc-criteria-hotels-tour-operators-destinations/criteria-for-hotels-tour-operators-industry.html?id=1296:global-sustainable-tourism-criteria-hotels (January 26, 2017).

must recognize GSTC criteria and offer indicators that the firms are making progress toward sustainable operations. Lodging facilities must address the following issues:[34]

Demonstrate effective sustainable management. Hoteliers must implement a management system that addresses social, ecological, and economic performance. These criteria must further address quality, health, human rights, safety, risk, and crisis management issues. The firm also agrees to communicate its sustainability policies to all stakeholders and ensure that employees are engaged in the implementation of the management system.

Maximize social and economic benefits to the local community and minimize negative impacts. The efforts of the hotelier must benefit the local community. Where possible, the firm should pursue local employment, local purchasing, and local entrepreneurship. The firm should favor equal opportunity, decent working conditions, and community services over exploitation and harassment.

Maximize benefits to cultural heritage and minimize negative impacts. Firms must be cognizant of indigenous communities and culturally or historically sensitive sites and strive to minimize adverse impacts while maximizing cultural benefits to local residents and visitors.

Maximize benefits to the environment and minimize negative impacts. Hotels further enhance their sustainability efforts by illustrating commitments to conserve resources, lower pollution, and conserve biodiversity and ecosystems.

Note that the hotel criteria listed above focus on sustainability issues germane to this industry. Tour operators represent a second group of firms (often much smaller entities) that seek approval for their sustainability efforts. While their general criteria are the same as those for hoteliers, the specific criteria differ between tour operators and hotels. Destination criteria, however, are generally directed at governmental entities. Although the general criteria are again consistent with those established for the hotel industry, there are different indicators between these groups. For example, hotel and destination criteria both recognize the need to maintain ecosystems, yet the indicators relevant to destinations are far more extensive than those for hotels.

Although the Global Sustainable Tourism Council plan provides guidelines for property development, it does not represent a form of accreditation that hotel properties can obtain. For example, Kimpton Hotels achieved accreditation from the Green Key Global Eco-Rating Program. Green Key is one of a number of a third-party firms that integrate Global Sustainable Tourism Council logic and other industry documentation into their ratings program. Lodging facilities are awarded a rating from 1 to 5 keys (5 keys is the highest level) based on the

[34] www.gstcouncil.org/en/gstc-criteria-hotels-tour-operators-destinations/criteria-for-hotels-tour-operators-industry.html?id=1296:global-sustainable-tourism-criteria-hotels (January 26, 2017).

results of a comprehensive environmental self-assessment. Similarly, tour operators and destinations can achieve GSTC approval by meeting the standards of accrediting bodies such as Biosphere Responsible Tourism and EarthCheck Destination Standard.[35]

Firms that engage in efforts to establish sustainability by conforming to GSTC guidelines provide substantial opportunities to marketing firms. Marketers who understand the nature of these criteria can use them to generate sales. Thus, a hotel that recognizes the need to monitor and control water usage will likely appreciate the benefits the firm can derive from a water purification system. Marketing organizations that identify firms aggressively pursuing sustainability in the hospitality industry are better equipped to market effectively to destinations, hotels, and tour operators.

SUMMARY

Introduction: Service Sector Contributors to Carbon Emissions

This chapter provides an overview of energy consumption in the services sector. This economic sector includes service businesses (e.g., retail stores and hotels), educational institutions, correctional facilities, religious groups, and fraternal organizations. On a global level, the service sector accounts for 9 percent of total final energy consumption and 12 percent of carbon emissions. The three primary sources of energy for services are electricity, natural gas, and fuel oil.

Sustainable Value in Services

Services are product offerings that possess several traits that distinguish them from goods and other product offerings. The delivery of most services is contingent of the action of people, and the personnel-based facet distinguishes these products from goods. Services are products that are essentially intangible and vary based on the provider. Because services are associated with the time the services provider has available to render the service, the amount of available service is perishable.

Ensuring Sustainable Delivery of Services

The customer experience in the delivery of services is crucial to success of the firm. Firms can ensure the sustainable delivery of services by recognizing potential gaps between expectations of the service provider and the client. The listening gap refers to the separation between customer expectations of a service and the firm's perceptions of the customer expectations. The service design gap refers to the separation between customer-driven service designs and management's perceptions of these service standards, whereas the service performance gap refers to separation between the customer service design and the service delivery by the provider. The communication gap refers to the separation between service delivery and the external communications to customers about the service.

---

[35] www.gstcouncil.org/en/get-involved/become-certified.html (January 26, 2017).

Educational Institutions

Education institutions refer to buildings used for academic or classroom instruction. Sustainability tracking, assessment and rating system (STARS) is a mechanism that evaluates universities and college efforts to attain sustainability in administration, climate change and energy, food and recycling, buildings/construction, endowment transparency, investment priorities, and shareholder engagement.

Health Care

The Green Guide to Health Care provides health facilities with guidelines about construction issues that include integrated design, sustainable sites, water efficiency, energy and atmosphere, materials, environmental quality, and innovation and design. The ongoing operations of the facility are also addressed with respect to energy efficiency, water conservation, chemical management, waste management, and environmental services.

Travel and Tourism

Firms operating in the lodging industry can increase the level of sustainability through proper building site and design, refurbishing and reusing existing buildings, and through sustainable construction.

KEY TERMS

services
intangibility
simultaneous production and
    consumption
heterogeneity

perishability
demand forecasting
listening gap
service design gap
service blueprints

service performance gap
communications gap
sustainability tracking, assessment and rating system
Green Guide for Health Care

DISCUSSION QUESTIONS

1. What makes services different from goods, and how do these differences affect efforts to enhance sustainability?
2. How does the perishability of services affect sustainability?
3. What is the service performance gap, and how does it affect sustainability efforts?
4. In a services organization, what employees need a marketing orientation? Why?
5. Describe two ways in which the communication gap affects sustainability.
6. Why would a preventative health organization benefit from a service blueprint?
7. What are the components of the sustainability tracking, assessment and rating system?

8. How does your college or institution rate on the sustainability tracking, assessment and rating system, and what can it do to enhance its performance?

9. What can your college or institution do to enhance the sustainability of the classroom in which your class is held?

10. What types of firms marketing to a hospital would benefit from knowing that the healthcare facility is using GGHC logic to direct its purchasing?

11. To what extent is the hotel and lodging industry engaging in sustainability efforts?

part four

Sustainability Reporting

14

Reporting Value to Stakeholders

INTRODUCTION

Apple, Inc.

In 2008, the environmental activist group Greenpeace released the 10th iteration of its Guide to Greener Electronics.[1] This guide urges producers of electronics to eliminate hazardous substances, responsibly recycle obsolete products, and reduce the climate impact of their products and operations. This guide also ranks the various producers of computers and electronics based on their environmental influences throughout the life cycles of their products. The guide notably ranked Apple below most of their competition due to their use of brominated fire retardants (BFRs). These chemicals are coated on printed circuit boards to prevent fires inside computers. The company also uses a polyvinyl chloride (PVC) coating on cables.[2] Some BFRs have been implicated as deterrents to neurological development and hormone system functionality,[3] whereas the incineration of PVCs produces chemicals that are toxic at low concentrations.[4]

Over the past 20 years, continued assessment of the environmental impact of the firm's products has enabled Apple to illustrate sustainability efforts and quantify progress in environmental concerns.[5] The negative evaluation by Greenpeace called public attention to the need for Apple to re-establish its commitment to the environment. Since the publication of this greener electronics guide, Apple has developed a number of initiatives to improve its environmental performance. Importantly, the company no longer uses PVC or BFR in its personal computers or in its iPhones and iPods.[6] These improvements have been praised by Greenpeace and have led the nongovernmental organization (NGO) to call competitors such as HP, Dell, Lenovo, Acer, and Toshiba to follow suit.[7] Soon after the publication of the Greenpeace guide, Apple began a television campaign that proclaimed Apple's MacBook line of laptops to be the world's greenest family of notebooks. The ads emphasized MacBook's low power consumption, the ability to recycle the enclosure, and the lack of hazardous materials.[8] These ads are not greenwashing as they are supported by environmental action within the firm and an increasing commitment to the environment that Apple initially publicized in 1990.

---

[1] www.greenpeace.org/international/PageFiles/43072/Guide-Greener-Electronics-9-edition.pdf (January 31, 2017).

[2] Hesseldahl, Arik (2008), "Apple is Greener than Greenpeace Says," *Businessweek Online* (December 12), 1.

[3] Legler, Juliette, and Abraham Brouwer (2003), "Are Brominated Flame Retardants Endocrine Disruptors?" *Environment International* 29 (6): 879–885.

[4] Menad, Nourreddine, Bo Björkman, and Eric G. Allain (1998), "Combustion of Plastics Contained in Electric and Electronic Scrap," *Resources, Conservation and Recycling* 24 (1), 65–85.

[5] images.apple.com/environment/pdf/Apple_Environmental_Responsibility_Report_2016.pdf (January 31, 2017).

[6] Burrows, Peter, and Arik Hesseldahl (2009), "Finally, a Big Green Apple?" *Businessweek*, (October 5), 68-69.

[7] Moren, Dan (2009), "Greenpeace Shows a Little Apple Love," *Macworld*, 26 (1), 28.

[8] Hesseldahl, Arik (2008), "Apple Is Greener than Greenpeace Says," *Businessweek Online* (December 12), 1.

Apple's efforts toward enhanced sustainability are made available to the public through a series of analyses of the supply chain for the company and each of its products. The company's environmental website outlines the influence of each step in the product life cycle (see Figure 14-1). The manufacture of products accounts for 77 percent of emissions; and transportation (4 percent), facilities (1 percent), and recycling (1 percent) are also factored into the emissions costs. Interestingly, product use account for 17 percent of all emissions associated with Apple products. Each product report provides analyses of climate change, energy efficiency, material efficiency, and restricted substances. Moreover, Apple provides sustainability reports that address its recycling efforts, facilities management, and suppliers. These reports are developed to reflect the Global Reporting Initiative (GRI) sustainability reporting guidelines.[10] GRI is a nonprofit organization established in 1997 that developed one the world's most widely used sustainability reporting framework. GRI provides guidelines on the development and use of sustainability reports and maintains a database of reports developed throughout the world. For example, Apple's 2016 report is one of over 1,000 sustainability reports collected by GRI in the year.

The Apple example illustrates how companies are following a closed-loop system in which they plan, implement, and report on their sustainability efforts. Cradle-to-cradle logic is employed in an effort to minimize energy use throughout a product's life. Firms that report on this activity are more inclined to yield sustainable results relative to their competition. In this chapter, we will look closely at the sustainability reporting practices of firms. We begin by examining the purposes and benefits of sustainability reporting. We proceed by outlining the components of sustainability reports, and we subsequently examine the reporting of financial, environmental, and social performance.

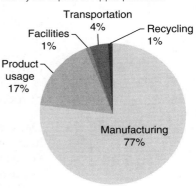

FIGURE 14-1

Life cycle impact of Apple products.[9]

PURPOSES OF SUSTAINABILITY REPORTING

The magnitude and urgency of the sustainability risks faced by organizations demand that firms provide complete information regarding their financial, environmental, and social performance. This information enables stakeholders of all types to make decisions about their relationships and commitments to the firm. If the firm offers complete disclosure of its actions as they relate to sustainability, stakeholders can make better decisions.

The ability of stakeholders to make evaluations about the firm is contingent on their ability to view the firm's operations. *Transparency* refers to the degree to which an entity provides complete disclosure of all activity related to economic, environmental, and relational performance.[11] Firms that provide complete disclosure concerning all interaction with stakeholders that is relevant to triple bottom-line

---

[9] images.apple.com/environment/pdf/Apple_Environmental_Responsibility_Report_2016.pdf (January 31, 2017).

[10] www.apple.com/environment/reports/gri-index.html (January 31, 2017).

[11] Adams, Carol A., and Richard Evans (2004)," Accountability, Completeness, Credibility and the Audit Expectations Cap," *Journal of Corporate Citizenship*," 14 (Summer), 97–115.

performance offer evidence of the transparency of their operations. In order to assess the level of transparency, it is germane to determine the sustainability topics and indicators that firm employs. Although firms are not required to report on all facets of triple bottom-line performance, they are increasingly providing financial and social performance indicators as well as environmental outcomes. In addition, it is essential for the firm to ensure the quality of the information provided in the report.

Transparent disclosure enables sustainability reports to be used for three purposes:[12]

Demonstrating. Firms demonstrate their commitment to sustainability by illustrating how the firm influences and is influenced by sustainable development. For example, the Best Buy 2015 sustainability report acknowledges the critical importance of electronics recycling, and it illustrates the measures undertaken by the firm to increase recycling rates.[13]

Benchmarking. Benchmarking refers to comparison of a firm's performance relative to laws, codes, norms, and voluntary initiatives. For example, Bayer Corporation's 2015 report indicates that approximately 93 percent of its production sites have been certified in accordance with the ISO 14001 or the European environmental management regulation Eco-Management and Audit Scheme (EMAS) standards.[14]

Comparing. Comparing enables a firm to illustrate changes in performance over time. These comparisons illustrate improvements in sustainability efforts by a company and illustrate its longitudinal performance relative to the competition. The Ford 2015/2016 sustainability report indicates, for instance, the performance of current auto models relative to previously sold products.[15] Firms that view themselves as industry leaders that engage in best practice can confirm these perceptions via comparison. For example, Apple's report that it no longer uses PVC or BFR in its products makes them stand out relative to the competition.[16]

Since sustainability reports provide insight to stakeholders, it is relevant to consider what should and should not be incorporated into these documents. The Global Reporting Initiative uses the following four criteria to guide the development sustainability reports:[17]

---

[12] Global Reporting Initiative (2011), G4 Sustainability Reporting Guidelines, www.globalreporting.org/ (January 31, 2017).

[13] corporate.bestbuy.com/wp-content/uploads/2015/06/fy15-full-report-final.pdf (January 31, 2017).

[14] www.annualreport2015.bayer.com/ (January 31, 2017).

[15] corporate.ford.com/content/dam/corporate/en/investors/reports-and-filings/Sustainability%20Reports/Sustainablilty-Report-15-16.pdf (January 31, 2017).

[16] Burrows, Peter, and Arik Hesseldahl (2009), "Finally, a Big Green Apple?" *Businessweek,* (October 5), 68–69.

[17] www.globalreporting.org/resourcelibrary/G3.1-Guidelines-Incl-Technical-Protocol.pdf (January 31, 2017).

Materiality. Because firms face a wide range of topics that could be the subject of these reports, it is relevant to establish what *material* is relevant. The firm must determine which facets of the economic, environmental, and social context substantially influence the evaluations made by stakeholders. Firms use internal and external factors to determine whether information is material. These factors include the firm's mission and competitive strategy as well as the concerns expressed by stakeholders.

Stakeholder Inclusiveness. The insight offered by the report is contingent on the interaction with all entities that are significantly affected by the firm's action.[18] These groups include employees, suppliers, customers, NGOs, government, and other groups with a vested interest in the firm's sustainability efforts. Stakeholder inclusiveness requires the firm to identify all these interest groups and report on how it has responded to the groups' expectations and interests. For example, the PepsiCo 2015 sustainability report emphasizes the need to gain input from consumers, customers, communities, investors, employees, and suppliers.[19]

Sustainability Context. The sustainability context criterion ensures that the organization explains how it is meeting the demands of achieving sustainability. The action of the firm must be viewed not in isolation but in the context in which the firm operates. Consequently, the firm should not only provide a summary of its sustainability efforts, but it should indicate how these efforts contribute to improvements to environmental, economic, and social conditions at the local, regional, and global levels.[20]

Completeness. Due to the breadth of issues associated with triple bottom-line performance, the firm faces a daunting task in determining the amount of information to present. Completeness refers to the provision of sufficient information about economic, environmental, and social performance to enable stakeholders to make informed decisions.[21] Completeness encompasses the dimensions of *time*, *scope*, and *boundary*. In order to track progress, it is essential to specify the time period associated with the report. The scope of the report should be broad enough to cover significant influences on triple bottom-line performance. The boundary of the report concerns the range of groups represented by the study. Firms need to consider their broad supply chains in this regard and examine the influences of upstream suppliers, employees,

---

[18] Hess, David (2008), "The Three Pillars of Corporate Social Reporting as New Governance Regulation: Disclosure, Dialogue, and Development," *Business Ethics Quarterly*, 18 (4), 447–482.

[19] www.pepsico.com/docs/album/sustainability-reporting/pep_gri15_v10.pdf (February 2, 2017).

[20] www.globalreporting.org/resourcelibrary/G3.1-Guidelines-Incl-Technical-Protocol.pdf (January 31, 2017).

[21] Hess, David (2008), "The Three Pillars of Corporate Social Reporting as New Governance Regulation: Disclosure, Dialogue, and Development," *Business Ethics Quarterly*, 18 (4), 447–482.

and downstream customers. For example, Apple recognizes that 17 percent of the energy impact of its products is associated with downstream product usage. The boundary of the report is a difficult consideration as different firms in the same industry may make different evaluations of the boundaries of their consumption. While sustainability reporting guidelines suggest that firms should report on any entity over which it has control or influence,[22] different companies may interpret their level of influence through contrasting decision logics.

BENEFITS OF SUSTAINABILITY REPORTING

Sustainability reporting is a relatively new phenomenon that is increasingly employed by firms in many sectors of the economy. It is difficult to state the origins of this type of reporting. Some annual reports, for instance, have addressed corporate interaction with the environment for decades. The first separate, environmental reports were developed in the late 1980s, and the number of these types of reports has risen substantially since that time.[23] This genre of reporting takes on a variety names that bear *social*, *environmental*, and *sustainability* monikers. Sustainability reports that address the role of the firm with respect to the triple bottom line of financial, relational, and environmental performance provide insight into the broadest spectrum of sustainability and its importance to the firm. Nevertheless, there are many forms of reporting that focus on environmental or social facets of sustainability without regard for other facets of triple bottom-line performance.

Over 15 years ago, the United Nations began analyzing the motivations for developing sustainability. Its research indicated a number of reasons why some firms do not participate develop sustainability reports. Some firms are skeptical of the advantage derived from this type of reporting, whereas other companies believe there are other ways to communicate a message about the environment to consumers. The motivation to develop a sustainability report also varies by market. Although most firms participating in the chemicals or computer industry publish these reports, firms operating in the retail and banking sectors develop substantially fewer sustainability studies.[24]

Some companies continue to refrain from developing sustainability reports, yet the number of these studies is increasing in most sectors of the economy. The benefits that accrue from sustainability reporting include:[25]

The Firm Becomes More Disciplined About Environmental Performance.
The Kyoto Protocol and other international activity designed to control greenhouse

---

[22] Global Reporting Initiative (2011), G4 Sustainability Reporting Guidelines, www.globalreporting.org/ (January 31, 2017).

[23] Kolk, Ans (2004), "A Decade of Sustainability Reporting: Developments and Significance," *International Journal of Environment and Sustainable Development*, 3 (1), 51–64.

[24] Kolk, Ans (2003), "Trends in Sustainability Reporting by the Fortune Global 250," *Business Strategy and the Environment* 12 (5), 279–291.

[25] Kolk, Ans (2000), "Green Reporting," *Harvard Business Review* 78 (1), 15–16.

gas emissions have prompted many firms to recognize that carbon rationing and trading affect an organization's business strategy and financial performance. Firms that report on efforts to control carbon emissions are simultaneously confronted with efforts to control the firm's interaction with the environment. Strategic cost management systems, for instance, provide the ability to evaluate the carbon emissions costs of products and services over their product life cycles. Firms that develop this information provide insight into human resource management, marketing, supply chain operations, and financial performance.[26] The organization that develops sustainability reports develops a broader awareness of environmental issues throughout organization, and this awareness should yield a smaller carbon footprint for the firm.

Conveys an Environmental Message to All Stakeholders. One of the primary benefits of sustainability reporting lies in the ability to promote dialogue with stakeholders. Recall from Chapter 3 that the stakeholders for the firm include consumers, suppliers, employees, competitors, the legal system, financial institutions, government, media, stockholders/owners, the scientific community, nongovernment organizations, and the general public. Companies recognize that they can enhance credibility with each of these groups through transparency. For example, Apple became vocal about its sustainability policies in 2007. At the time, CEO Steve Jobs noted Apple ordinarily does not proclaim its plans for the future, but the current policies had left important stakeholders (customers, shareholders, and employees) in the dark.[27] By taking a proactive stance toward sustainability reporting, Apple and other firms can have a strong influence on the way they are perceived in the markets in which they compete. Thus, sustainability reporting provides a context which enables the firm to model changes in employees' values, beliefs, and core assumptions about the organization.[28]

Track Progress Versus Targets. When sustainability reporting is completed on an annual or regular basis, it enables the organization to chart its progress against objectives over time. For example, Electrolux has been developing sustainability reports since 1998. In its 2015 report, the company identifies its objectives over the past several years, and it identifies the extent to which it has achieved these objectives. The report not only identifies past progress, it lists specific targets for the future.[29] Charting performance over time indicates progress to all stakeholders and further emphasizes the gravity of the firm's sustainability interests.

---

[26] Ratnatunga, Janek T. D., and Kashi R. Balachandran (2009), "Carbon Business Accounting: The Impact of Global Warming on the Cost and Management Accounting Profession," *Journal of Accounting, Auditing and Finance*, 24(2), 333–355.

[27] Truini, Joe (2007), "Jobs Finally Unveils 'Greening of Apple' Plan," *Waste News*, 13 (1), 22.

[28] Linnenluecke, Martina K., and Andrew Griffiths (2009), "Corporate Sustainability and Organizational Culture," *Journal of World Business* 45 (4), 357–366.

[29] www.electroluxgroup.com/en/wp-content/uploads/sites/2/2016/04/Electrolux-Sustainability-In-Brief-2015.pdf (January 31, 2017).

Reduce Environmental Risk. Sustainability poses a series of risks that are distinct from other forms of risk. Firms must address risks associated with climate change, boycotts, ecosystem services risk, social justice, and harmful substances; and these risks can pose specific liabilities for directors and officers of the firm.[30] Firms that examine the risks encountered in the procurement, processing, consumption, and disposition of products can reduce their liabilities due to environmental factors.

Identify Savings and Efficiencies. Organizations that begin to monitor the use of energy subsequently begin to recognize the magnitude of energy expenses and the distribution among alternative needs. Firms that annually provide sustainability reports quantify their energy and begin to find ways to reduce these expenditures. For example, by charting energy use over successive years, IBM was able to reduce consumption throughout the company by more 6.3 percent in 2015.[31]

Identify New Business Opportunities. In order to develop a sustainability report, a firm must necessarily review all of its business operations. In this review, firms on occasion find that resources within the firm that are not been marketed. For example, Shell Oil pumps carbon dioxide from Dutch refineries to greenhouses. Before it assessed the sustainability of the refinery, this carbon dioxide was released into the atmosphere.[32]

OVERVIEW OF SUSTAINABILITY REPORTS

Many firms adopt contrasting styles and formats to present their efforts to achieve some level of sustainability. Despite these alternative styles, several essential elements should be addressed if the firm is to offer a meaningful discussion of its sustainability efforts and performance. The firm initially outlines its strategy with respect to sustainability, and it then provides specific economic, environmental, and social indicators of its efforts. Although the firm may use a variety of styles to present this information, many companies illustrate how their sustainability analyses dovetail with the Global Reporting Initiative (GRI) sustainability reporting guidelines. For example, General Electric indexes their 2015 sustainability report with the point-by-point criteria outlined by GRI. Figure 14-2 provides an overview of the elements of a sustainability report.

Strategy and Analysis

The initial component of a sustainability report provides a summary of the corporate strategy and the managerial approach to sustainability. The discussion of corporate strategy should focus on the relationship between the firm and its stakeholders with respect to economic, environmental, and social conditions. Importantly, the strategic overview should include a letter from the senior decision-maker of the organization about the relevance of sustainability to the organization and its

[30] Anderson, Dan R. (2006), "Sustainability Risk Management," *CPCU eJournal*, (May), 1–17.

[31] www.ibm.com/ibm/responsibility/2015/assets/downloads/IBM_2015_CR_report .pdf (January 31, 2017).

[32] Deliser, H. (2006), "Gas for the Greenhouse," *Nature* 442, 499PP.

I. Summary of Corporate Sustainability Strategy

   Strategy and analysis

   Organizational profile

   Report parameters

   Governance, commitments and engagement

II. Performance Indicators

   Economic indicators

   Environmental indicators

   Social indicators

III. Third-party Validation

FIGURE 14-2
Elements of a sustainability report.

strategy.[33] In addition, this initial discussion should provide a review of the key influences of the firm as well as a treatment of its risks and opportunities in the markets it serves. For example, the General Electric 2015 sustainability report provides a letter from Chairman Jeff Immelt's commitment to sustainability. The report also provides a review of the commitments and progress made by the firm over the last year's report and the progress made toward achieving those objectives in 2015, as well as expectations for 2016.[34]

Organizational Profile

The organizational profile identifies the name of the company, the nature of its ownership, and its headquarters. In addition, the company describes the countries and the markets served as well as its primary products, brands, and services. The company also indicates its level of involvement in the production and the amount of outsourcing employed during production.

Report Parameters

The report parameters concern the period represented by the study and the frequency of reporting by the company. The firm also identifies the scope and the boundary of the study at this point, and it recognizes known limitations with respect to these parameters. The firm also provides a review of its measurement techniques, and it describes the policies and practices associated with gaining external assurance about the report.

Governance, Commitments, and Engagement

The governance system provides an overview of how the firm seeks to attain its objectives. Governance includes the structure of the organization and the

---

[33] www.globalreporting.org/resourcelibrary/G3.1-Guidelines-Incl-Technical-Protocol .pdf (January 31, 2017).

[34] www.gesustainability.com/performance-data/a-letter-from-the-ceo/ (January 31, 2017).

committees responsible for the firm's strategy and organizational oversight. The firm also outlines its mission and values with respect to economic, environmental, and social performance. The incentive structures of the senior officers are outlined, and the firm indicates procedures for employees and other stakeholders to provide recommendations.

The firm also outlines its commitments external to the firm. One vital part of a firm's commitment lies in its participation in the development of industry standards. Companies supply lists of industrial groups and affiliates. In addition, they report on externally developed triple bottom-line principles that they endorse. For example, GE's 2015 sustainability report recognizes the company's partnerships with energy (e.g., Statoil and Masdar), retailing (e.g., Wal-Mart), financial services (e.g., Goldman Sachs), and other industries.[35]

The final component of the strategic overview is the engagement of stakeholders. Since all of the information in the report derives from these groups, it is essential to identify their level of involvement. The firm provides its rationales for the selection and identification of stakeholders, and it describes the frequency of engagement with each type of stakeholder. The company also provides a review of the topics addressed in meetings with stakeholders.[36]

Third-party Validation

When the firm has completed its summary of the corporate sustainability strategy, it then reports on the economic, environmental, and social performance as outlined in the following sections. After these performance indicators have been provided, firms increasingly provide some evidence of assurance via a third party.[37] Although many firms have established procedures for determining sustainable action, assurance is significantly enhanced through evaluation by some entity external to the organization. In reporting on third-party evaluations, firms indicate that the evaluation is performed by an external party that uses individuals who are not limited by their relationship with the firm. The third-party reports should be completed by persons competent in the subject matter and related practices. In addition, the report should be developed in a systematic, documented approach, and it should result in the development of a publicly available opinion of the firm's sustainability performance.

REPORTING ECONOMIC VALUE

The economic value provided by an organization is not a substitute or a replacement for accounting and financial reporting. On the contrary, this part of the sustainability report is designed to illustrate the flow of capital among stakeholders

---

[35] dsg.files.app.content.prod.s3.amazonaws.com/gesustainability/wp-content/uploads/2015/01/26171807/Partnerships_Infographic-10.26.15.png (January 31, 2017).

[36] Global Reporting Initiative (2011), G4 Sustainability Reporting Guidelines, www.globalreporting.org/ (January 31, 2017).

[37] Kolk, Ans (2008), "Sustainability, Accountability and Corporate Governance: Exploring Multinationals' Reporting," *Business Strategy and the Environment*, 17 (1), 1–15.

Source of funds	€ millions	Relative Value
Total sales	18,089	99.9%
Other income	11	0.1%
Distribution of funds		
Cost of materials	7,839	43.3%
Depreciation and amortization	460	2.5%
Other expenses	4,027	22.3%
Value added	5,774	31.9%
Employees	3,047	52.8%
Central and local government	685	11.8%
Interest expense	74	1.3%
Shareholders	639	11.1%
Minority shareholders	47	0.8%
Reinvested in the company	1,282	22.2%

FIGURE 14-3
Henkel value-added statement 2015.[39]

and illustrate the economic influence of the firm throughout society.[38] Economic reporting includes reviews of *financial performance*, *local market presence*, and *indirect economic influences* of the firm (see Figure 14-3).

Financial Performance

Financial performance refers to the presentation of the firm's value in terms of accounting and financial standards. The *value-added statement* identifies the direct economic value generated and distributed to capital providers and government. This section of the report summarizes revenues, employee compensation, operating costs, donations and other community investments, retained earnings, and payments. For example, Henkel is one of the world's leading suppliers of laundry and home care products (e.g., *Purex*), cosmetics and toiletries (e.g., *Schwarzkopf Professional* hair care), and adhesives (*Loctite* glue). Figure 14-3 illustrates the value added to the company in financial terms.

A second financial consideration is the disclosure of the financial implications of climate change for the firm. As the level of regulation associated with climate change increases, firms face regulatory risk due to increased costs. These regulations also provide opportunities through new markets and technologies. Firms report on these considerations to illustrate their planning efforts and control risks. For example, Timberland reports on its efforts to source 50 percent of its energy needs from renewable sources. This strategy notably involves reductions in its demand for energy, procurement of renewable energy, and investing in renewable energy through carbon offset purchases.[40]

---

[38] Global Reporting Initiative (2011), G4 Sustainability Reporting Guidelines, www .globalreporting.org/ (January 31, 2017).

[39] www.henkel.de/blob/638616/055568a710b212cb4eb8a55fe13095fc/data/2015-sustainability-report.pdf (January 31, 2017).

[40] www.timberland.com/responsibility.html (February 1, 2017).

Reporting firms supply two additional pieces of information that are pertinent to employees, investors, and other stakeholders. Firms disclose the financial obligations associated with benefit plans.[41] In addition, they indicate whether they receive significant financial assistance from government.[42]

Local Market Presence

The second set of economic indicators addresses the role of the firm in the local markets in which it has a significant presence. The firm reports on the relative wage rate by illustrating the relationship between company wages and local minimum wages.[43] It also reports on the policies and the practices associated with hiring personnel from the local community. Similarly, firms also report on the procedures associated with securing locally based suppliers. For example, Unilever's 2015 sustainability report outlines the company's efforts in the areas of leadership development and corporate diversity. It further outlines its business partner code that specifies sourcing requirements for business ethics, health and safety, labor standards, and the environment.[44]

Indirect Economic Influences

The indirect economic influences refer to the firm's effort to enhance public welfare. The organization reports on the development of infrastructure and services. For example, Coca-Cola reports that it invested more than $126 million (€117million) to communities in 2015, enabling them to support communities and organizations around the globe. In addition to investments in infrastructure, firms also report on other economic activity derived from their sustainability efforts. The Coca-Cola 2015 report, for example, reports on the company's ongoing efforts to bring safe water access to 1 million people in 37 African countries.[45]

....

REPORTING ENVIRONMENTAL VALUE

The reporting of environmental performance addresses the extent to which the action of the firm is associated with *material usage, energy, water, biodiversity, by-products and waste, products and services*, and *transportation*.[46] Consider first the firm's material use.

---

[41] Hansen, Fay (2007), "A Home for HR Metrics," *Workforce Management*, 86 (2), 10–11.

[42] Global Reporting Initiative (2011), G4 Sustainability Reporting Guidelines, www.globalreporting.org/ (January 31, 2017).

[43] Hansen, Fay (2007), "A Home for HR Metrics," *Workforce Management*, 86 (2), 10–11.

[44] www.unilever.com/Images/uslp-mobilising-collective-action-summary-of-progress-2015_tcm244-424809_en.pdf (February 1, 2017).

[45] assets.coca-colacompany.com/29/0b/1c0121a84941aa46b9c9f6201ac9/2014-2015-sustainability-report.15_080415.pdf (February 1, 2017).

[46] Global Reporting Initiative (2011), G4 Sustainability Reporting Guidelines, www.globalreporting.org/ (January 31, 2017).

Materials

Material usage directly addresses the overall cost of operations, and the tracking of this factor enables the firm to monitor material efficiency and costs associated with the flow of material. Companies report on raw material, processed material, semi-manufactured goods, and packaging materials. They also report on the extent to which they use recycled materials as inputs. For instance, the 2014/2015 Ford Motor Company sustainability report indicates the amount of recycled materials used in its production processes worldwide.[47] The report also indicates that Ford employs a life-cycle design strategy.

Energy

The monitoring of energy usage is instrumental to achieving fuel efficiency. Firms monitor direct and indirect energy consumption. *Direct energy* refers to consumption of energy without conversion, whereas *indirect energy* refers to use of energy that has been transformed through some process. For example, an electrical plant has a direct use of coal to produce its output—electricity. The use of this electricity by an auto plant is a form of indirect energy use. In the direct energy category, firms provide reports of the use of nonrenewable forms of energy that include coal, natural gas, gasoline, and other forms. Direct energy also includes renewable sources of energy such as biofuels, ethanol, and hydrogen. Similarly, reporting on indirect energy use distinguishes nonrenewable energy purchases of electricity, heating/cooling, steam, and nuclear energy from renewable sources such as solar, geothermal, and wind energy.

Reporting on energy utilization over time enables companies to illustrate results of their efforts to limit the amount of energy consumed. For example, the Merck 2015/2016 sustainability report tracks purchases of coal, fuel oil, and electricity over five years.[48] Firms offer evidence of the degree to which conservation activities increase energy efficiency leading to reductions in direct and indirect energy consumption. They also indicate the extent to which they provide products that rely on energy-efficient technologies or that employ renewable sources of energy. For example, the Ford 2014/2015 sustainability report outlines the firm's efforts to reduce its direct and indirect energy consumption. The report also highlights Ford's development of products that strive to achieve efficiency through alternative fuels, electrification, and new drive train technologies.[49]

Water

Because access to clean freshwater is declining, the firm's reporting on its use of water provides insight into the financial and social risks faced by the organization.[50] Firms report on the amount of water withdrawn from surface (*rivers, lakes, oceans,* and *wetlands*) sources, ground water, rainwater, municipal sources, and

[47] corporate.ford.com/microsites/sustainability-report-2014-15/doc/sr14.pdf (February 1, 2017).

[48] www.msdresponsibility.com/environmental-sustainability/ (February 1, 2017).

[49] corporate.ford.com/microsites/sustainability-report-2014-15/doc/sr14.pdf (February 1, 2017).

[50] Global Reporting Initiative (2011), G4 Sustainability Reporting Guidelines, www.globalreporting.org/ (January 31, 2017).

waste water. They further identify sources of water significantly influenced by water removal. They also indicate the total volume of water reused or recycled. The Abbott Laboratories 2015 sustainability report, for example, indicates a outlines 19 percent reduction in water intake as compared to 2010.[51]

Biodiversity

Given the imminent risks to flora and fauna, it is essential that environmental reviews take stock of the firm's efforts associated with enhancing habitat. Firms report on their strategies, operations, and influences on wildlife in areas of high biodiversity value and in protected areas. The reporting further indicates the number of endangered species affected by operations and the habitats restored or protected by the firm. For example, Shell Oil indicates how it uses its partnerships with Wetlands International and the International Union for the Conservation of Nature to conserve tundra ecosystems in the Arctic. This partnership also enables them protect wetlands along the flight paths of migratory birds.[52]

By-products and Waste

By-products and waste refer to the gaseous, liquid, and solid output discarded in the supply chain. Gaseous by-products include *greenhouse gas emissions* as well as *ozone-depleting substances*. Firms report on the process used to determine the level of these outputs as well as their initiatives to lower emissions. Vodafone's energy performance report, for instance, indicates its total direct and indirect greenhouse gas emissions.[53]

Firms also report on the total waste and the methods of disposal for waste. This material includes liquid and solid waste, and it includes hazardous and nonhazardous waste. Abbott Laboratories, for example, indicates that in 2015 redesign and remanufacture of its patented glucose monitors yielded a 25 percent reduction in raw materials usage.[54] Firms indicate the degree to which they use composting, reuse, recycling, recovery, deep-well injection, onsite storage, incineration, or landfills to dispose of by-products.

Products and Services

Conservation efforts associated with products address the inputs into development and production. Firms provide summaries of the material, water, emissions, and other factors associated their products. Apple's annual sustainability report, for example, provides an account of the life cycle costs associated with its products.[55] Product reporting also considers the degree to which the firm engages in efforts to reclaim products. Since many products (e.g., computers) have historically been

---

[51] http://dam.abbott.com/global/documents/pdfs/abbott-citizenship/global-reports/ Abbott_Global_Citizenship_Report.pdf (may 2, 2017).

[52] www.shell.com/sustainability/sustainability-reporting-and-performance-data/ sustainability-reports.html (February 1, 2017).

[53] www.vodafone.com/content/index/about/sustainability/sustainablebusiness2016 .html (February 1, 2017).

[54] prod3.dam.abbott.com/global/documents/pdfs/abbott-citizenship/global-reports/ Abbott_Global_Citizenship_Report.pdf (February 1, 2017).

[55] TN> www.apple.com/environment/climate-change/ (February 1, 2017).

made with hazardous material such as brominated flame retardants, it is pertinent to develop programs to reclaim these products and dispose of them properly. The Lexmark sustainability program, for instance, reports on the company's efforts to reclaim inkjet cartridges, laser toner cartridges, printers, and other products.[56]

Compliance

This facet of reporting concerns the extent to which a company complies or fails to comply with environmental regulations. Compliant firms generally face less financial risk and are better positioned to gain permits or otherwise expand operations.[57] In some sustainability reports, firms provide a review of their environmental policy and provide evidence of their compliance with acceptable industry standard. For example, Merck's 2014/2015 sustainability report outlines its commitment to safety and environmental performance and indicates its compliance with prevailing environmental law concerning spills. Firms also explain conditions under which they have failed to comply with prevailing standards by reporting monetary fines and nonmonetary sanctions associated with environmental regulations. The Merck 2014/2015 report, for example, indicates that the company paid over $157K (€145.7K) associated with seven environmental fines.[58]

Transportation

Since the distribution and supply chain for products are primary sources of value for many firms, it is important for companies to report on the influence of transportation. Firms identify their strategies to mitigate transportation costs. Importantly, they report on the energy used in transportation, the emissions associated with transportation, and the waste, noise, and spills associated with transportation. The 2015 United Parcel Service (UPS) environmental stewardship report, for example, provides summary statistics on energy use for shipping by road, rail, and air. The report indicates that efforts over the past five years to move to more efficient transportation yielded savings comparable to taking over 4 million cars off the road.[59]

REPORTING SOCIAL VALUE

Reporting on social value provides the third component of sustainability reporting. This section includes reporting on human rights, labor practices, product responsibility, and society.

Human Rights

In the human rights sector, the firm indicates how it maintains and respects the basic rights of human beings.[60] The firm indicates the extent to which investment

---

[56] csr.lexmark.com/gri.html (February 1, 2017).

[57] www.globalreporting.org/resourcelibrary/G3.1-Guidelines-Incl-Technical-Protocol .pdf (January 31, 2017).

[58] www.msdresponsibility.com/environmental-sustainability/ (February 1, 2017).

[59] https://sustainability.ups.com/media/ups-pdf-interactive/index.html (May 2, 2017).

[60] www.globalreporting.org/resourcelibrary/G3.1-Guidelines-Incl-Technical-Protocol. pdf (January 31, 2017).

agreements and trading partners have been reviewed for human rights considerations. For example, Ford Motor Company's 2014/2015 sustainability report discusses collaboration on human rights issues with its partners in the supply chain.[61] Firms report on the extent to which they have invested in training employees about human rights issues, and they report on the number of incidents of discrimination.

The human rights section also outlines some policies that concern working conditions. Firms report on operations that have a significant potential to limit *freedom of association* and *collective bargaining*. They also report on operations with the potential to engage in child labor or compulsory labor. For example, Starbuck's 2015 sustainability report outlines the firm's effort to achieve a goal of 100 percent responsibly grown, ethically grown coffees.[62] Coffee grown under these criteria are unlikely to violate working condition standards.

Labor Practices

The analysis of labor practices centers on the concept of decent work.[63] The firms discloses the scope and the diversity of its workforce and emphasizes aspects of gender and age distribution. The firm also provides an account of its employee benefits and discloses the extent to which it uses collective bargaining agreements. In addition, it provides demographic and financial reports of employee data to provide evidence of diversity and equal opportunity. For example, Unilever's 2015 strategic report outlines progress towards empowering women in the workforce.[64]

The well-being and physical protection of employees is covered by occupational *health and safety standards* and the ongoing training provided by the firm. These safety and occupational health indicators chart statistical performance and enable firms to communicate their health and safety programs to employees. Companies report on the amount of training and counseling dedicated to informing community members about serious illness and disease. For example, Coca-Cola reports on the company's efforts to address human rights risks in the countries where it sources sugar.[65]

Product Responsibility

Product responsibility reporting addresses the effects of products and services on customers and users. Organizations are expected to exercise diligence to ensure that products are fit for intended use and do not pose any unintended hazards to health and safety. Companies report on the health and safety impacts of their

---

[61] corporate.ford.com/microsites/sustainability-report-2014-15/doc/sr14.pdf (February 2, 2017).

[62] globalassets.starbucks.com/assets/ee8121c1a6554399b554d126228d52ed.pdf (February 2, 2017).

[63] Global Reporting Initiative (2000-2011), *Labor Practices and Decent Work Performance Indicators,* Amsterdam, Netherlands: Global Reporting Initiative.

[64] www.unilever.com/Images/annual_report_and_accounts_ar15_tcm244-478426_en.pdf (February 2, 2017).

[65] www.coca-colacompany.com/content/dam/journey/us/en/private/fileassets/pdf/2016/SR16-HWR.pdf (February 2, 2017).

products and report on the incidents of noncompliance with regulations. For example, Mercedes-Benz reports on the health and safety from concept development to post-consumption disposal.[66] Firms also indicate the type of product labeling and specify the number of incidents of noncompliance.

Product responsibility reporting also includes consideration of the marketing communications and the security of customer information. Companies must outline programs for adherence to standards and laws concerning advertising, promotion, sponsorship, and other marketing communiqués.[67] For example, Shaw Industries' 2015 sustainability report indicates its commitment to upholding the U.S. Federal Trade Commission's Green Guides for communicating environmental initiatives and sustainability of its carpeting and other products.[68] Reporting firms must also reveal the number of incidents of noncompliance with regulations and report any fines incurred due to noncompliance. Customer privacy is also a concern addressed within product responsibility reporting. The organization indicates the number of substantiated complaints regarding breaches of privacy and losses of consumer data.

Society

Whereas human rights, labor, and product considerations focus on a specific stakeholder group, the society performance indicators reflect interaction with the community at large.[69] The firm provides an overview of its programs designed to manage and assess the influence of its operations on the community. For example, Shell Oil reports on its efforts to reduce the influence of operations on local communities. It partners with the Galveston Bay Foundation in the Bike Around the Bay Race that helps preserve wetlands, protect natural habitat, and enhance the water quality in the bay.[70] The reporting company also provides a discussion of its participation in public policy development and lobbying. It also offers an account of its contributions to political parties, politicians, and related institutions in all the markets it serves.

The firm also reports on its compliance with laws and regulations, and it reports judgments associated with corruption or anti-competitive behavior. Johnson & Johnson, for instance, outlines a code of conduct that specifically outlines policies associated with bribery and corruption, conflicts of interest, gifts and hospitality, insider dealing, and political action.[71] The reporting firm also identifies the number of business units analyzed for risk of corruption, and it describes the extent to which employees have been trained in the firm's anti-corruption practices.

---

[66] www.daimler.com/sustainability/product/ (February 2, 2017).

[67] Global Reporting Initiative (2000-2011), *Labor Practices and Decent Work Performance Indicators*, Amsterdam, Netherlands: Global Reporting Initiative.

[68] shawinc.com/getattachment/68d2a10c-bdc5-4279-b7a2-bc706dbf23a1/attachment.aspx (February 2, 2017).

[69] Global Reporting Initiative (2000-2006), *Society Performance Indicators*, Amsterdam, Netherlands: Global Reporting Initiative.

[70] www.shell.us/sustainability/conservation/latest-news/bike-around-the-bay.html (February 2, 2017).

[71] www.jnj.com/sites/default/files/pdf/Code-of-Business-Conduct-English-US.pdf (February 2, 2017).

Introduction

The goal of this chapter has been to outline the logic, the merits, and the processes associated with sustainability reporting. Firms that report on this activity are more likely to yield sustainable results relative to their competition. We examine the purposes and the benefits of sustainability reporting, and we outlining the components of sustainability reports. We also examine the reporting of financial, environmental, and social performance.

Purposes of Sustainability Reporting

Sustainability reporting serves three primary purposes for the firm. First, these reports enable firms to demonstrate their commitment to sustainability. Second, sustainability reporting enables companies to compare their performance to laws, codes, norms, and voluntary initiatives. Third, these reports enable companies to illustrate their longitudinal performance relative to the competition.

Benefits of Sustainability Reporting Value

Companies can realize multiple benefits from sustainability reporting. Firms can become more disciplined about environmental performance, and they can convey environmental messages to all stakeholders. They can also track progress relative to targets and reduce their overall risk due to sustainability reporting. Furthermore, this reporting enables companies to identify savings and efficiencies, and it enables them to identify new business opportunities.

Overview of Sustainability Reports

Sustainability reports provide an overview of the firm's sustainability strategy by reviewing corporate strategy and governance and by profiling the organization's approach to the markets it pursues. The company also provides detailed reviews of its economic, environmental, and social performance. Third-party verification of these reports provides assurance of a level of quality for these reports.

Reporting Economic Value

Economic performance includes analyses of financial performance, market presence, and indirect market influences. Financial performance addresses the flow of capital between the firm and its stakeholders, and market presence concerns the local market performance of the firm relative to alternative employers. Indirect influences refer to the contributions in the forms of services and infrastructure.

Reporting Environmental Value

Environmental performance concerns the extent to which the action of the firm is associated with material usage, energy, water, biodiversity, by-products and waste, products and services, and transportation. Material usage directly addresses the overall cost of operations, and the tracking of this factor enables the firm to monitor material efficiency and costs. The monitoring of energy usage addresses direct and indirect energy consumption. Firms also report on the amount of water withdrawn from multiple sources, and they identify water sources significantly influenced by water removal. Biodiversity reporting concerns the influence of the firm on flora and fauna, whereas by-product reporting outlines the firm's procedures for treating waste and other nonproduct outputs of production. Product reporting summarizes material, water, emissions, and other factors associated products, and transportation reporting identifies strategies employed to control transportation-related costs.

Reporting Social Value

Reporting on social value includes discussions of human rights, labor practices, product responsibility, and society. The firm reports on its basic human rights policies, and it reports on the use of collective bargaining. Labor reporting discloses the scope and the diversity of the workforce as well as the firm's occupational health and safety standards. Product responsibility reporting addresses the effects of products and services on customers, and societal reporting addresses the firm's interaction with the community at large.

KEY TERMS

transparency
financial performance
value-added statement
direct energy

indirect energy
greenhouse gas emissions
ozone-depleting substances
freedom of association

collective bargaining
health and safety standards

DISCUSSION QUESTIONS

1. If sustainability reporting is not required by law, why do firms bother to develop these reports?
2. How is sustainability reporting related to triple bottom-line performance?
3. How do firms illustrate transparency, and how does this effort help stakeholders?
4. What stakeholders are relevant to sustainability reporting? Why might the number of stakeholder groups vary for different types of organizations?
5. What is the role of stakeholders in developing sustainability reports?
6. Why is it essential for companies to describe their corporate strategy and governance in sustainability reports?
7. How does third-party verification influence evaluations of sustainability reports by stakeholders?

8. To what extent is the economic part of the sustainability report redundant with the firm's annual report? Why do firms include indirect economic consequences in the economic section of sustainability reports?

9. What are the elements of the environmental section of the sustainability reports? How does reporting of each facet of the environment contribute to ecological performance?

10. Who benefits from reporting on social performance, and how do they benefit from this practice?

Macro-Economic Energy Consumption

appendix

A-1

The Environment and Consumption

In this appendix you will learn about:

Climate Change and Consumption

Greenhouse Gases and Their Contributions to Climate Change

Sources of Energy and Their Use across International Regions

Human Influences on the Atmosphere

Human Influences on Water

Human Influences on Land

Human Influences on Biodiversity

The goal of this appendix is to characterize influences of consumption on the physical environment. We outline influences of consumption on climate change, energy, the atmosphere, water, and land. The analysis of climate change examines the production of greenhouse gases. Our discussion of the atmosphere addresses ozone depletion and air pollution. Our examination of water includes reviews of freshwater, oceans and fisheries, and water purity. Our analysis of land examines urban expansion, land degradation, deforestation, desertification, and waste management.

We distinguish among climatic, atmospheric, water, land, and biodiversity facets of the environment to provide background on trends in the environment. These environmental issues are interactive rather than independent. Moreover, factors that have a primary influence on one facet of the environment likely also influence other facets of the environment. For example, ozone depletion is an aspect of the atmosphere, but it influences water and biodiversity.[1]

CLIMATE CHANGE AND CONSUMPTION

The United Nations reports that 11 of the hottest years since 1850 have occurred in the last 20 years, and the last decade is the hottest on record.[2] This report underscores the critical level of climate change faced on the planet. Indeed, climate change is shaping up to be the biggest environmental issue that business has ever faced.[3]

Climate change refers to any change in climate over time, whether due to natural variability or as a result of human activity.[4] The Earth is surrounded by a natural blanket of gases that keep the planet warm enough to sustain life. Solar enegy in the form of visible light that hits the Earth's surface warms the planet. The Earth emits energy back out to space in the form of thermal radiation. Greenhouse gases block the radiation from escaping resulting in the *natural greenhouse effect*. This natural effect raises the Earth's temperature by approximately 30°C and is essential for life.[5]

Since the beginning of industrial revolution, increasing emissions of greenhouse gases have been making the blanket thicker. This artificial influence on the environment is known as the *enhanced greenhouse effect*. The Earth must rid itself of energy at the same rate at which it receives from the sun. As the blanket of greenhouse gases thickens, less energy is lost to space. The system primarily restores balance through global warming of the Earth's lower atmoshere and surface. Thus, increases in greenhouse gases lead to increases in the Earth's surface temperature.

---

[1] Lemonick, M.D., and D. Cray (1992), "The Ozone Vanishes," *Time* February 17, 60–63.

[2] Held, David, Mary Kaldor, and Danny Quah (2010), "The Hydra-headed Crisis," *LSE Global Governance* 297–317.

[3] Esty, Daniel C., and Andrew S. Winston (2006), *Green to Gold*, New Haven, CT: Yale University Press.

[4] Alley, Richard, et al. (2007), "Climate Change 2007: The Physical Science Basis Summary for Policymakers," 1–18, Cambridge University Press.

[5] Karl, Thomas R., and Kevin E. Trenberth (2003), "Modern Global Climate Change," *Science* 302 (5651), 1719–1723.

Climate change has several critical influences that include:[6]

1. **Erratic climate and weather extremes lead to increased risks**:
   a) **Higher temperatures and increased risk**. The climate takes time to respond to emissions, and the actual period of time can take decades. Furthermore, oceans absorb and release heat more slowly than the atmosphere. The result of these effects is higher temperatures for centuries after stabilization of greenhouse gases. A substantial portion of the strain is associated with higher and more frequent temperature spikes such as those that Europe faced in the summer of 2003. Excess mortality in France alone for the August 1-15 period was 11,435 deaths.[7] Evidence also suggests that human influence has more than doubled the risk of summers becoming as hot as 2003, with the likelihood of such events to increase 100-fold over the next four decades.[8]

2. **Altered ecosystems and habitats have several influences on commerce**:
   a) **Decline in the quantity and quality of freshwater**. Rising temperatures influence the level of moisture in the air. Warmer atmospheres hold more moisture and produce more precipitation, especially in the form of heavy cloud bursts. In addition, greater heat speeds up evaporation. Together these changes in the cycling of water reduce the quantity and quality of freshwater supplies across all major geographic regions.
   b) **Decline in the terrestrial and inland water ecosystems**. As climate change exacerbates and water quality lowers, the viability of ecosystems suffers. The functions and the services provided by these ecosystems can suffer markedly. For example, in the last 50 years, the area of the Aral Sea has shrunk by 74 percent, and its volume has decreased by 90 percent.[9] The influences of climate change on this region have led to decimation of native fish species and increased intensity of dust storms.[10]
   c) **Rising sea levels**. Climate change associated with higher temperatures is resulting in higher sea levels. Evidence indicates that the Antarctic and Greenland ice sheets are losing mass and contributing to rising sea levels.[11] The rise in sea levels over the last 20 years is twice as fast as the average over the twentieth century, and the

---

[6] www.edf.org/climate/climate-change-impacts (June 17, 2015).

[7] WHO (2003), "The Health Impacts of 2003 Summer Heatwaves," *Briefing Note for the 53rd Session of the World Health Organization Regional Committee for Europe.*

[8] Stott, Peter A., D. A. Stone, and M. R. Allen (2004), "Human Contribution to the European Heatwave of 2003," *Nature* 432 (7017), 610–614.

[9] Micklin, P. (2007). "The Aral Sea Disaster." *Annual Review of Earth and Planetary Sciences*, 35, 47–72.

[10] Small, Eric E., Filippo Giorgi, Lisa Cirbus Sloan, and Steven Hostetler (2001), "The effects of desiccation and climatic change on the hydrology of the Aral Sea," *Journal of Climate* 14 (3), 300–322.

[11] Shepherd, Andrew, and Duncan Wingham (2007), "Recent sea-level contributions of the Antarctic and Greenland ice sheets," *Science* 315 (5818), 1529–1532.

twentieth century experienced a growth rate substantially greater than the previous two millennia.[12] These rising sea levels increase coastal flooding and erosion.

d) **Threats to biodiversity**. Biodiversity refers to the animal and plant life that surrounds us. Climate change over the last 40 years has modified the distribution and the location of many species. Increases in average temperatures are associated with increasing levels of species extinction such that 20 to 30% of species face an increased risk of extinction.[13] This trend is attributed to shifts in vegetation zones, shifts in ranges of individual species, interaction between climate change and habitat fragmentation, and changes in ecosystem functioning. Species extinction is likely to occur across regions on the planet. Consequently, the services they offer to society are jeopardized.

3. **Risks to human health and society include**:

a) **Increased health risk**. Although climate change likely reduces the number of deaths due to exposure, it generally has a negative effect on health. Climate change increases the risks of death or injury due to storm surges, coastal and inland flooding, and rising sea levels. Exposure to extreme weather conditions increases mortality and morbidity for workers.[14] Climate change alters distribution patterns of malarial mosquitoes and other carriers of infectious diseases.[15] It also affects the seasonal distribution of allergy-causing pollen.

b) **Affects the most vulnerable**. Exposure to climate change is greatest among the poor and those with limited resources to invest in mitigating and preventing effects of climate change. Changes in climate have the potential to force departures from the Arctic climates due to lack of biodiversity and degradation of habitat. Simultaneously, climate change may force departures from tropical areas where inhabitants live just above sea level. These trends will lead to increased displacement and higher numbers of environmental refugees.[16]

Climate change also has several direct influences on business that include:[17]

a) **Agriculture**. Rising and volatile weather patterns adversely affect the agricultural sector and complicate efforts to speculate on future values

---

[12] Church J. A., Woodworth P. L., Aarup T., Wilson S. W. (Eds.) (2010) *Understanding sea-level rise and variability*. Chichester, UK: Wiley-Blackwell Publishing.

[13] Burns, William C. G., and Hari M. Osofsky (2009), Adjudicating climate change: state, national, and international approaches. Cambridge University Press.

[14] United Nations (2012), *Global Environmental Outlook 5*, Valetta, Malta: Progress Press.

[15] Patz, J. A., Campbell-Lendrum, D., Holloway, T., and Foley, J. A. (2005). "Impact of regional climate change on human health," *Nature*, 438(7066), 310–317.

[16] Esty, Daniel C., and Andrew S. Winston (2006), *Green to Gold*, New Haven, CT: Yale University Press.

[17] Parry, Martin L. (Ed.) (2007), *Climate Change 2007: Impacts, adaptation and vulnerability: Contribution of Working Group II to the fourth assessment report of the Intergovernmental Panel on Climate Change* (Vol. 4), Cambridge University Press.

of agricultural-based commodities (e.g., frozen orange juice and pork bellies).[18]

b) **Tourism**. Winter and summer-based tourism sites stand to lose considerably due to climate change.[19] Rising temperature eliminate ski resorts, and rising sea levels *drown* beaches. In addition, severe thunderstorms are problematic for airlines and other transportation systems.

c) **Insurance**. The insurance industry is particularly susceptible to climate change. As the premiums and the costs associated with underwriting policies become more difficult to assess, costs increase, and the numbers of providers decrease.[20]

d) **Transportation and related costs**. As climate change increases, government will likely act to control greenhouse gas emissions. Consequently, industries that have heavy transportation needs (e.g., automobile production) face higher costs of operations. Similarly, industries that use petroleum-related raw materials (e.g., plastics production) face greater costs.[21]

e) **New product/solution development**. Although climate change has many negative consequences, it presents enormous opportunities for entrepreneurs who develop technologies, services, and products. Consumer demand for products that reduce energy costs or eliminate the need to rely on carbon-based fuels will receive greater attention.[22].

GREENHOUSE GASES AND THEIR CONTRIBUTIONS TO CLIMATE CHANGE

Given its strong influence on the environment, it is essential to examine factors that accelerate the extent of climate change. Gases with a direct influence on climate change include naturally occurring gases and synthetic gases that are the result of industrial activity. The naturally occurring gases include carbon dioxide (CO_2), methane (CH_4), and nitrous oxide (N_2O). Synthetic gases include hydrofluorocarbons (HFCs), perfluorocarbons (PFCs), and sulfur hexafluoride (SF_6). These fluorinated gases are also referred to as *F gases*. Some gases do not have a direct effect on global warming but influence the formation and the destruction of other greenhouse gases, including carbon monoxide (CO), oxides of nitrogen (NO_x), and nonmethane volatile organic compounds. Figure AP1-1

---

[18] Vermeulen, Sonja Joy, et al. (2012), "Options for support to agriculture and food security under climate change," *Environmental Science & Policy* 15 (1), 136–144.

[19] Cabrini, Luigi, Murray Simpson, and Daniel Scott (2009), "From Davos to Copenhagen and beyond: Advancing tourism's response to climate change," UN World Tourism Organization (UNWTO) background paper (2009).

[20] Geneva Association. (2014). "The insurance industry and climate change-Contribution to the global debate," *The Geneva Reports*, 2(1), 1–152.

[21] Mashayekh, Yeganeh, et al. (2012), "Potentials for sustainable transportation in cities to alleviate climate change impacts," *Environmental Science & Technology* 46 (5), 2529–2537.

[22] Gans, Joshua S. (2012), "Innovation and climate change policy," *American Economic Journal: Economic Policy* 4 (4), 125–145.

FIGURE AP1-1[23]

Trend in global emissions of greenhouse gases 1970-2010

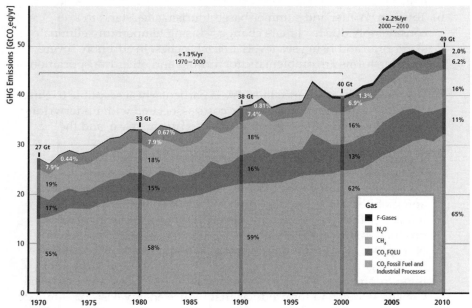

Total Annual Anthropogenic GHG Emissions by Groups of Gases 1970–2010

FIGURE AP1-2A[24]

Global anthropogenic greenhouse gas emissions in 2004

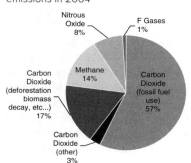

FIGURE AP1-2B[25]

Greenhouse gas emissions by sector in 2004

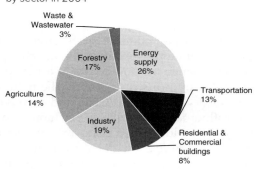

indicates increases in each of these gases over the 1970-2010 horizon. Over this 30-year period, greenhouse gas emissions increased by 60 percent. Figure AP1-2 provides an overview of the emissions for each gas with direct influences on global warming.

Figure AP1-2b indicates the global sources of these greenhouse gases by industrial sector. Energy accounts for more than 25 percent of greenhouse emissions,

[23] IPCC (2014), Summary for Policymakers, In: *Climate Change 2014, Mitigation of Climate Change. Contribution of Working Group III to the Fifth Assessment Report of the Intergovernmental Panel on Climate Change.* Edenhofer, O., et al. (Eds.), Cambridge, UK and New York: Cambridge University Press.

[24] www.epa.gov/climatechange/ghgemissions/global.html#three (June 24, 2015).

[25] www.epa.gov/climatechange/ghgemissions/global.html#three (June 24, 2015).

Gas		Global Warming Potential	Gas		Global Warming Potential
CO2	Carbon dioxide	1	HFC-227ea	F-gas	3,220
CH4	Methane	25	HFC-236fa	F-gas	9,810
N2O	Nitrous oxide	298	HFC-4310mee	F-gas	1,640
HFC-23	F-gas	14,800	CF4	F-gas	7,390
HFC-32	F-gas	675	C2F6	F-gas	12,200
HFC-125	F-gas	3,500	C4F10	F-gas	8,860
HFC-134a	F-gas	1,430	C6F14	F-gas	9,300
HFC-143a	F-gas	4,470	SF6	F-gas	22,800
HFC-152a	F-gas	124	NF3	F-gas	17,200

TABLE AP1-1
Global Warming Potentials
(100-year time horizon)[26]

and a substantial portion of these emissions are associated with coal. The industrial sector represents the second largest contributor at 19 percent. Forestry, including deforestation and decay from logging and deforestation, accounts for another 17 percent, whereas agriculture accounts for 14 percent. The transportation sector, by contrast, represents 13 percent of greenhouse gas emissions.

In order to compare gases, scientists have developed an index of global warming potential that compares the ability of a greenhouse gas to trap heat in the atmosphere relative carbon dioxide emissions. Table AP1-1 identifies the global warming potential of greenhouse gases with a direct effect on the climate. Thus, sulfur hexafluoride has 22,800 times the warming potential as an equivalent amount of carbon dioxide.

Carbon Dioxide

Carbon dioxide (CO_2) accounts for over 80 percent of the greenhouse emissions worldwide. Since 1750, global atmospheric concentrations of carbon dioxide have increased by about 35 percent.[27] Currently, China has the largest emissions of any country, yet the United States has the largest emissions per capita. The two countries alone account for 40 percent of carbon dioxide emissions, with Europe providing an additional 15 percent.[28]

On a global level, emissions have risen by 22 percent over the 2000-2010 period.[29] Factors that contribute to this increase include a growing domestic economy as well as significant increases in emissions from electricity generation

[26] www.epa.gov/climatechange/Downloads/ghgemissions/US-GHG-Inventory-2015-Main-Text.pdf (June 24, 2015).

[27] Hofmann, David (2004). *Long-lived Greenhouse Gas Annual Averages for 1979–2004*. Boulder, CO: National Oceanic and Atmospheric Administration, Earth Systems Research Laboratory, Global Monitoring Division. www.blackwellsynergy.com/doi/ abs/10.1111/j.1600-0889.2006.00201.x.

[28] *Business & the Environment with ISO 14000 Updates* (2007), "Momentum for Greenhouse Gas Cuts Grows," 18 (7), 1–4.

[29] IPCC (2014), *Summary for Policymakers, In: Climate Change 2014, Mitigation of Climate Change. Contribution of Working Group III to the Fifth Assessment Report of the Intergovernmental Panel on Climate Change*. Edenhofer, O. et al. (Eds.), Cambridge, UK and New York: Cambridge University Press.

and transportation. The burning of fossil fuels represents the largest source of greenhouse emissions in the world. Coal used in electricity generation and transportation represents the single largest contributor to carbon dioxide emissions. Petroleum used in transportation also contributes substantially to carbon dioxide emissions. Iron and steel production as well as cement manufacture also contribute significantly to carbon dioxide emissions. Waste combustion is also a significant contributor to carbon dioxide emissions. Due in part to the increased amounts of plastics and other fossil-carbon containing materials in municipal solid waste, the amount of waste combustion-based carbon dioxide emissions has increased significantly since 1990.[30] Emissions in the residential sector are largely (77 percent) associated with the use of natural gas as a source of heat. Electrical power generation generally yields emissions through the burning of coal (41 percent) and natural gas (25 percent) as well and nuclear power (21 percent).

Methane

Methane (CH_4) is the second largest contributor to greenhouse gas emissions. As Table AP1-1 illustrates, methane is more than 20 times as effective as carbon dioxide at trapping heat in the atmosphere. Since 1750, methane emissions have increased by 143 percent.[31] Methane emissions are associated with agriculture (53 percent), energy (28 percent), and waste (15 percent)[32]. *Enteric fermentation* refers to intestinal processing of methane associated with the digestion process for cattle. This source of methane is the largest global contributor to methane emissions, but it is in decline due to decreases in populations of beef and dairy cattle as well as improved feed quality for cattle. Across the globe, manure management, rice cultivation, and other agricultural activity account for another 26 percent of emissions. Methane is also released in oil and gas extraction as well as in coal mining. Landfills represent the largest man-made sources of methane emissions at 25 percent of U.S. output, yet they reflect only 10 percent of global emissions. Although the amount of solid waste continues to increase, methane levels are declining due to the portion that is captured and burned at landfills. Similarly, methane emissions from natural gas systems (6 percent of total CH_4) are in decline due to improvements in technology and management practices.

Nitrous Oxide

Nitrous oxide (N_2O) is third largest contributor to greenhouse gas emissions. Although emissions are substantially lower than those of carbon dioxide, nitrous oxide is 298 times more powerful than CO_2 in its ability to trap heat in the

---

[30] www.epa.gov/climatechange/ghgemissions/global.html (June 28, 2015).

[31] Hofmann, David (2004). *Long-lived Greenhouse Gas Annual Averages for 1979–2004.* Boulder, CO: National Oceanic and Atmospheric Administration, Earth Systems Research Laboratory, Global Monitoring Division. www.blackwellsynergy.com/doi/abs/10.1111/j.1600-0889.2006.00201.x.

[32] Yusuf, Rafiu O., Zainura Z. Noor, Ahmad H. Abba, Mohd Ariffin Abu Hassan, and Mohd Fadhil Mohd Di (2012), "Methane emission by sectors: A comprehensive review of emission sources and mitigation methods," *Renewable and Sustainable Energy Reviews* 16 (7), 5059–5070.

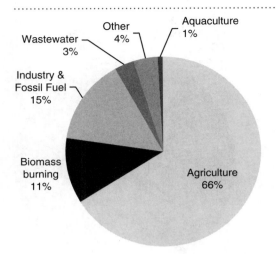

FIGURE AP1-3[33]
2004 global nitrous oxide emissions

atmosphere (see Table AP1-1). Since the Industrial Revolution (i.e., about 1750), nitrous oxide emissions have increased by approximately 25 percent. Fertilizer applications and related soil management practices account for 66 percent of N_2O emissions worldwide. Historical data do not indicate long-term increases or decreases in this source of emissions.

Fluorinated Gases

F-gases is a collective term that describes hydrofluorocarbons (HFCs), perfluorocarbons (PFCs), and sulfur hexafluoride (SF_6). In contrast to the previous three gases, which occur naturally in the atmosphere, F-gases are produced almost exclusively through industrial activity. These gases represent about 2 percent of U.S. emissions, but they have global warming potentials that range from 124 (HFC-152a) to 22,800 (SF_6), the potential for carbon dioxide. In addition, sulfur dioxide and PFCs have long atmospheric lifetimes that result in nearly irreversible atmospheric accumulation once emitted. The largest and fastest growing source of HFCs and PFCs is through their use as alternatives to ozone-depleting substances (ODS). HFCs largely accrue due to the use of HFCs as a refrigerant. HFC gases also are by-products of foam, aerosol, and fire protection products. PFCs primarily are released in aluminum production, whereas sulfur hexafluoride is employed as an insulator for electrical power transmission and as a cover gas in magnesium production.

Emissions of these gases has increased markedly since the *Montreal Protocol* came into effect requiring the phase-out of ozone-depleting substances. Although current contributions to greenhouse gases are marginal (at 2 percent), research suggests that the gases could contribute 7.9 percent of emissions by 2050.[34]

---

[33] UNEP (2013). *Drawing Down N2O to Protect Climate and the Ozone Layer. A UNEP Synthesis Report*. United Nations Environment Programme (UNEP), Nairobi, Kenya

[34] Gschrey, Barbara, Winfried Schwarz, Cornelia Elsner, and Rolf Engelhardt (2011), "High increase of global F-gas emissions until 2050," *Greenhouse Gas Measurement & Management* 1 (2), 85–92.

FIGURE AP1-4[35]

2010 global F-gas emissions

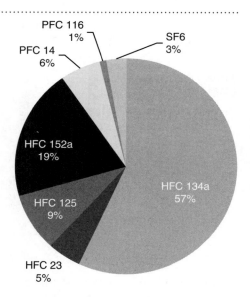

UNDERSTAND SOURCES OF ENERGY AND THEIR USE ACROSS
INTERNATIONAL REGIONS

The examination of energy use complements the analysis of climate change since many of the antecedents to climate change are energy related. Figure AP1-5 illustrates how the mix of energy sources has evolved worldwide since 1971. Although it represents a smaller portion of the energy supply than it once did, at 31.4 percent, oil remains the primary energy used worldwide. Oil consumption remains high due to the rising transportation sector (i.e., increases in passenger travel and freight transport) and expansion in the service economy.[36] At 29 percent and 21.3 percent respectively, coal and gas together account for another 50.3 percent of consumption. Combustible renewables and waste that are primarily employed in emerging economies account for 10 percent of consumption. The remaining 8.3 percent includes nuclear, hydroelectric, geothermal, solar, wind, and heat power. Although there have been substantial strides in these sources of energy, they currently represent a small fraction of consumption.

The data in Table AP1-2 indicate some intriguing trends. The data underscore the merits of contrasting energy use in Organisation for Economic Cooperation and Development (OECD) countries (Australia, Austria, Belgium, Canada, the Czech Republic, Denmark, Finland, France, Germany, Greece, Hungary, Iceland, Ireland, Italy, Japan, Korea, Luxembourg, Mexico, the Netherlands, New Zealand, Norway, Poland, Portugal, the Slovak Republic, Spain, Sweden, Switzerland, Turkey, the United Kingdom, and the United States) and the rest of the world. As a percentage of overall consumption, non-OECD countries spend more (12.5 percent) than OECD countries on manufacturing and industry. By contrast, OECD countries

---

[35] Montzka, S. A., et al. (2011), "Scientific assessment of ozone depletion: 2010," *Global Ozone Research and Monitoring Project-Report No. 51*(2011).

[36] International Energy Agency (2014), *Key World Energy Statistics*, Paris: International Energy Agency.

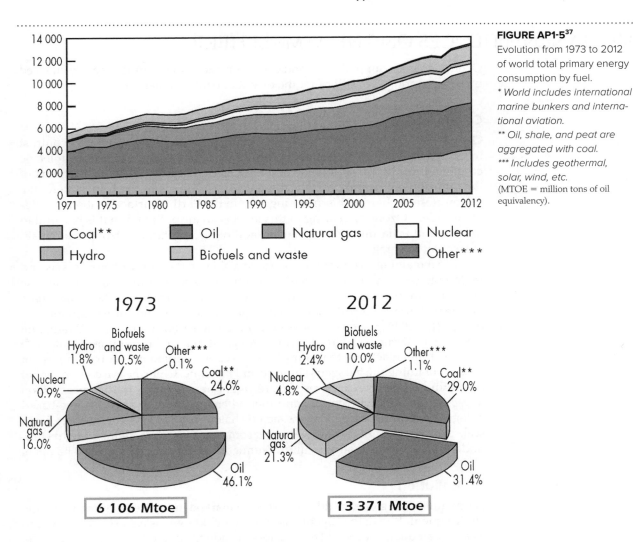

Evolution from 1973 to 2012 of world total primary energy consumption by fuel.

* World includes international marine bunkers and international aviation.

** Oil, shale, and peat are aggregated with coal.

*** Includes geothermal, solar, wind, etc.

(MTOE = million tons of oil equivalency).

Coal** Oil Natural gas Nuclear

Hydro Biofuels and waste Other***

1973

Hydro 1.8%
Biofuels and waste 10.5%
Other*** 0.1%
Coal** 24.6%
Nuclear 0.9%
Natural gas 16.0%
Oil 46.1%

6 106 Mtoe

2012

Hydro 2.4%
Biofuels and waste 10.0%
Other*** 1.1%
Coal** 29.0%
Nuclear 4.8%
Natural gas 21.3%
Oil 31.4%

13 371 Mtoe

spend more (13.5 percent) than non-OECD countries on transportation. Other energy use (primarily associated with households and services) and nonenergy use does not vary markedly between OECD and non-OECD countries.

	OECD		Non-OECD	
Industry	792[1]	22.2%[2]	1748[1]	34.6%[2]
Transportation	1185	33.2%	973	19.3%
Other (includes households and services)	1275	35.7%	1849	36.6%
Nonenergy use	318	8.9%	476	9.4%

TABLE AP1-2[38]

Shares of Global Final Energy Consumption

1 – Values represent millions of tons of oil equivalent.

2 – Values represent percentage of energy consumption.

[37] International Energy Agency (2014), *Key World Energy Statistics*, Paris: International Energy Agency.

[38] International Energy Agency (2014), *Energy Efficiency Indicators: Fundamentals on Statistics*, Paris: International Energy Agency.

HUMAN INFLUENCES ON THE ATMOSPHERE

Ozone depletion, air pollution, and energy are facets of the atmosphere influenced by consumption. Consider first the extent of ozone depletion.

Ozone

Ozone is a form of oxygen naturally occurring in the atmosphere. In contrast to the typical oxygen molecule that has two oxygen atoms, the ozone molecule contains three atoms and is labeled O_3. Ozone is observed in two regions of the atmosphere. Approximately 10 percent of ozone is in the troposphere, the region closer to Earth. This area ranges from the Earth's surface to about 6 miles in altitude.[39] Ozone appearing in this level is an air pollutant that is harmful to breathe and is harmful to crops, trees, and other vegetation. Ozone is the main ingredient in smog.[40]

The remaining 90 percent of the ozone resides in the stratosphere. This second region ranges from the top of the troposphere to about 31 miles in altitude. The large amount of ozone in the stratosphere is often referred to as the *ozone layer*. Ozone in this layer absorbs some of the sun's biologically harmful ultraviolet radiation (UV).[41] Depletion of this ozone leads to increased amounts of UV radiation reaching the Earth, which leads to more lung, asthma, and respiratory problems.[42]

The human activity that contributes to ozone depletion involves the use of gases containing the halogens chlorine and bromine. Chlorine is a component of chlorofluorocarbons (CFCs) used in refrigerators and air conditioners. Carbon tetrachloride, methyl chloride, and methyl chloroform are also chlorine-based halogens. Bromine-based halogens include halons used in fire extinguishers, large scale computers, military hardware, and commercial aircraft engines. Methyl bromide, which is used as an agricultural fumigant, is also a bromine-based halogen.

Air Pollution

Air pollution is a global health concern with marked influence on humans and the environment. Regulatory agents use six factors known as *criteria pollutants* to establish air quality levels.[43] These factors include sulfur dioxide, nitrogen dioxide, carbon monoxide, ozone oxygen, lead, and particulate matter (PM). Particulate matter includes chemical compounds (sulfate, nitrate, ammonium, organic carbon, elemental carbon, and soil dust), heavy metals (arsenic, cadmium, and mercury), volatile organic compounds (e.g., benzene), polycyclic aromatic hydrocarbons, and persistent organic pollutants (dioxins and furans). Most forms of particulate

---

[39] ozone.unep.org/Assessment_Panels/SAP/Scientific_Assessment_2010/SAP-2010-FAQs-update.pdf (June 30, 2015).

[40] dnr.wi.gov/files/PDF/pubs/am/AM318.pdf (June 30, 2015).

[41] ozone.unep.org/Assessment_Panels/SAP/Scientific_Assessment_2010/SAP-2010-FAQs-update.pdf (June 30, 2015).

[42] dnr.wi.gov/files/PDF/pubs/am/AM318.pdf (June 30, 2015).

[43] www.epa.gov/airquality/urbanair/ (June 30, 2015).

matter become pollutants through the burning of fossil fuels, biomass, and solid waste, whereas ammonium as a pollutant primarily derives from agriculture.

It is important to distinguish between outdoor and indoor pollution. Outdoor air pollution accounts for 1.4 percent of total global mortality and amounts to 800,000 deaths annually. Eighty-one percent of the mortality occurs in people 60 years of age or older. The incidence of death is strongly related to geography, as 49 percent of the deaths occur in the region that includes Bangladesh, Bhutan, Democratic People's Republic of Korea, India, Maldives, Myanmar, Nepal, or Timor-Leste. Another 19 percent of deaths occur in Southeast Asia. In addition to the mortality data, outdoor pollution increases hospitalization and emergency room visits, asthmas attacks, bronchitis, respiratory symptoms, and lost workdays.[44]

Indoor air pollution is the more egregious form of airborne contamination as it is implicated in more than 4.3 million deaths per year.[45] Household air pollution leads to increased deaths associated with pneumonia, stroke, heart disease, chronic obstructive pulmonary disease (COPD), and lung cancer. The incidence of death related to indoor air pollution is related to geography. Indoor air pollution is responsible for 1.2 million deaths per year in Afghanistan, Angola, Bangladesh, Burkina Faso, China, the Democratic Republic of the Congo, Ethiopia, India, Nigeria, Pakistan, and the United Republic of Tanzania. Moreover, in the 20 most affected countries (Afghanistan, Angola, Benin, Burkina Faso, Burundi, Chad, the Democratic Republic of the Congo, Eritrea, Ethiopia, Guinea-Bissau, Liberia, Madagascar, Malawi, Mali, Niger, Rwanda, Sierra Leone, Somalia, and Tajikistan), indoor air pollution is implicated as the cause of 5 percent or more of the total burden of disease.[46]

The likelihood of experiencing health problems due to indoor air pollution is associated with income, gender, and age. Figure AP1-6 outlines the relationship between prosperity and fuel usage. Electricity is used in the most affluent societies and is relatively clean and efficient. By contrast, the crop waste and wood used in emerging economies is relatively unclean and inefficient. These fuels produce indoor smoke with several health-damaging pollutants, including particulate matter, carbon monoxide, nitrous oxides, sulfur oxides, formaldehyde, and carcinogens (chemical substances that increase the risk of cancer).[47]

Increasing cleanliness, efficiency, cost, cleanliness

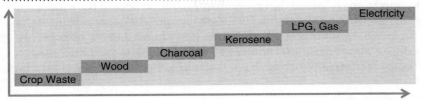

Increasing prosperity

FIGURE AP1-6[48]

Relationship of prosperity with fuel cleanliness, efficiency, cost, and convenience

[44] Ostro, B. (2004), *Outdoor Air Pollution: Assessing the Environmental Burden of Disease at National and Local Levels*, Geneva: World Health Organization.

[45] www.who.int/mediacentre/factsheets/fs292/en/ (June 30, 2015).

[46] www.who.int/indoorair/health_impacts/burden_national/en/ (June 30, 2015).

[47] www.who.int/mediacentre/events/HSD_Plaq_10.pdf (June 30, 2015).

[48] www.who.int/mediacentre/events/HSD_Plaq_10.pdf (June 30, 2015).

In many countries, women bear the primary responsibility for food preparation. In emerging economies, women typically cook with crop waste or wood. Wood provides around 15 percent of the energy needs in developing countries and rises to 75 percent in tropical Africa. In over 30 countries, wood still provides more than 70 percent of energy used, and in 13 countries, it accounts for over 90 percent. Because women do the majority of the cooking, they are more susceptible to indoor air pollution than men. In addition, young children present during cooking are exposed to indoor smoke. This air pollution increases the risk of chronic obstructive pulmonary disease, the leading cause of death among children under 5 years of age in developing countries.[49]

Air pollution has a number of ancillary environmental effects. First, the level of ozone in the troposphere results in worldwide crop losses of over $14 to $26 billion annually.[50] Second, acid rain associated with sulfur and nitrogen historically leads to lake acidification and forest decline in North America and Europe. Although this trend has been markedly reduced, there is growing concern about acidification in other regions, notably Asia. Finally, nitrogen deposits continue to drive losses in the number of species present in sensitive ecosystems. These settings include heaths, bogs, and mires in North America and Europe.[51]

HUMAN INFLUENCES ON WATER

Access to Clean Drinking Water

Water is essential for life, yet the influence of consumption on water use is not well understood. Ninety-seven percent of the world's water supply is saline, leaving 2.5 percent freshwater.[52] Almost 70 percent of the freshwater is frozen in the icecaps of Antarctica and Greenland. The remainder is primarily present as soil moisture or lies in deep underground aquifers as groundwater not accessible to human use. Less than 1 percent of the world's water is available for human use. This water is found in lakes, rivers, reservoirs, and underground sources shallow enough to be tapped at an affordable cost. The three primary uses of freshwater include irrigation (70 percent), industry (20 percent), and residential purposes (10 percent).[53]

The availability of freshwater is related to geographic location. The World Health Organization estimates that more than 2.6 billion people have gained access to improved drinking water since 1990 (see Figure AP1-7a). Nevertheless, 663 million people still use unimproved drinking water. Almost half of this population resides in sub-Saharan Africa, and another 40 percent lives in Asia. 2015 estimates indicate that 2.4 billion people do not have access to adequate sanitation services.[54]

[49] www.who.int/mediacentre/events/HSD_Plaq_10.pdf (June 30, 2015).

[50] Avnery, Shiri, Denise L. Mauzerall, Junfeng Liu, and Larry W. Horowitz (2011), "Global crop yield reductions due to surface ozone exposure: 1. Year 2000 crop production losses and economic damage," *Atmospheric Environment* 45 (13): 2284–2296.

[51] McCormick, John. (2013), *Acid Earth: The Global Threat of Acid Pollution*. Vol. 4. New York: Routledge.

[52] ga.water.usgs.gov/edu/waterdistribution.html (June 30, 2015).

[53] Brown, Lester R. (2008), "Draining Our Future," *Futurist*, (May-June), 16–22.

[54] www.who.int/docstore/water_sanitation_health/Globassessment/.

FIGURE AP1-7A.

Population without access to improved sources of drinking water in 2015[55]

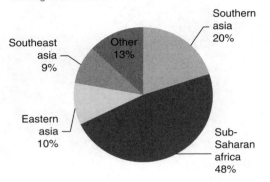

FIGURE AP1-7B.

Population without improved sanitation in 2015[56]

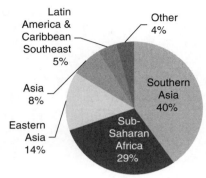

Figure AP1-7b illustrates the distribution of this population across the globe. The data underscore the magnitude of the problem in Asia and Africa. These water issues are particularly problematic for people living in rural areas where proper infrastructure is not available.

Although there are deep underground aquifers that can be drilled for human use, only lakes, rivers, reservoirs, and shallow underground sources are renewed by rain and snowfall. Consequently, only this freshwater is available on a sustainable basis.[57]

Several critical consequences of inadequate and unsanitary water include:

a) **Falling water tables**. While freshwater derived from lakes, rivers, and shallow underground resources is replenishable, water from connate or fossil aquifers cannot be recharged.[58] The Ogallala aquifer in the United States, the deep aquifer in the North China Plain, and the Saudi aquifer are prime examples of such water repositories. Because these aquifers cannot be replenished, their depletion means the end of irrigation and, consequently, a marked change or end of agriculture in the dependent area.[59]

b) **Floods and droughts**. Too much water and too little water are the result of variability in the hydrologic cycle influenced by climate change and alterations in land use patterns.[60] Every continent has experienced severe flooding during the last decade, and there is evidence that the

---

[55] www.who.int/water_sanitation_health/publications/jmp_2015_update_compressed.pdf (June 30, 2015).

[56] www.who.int/water_sanitation_health/publications/jmp_2015_update_compressed.pdf (June 30, 2015).

[57] Postel, Sandra L., Gretchen C. Daily, and Paul R. Ehrlich (1996), "Human Appropriation of Renewable Fresh Water," *Science*, 271 (5250), 785–788.

[58] Fetter, C. W. (1994), *Applied Hydrogeology*. New York: Macmillan.

[59] Brown, Lester R. (2008), *Plan B 3.0: Mobilizing to Save Civilization*, New York: W.W. Norton.

[60] Somlyody, Laszlo, and Olli Varis (2003), "Freshwater Under Pressure," *International Review for Environmental Strategies*, 6 (2), 181–204.

FIGURE AP1-8[61]
Diseases contributing to
the water-, sanitation-, and
hygiene-related disease
burden

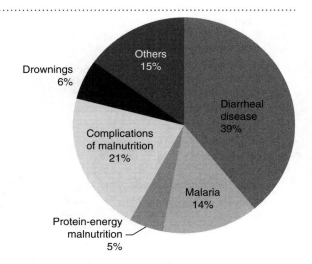

number of flood and drought disasters is increasing.[62] Over the past
three decades, the proportion of the world's population living in flood-
prone river areas has increased by 114 percent, and those living on
cyclone-exposed coastlines has increased by 192 percent. The number
of reports of extreme weather events and disasters has more than
tripled since the 1960s, and scientists anticipate that such events will
become more frequent and severe in the future due to climate change.

c) **Disease**. Figure AP1-8 outlines the global burden of disease associated
with lack of adequate water. The World Health Organization estimates
that over 361 million children die every year due to diarrhea acquired
due to unsafe water, inadequate sanitation, or insufficient hygiene.[63]
Inadequate water supplies raise the number of fatalities associated
with malnutrition, malaria, drowning, and other diseases.

d) **Farmers losing to cities**. The economics of production do not favor
agriculture over other industries when water is considered. For
example, it takes 14 tons of water to make a ton of steel worth $560,
yet it takes 1000 tons of water to grow a ton of wheat worth $200.[64]
Countries focused on expanding their economies and creating jobs are
increasingly favoring industry over agriculture.

e) **Political tension**. The water resources of the 232 international rivers
that exist today are ordinarily shared by several countries.[65] The
Jordan, Ganges, Colorado, Nile, Zambezi, Amazon, Danube, and
Rhine are all examples of international rivers. Conflicts occur between

[61] Prüss-Üstün A, R. Bos, F. Gore, and J. Bartram (2008), *Safer Water, Better Health: Costs, Benefits and Sustainability of Interventions to Protect and Promote Health*, Geneva: World Health Organization.

[62] library.wmo.int/pmb_ged/wmo_1098_en.pdf. (July 1, 2015).

[63] www.who.int/mediacentre/factsheets/fs391/en/ (July 1, 2015).

[64] Brown, Lester R. (2008), "Draining Our Future," *Futurist*, (May-June), 16–22.

[65] Hashimoto, Ryutaro (2002), "Current Status and Future Trends in Freshwater Management," *International Review of Environmental Strategies*, 3 (2), 222–239.

nations due to water scarcity, inadequate distribution, or due to a lack of agreements for distribution.

Factors that contribute to inadequate and unsanitary water include:

a) **Population growth and urbanization**. Increases in population are highly related to water resources. As the population increases, land, clean water, and other natural resources become scarce. Moreover, urbanization exacerbates this problem as growing cities demand increases in the water supply.[66] Estimates suggest that the population will increase by 3 billion people by 2050, with the great majority of this increase in urban areas.[67]

b) **Poverty and low human development**. Not surprisingly, the level of poverty and the extent of human development are associated with the water supply.[68] The impoverished are exposed to malnutrition, unclean water, and inadequate sanitation services.[69] Improved education constrains the influences of the environment, yet individuals in many emerging economies do not have access to higher education.

c) **Food security**. Food security refers to access by all people at all times to enough food for an active, healthy life. It includes the ready availability of nutritionally adequate and safe foods as well as the assured ability to acquire personally acceptable foods in a socially acceptable way.[70] Food insecurity affects 1 out of every 9 people on the planet.[71] Although food production has increased in many parts of the world over the past few decades, malnutrition remains a problem due to rapid population growth and urbanization.

Oceans and Fisheries

Oceans. Consumption has a marked influence on oceans and fisheries. Mounting evidence indicates that the Arctic is warming twice as fast as the rest of the planet, with the summer sea ice shrinking at 9.1 percent per decade from 1979 to 2006.[72] At this rate, the sea could be ice-free as early as 2030.[73] If all the ice melts,

---

[66] Somlyody, Laszlo, and Olli Varis (2003), "Freshwater Under Pressure," *International Review for Environmental Strategies,* 6 (2), 181–204.

[67] Brown, Lester R. (2008), *Plan B 3.0: Mobilizing to Save Civilization,* New York: W.W. Norton.

[68] www.ifrc.org/Global/Documents/Secretariat/201410/WDR%202014.pdf (July 1, 2015).

[69] Somlyody, Laszlo, and Olli Varis (2003), "Freshwater Under Pressure," *International Review for Environmental Strategies,* 6 (2), 181–204.

[70] Campbell, Cathy C. (1991), "Food Insecurity: A Nutritional Outcome or a Predictor Variable," *Journal of Nutrition* 121, 408–415.

[71] FAO, IFAD, and WFP (2015), *The State of Food Insecurity in the World 2015. Meeting the 2015 international hunger targets: Taking stock of uneven progress.* Rome, FAO.

[72] Overland, James E., Rune Grand Graversen, and Meiji Honda (2010), "Hot Arctic—Cold Continents: Global Impacts of Arctic Change: International Polar Year Oslo Science Conference, Oslo, Norway, 8–12 June 2010" *EOS, Transactions American Geophysical Union* 91, No. 41 (2010): 373-373.

[73] Adam, David (2006), "Meltdown of Winter Ice Linked to Greenhouse Gases," *Guardian* May 15.

it will not directly affect sea levels as the ice is already in the water. Nevertheless, substantially more heat is absorbed through water rather than ice, leading to the melting of the Greenland ice sheet. As the ice melts, some water filters through the cracks in glaciers and increases the break-off of icebergs into the ocean. A similar process is occurring in Antarctica, and together these trends indicate the potential for rising sea levels. If the sea were to rise 10 meters, one-eighth of the world's population would be vulnerable.[74] China, India, Bangladesh, Vietnam, Indonesia, Japan, Egypt, and the United States would have millions of potential climate change refugees. Some of the world's largest cities—New York, London, Shanghai, and Calcutta—would be partially or totally inundated, and considerable amounts of productive farmland would be lost.

Rivers. Over the past century, the demand for water has tripled, and the demand for water for human purposes multiplied sixfold.[75] Consequently, the worldwide number of dams over 15 meters' high has increased to 47,000 from 5,000.[76] These dams deprive rivers of some of their flow, and the associated evaporation is 10 percent of their capacities.[77] For example, Colorado River water usage by Colorado, Utah, California, Arizona, and Nevada results in very little water reaching the Gulf of California. Similar conditions in multiple continents markedly inhibit river ecosystems and their fisheries.

Lakes. On every continent, lakes are shrinking and in some cases disappearing as a result of consumption. The dissolution of lakes is due to excessive diversion of water from rivers and the overpumping of aquifers.[78] For example, the Aral Sea in Central Asia has lost 85 percent of its area and 92 percent of its volume since 1960[79]. Expansion of the Soviet cotton industry led to the diversion of two rivers from the sea. As the sea shrank and the water became more saline, fish died along with a maritime industry that produced 50,000 tons of seafood annually.

Water Impurities

Unless it has been distilled, water is not pure. Water impurities emerge from naturally occurring substances, agriculture, urbanization, industry, and water treatment.[80] Consider first naturally occurring substances.

---

[74] McGranahan, Gordon, Deborah Balk, and Bridget Anderson (2007), "The Rising Tide: Assessing the Risks of Climate Change and Human Settlements in Low Elevation Coastal Zones," *Environment and Urbanization* 19 (1), 17–37.

[75] Cosgrove, William J., and Frank R. Rijsberman (2014), *World water vision: Making water everybody's business*. London: Routledge, 2014.

[76] Cohen, Andrew (2014), "Dams and the Dilemmas of Development," *African Historical Review* 46 (1), 70–81.

[77] Brown, Lester R. (2008), *Plan B 3.0: Mobilizing to Save Civilization*, New York: W.W. Norton.

[78] Brown, Lester R. (2008), "Draining Our Future," *Futurist*, (May-June), 16–22.

[79] Micklin, Philip (2014), "Efforts to Revive the Aral Sea," *The Aral Sea*. Springer Berlin Heidelberg, 361–380.

[80] Thompson, Terrence, et al. (2007), *Chemical Safety of Drinking Water: Assessing Priorities for Risk Management*, Geneva: World Health Organization.

Naturally occurring substances. Substances that occur in nature that influence water purity include inorganic and organic materials. Inorganic materials are those that do not contain carbon. These chemicals accrue due to water flowing over rocks and soil. Four substances known to be associated with adverse health effects are fluoride, arsenic, selenium, and nitrate. Given their adverse health consequences, it is essential to monitor their levels prior to examining human influence. The pH level of the water should also be monitored as the influence of these chemicals is exacerbated by the level of acidity in the water. Organic compounds (i.e., chemicals that contain carbon) emerge from the breakdown of plants or algae and other microorganisms.

Agriculture. The farming sector plays a significant role in the quality of water as agricultural runoff is the leading source of impurities in lakes and rivers.[81] Fertilizer in the form of manure or human excrement increases levels of nitrates, ammonium salts, and organic nitrogen compounds, whereas chemical fertilizers increase nitrogen levels when these nutrients are used in excess. Biosolids used as fertilizer are treated residues from industrial or municipal waste or septic soil. These biosolids similarly lead to increased nitrate levels in water. Animal practices such as feedlots produce large amounts of waste that also lead to higher levels of nitrates. Pesticides refer to a broad mix of chemicals that have chemical and physical properties that contribute to runoff. Irrigation and drainage transport pollutants and alter salt balances in the soil. Consequently, they raise the level of nitrates and selenium in the soil.

Urbanization. The increasing population in urban areas is traced to three categories of contaminant sources.[82] Point sources refer to pollution discharged from a specific location and includes onsite sanitation waste disposal locations. These point sources increase the levels of nitrate and ammonium in water. Nonpoint sources are widely spread and difficult to identify origins of pollutant. Three primary forms of nonpoint polluters are fuel storage locations, chlorinated solvents, and pesticides. Diffuse point sources refer conditions under which there are many small point sources. For example, urban runoff from small point sources raises levels of nitrates, ammonium, and heavy metals in water.

Industry. Industrial practices include mining and manufacturing. Mining increases multiple types of metals in water, including arsenic, antimony, barium, cadmium, fluoride, and nickel. Manufacturing and processing of materials contribute a variety of chemicals with diverse properties that influence water purity.

Water treatment. Ironically, the efforts to treat water can also contribute to impurities. Chlorine is used as a disinfectant in the purification process, but in excess, it reacts naturally with organic matter to produce unwanted by-products

---

[81] water.epa.gov/polwaste/nps/upload/2005_4_29_nps_Ag_Runoff_Fact_Sheet.pdf (July 1, 2015).

[82] Thompson, Terrence, et al. (2007), *Chemical Safety of Drinking Water: Assessing Priorities for Risk Management*, Geneva: World Health Organization.

such as chloroform. ***Coagulants*** such as aluminum and iron salts are important barriers to microbiological contaminants. Although these chemicals are not significant health risks, they may lead to discoloration or sediment. ***Conveyors*** refer to the pipes and the fittings used to transport water. The most common conveyor is iron, a substance prone to corrosion. Corrosion due to low alkalinity, sediment, and microbes leads to water discoloration. Lead, copper, and zinc are also conveyors that may be present in water. Although lead is more likely to be present at unacceptable levels, copper and zinc are more prevalent in newer buildings. Finally, polyvinyl chloride (PVC) is a form of plastic often used as a conveyor of water. Because lead is often used as a stabilizer for PVC, use of this material may lead to elevated levels of lead.

HUMAN INFLUENCES ON LAND

Urban Expansion

Urban expansion refers to the increasing use of land associated with increases in urban populations. In 2007, the urban population on the planet exceeded the rural population for the first time.[83] Current estimates project that the population in developing-country cities will double in the next 20 years from 2 to 4 billion people. These cities will more than triple their land area. By contrast, the urban population in industrialized countries is expected to grow by 11 percent from 0.9 to 1 billion people over the same period. Urban land use in these areas is expected to double over the next two decades.[84]

Research examining of the role of urbanization indicates that many factors are associated with the rise in urban population. Urbanization may be both the cause and the consequence of these factors. Forces that seem to shape expansion include aspects of the local natural environment (e.g., existence of drillable water aquifers), demographic factors (e.g., level of urbanization in a country), economics (e.g., property taxes), prevailing transport systems, consumer preferences (e.g., preference for urbanism), and metropolitan governance. ***Greenfield development*** refers to the construction on a previously unused piece of property. This type of development has been implicated as a factor that yields air pollution, excessive energy use, greenhouse gas production, and traffic congestion. Furthermore, cities draw upon rural areas for water and waste disposal. As cities increase their land masses, the interaction with environment must remain a central concern.

Land Degradation

Land degradation is a collective term that refers to the long-term loss of ecosystem function and productivity.[85] Degradation includes productivity losses due

---

[83] Angel, Shlomo, et al. (2005), *The Dynamics of Global Urban Expansion* Washington: The World Bank.

[84] Angel, S., Parent, J., Civco, D. L., Blei, A., and Potere, D. (2011), "The dimensions of global urban expansion: Estimates and projections for all countries, 2000–2050," *Progress in Planning*, 75(2), 53–107.

[85] Bai, Zhanguo G., David L. Dent, Lennart Olsson, and Michael E. Schaepman (2008), "Proxy global assessment of land degradation," *Soil Use and Management* 24 (3), 223–234.

to water erosion, wind erosion, soil fertility decline, salinization, waterlogging, and lowering of the water table.[86] Current estimates indicate significant land degradation of 24 percent of the global land area over the past quarter century. The global cost of degradation exceeds $490 billion—a figure that is much higher than the cost of action to prevent it.[87] This land area is home to about 1.5 billion people. The primary areas of concern for degradation are subequatorial Africa; the Indo-China, Myanmar, Malaysia and Indonesia region; south China; north-central Australia and the western slopes of the Great Dividing Range; the Pampas; as well as the high-latitude forest belts in North America and Siberia.[88]

The degradation of land yields problems at three levels.[89] At the field level, degradation reduces productivity; at the national level, it is associated with flooding and sedimentation; and globally it contributes to climate change, international waters declines, and biodiversity losses.[90]

Deforestation and Desertification

Forests are important parts of ecosystems that sustain life. Forests cover 31 percent of the land area, and the five most forest-rich countries (Russian Federation, China, the United States, Canada, and Brazil) account for over half of the forested area. Forests prevent soil erosion, maintain soil fertility, support biodiversity, and provide homeopathic and traditional medicines. Furthermore, forests support local economies and provide important sources of fuel.[91] Over the past 15 years, the global forest area has shrunk at an annual rate of 0.05 percent per year.[92] Although the forest area has expanded in the Caribbean, Europe, Oceania, North America, and China, deforestation has been observed in Africa, Latin America, and Australia. Although the rate of change is decreasing, degradation remains a critical problem.

Deforestation is associated with several factors.[93] In many cases, trees are removed from forests for use as fuel or as raw materials in production. Deforestation also occurs due to climate change, disease, invasive species, pests, and air pollution. Economic factors—notably agriculture and mining—increase the level of deforestation. Demographic trends such as changes in population density and urbanization raise demands for timber and firewood, and they increase the demand for water resources. The demographic trends increase the amount of deforestation.

---

[86] www.fao.org/docrep/v4360e/V4360E03.htm#Chapter 2 - Types of land degradation (July 2, 2015).

[87] United Nations Convention to Combat Desertification (2012), *Land Degradation Neutrality: Resilience at Local, National and Regional Levels* Bonn, Germany.

[88] Bai, Zhanguo G., David L. Dent, Lennart Olsson, and Michael E. Schaepman (2008), "Proxy global assessment of land degradation," *Soil Use and Management* 24 (3), 223–234.

[89] www.fao.org/docrep/v4360e/V4360E08.htm#Direct causes of degradation (July 2, 2015).

[90] Pagiola, Stefano (1999), *The global environmental benefits of land degradation control on agricultural land: global overlays program. Vol. 16.* Washington: World Bank Publications, 1999.

[91] United Nations (2012), Global Environmental Outlook 5, Valetta, Malta: Progress Press.

[92] www.earth-policy.org/indicators/C56 (July 2, 2015).

[93] Food and Agriculture Organization (2006a). *Global Forest Resources Assessment 2005 – Progress Towards Sustainable Forest Management.* Forestry Paper 147. United Nations: Rome.

Increased deforestation has several notable consequences for the environment.[94] Reductions in forest acreage result in loss of habitat and consequently lead to limited biodiversity. Deforestation reduces the amount of stored carbon and disturbs biological cycles. In addition, fewer forests mean diminished water resources, lower water quality, and less soil water retention.

Desertification refers to land degradation in arid, semi-arid, or dry subhumid areas due to climatic variations and human activities.[95] When individual land degradation processes combine to affect large areas of drylands, desertification occurs.[96] Populations living in poor countries suffer the most due to desertification. Across the globe, drylands cover 40 percent of the Earth's land surface and support over 2 billion people. Although 90 percent of this population lives in developing countries, Western countries are also vulnerable to deforestation. One-third of the Mediterranean and 85 percent of the rangeland in the United States are susceptible to deforestation.

Because desertification occurs over a prolonged period of time in large areas, there is not a consistent measure to chart transition to deserts. The direct cause of deforestation is usually the expansion of cropping, grazing, or wood harvesting. As the level of deforestation increases, ecosystems become less resilient to other environmental conditions.

Global concerns about deforestation have important repercussions for every company that uses wood, paper or cardboard packaging.[97] Although activists initially targeted prominent retailers about their packaging, today these organizations are focused on a broader mix of companies that use wood-related products in production, marketing, and distribution.

HUMAN INFLUENCES ON BIODIVERSITY

Biodiversity refers to the variety of life on Earth.[98] It includes genetic diversity among individual beings in a population, diversity of species, and diversity of ecosystems and habitats. Biodiversity is the basis of agriculture in that it enables the production of wild and cultivated foods while also contributing to the health and nutrition of humans, animals, and plants.

Biodiversity provides provisional, regulatory, supportive, and cultural services to an ecosystem.[99] *Provisional services* refer to the supply of food, fuel, or fiber made available for consumption in an ecosystem. For example, aquaculture and capture fisheries supplied the world with about 148 million tons of fish in 2010

[94] United Nations (2012), Global Environmental Outlook 5, Valetta, Malta: Progress Press.

[95] United Nations General Assembly (1994) United Nations General Assembly Document A/AC.241/27.

[96] United Nations (2012), Global Environmental Outlook 5, Valetta, Malta: Progress Press.

[97] Esty, Daniel C., and Andrew S. Winston (2006), *Green to Gold*, New Haven, CT: Yale University Press.

[98] United Nations Environment Programme (2007), *Global Environment Outlook GEO4*. Valletta, Malta: United Nations Environment Programme.

[99] www.unep.org/maweb/documents/document.300.aspx.pdf (July 2, 2015).

with a total value of $217.5 billion.[100] The *regulatory services* control interaction between factors in an ecosystem. For example, honeybee pollination of agricultural products is a regulatory service whose value to the US economy is estimated at between $6 and 14 billion per year.[101] *Supporting services* maintain the conditions for life on Earth and include soil formation, soil protection, nutrient cycling, and water cycling. *Cultural services* refer to the spiritual, recreational, and aesthetic benefits afforded to an ecosystem through biodiversity. For instance, coral reefs for fisheries and tourism provide worldwide cultural services of $30 billion.[102]

When biodiversity is threatened, the provisional, regulatory, supportive, and cultural benefits enjoyed in the ecosystem are also affected. Unfortunately, 60 percent of ecosystems that have been assessed are degraded or used unsustainably.[103] Rates of species extinction are 100 to 1000 times higher than baseline rates based on fossil records.[104] Among major vertebrate groups that have been examined, 21 percent of mammals, 12 percent of birds, 30 percent of reptiles, 31 percent of amphibians, and 3 percent of fish are threatened with extinction.[105] The percentage among plants is greater such that 70 percent of species are threatened (see Table AP1-3).

The principal factors that account for reduced vertebrate biodiversity include habitat loss and degradation, overexploitation, invasive alien species, climate change, and pollution (see Figure AP1-9). Habitat conversion such as deforestation reduces the amount of available natural habitat, homogenizes species composition, fragments landscapes, and degrades soil. Invasive alien species refer to the introduction of new species into an ecosystem. The new species may be competitors or predators of existing species and lead to genetic contamination. Overexploitation, or the harvesting of species above sustainable rates, leads to decreased populations and extinctions. Climate change robs species of their habitats, resulting in contraction of species ranges, changes in species compositions, and extinction. Pollution yields higher mortality rates, influences nutrient availability, and raises levels of acidification in soil and water. Importantly, all these effects on biodiversity constrain the level of (provisional, regulatory, supportive, and cultural) services in an ecosystem and have significant consequences for the well-being of humans.

---

[100] FAO (2004). *The State of the World's Fisheries and Aquaculture 2012.* Food and Agriculture Organization of the United Nations, Rome.

[101] Mburu, John, Lars Gerard Hein, Barbara Gemmill, and Linda Collette (2006), *Tools for Conservation and Use of Pollination Services Economic Valuation of Pollination Services: Review of Methods.* Food and Agriculture Organization of the United Nations, Rome.

[102] Cesar, H. J. S., Burke, L., and Pet-Soede, L. (2003). The Economics of Worldwide Coral Reef Degradation Cesar Environmental Economics Consulting, Arnhem, and WWF-Netherlands, Zeist, The Netherlands.

[103] United Nations (2012), *Global Environmental Outlook 5*, Valetta, Malta: Progress Press.

[104] De Vos, Jurriaan M., Lucas N. Joppa, John L. Gittleman, Patrick R. Stephens, and Stuart L. Pimm (2014), "Estimating the Normal Background Rate of Species Extinction," *Conservation Biology* 29 (2), 452–462.

[105] IUCN (2006). *2006 IUCN Red List of Threatened Species.* www.iucnredlist.org/ (last accessed August 8, 2008); and Baillie, Jonathan E. M., Janine Griffiths, Samuel T. Turvey, Jonathan Loh, and Ben Collen (2010), "Evolution Lost: Status and Trends of the World's Vertebrates," London: Zoological Society of London.

TABLE AP1-3[106]
Threatened Species by
Major Groups

	Estimated Number of Described Species	Number of Species Evaluated	Number of Threatened Species	Number Threatened, as % of Species Described	Number Threatened, as % of Species Evaluated
Vertebrates					
Mammals	5,488	5,488	1,141	21%	21%
Birds	9,990	9,990	1,222	12%	12%
Reptiles	8,734	1,385	423	5%	31%
Amphibians	6,347	6,260	1,905	30%	30%
Fishes	30,700	3,481	1,275	4%	37%
Subtotal	**61,259**	**26,604**	**5,966**	**10%**	**22%**
Invertebrates					
Insects	950,000	1,259	626	0%	50%
Mollusks	81,000	2,212	978	1%	44%
Crustaceans	40,000	1,735	606	2%	35%
Corals	2,175	856	235	11%	27%
Arachnids	98,000	32	18	0%	56%
Velvet Worms	165	11	9	5%	82%
Horseshoe Crabs	4	4	0	0%	0%
others	61,040	52	24	0%	46%
Subtotal	**1,232,384**	**6,161**	**2,496**	**0.20%**	**41%**
Plants					
Mosses	16,000	95	82	1%	86%
Ferns and Allies	12,838	211	139	1%	66%
Gymnosperms	980	910	323	33%	35%
Dicotyledons	199,350	9,624	7,122	4%	74%
Monocotyledons	59,300	1,155	782	1%	68%
Green Algae	3,962	2	0	0%	0%
Red Algae	6,076	58	9	0%	16%
Subtotal	**298,506**	**12,055**	**8,457**	**3%**	**70%**
Others					
Lichens	17,000	2	2	0%	100%
Mushrooms	30,000	1	1	0%	100%
Brown Algae	3,040	15	6	0%	40%
Subtotal	**50,040**	**18**	**9**	**0.02%**	**50%**
TOTAL	**1,642,189**	**44,838**	**16,928**	**1%**	**38%**

[106] Baillie, Jonathan E. M., Janine Griffiths, Samuel T. Turvey, Jonathan Loh, and Ben Collen (2010), "Evolution Lost: Status and Trends of the World's Vertebrates," London: Zoological Society of London.

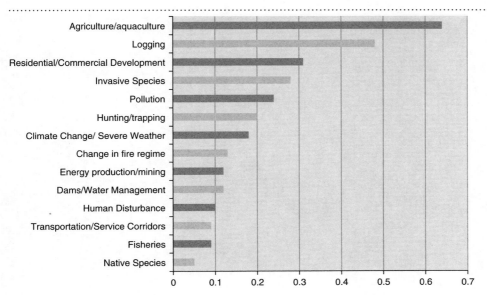

FIGURE AP1-9[107]

Major threats to vertebrates listed as critically endangered, endangered, or vulnerable on the IUCN red list

[107] Baillie, Jonathan E. M., Janine Griffiths, Samuel T. Turvey, Jonathan Loh, and Ben Collen (2010), "Evolution Lost: Status and Trends of the World's Vertebrates," London: Zoological Society of London.

A-2

Geopolitical Action and Consumption

IDENTIFY ENVIRONMENTAL ACTION DESIGNED TO REDUCE CLIMATE CHANGE

In Appendix 1, we focused on the influences that consumption has on the environment. In this appendix, we identify activity occurring outside the firm designed to influence consumption. Our discussion considers political and economic forces that shape operations in an industry. We begin by examining efforts to regulate climate change and then engage in a discussion of efforts to influence the supply and demand for energy. In the subsequent sections, we identify macroenvironmental efforts to reduce human influence on the atmosphere, water, land, and biodiversity.

Numerous efforts have been launched to address the influences of consumption and other human activity on the environment, and these activities have taken place at the international, national, regional, and local levels. Although international agencies and national governments enact policies and legislation, local activity determines whether these initiatives are successful.

Consider now macroenvironmental efforts to limit climate change.

The United Nations Convention on Climate Change was established in 1994. Since this time, the UN has introduced a number of climate change directives, including the 2007 Kyoto Protocol, the 2012 Doha Amendment to the Kyoto Protocol, and the 2016 Paris Agreement.[1] The Kyoto Protocol designated emissions levels for participating countries and created a market for the sale and purchase of greenhouse gas emissions. Three Kyoto mechanisms that facilitate the exchange of emission credits are:

Emissions trading. Emissions trading refers to the exchange of carbon trading units. The participating countries allocate carbon trading units to industries such as manufacturing and utilities. Companies in these industries within these countries were required to reduce emissions to the target levels. If companies attained emissions levels below targeted rates, they can sell the emission credits on an exchange. If companies surpass their emission levels, they must go to a market and buy *carbon offsets*. These offsets often are investments in developing countries such as China and India. Investments in carbon offsets reduce the emissions in the emerging markets and thereby contribute to lower global emissions.[2]

Clean development mechanism (CDM). The clean development mechanism enables emission reduction or removal projects in developing countries to earn *certified emission reduction* (CER) credits.[3] Each CER is equivalent to 1 ton of carbon dioxide. CERs can be traded, sold, or used to meet emission targets outlined by the Kyoto Protocol.

Joint implementation (JI). Joint implementation is similar to the clean development mechanism given that it relies on collaboration between countries to lower GHG emissions. In contrast to CDMs that involve an industrialized country and a developing country, however, joint

---

[1] unfccc.int/paris_agreement/items/9485.php (January 10, 2017).

[2] Bartlett, Chris (2007), "Carbon Markets Go Global," *Airfinance Journal*, October, 22.

[3] cdm.unfccc.int/about/index.html (January 10, 2017).

implementation projects involve industrialized countries.[4] Participants to JI arrangements earn *emission reduction units* (ERUs), each equivalent to 1 ton of carbon dioxide that can be counted towards Kyoto Protocol targets.

The goal of the Paris Agreement is to strengthen the global response to the threat of climate change. The agreement seeks to prevent a global temperature rise this century above 2 degrees Celsius above pre-industrial levels. In addition, it seeks to limit the temperature increase to 1.5 degrees Celsius. Table A2-1 identifies parties to the convention. Ratification occurs on a country-by-country basis.

The Paris Agreement seeks to reach a peak in emissions in the near future. It requires committed countries to develop a nationally determined contribution to the mitigation of GHG emissions. To ensure transparency, the agreement requires international verification of reported GHG emissions.

UNDERSTAND EFFORTS TO INFLUENCE THE SUPPLY AND DEMAND FOR ENERGY

Many countries throughout the world have established regulations designed to enhance the sustainability and the efficiency of energy consumption. The desire to conserve energy is not a new phenomenon, but it is gaining increasing interest due to climate change and rising oil prices. One way to examine energy is on the basis of its supply and demand. Renewable energy sources provide contributions to the supply of energy. To the extent that these sources are employed as substitutes for fossil fuels, the environment does not encounter the negative consequences of oil or other fossil fuel consumption.

Renewable energy sources will increase throughout the world, but the demand for energy will also continue to rise. It is, therefore, important to consider the mechanisms that influence the demand for energy. Figure A2-1 indicates the share of energy and electricity use throughout the world. Note that of the 19.2 percent associated with renewable forms of energy, 8.9 percent of this total is associated with traditional biomass. Other forms of renewable energy account for 10.3 percent of usage throughout the world. Renewable energy technologies have made tremendous advances over the last 20 years and offer significant advantages over conventional fuels for meeting energy needs.

Research indicates that adding renewable energy to a fossil-fuel dominated energy portfolio reduces generating costs and enhances energy security.[5] The Renewable Energy Policy Network[6] emphasizes the following benefits to renewable energy:

1. Use of locally available, renewable resources such as the sun, wind, biomass, geothermal, and hydropower.
2. Reduced reliance on fossil fuels and their associated international trade consequences.
3. Heightened energy security by developing a diverse energy portfolio.

[4] unfccc.int/kyoto_protocol/mechanisms/items/1673.php (January 10, 2017).

[5] Awerbuch, Shimon (2006), "Portfolio-Based Electricity Generation Planning: Policy Implications for Renewables and Energy Security," *Mitigation and Adaptation Strategies for Global Change*, 11 (3), 693–710.

[6] www.ren21.net/status-of-renewables/global-status-report/ (January 11, 2017).

TABLE A2-1
Parties to the Paris
Convention[7]

Afghanistan	Dominica	Luxembourg	Saint Vincent & The Grenadines
Albania	Dominican Republic	Macedonia	Samoa
Algeria	Ecuador	Madagascar	San Marino
Andorra	Egypt	Malawi	Sao Tome & Principe
Angola	El Salvador	Malaysia	Saudi Arabia
Antigua & Barbuda	Equatorial Guinea	Maldives	Senegal
Argentina	Eritrea	Mali	Serbia
Armenia	Fiji	Malta	Seychelles
Australia	Finland	Marshall Islands	Sierra Leone
Austria	France	Mauritania	Singapore
Azerbaijan	Gabon	Mauritius	Slovakia
Bahamas	Gambia	Mexico	Slovenia
Bahrain	Georgia	Micronesia	Solomon Islands
Bangladesh	Germany	Monaco	Somalia
Barbados	Ghana	Mongolia	South Africa
Belarus	Greece	Montenegro	South Korea
Belgium	Grenada	Morocco	South Sudan
Belize	Guatemala	Mozambique	Spain
Benin	Guinea	Myanmar	Sri Lanka
Bhutan	Guinea-Bissau	Namibia	Sudan
Bolivia	Guyana	Nauru	Suriname
Bosnia & Herzegovina	Haiti	Nepal	Swaziland
Botswana	Honduras	Netherlands	Sweden
Brazil	Hungary	New Zealand	Switzerland
Brunei Darussalam	Iceland	Niger	Tajikistan
Bulgaria	India	Nigeria	Tanzania
Burkina Faso	Indonesia	Niue	Thailand
Burundi	Iran	Northern Ireland	Timor-Leste
Cabo Verde	Iraq	Norway	Togo
Cambodia	Ireland	Oman	Tonga
Cameroon	Israel	Pakistan	Trinidad & Tobago
Canada	Italy	Palau	Tunisia
Central African Republic	Jamaica	Palestine	Turkey
Chad	Japan	Panama	Turkmenistan
Chile	Jordan	Papua New Guinea	Tuvalu
China	Kazakhstan	Paraguay	Uganda
Colombia	Kenya	Peru	Ukraine
Comoros	Kiribati	Philippines	United Arab Emirates

[7]unfccc.int/paris_agreement/items/9444.php (January 10, 2017).

Congo	Kuwait	Poland	United Kingdom
Cook Islands	Kyrgyzstan	Portugal	United States of America
Costa Rica	Laos	Qatar	Uruguay
Côte d'Ivoire	Latvia	Republic of Korea	Vanuatu
Croatia	Lebanon	Republic of Moldova	Venezuela
Cuba	Lesotho	Romania	Vietnam
Cyprus	Liberia	Russian Federation	Yemen
Czech Republic	Libya	Rwanda	Zambia
Denmark	Liechtenstein	Saint Kitts And Nevis	Zimbabwe
Djibouti	Lithuania	Saint Lucia	

4. Increased price stability during volatile periods for fossil fuel prices.
5. Reduced risk of future energy costs.
6. Income, revenue, and job opportunities. Renewable energy supports over 8 million jobs globally.
7. Conserve the natural resource base in a country.
8. Provide health benefits, notably to women and children, through improved cooking facilities.
9. Contribute to economic and social development through provision of modern energy services, including lighting, heating, cooking, cooling, water pumping, transportation, and communications.
10. Renewable energy is environmentally friendly because it does not rely on nitrogen and sulfur oxides that are harmful to humans, animals, and plants. It also does not generate carbon dioxide that contributes to climate change.

GEOPOLITICAL ACTION CONCERNING ATMOSPHERE

Air Pollution

International action focused on controlling air pollution is implemented on a regional basis in Europe, North America, and Asia. In 1947, the United Nations established the United Nations Economic Commission for Europe (UNECE) as one of five regional commissions. The UNECE establishes standards to facilitate international cooperation within and outside the region.[8] Since 1979, this group has developed the Convention on Long-range Transboundary Air Pollution. This treaty has been extended via eight protocols identifying specific measures to be taken by parties to reduce air pollution. Here is a brief synopsis of these protocols:

1. **The 1984 Geneva Protocol on Long-term Financing of the Cooperative Programme for Monitoring and Evaluation of the Long-range Transmission of Air Pollutants in Europe.** This protocol provides for international cost-sharing of monitoring programs. The protocol calls for collection of emission data for SO_2, NO_x, VOCs, and other air pollutants;

[8] www.unece.org/about/about.htm (September 2, 2008).

air and precipitation quality measurement; and modeling of atmospheric dispersion.[9]

2. **The 1985 Helsinki Protocol on the Reduction of Sulfur Emissions.** The Helsinki protocol sought sulfur reductions of at least 30 percent over 1980 levels. The 21 parties to this protocol had reduced 1980 sulfur emissions by more than 50 percent by 1993.[10]

3. **The 1988 Sofia Protocol concerning the Control of Emissions of Nitrogen Oxides.** The Sofia protocol seeks a reduction in emissions of NO_x of 9 percent compared to 1987. Nineteen of the 25 parties to the protocol have reached the target emissions at 1987 (or 1978 for the United States) levels or reduced emissions.[11]

4. **The 1991 Geneva Protocol concerning the Control of Emissions of Volatile Organic Compounds.** This directive sought a 30 percent reduction in emissions of volatile organic compounds (VOCs) using a year between 1984 and 1990 as a basis.[12]

5. **The 1994 Oslo Protocol on Further Reduction of Sulfur Emissions.** This protocol augments the 1985 Helsinki directive by adding criteria that led to a differentiation of emission reduction obligations of parties to the protocol.[13]

6. **The 1998 Aarhus Protocol on Persistent Organic Pollutants (POPs).** The goal of this protocol is to eliminate discharges of POPs. The protocol bans the production and use of some products outright (e.g., chlordane), and limits the use of POP's, and schedules them for elimination at a later stage (e.g., DDT).[14]

7. **The 1998 Aarhus Protocol on Heavy Metals.** This protocol calls for reduced emissions for cadmium, lead, and mercury beyond their levels in 1990. It also requires participating parties to phase out leaded gasoline.[15]

8. **The 1999 Gothenburg Protocol to Abate Acidification, Eutrophication and Ground-level Ozone.** This protocol sets limits for sulfur, NO_x,

---

[9] Fraenkel, Amy A. (1989), "The Convention on Long-Range Transboundary Air Pollution: Meeting the Challenge of International Cooperation," *Harvard International Law Journal* 30, 447–476.

[10] Ringquist, Evan J., and Tatiana Kostadinova (2005), "Assessing the effectiveness of international environmental agreements: The case of the 1985 Helsinki Protocol," *American Journal of Political Science* 49 (1), 86–102.

[11] Vestreng, V., et al. (2009). "Evolution of NO x Emissions in Europe with Focus on Road Transport Control Measures," *Atmospheric Chemistry and Physics*, 9(4), 1503–1520.

[12] ECE, U. (1991), "Protocol to the 1979 Convention on Long-range Transboundary Air Pollution Concerning the Control of Emissions of Volatile Organic Compounds or Their Transboundary Fluxes," ECE/EB. AIR/30. United Nations Economic Commission for Europe, Geneva, Switzerland.

[13] Finus, Michael, and Sigve Tjøtta (2003), "The Oslo Protocol on Sulfur Reduction: The Great Leap Forward?" *Journal of Public Economics* 87 (9), 2031–2048.

[14] Buccini, John (2003), "The Development of a Global Treaty on Persistent Organic Pollutants (POPs)," *Persistent Organic Pollutants*, Springer Berlin Heidelberg, 13–30.

[15] Pacyna, Elisabeth G., et al. (2007), "Current and Future Emissions of Selected Heavy Metals to the Atmosphere from Anthropogenic Sources in Europe," *Atmospheric Environment*, 41(38), 8557–8566.

volatile organic compounds (VOCs), and ammonia. When the protocol is fully implemented, Europe's sulfur emissions will be cut by at least 63 percent, NO_x emissions by 41 percent, VOC emissions by 40 percent, and its ammonia emissions by 17 percent compared to 1990.[16]

These protocols offer pollution standards adopted by countries outside of Europe. Canada and the United States have participated in several of these protocols. Both countries have ratified the 1984 Geneva Protocol, the 1988 Sofia Protocol, and the 1998 Heavy Metals Protocol. Canada has also ratified the 1985 Helsinki Protocol and the 1998 Aarhus Protocol for heavy metals, whereas the United States has ratified the 1999 Gothenburg Protocol.

In addition to the ratification of these protocols, the United States has been working to enhance air quality since the enactment of the Clean Air Act of 1970. The U.S. Environmental Protection Agency (EPA) sets national air quality standards for common air pollutants (carbon monoxide, ozone, lead, nitrogen dioxide, particulate matter, and sulfur dioxide). In 1990, a new Clean Air Act introduced a nationwide approach to the reduction of acid rain. The law is designed to reduce acid rain and improve public health by reducing emissions of sulfur dioxide and nitrogen oxides. The program sets a permanent limit on the total amount of sulfur dioxide emitted by electric power plants nationwide.[17]

Asian countries have also enacted policies to limit air pollution. The Association of Southeastern Nations (ASEAN) has adopted a Haze Fund designed to coordinate response to forest fires and the resulting smoke and fog.[18] In China, a country with tremendous need to curb pollution, environmental law is under-developed and neglected. China has revised its pollution laws in 1995 and 2005, but these changes have had limited effect on air quality.[19]

Ozone

The United Nations and affiliated countries have been taking action to reduce ozone depletion for over 20 years. In 1987, the United Nations developed the Montreal Protocol.[20] This directive and other regulations banning ozone-depleting substances have reversed the destructive trend toward ozone depletion. Chloro-fluorocarbons (CFC) previously used in refrigerants, blowing foams, and solvents have been temporarily replaced with hydrofluorocarbons (HFC). Although HFCs

---

[16] Vestreng, V., et al. (2009). "Evolution of NO x Emissions in Europe with Focus on Road Transport Control Measures," *Atmospheric Chemistry and Physics*, 9(4), 1503–1520.

[17] Schennach, Susanne M. (2000), "The Economics of Pollution Permit Banking in the Context of Title IV of the 1990 Clean Air Act Amendments," *Journal of Environmental Economics and Management*, 40(3), 189–210.

[18] Tacconi, Luca, Frank Jotzo, and R. Quentin Grafton (2008), "Local Causes, Regional Co-operation and Global Financing for Environmental Problems: The Case of Southeast Asian Haze Pollution," *International Environmental Agreements: Politics, Law and Economics* 8 (1), 1–16.

[19] Alford, William P., and Benjamin L. Liebman, (2000), "Clean Air, Clean Processes—The Struggle over Air Pollution Law in the People's Republic of China," *Hastings Law Journal* 52 (2000): 703–748.

[20] United Nations Environment Programme (1987), *Montreal Protocol on Substances that Deplete the Ozone Layer* United Nations Environment Programme: Nairobi.

also contribute to ozone depletion, their influence is substantially lower (88 to 98 percent less effective ozone depletion) than that of CFCs. The UN directives, however, call for the long-term elimination of these chemicals as well. HFCs are also used as substitutes for CFCs. Although these chemicals do not deplete the ozone, they contribute to global warming.

Despite the fact that bromide-based emissions continue to be problematic, there is evidence that the Montreal Protocol is working. Recent research indicates evidence of a decrease in the atmospheric burden of ozone-depleting substances in the lower atmosphere. There is also evidence of some early signs of the expected stratospheric ozone recovery.[21] Given that ozone-depleting gases typically last 40 to 100 years in the atmosphere, full recovery is not expected before 2070. Nevertheless, failure to continue to comply with the Montreal Protocol could delay or prevent recovery of the ozone layer.

GEOPOLITICAL ACTION DESIGNED TO INFLUENCE WATER CONSUMPTION

Consumption simultaneously influences multiple factors associated with water. We examine three related aspects of water. These include the availability of clean drinking water, the impurities in water, and the oceans and fisheries as bodies of water.

Access to Clean Drinking Water

Efforts to increase the accessibility of freshwater are underway in many parts of the world. The percentage of the global population that has access to improved sanitation has increased from 76 percent in 1990 to 91 percent in 2015. Nevertheless, 12 percent of the world's population still does not have access to clean drinking water.[22] The availability of freshwater is increasingly a more significant problem across the globe, but at present, it is most pronounced in Asia and Africa (see Figure A2-1).

Although there are ongoing efforts on each continent to enhance the quality of freshwater, more work is needed to secure suitable drinking water. If appropriate action is not taken, environmental science projects that the majority of the world population will live in conditions of very low water availability by 2025.[23] Science underscores the need for a drastic decrease in water consumption, especially in irrigated land use and industry. In addition, environmental researchers call for reduction of wastewater discharges into the water supply, long-term river runoff regulation, and the redistribution of water resources across territories.[24]

---

[21] Barnes, Elizabeth A., Nicholas W. Barnes, and Lorenzo M. Polvani (2014), "Delayed Southern Hemisphere Climate Change Induced by Stratospheric Ozone Recovery, as Projected by the CMIP5 models," *Journal of Climate* 27 (2), 852–867.

[22] Byrne, John Anthony, Pilar Fernández-Ibáñez, and Preetam Kumar Sharma (2016), "9 Water Scarcity in Developing Regions," *Sustainable Water Management*.

[23] Shiklomanov, I. A. (2000), "World Water Resources and Water Use: Modern Assessment and Outlook for the 21st Century," Paris: IHP/UNESCO.

[24] Shiklomanov, Igor A. (2000), "Appraisal and Assessment of World Water Resources," *Water International*, 25, (1), 11–32.

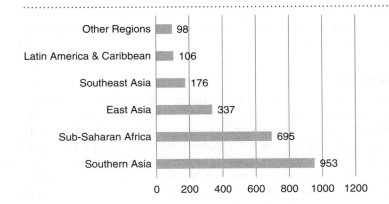

FIGURE A2-1[25]
Population (in millions)
without access to improved
sanitation in 2015

Water Impurities

The *World Health Organization* **(WHO)** has established guidelines designed to limit the impurities in the water supply. The guidelines offer health-based targets implemented by national water authorities. The guidelines indicate generally acceptable levels of biological and chemical (i.e., anthropogenic) water contaminants for water suppliers. For example, the WHO recognizes that manganese in water supplies causes an undesirable taste in beverages and stains laundry. Consequently, the guidelines call for a maximum of 0.4 milligrams/liter in the water supply. The WHO guidelines also offer background information on microbial, chemical, and radiological aspects of contaminants. In addition, the health-based guidelines indicate procedures for monitoring of control measures for drinking water safety as well as independent surveillance systems to ensure that water supplies remain healthy.

Although the WHO provides the guidelines, the determination of water quality is administered on a national and regional basis. The quality of drinking water is an increasing concern in every region. For instance, the European Union introduced the Water Framework Directive in 2000 and a flood risk management directive in 2007. Similarly, the United States passed the Safe Drinking Water Act in 1974. This law has been modified on several occasions to curb exposure to microbial contaminants and disinfectants.

Water contaminants continue to be problematic in Asia despite multiple efforts to enhance water quality. There have been attempts to reform the water and sanitation sector in South Asia and Southeast Asia, including large-scale subsidization of water for the poor. For instance, Laos is developing the infrastructure to ensure greater access to safe water and sanitation, especially for the rural population.

In Africa, suitable water and sanitation facilities have been extended to many more people during the past decade, but there is a strong need to increase the access to clean water and sanitation.[26] South Africa has passed a National

---

[25] WHO (2015), *Progress on Sanitation and Drinking Water—2015 Update and MDG Assessment*.Geneva, Switzerland: UNICEF and World Health Organization.

[26] United Nations Environment Programme (2012), Global Environment Outlook GEO5. Valletta, Malta: United Nations Environment Programme.

Water Act designed to protect ecosystems and enhance the quality of water.[27] Nevertheless, more regulation is needed to ensure that citizens have access to clean drinking water and sanitation.

Oceans and Fisheries

The United Nations Convention on the Law of the Sea was developed in 1982 to address coastal state sovereignty and jurisdiction. This edict addresses the broader interest of the international community concerning the deep seabed, fish stocks, high seas, scientific marine research, marine environmental protection, and military use of oceans.[28] This law outlines rights and obligations of countries, and it further provides the international basis for the protection and sustainable development of the marine and coastal environment. The Convention entered into force in 1994 and has been ratified by 135 nations. Increasingly, nations are codifying requirements for coastal management. Standards developed by the United Nations and the World Bank provide direction in the development of these regulations. The 1995 Global Programme of Action (GPA) for the Protection of the Marine Environment from Land-based Activities provided additional incentive to develop methods for preventing the degradation of the marine environment. GPA provides conceptual and practical guidance to national water authorities and facilitates cooperation among nations.[29]

Although the level of cooperation among nations has increased, estimates indicate that at least 63 percent of world fish stocks still require rebuilding, and lower exploitation rates are required to reverse the collapse of vulnerable species.[30] The Food and Agriculture Organization (FAO) of the United Nations Code of Conduct for Responsible Fisheries has influenced many countries to modify fisheries laws. This organization developed the Code of Conduct for Responsible Fisheries in 1995. This code is the foundation for promotion of sustainable fisheries and aquaculture. The FAO also has outlined international plans of action to improve shark management, and to control fishing. Despite these regulations, illegal, unregulated, and unreported fishing remain severe problems affecting world fisheries.

GEOPOLITICAL ACTION DESIGNED TO INFLUENCE LAND UTILIZATION

Urban Expansion

2007 marked the first year that the population in urban settings exceeded the rural population.[31] Urban expansion is an issue on every continent, but there are varying levels of response to this issue. Interestingly, in Latin America, countries

---

[27] portal.unesco.org/en/ev.php-URL_ID=47385&URL_DO=DO_TOPIC&URL_SECTION=201.html (January 13, 2017).

[28] Rothwell, Donald R., and Tim Stephens (2016), *The International Law of the Sea*, London: Bloomsbury Publishing.

[29] www.unep.org/gpa/documents/gpa/GPAFactsheet.pdf (January 13, 2017).

[30] Worm, Boris, et al. (2009), "Rebuilding global fisheries," *Science* 325 (5940), 578–585.

[31] Angel, Shlomo, et al. (2005), *The Dynamics of Global Urban Expansion* Washington: The World Bank.

with the lowest percentages of urban citizens are witnessing the fastest urbanization rates. The urban growth rates in Paraguay, Chile, and Bolivia are now faster than in Argentina and Ecuador.[32] Africa is the least urbanized inhabited region, but it has the world's highest rate of urbanization.

Increasing urbanization is an issue on every continent, but the primary impetus for change has been in mature economies. The U.S. EPA funds the *Smart Growth Network* , an organization focused on enhancing the quality of living conditions in cities. Smart growth refers to a set of policy options that relates the reshaping of urban growth to transportation priorities. This network seeks to enhance urban lifestyles by promoting a range of housing opportunities and walkable neighborhoods. It encourages community and stakeholder collaboration and fosters attractive communities that make fair development decisions. In addition, it seeks to provide transportation alternative within cities and promotes preservation of open space, farmland, and natural beauty.[33]

In contrast to urban sprawl that follows freeways, smart growth relies on compact urban development and revitalization of older areas in cities in conjunction with renewed public transit systems. Recent evidence indicates that adoption of Smart Growth principles and guidelines reaps benefits for citizens and cities. Smart growth factors such as mixed land use, diverse housing types, compact development plans, housing density, and levels of open space have been associated with increased levels of physical activity and walking.[34] It also serves as an effective means for changing development patterns and constraining urban sprawl.[35]

Land Degradation

Degradation of land is related to several other facets of the environment, especially water quality and biodiversity. One of the primary issues on land degradation is the international movement of hazardous materials. The *Basel Convention on the Control of the Trans-boundary Movement of Hazardous Waste and Their Disposal* was adopted in 1989 and entered into force in 1992. This convention was created to prevent the economically motivated dumping of hazardous wastes from richer to poorer countries. The *Basel Ban Amendment*, adopted in 1995, prohibits all exports of hazardous wastes from the Organisation for Economic Cooperation and Development (OECD), EU, and Liechtenstein to all other parties to the Convention. The United States is the only OECD country that has not ratified the Basel Convention or the Basel Ban Amendment.[36] China, India, Myanmar, and Pakistan become the home of more than 90 percent of 20 to 50 million tons of electronic

---

[32] Dufour, D. L. and B. A. Piperata (2004), "Rural-to-urban migration in Latin America: An Update and Thoughts on the Model," *American Journal of Human Biology*, 16 (4), 395–404.

[33] Downs, Anthony (2005), "Smart Growth," *Journal of the American Planning Association* 71(4), 367–380.

[34] Durand, C. P., M. Andalib, G.F. Dunton, J. Wolch, and M. A. Pentz (2011), "A Systematic Review of Built Environment Factors Related to Physical Activity and Obesity Risk: Implications for Smart Growth Urban Planning," *Obesity Reviews*, 12(5), e173–e182.

[35] Goetz, Andrew (2013). Suburban Sprawl or Urban Centres: Tensions and Contradictions of Smart Growth Approaches in Denver, Colorado," *Urban Studies* 50(11), 2178–2195.

[36] Kelemen, R. Daniel, and David Vogel (2010), "Trading Places: The Role of the United States and the European Union in International Environmental Politics," *Comparative Political Studies* 43 (4), 427–456.

waste produced each year.[37] Export of e-waste to these countries is a violation of the Basel Convention and the Basel Ban Amendment. In other parts of Asia, Japan and South Korea are lowering waste generation through the reduced use of natural resources in production and more sustainable consumption.

The New Partnership for African Development (NEPAD) program addresses soil erosion, salinization, declining fertility, soil compaction, and pollution on the continent. Through a network of regional organizations, NEPAD promotes sustainable land use, rational use of rangelands, sustainable agriculture, and integrated natural resource management.[38] Similar problems plague West Asia where poorly managed irrigation systems are associated with higher levels of salinity. Although there are efforts to improve degraded lands, most of this action is focused on 16 percent of the land mass located in the Arabian Peninsula and Mashriq.

Deforestation and Desertification

Recognizing the worldwide concerns for deforestation, the United Nations has developed some nonbinding instruments for the management of forests. The UN calls for the reverse of loss of forest cover through sustainable forestry that enhances ecosystem economic, social, and environmental benefits. In addition, it calls for increases in the area of protected forests as well as increases in funding for sustainable forest management.[39] Despite this initiative, subregional issues continue to limit the amount forestation. For example, the European Union has adopted a sustainability strategy for forest management, yet Eastern Europe continues to try to limit illegal logging as well as human-induced forest fires. Deforestation is rampant in the Middle East, but the balancing of this activity with reforestation in other areas has resulted in no major changes in the level of forestation over the past 15 years.

Efforts to curb desertification recognize that the increased frequency and severity of droughts due to climate change will likely to exacerbate desertification. Consequently, the *United Nations Convention to Combat Desertification* offers a platform for mitigation of this issue. This convention outlines necessary financing, information, and technology to reduce desertification, and it also outlines national action programs.[40]

Implementation of the UN efforts to combat desertification occurs on a regional level, with the greatest attention focused on Africa, Asia, northern Mediterranean, Central and Eastern Europe, Latin America, and the Caribbean. Given that two-thirds of Africa is desert or drylands, the implementation plan is the most detailed of all regions. The plan calls for adoption on a national basis of legal, political, economic, financial, and social measures to limit desertification. Asia faces similar problems due to the high percentage of land that is desert. About 27

[37] Schwarzer, S., A. De Ono, P. Peduzzi, G. Giuliani, and S. Kluser (2005), "E-waste, the Hidden Side of IT Equipment's Manufacturing and Use," Geneva: United Nations Environmental Program.

[38] Omona, Julius (2010), "New Partnership for Africa's Development," In *International Encyclopedia of Civil Society*, 1029–1030. New York: Springer-Verlag.

[39] United Nations (2005), "United Nations Forum on Forests," New York: United Nations.

[40] United Nations (2008), "Review of Implementation of Agenda 21 and the Johannesburg Plan of Implementation (JPOI): Desertification," New York; United Nations.

percent of China is desertified, and nearly 400 million people live in these areas. China has responded to this environmental threat by passing laws and drawing up a national plan to limit desertification.[41] In the northern Mediterranean, land degradation is often linked to poor agricultural practices.[42] Thus, Greece, Italy, Portugal, Spain, and Turkey have launched a subregional program for scientific cooperation, exchange of information and documentation, and organization of regional training courses. Similarly, countries in Central and Eastern Europe are coordinating efforts in scientific research, data management, information exchange, training, drought mitigation, and disaster preparedness. The Latin American regional plan outlines the need to eliminate unsustainable practices such as excessive irrigation and inappropriate agricultural practices, inadequate legal support, inappropriate use of soil, fertilizers and pesticides, overgrazing, and intensive exploitation of forests.

GEOPOLITICAL ACTION DESIGNED TO INFLUENCE BIODIVERSITY

Biodiversity concerns variation among species of plant and animal life. In 1992, members of the United Nations signed the *Convention on Biological Diversity*. This document sought to conserve biodiversity, promote sustainable use of the components of biodiversity, and share the benefits of utilization of genetic resources in a fair manner. The convention offers guidance based on the precautionary principle that where there is a threat of significant reduction or loss of biological diversity, lack of full scientific certainty should not be used as a reason for postponing measures to avoid or minimize such a threat. The convention recognizes that substantial investments are required to conserve biological diversity. Current evaluations of progress of the convention indicate that strong increases in the coverage of protected areas for various species. The abundance of species and respected habitats, however, is decreasing. Moreover, threatened species face greater risks than in previous eras.

The Convention on Biodiversity provides guidelines for implementation on a regional or national level. Due in part to the rapid development in the region, the Asia Pacific region has encountered tremendous pressure on ecosystems over the past two decades. Asian countries participate in protection of coastal ecosystems by affiliation with one of four Regional Sea Action Plans: East Asia, Northwest Pacific, South Asia, and the Pacific. Despite this affiliation, East Asia and South Asia discharge more than 85 percent of their wastewater directly into the sea. In the South Pacific, local communities are collaborating through locally managed marine areas designed to protect coastal areas.

The EU initiatives to deter biodiversity loss are more stringent than those established by the UN convention. The Pan-European Ecological Network (PEEN) is a nonbinding framework that promotes cooperative action across Europe

---

[41] Yoon, Esook (2013), "Combating Desertification and DSS in Northeast Asia," 환경정책 21 (2), 85–113.

[42] Geist, Helmut J., and Eric F. Lambin (2004), "Dynamic Causal Patterns of Desertification," *Bioscience* 54 (9), 817–829.

contributing to the evolving international process of developing a stronger strategic component to nature conservation in Europe.[43] The EU Commission on a European Biodiversity Strategy seeks to anticipate, prevent, and attack causes of reduction or loss of biodiversity at the source. It focuses on the reversal of present trends in biodiversity reduction or losses. It also provides a clearing house that facilitates public access to information relevant for biodiversity.[44]

Protection of biodiversity is also a vital concern in Latin America. Over the past 15 years, the amount of protected marine and terrestrial land has nearly doubled. The Mesoamerican Biological Corridor is designed to support biodiversity in Mexico, Belize, Guatemala, Honduras, Nicaragua, Costa Rica, and Panama.[43] Similarly, the pilot program to conserve the Brazilian rain forest is a joint undertaking of the Brazil, and the international community seeks to find ways to conserve the tropical rain forests of the Amazon and Brazil's Atlantic coast.[46]

Although there has been some progress toward biodiversity targets, the UN recognizes that much work is needed to achieve a significant reduction of the current rate of biodiversity loss. To limit biodiversity loss, it is imperative to improve agricultural efficiency and plan for agricultural expansion. Furthermore, the demand for meat by the more affluent sectors of society should be lowered, and over-fishing should be eliminated. Biodiversity should be integrated into trade decisions, and it should be integral to poverty reduction strategies. Finally, regulators should recognize that biodiversity will be better protected through actions that are justified on their economic merits.[47]

[43] http://www.eeconet.org/eaf/network/ (January 13, 2017).

[44] Maes, J., M.L. Paracchini, G. Zulian, M.B. Dunbar, and R. Alkemade (2012), "Synergies and Trade-offs between Ecosystem Service Supply, Biodiversity, and Habitat Conservation Status in Europe," *Biological Conservation*, 155, 1–12.

[45] Harvey, Celia A., et al. (2008). "Integrating Agricultural Landscapes with Biodiversity Conservation in the Mesoamerican Hotspot," *Conservation Biology*, 22(1), 8–15.

[46] Goncalves, Marco Antonio (2002), "Pilot program to conserve the Brazilian rain forests: An innovative experience in international cooperation for sustainable development," agris.fao.org/agris-search/search.do?recordID=XF2015000893 (January 13, 2017).

[47] Secretariat of the Convention on Biological Diversity (2014) *Global Biodiversity Outlook 4*. Montreal: United Nations.

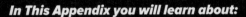

A-3

The Role of Household Consumption

In This Appendix you will learn about:

The Environmental Impact of Home Energy Consumption

Factors Affecting Space Heating

The Impact of Appliances

The Impact of Water Heating

The Impact of Lighting and Cooking

The Impact of Food Consumption

In order to influence energy consumption in the home, it is necessary to examine the amount and manner of this consumption. Home energy consumption represents 17 percent of total energy consumption.[1] Figure A3-1 provides an overview of how households consume this energy and how their consumption of energy has changed over time. Households consume energy through space heating, appliances, water heating, lighting, and cooking. In addition, households are involved in indirect energy use associated with food purchases.

Energy usage varies markedly with per capita consumption in the United States and Canada at twice the rate of all other Organisation for Economic Cooperation and Development (OECD) countries.[2] Moreover, the rate of consumption in these two countries is more than seven times the rate of consumption for most other markets. Individuals in these two markets and in other parts of the world are making efforts to enhance fuel efficiency, and consumers in North America have the greatest opportunity to have an influence on energy conservation in the household. Consider first energy consumption associated with space heating.

Space Heating. At 53 percent, space heating represents the largest portion of energy consumption in the household. Since the oil crisis of the 1970s, many OECD countries have established mandatory energy efficiency codes that focus on improving energy consumption related to heating equipment, building design, and insulation.[3] Importantly, analysis of space heating must examine the productivity of the entire system rather than a single facet of space heating. The *whole building concept* encompasses consideration of the location, infrastructure, utilities, and ancillary devices within the home.[4] Ancillary devices, including appliances and lighting, are addressed in a subsequent section.

Consumers who seek to limit their space heating costs should consider all facets of the whole building concept. The first consideration is the location. Location consideration includes the climate and the specific housing location. The U.S. Department of Energy, for example, portions the climates in the contiguous 48 states outlined in Figure A3-3. Climate dictates the need for heating and cooling as well as the efficiency of alternative forms of these home utilities and components of the infrastructure of the house. For example, windows that offer optimal insulation in cold climates are less than effective in southern regions because they tend to localize overheating and sun glare.

Another important location consideration is the actual site of the home. Management of energy and light from the sun should be considered in location decisions. Proper orientation of a house can result in substantial savings of heating and cooling costs, and the orientation is dependent on specific site conditions and house designs. For most designs, homes that favor exposure to the north or the south generally encounter less sunlight and are, therefore, preferred to

---

[1] International Energy Agency (2016), *Key World Energy Trends - International Energy Agency*, Paris: International Energy Agency.

[2] www.iea.org/publications/freepublications/publication/Indicators_2008.pdf (February 28, 2017).

[3] United Nations Department of Social and Economic Affairs (2007), "Sustainable Consumption and Production," United Nations.

[4] energy.gov/energysaver/whole-house-systems-approach (February 28, 2017).

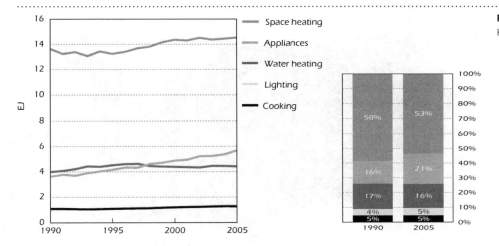

FIGURE A3-1
Household energy use[5]

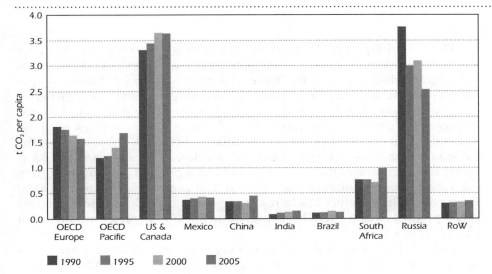

FIGURE A3-2
Household CO_2 emissions
per capita[6]

homes with pronounced exposure to the east and west.[7] Planting of shade trees limits a home's exposure to sun, whereas site grading and landscaping assist in maintaining the integrity of the building.[8]

---

[5] International Energy Agency (2008), *Worldwide Trends in Energy Use and Efficiency*, Paris: International Energy Agency.

[6] International Energy Agency (2008), Worldwide Trends in Energy Use and Efficiency, Paris: International Energy Agency.

[7] www.fsec.ucf.edu/en/consumer/buildings/homes/priorities.htm (February 28, 2017).

[8] blog.davey.com/2016/05/the-benefits-of-shade-trees-nature-s-sunscreen/ (September 24, 2008).

FIGURE A3-3

Five climactic regions
of the United States[9]

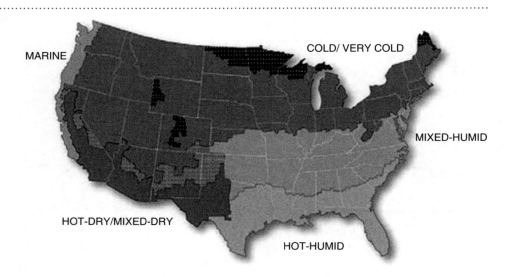

MARINE

COLD/ VERY COLD

MIXED-HUMID

HOT-DRY/MIXED-DRY

HOT-HUMID

The second aspect of the home-related heating cost is the infrastructure. The infrastructure includes walls, roof, foundation, windows and doors, natural lighting, and duct system in the home. The energy efficiency of most components of the infrastructure varies based on environmental factors, design needs, and climate zone. Windows and doors that use multiple panes of glass and incorporate argon or krypton gases offer substantial energy savings, resulting in the need for smaller heating and ventilation systems.[10] Nevertheless, the value to the consumer of these doors and windows varies by climactic zone. U-factor is the measure that indicates how well a product prevents heat from escaping a home or building, and the solar heat gain coefficient (SCHG) measures how well a product blocks heat from the sun. While northern climates prefer products that prevent heat loss, southern climates prefer products that provide shade.[11]

Examination of the infrastructure must also consider areas where air is transferred between the inside and the outside of the home. Figure A3-4 illustrates potential sources of heat and energy transfer in a single-family dwelling. The U.S. EPA estimates that a homeowner can save 11 percent of a home's total energy costs by air sealing the home and providing proper insulation materials in the attic, over the crawl space, and in the basement.[12]

The utilities in the home refer to the heating and air conditioning systems. Since the mid-1970s, governments have been establishing standards for these home utilities. As technology has advanced, the productivity of these systems

---

[9] www.eia.gov/consumption/commercial/maps.php (February 28, 2017).

[10] www.fsec.ucf.edu/en/consumer/buildings/homes/windows/q_a.htm (February 28, 2017).

[11] www.windowreplacement.net/u-factor.html (February 28, 2017).

[12] www.energystar.gov/index.cfm?c=home_sealing.hm_improvement_methodology (February 28, 2017).

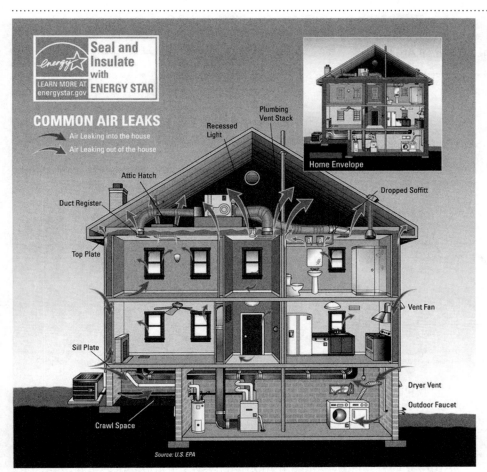

FIGURE A3-4
Potential sources of air
transfer[13]

has increased along with increases in the efficiency standards. Cumulative operating cost savings from all standards in effect since 1987 will reach nearly $2 trillion by 2030.[14]

Although space heating capabilities and insulation have improved, these gains have been offset by a higher number of dwellings occupied by fewer people. Although fewer people may live in a dwelling, the heating costs may not be reduced.[15] In some markets, the space heating needs are further increased by increases in home size. For example, homes built in the current decade are 80 percent larger than a typical home of the 1940s. [16]

---

[13] www.epa.gov/indoorairplus/indoor-airplus-program-documents (February 28, 2017).

[14] www1.eere.energy.gov/buildings/appliance_standards/residential/pdfs/fb_fr_tsd/chapter_1.pdf (February 28, 2017)

[15] International Energy Agency (2008), *Worldwide Trends in Energy Use and Efficiency*, Paris: International Energy Agency.

[16] www.forbes.com/sites/trulia/2013/05/02/american-homes-by-decade/#233842381045 (February 28, 2017).

FIGURE A3-5A

Energy share usage of large and small appliances[17]

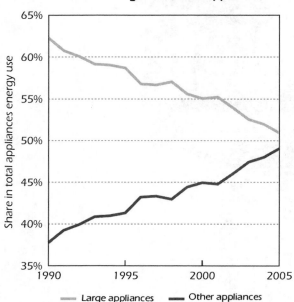

FIGURE A3-5B

Average unit energy consumption[18]

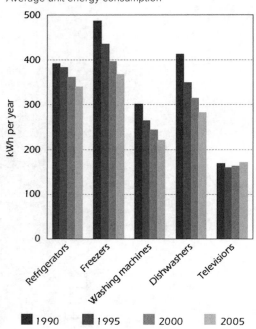

The Energy Star branding has also been expanded to include the housing sector. Through the U.S. EPA website, consumers can gain access to builders of onsite and modular homes that offer Energy Star homes. In addition, consumers can also gain access to lenders that offer special rates for energy-efficient housing.

Appliances. Energy consumption analysis for appliances distinguishes between large and other appliances. Large appliances include refrigerators, freezers, washing machines, dishwashers, and televisions. Figure A3-5 illustrates how the usage of energy among these products has changed over time. Although large appliances once represented over 60 percent of fuel consumption (Figure A3-5a), all large appliances except televisions have reduced their average energy consumption with time (Figure A3-5b). Television technology is more energy efficient than 20 years ago, but the average screen is substantially larger than the previous era.

The proliferation of small appliances represents an increasingly more important part of household energy consumption. These devices include mobile phones, personal computers, personal audio equipment, and other home electronics. Many of these products continue to draw energy even though their batteries are recharged and the products are not currently in use. Consequently, product developers have strived to achieve minimal levels of energy absorption during inactive modes. Another aspect of productivity for these devices is the level of

---

[17] International Energy Agency (2008), *Worldwide Trends in Energy Use and Efficiency*, Paris: International Energy Agency.

[18] International Energy Agency (2008), *Worldwide Trends in Energy Use and Efficiency*, Paris: International Energy Agency.

efficiency during operational mode. These supplies may be located inside or outside of devices such as cordless phones, answering machines, video games, computer speakers, and cordless tools.

Water heating. The third largest percentage of home energy consumption is water heating. Multiple means for heating water are employed in various countries, but in many cases, data outlining the extent to which sustainable sources of energy are used are unavailable.[19] In the United States, most traditional storage units are either gas or electric. Of the 9.8 million water heater shipments in 2006, 4.8 million were conventional electric-resistance, and 4.7 million were conventional gas storage.[20] Advanced water heating technologies constitute a small portion of the market. Of the advanced technologies, gas tankless water heaters represent 2.6 percent of the market (254,600 units in 2006). Tankless water heaters do not contain a storage tank and operate when there is a demand for hot water. The elimination of standby losses from the tank reduces energy consumption by 10 to 15 percent. Solar water heater shipments were estimated at 2,430 units in the same year.

The use of solar energy for heating water varies markedly by country. The current volume of solar energy usage for water heating amounts to an annual avoidance of 34.1 million tons of carbon dioxide emissions and the equivalent to 12.1 billion liters of oil.[21] At the end of 2005, worldwide operation of solar thermal energy was 111.0 GW (gigawatts), while 86.3GW was associated with flat-plate and evacuated tube collectors primarily used for home water heating, and the remaining 23.9 GW was associated with unglazed plastic collectors used for heating swimming pools. China, which is the largest market for the flat-plate technology, represents 48 percent of the world market. Turkey, Japan, Germany, Israel, and Greece are also leading countries in terms of the total demand for flat-plate and evacuated tube technology. The United States is the primary market for the unglazed plastic collector technology.

Lighting and Cooking. Lighting and cooking together represent about 10 percent of energy consumption in the home. In many regions of the world, marketers of lighting and cooking appliances have developed mandatory efficiency standards. Standards such as *Energy Star* have been effective in eliminating the most inefficient models from the market. In addition, countries have implemented labeling that identifies the energy consumption of products and endorsement labels (e.g., *Energy Star*) that promote the most energy efficient products.[22] The efficient lighting initiative (ELI) is an international branding system for high-quality, energy-efficient lighting products. In 2005, the China Standard Certification Center (CSC) was commissioned to develop ELI certification and branding system globally. The expanded ELI program is operated by the ELI Quality Certification Institute. This institute is led by CSC with assistance from a team of international experts from Asia, North America, and Latin America. The ELI Quality Certification Institute is currently promoting voluntary technical specifications for energy fluorescent

---

[19] United Nations Department of Social and Economic Affairs (2007), "Sustainable Consumption and Production," United Nations.

[20] www.energystar.gov/ia/partners/prod_development/new_specs/downloads/water_heaters/WaterHeaterDraftCriteriaAnalysis.pdf (February 28, 2017).

[21] Weiss, Werner, Irene Bergmann, and Gerhard Faninger (2008), *Solar Heat Worldwide*, International Energy Agency: Gleisdorf, Austria.

[22] United Nations Department of Social and Economic Affairs (2007), "Sustainable Consumption and Production," United Nations.

lighting. It is focusing on the developing countries of Asia/Asia Pacific, Latin America, and Africa and seeks to harmonize its test methods and performance specifications with other voluntary labeling programs internationally.[23]

Food. The energy use associated with food consumption includes direct energy consumption associated with shopping trips as well as with the storing and cooking of food. The indirect costs are those associated with agricultural production, food processing, and distribution. The indirect costs are substantially larger than the direct costs.[24] In addition to fossil fuel usage, food production is also a source of methane and nitrous oxide. Methane is associated with animal production, and nitrous oxide is derived from fertilizer. Although these gases are powerful greenhouse gases, they do not represent the primary sources of energy use in food consumption.

The primary source of energy use is the processing and distribution of food. In the United States, approximately 10 percent of the total primary energy supply is associated with food production. Only 20 percent of this energy is attributed to farm production. Thirty-four percent of farm production energy use is for farm vehicles, 28 percent is in fertilizer use, and the remainder is used for irrigation, crop drying, pesticides, and other farm operations. By contrast, the remaining 80 percent of energy is used for food processing, storage, packaging, and retail distribution. Processed foods make up three-fourths of total world food sales, and the costs to process food are substantial. For instance, processing breakfast cereals requires more than five times as much energy as is contained in the cereal itself. These processed foods are often individually wrapped, bagged, and boxed. This packaging requires large amounts of energy and raw materials to produce, yet most of it ends up in landfills.[25]

The recognition that food processing is a central issue in food energy costs has prompted speculation about reduction measures. The use of organic food has been touted as a way to eliminate fertilizer and pesticide costs while enhancing food quality. Because organic farms have lower yields per acre, however, more fuel is required for clearing land, cultivation, and harvesting.[26] A second consideration is the degree to which the consumer diet relies on meat products versus grain, vegetables, and fruits. Meat tends to require more energy for production than vegetables, and reductions in this area should influence carbon emissions. Nevertheless, a recent Swedish study suggested that transition to a nutritionally and environmentally sustainable diet would result in a negligible change in energy use and greenhouse gas emission.[27] These findings suggest that there is a need to develop a keener understanding of consumption and its ramifications for energy use and other essential areas.

---

[23] www.efficientlighting.net/index.php?option=com_content&task=view&id=18&Itemid=41 (February 28, 2017).

[24] United Nations Department of Social and Economic Affairs (2007), "Sustainable Consumption and Production," United Nations.

[25] Murray, Daniel (2005), "Oil and Food: A New Security Challenge," *Asia Times*, June 3.

[26] United Nations Department of Social and Economic Affairs (2007), "Sustainable Consumption and Production," United Nations.

[27] Wallén, Anna, Nils Brandt, and Ronald Wennersten (2004), "Does the Swedish Consumer's Choice of Food Influence Greenhouse Gas Emissions?" *Environmental Science and Policy*, 7(6), 525–535.

Energy Consumption in the Services Sector

INTRODUCTION: SERVICE SECTOR CONTRIBUTORS TO CARBON EMISSIONS

This appendix provides an overview of carbon emissions in the services sector of the economy. Services are product offerings that possess several traits that distinguish them from goods and other product offerings. The delivery of most services is contingent of the action of people, and the personnel-based facet distinguishes these products from goods. Services are products that are essentially intangible and vary based on the provider. Because services are associated with the time the services provider has available to render the service, the amount of available service is perishable.[1]

The services sector includes service businesses (e.g., retail stores and hotels), educational institutions, correctional facilities, religious groups, and fraternal organizations. The services sector of an economy is an important source of employment and gross domestic product (GDP). In the United States, for example, the services sector accounts for over 80 percent of the jobs in the economy as well as 80 percent of the GDP.[2]

On a global level, the services sector accounts for 9 percent of total final energy consumption and 12 percent of carbon emissions.[3] The three primary sources of energy for services are electricity, natural gas, and fuel oil. Electricity usage represented 47 percent of all energy use, with the largest uses associated with air cooling, lighting, office equipment operations, refrigeration, and ventilation. Natural gas represents nearly 40 percent of energy use, and it is the primary source of energy for space heating, water heating, and cooking. Electricity is also used for these purposes, but gas is generally a more efficient and more popular energy source for these applications. Fuel oil is predominantly used for space heating.[4]

Figure AP4-1 illustrates the primary uses of energy in commercial buildings. Space heating accounts for 25 percent of energy use, whereas lighting, water heating, ventilation, and refrigeration each account for another 10 percent. It is noteworthy that the number of commercial buildings and the amount of floor space has steadily increased, yet total energy consumption in this sector has not risen at comparable levels. In virtually every application—from computers to space heating—there have been significant enhancements to energy efficiency. Space heating is primarily achieved through boilers and furnaces. Furnaces heat air and distribute it through ducts; boilers heat water, providing either hot water or steam for heating. Steam is distributed through pipes to steam radiators, and hot water can be distributed through baseboard radiators or radiant floor systems.[5] Boilers are more likely used in larger buildings, whereas furnaces are more prevalent in smaller facilities.

---

[1] Parasuraman, A., Valarie A. Zeithaml, and Leonard L. Berry (1985), "A Conceptual Model of Service Quality and Its Implications for Future Research," *Journal of Marketing*, 49 (4), 41–50.

[2] Berg, Daniel (2006), "Analysis of the Service Sector," *International Journal of Information Technology & Decision Making*, 5 (4), 699–701.

[3] International Energy Agency (2008), *Tracking Industrial Energy Efficiency and CO2 Emissions*, Paris, France: OECD/IEA.

[4] International Energy Agency (2008), Tracking Industrial Energy Efficiency and CO2 Emissions, Paris, France: OECD/IEA.

[5] energy.gov/energysaver/home-heating-systems (March 2, 2017).

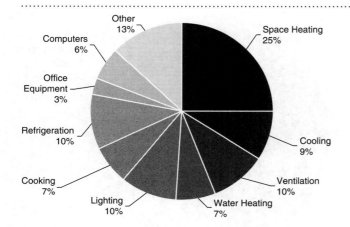

FIGURE AP4-1.
Energy use in commercial
buildings—2012.[6]

The energy efficiency of a furnace or boiler is measured by ***annual fuel utilization efficiency*** (AFUE). The U.S. Federal Trade Commission requires new furnaces or boilers to display each unit's AFUE for consumer comparison purposes. AFUE is the ratio of heat output of the furnace or boiler compared to the total energy consumed by a furnace or boiler. For example, a furnace with an AFUE of 95 percent uses 95 percent of the energy as heat, whereas the remaining 5 percent escapes through the chimney or elsewhere. The U.S. Department of Energy has established federal minimums of 80 percent efficiency for gas-fired furnaces, 82 percent for oil-fired furnaces, 84 percent gas fired-boilers, and 83 percent for oil fired-boilers. These minimums are below *Energy Star* requirements that are currently set at 90 percent for furnaces and 85 percent for boilers.[7]

The fuel efficiency of furnaces and boilers has improved markedly over the years. As a result of this enhanced efficiency, there are substantial savings and, simultaneously, reduced carbon emissions realized from upgrading space heating systems. For example, many furnaces installed in the 1970s had AFUE's of 60 percent. The replacement of one of these systems with a highly fuel efficient system with an AFUE of 95 percent lowers fuel consumption costs substantially. Consequently, carbon emissions and fuel cost are both reduced through the upgrade to more efficient space heating technology.

One area of energy consumption that has changed markedly over the past 10 years is in the form of lighting used within this sector. In contrast to the household sector, the services sector has substantially more locations that rely on fluorescent lighting rather than incandescent lighting. There are some energy savings to be realized from replacing fluorescent lighting with more efficient LED-based lighting. Improvements in electronic control technology complement advances in the efficiency of lighting and space heating equipment. The development of digital thermostats enables one to control the temperature in a home by the day, week, and hour. Thus, facilities operated in climates that demand air conditioning and

---

[6] www.eia.gov/consumption/commercial/reports/2012/energyusage/ (March 2, 2017).

[7] *Energy Design Update* (2006), "DOE Updates Furnace *Efficiency Standards*," *Energy Design Update* 26(12), 2–4.

FIGURE AP4-2.
Commercial buildings
consumption by energy
source[8], 2003 (6523 trillion
BTUs).
** Other includes public
assembly, public order and
safety, religious worship,
warehouse and storage, and
vacant properties.*

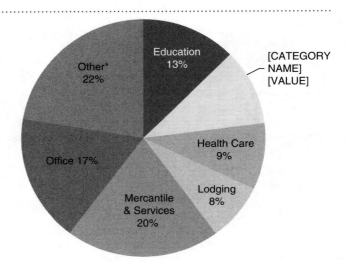

heating in the same day can be managed effectively. Moreover, the electronic programming of the heaters enables one to raise or lower the temperature in a location. Properly programmed digital thermometers can lower heating costs and limit the amount of carbon emissions associated with the location.

Digital control devices also lower fuel costs and emissions. The lighting control devices include dimmers, sensors, and timers. Dimmers used with fluorescent lighting are dedicated fixtures and bulbs that provide even greater energy savings than a regular fluorescent lamp. By contrast, dimmers used with incandescent lighting do not increase energy efficiency. Sensors are devices that sense motion, light (photo sensors), and occupancy. These devices enhance fuel efficiency by reducing the use of power when conditions do not warrant energy consumption. For example, photo sensors are used in outdoor applications to turn appliances off during daylight hours. Similarly, timers attempt to limit energy use through programs that allow energy to flow to lighting appliances on predetermined schedules.

Figure AP4-2 illustrates the various facets of the services sector as well as their respective energy consumption in the United States. At 20 percent of total energy consumption, the mercantile section represents the largest user of energy in the services sector of the economy. Mercantile services include the malls and strip centers that house nonfood, nonlodging components of retailing. At 17 percent of total energy usage, offices are the second largest consumers in the services sector. Education facilities account for 13 percent of energy consumption, whereas food service, health care, and lodging are each associated with at least 8 percent of total energy consumption. Consider first the role of the mercantile sector.

NONFOOD RETAILING

The mercantile component of the services sector includes all buildings used for the sale and the display of goods other than food. This category includes enclosed malls, strip shopping centers, car dealerships, liquor stores, video rental stores, and every type of retail building other than food retailing. In order to assess the

[8] www.eia.gov/totalenergy/data/annual/showtext.php?t=ptb0209 (March 2, 2017).

potential to enhance sustainability in the nonfood retail sector, it is valuable to look at the *inputs, processes, and outputs*. Two inputs associated with carbon emissions are packaging and energy sourcing. Manufacturers and distributors are increasingly examining ways to enhance sustainability while simultaneously shoring up logistics costs associated with marketing to retailers.

A second input that is being aggressively modified is the form of energy employed at the retail location. For example, Wal-Mart has a long-term goal to use 100 percent renewable forms of energy in its retail stores. Wal-Mart has entered into a four-year power purchase agreement with Duke Energy whereby they will purchase wind power at competitive rates from Duke's Notrees, Texas, facility. By purchasing clean, renewable energy, Wal-Mart will avoid producing more than thousands of metric tons of carbon dioxide (CO_2) emissions per year.[9]

The process component of nonfood retailing concerns the management of energy usage at a retail location. Wal-Mart and Target have implemented programs designed to reduce energy consumption without affecting the consumer shopping experience. Wal-Mart uses dimmable fluorescent lighting systems and light-emitting diode (LED) technologies that are more efficient than older fluorescent lights. Since about 80 percent of the energy consumed in a retail location is associated with heating and cooling, Target has made substantial strides to enhance the energy efficiency of these systems. Heating and air conditioning systems within Wal-Mart stores are well above retailing requirements, and humidification systems are energy efficient systems that make the trip to the market more enjoyable. Wal-Mart also has implemented a plan to reduce store water consumption through the installation of new faucets and other plumbing that limits the flow of water. In addition, Wal-Mart is replacing some percentage of cement with fly ash and slag. The company also uses recycled materials in its cabinetry and counters, and it uses 100 percent recycled plastics (most from unused diaper scraps) in its baseboards.

The third aspect of nonfood retailing concerns the waste derived from a retail location. Retailers have collected paper waste for recycling for many decades, but the attention to waste reduction has increased dramatically in the last few years. Target, for instance, now recycles or reuses over 70 percent of waste that would have been thrown into landfills a few years ago. Municipalities are mandating that retailers recycle plastic bags. For example, in 2008 New York City passed a law that requires retailers to establish in-store recycling programs for plastic bags.[10] In response to the criticism of plastic bags, retailers are actively switching to other bags.

FOOD RETAILING

Food retailing represents 10.4 percent of consumption in the services sector.[11] The *food service* component refers to buildings used for the preparation and the sale of food and beverages. These buildings include restaurants, cafeterias, and fast food restaurants. *Food sales* refers to buildings used to sell food at the retail or wholesale level and include grocery stores, food markets, and convenience stores.

---

[9] www.supermarketnews.com/latest-news/wal-mart-buys-wind-energy-texas-stores (March 2, 2017).

[10] *Paper, Film & Foil Converter* (2008), "NYC Mandates Plastic Bag Recycling," *Paper, Film & Foil Converter*, 82 (6), 17.

[11] www.eia.gov/totalenergy/data/annual/showtext.php?t=ptb0209 (March 2, 2017).

Food service accounts for 6.8 percent of total energy consumption, whereas food sales represent 3.8 percent of total energy consumption.

Although food retailing represents slightly more than 10 percent of consumption in the services sector, the energy intensity for food marketing is more than twice the average among all commercial buildings. In the food service subsector, electricity represents slightly more than 50 percent of energy usage, with the remainder primarily associated with natural gas. Companies operating in this market are addressing ways to reduce fuel input costs, operating costs, and waste removal. Food retailers have taken measures to conserve energy and use sustainable sources of fuel. McDonald's, for instance, has implemented The Energy-Efficient McDonald's (TEEM) strategies that save each restaurant more than $2,000 annually. The design elements include skylights that allow fluorescent lights to be dimmed during the day as well as windows with specially treated glass that filter out the sun's infrared and ultraviolet light. Infrared rays raise the temperature in dining areas, whereas ultraviolet light fades colorful fabrics inside restaurants.[12]

Many other restaurateurs are recognizing financial and brand advantages. The Austin Grill, for example, made the switch to wind power in 2003, and it was the first multiunit restaurant in the United States powered exclusively by wind power. The switch to wind power cost the restaurant chain about 2 percent more per kilowatt hour versus fuels generated from traditional sources.[13] Similarly, Holland Inc. began using wind power for all of its electrical needs at Burgerville and Noodlin' restaurants in 2005. By converting 40 restaurants to wind power, Holland Inc. avoids adding 17.4 million pounds of carbon dioxide to the air each year.[14]

A second facet of sustainability associated with inputs to the restaurant and food service industry concerns food sourcing. Restaurateurs can lower their carbon footprint by purchasing sustainably grown products and products sourced locally. Sustainably-grown products are generally associated with lower carbon emissions, but they can cost more than their counterparts.[15] Local purchasing offers many benefits to the restaurateur and the community. The purchase of locally produced products lowers the carbon emissions costs associated with delivery and results in generally lower shipping costs. In addition, the firm can support its claims associated with freshness by buying locally grown products. The purchase of these products also supports the local community that is vital to the success of the restaurants.[16]

Retailers are also recognizing the multiple benefits associated with limiting fuel consumption. Since heating/air conditioning, lighting, cooking, and refrigeration account for about 75 percent of fuel costs in the sector, companies are looking for efficiencies realized through equipment purchases and operations. Commercial restaurant equipment that bears the *Energy Star* label offer significant fuel savings and carbon reductions. *Energy Star* fryers are more than 50 percent more efficient than other fryers. Similarly, *Energy Star* steamers are 25 to 60 percent more efficient,

---

[12] Zuber, Amy (2000), "Go, T.E.E.M.! New McDonald's Units Conserve Energy, Save Money," *Nation's Restaurant News*, 34 (11), 30.

[13] Johnson, Jim (2003), "Restaurant Chain Converts to Wind," *Waste News*, 9 (6), 31–35.

[14] Johnson, Jim (2005), "Restaurant Chain to Devour Wind," *Waste News*, 11 (9), 16.

[15] Walkup, Carolyn (2008), "Chicago's Epic Burger Serves Up 'More Mindful' Menu in Quest to Minimize Its Carbon Footprint," *Nation's Restaurant News*, 40 (24), 1–4.

[16] Parseghian, Pamela (2006), "Restaurants Get Help Finding Produce," *Nation's Restaurant News*, 40 (39), 30.

and food warming/heating equipment is up to 137 percent more efficient than products that do not carry the *Energy Star* label.[17] In addition, restaurateurs can invest in tankless water heaters that reduce water consumption and are up to 70 percent more efficient than conventional water heaters.

Energy management for refrigeration equipment requires retailers to examine ozone depletion and global warming.[18] Retailers can reduce energy expenses by investing in refrigeration equipment that offers the highest possible evaporation temperature and the lowest possible condensing temperature while maintaining optimal storage temperature.[19] Newer model commercial refrigerators meet these specifications and are 30 percent more efficient than older models. In addition, these units may use coolants that are more environmentally friendly than chlorofluorocarbon (CFC) or hydrofluorocarbon (HFC)-based refrigerators. Since moisture removal is more energy-intensive than lowering air temperature, it is essential to regulate humidity.[20] Proper dehumidification makes the shopping experience more enjoyable and can make supermarket refrigeration cases up to 20 percent more efficient. Furthermore, moisture elimination is a main factor in the control of biological contamination, particularly for meat and poultry. Retailers must simultaneously consider the energy efficient rating (EER) and the moisture removal efficiency (MRE). Whereas the former measures the kilowatt cost per hour to maintain temperature, the latter addresses the amount of condensate per kilowatt hour.[21]

Importantly, refrigerators and cooking equipment only realize energy savings when installations are maintained properly. Store-level operations must, for example, regularly clean evaporator coils and condensers to ensure fuel efficiency and avoid wear on compressors. Refrigerators should also be maintained and properly loaded to ensure quick access to products without affecting the flow of air throughout the units. When proper maintenance is part of the energy, the life cycle savings of commercial products can be realized.[22]

The final aspect of energy conservation for food retailing concerns the amount of waste produced. These costs are curtailed by recycling, reusing, donating, and composting materials. Recycling centers, for example, pay retailers for noncontaminated paper, glass, and aluminum. By contrast, retailers lower their costs by reusing cardboard, paper, and plastic. They can also lower overall costs by donating food, used uniforms, furniture, and appliances to the needy. Finally, retailers recognize the financial rewards associated with composting.

---

[17] Stys, Brian (2008), "Green Restaurants: Commercial Kitchens Face Unique Challenges as well as Opportunities for Saving Energy and Materials," *Environmental Design & Construction*, 11 (5), 64.

[18] Wilson, Marianne (2007), "Energy Management: Changes in Refrigerants and Energy Procurement Are Major Concerns," *Chain Store Age*, 83 (5), 164–166.

[19] *Nation's Restaurant News* (2003), "Electric End Use Cools off Proper Refrigeration Improves Energy Efficiency in Quick-Serve Restaurants," *Nation's Restaurant News*, 2 (2 supplement), 18.

[20] Wilson, Marianne (2007), "Energy Management: Changes in Refrigerants and Energy Procurement Are Major Concerns," *Chain Store Age*, 83 (5), 164–166.

[21] Jackson, Dusty (2007), "Upping Energy Efficiency Through Dehumidification," *Chain Store Age*, 82 (11), 92.

[22] Stys, Brian (2008), "Green Restaurants: Commercial Kitchens Face Unique Challenges as well as Opportunities for Saving Energy and Materials," *Environmental Design & Construction*, 11 (5), 64.

OFFICES AND ADMINISTRATIVE BUILDINGS

Office buildings include locations used for general office space, professional offices, and administrative offices. Twenty-nine percent of the energy used in these locations is associated with electricity for lighting, and another 16 percent is associated with office equipment. They also rely on natural gas and electricity for space heating. Together, space heating fuels account for 25 percent of energy use in office buildings.

Efforts to control energy expenditures for commercial offices include *green design* and *office equipment* operations. Green design refers to the development and maintenance of buildings that are sensitive to the environment, resource and energy consumption, the quality of the work setting, cost effectiveness, and the world at large.[23] In the United States, the nonprofit Green Building Council (USGBC) has established the leadership in energy and environmental design (LEED) rating system. LEED includes 34 performance criteria associated with sustainable sites, water efficiency, energy and atmosphere, materials and resources, indoor environmental quality, and innovation and design processes. Four levels of certification (certified, silver, gold, and platinum) correspond to increasingly higher levels of sustainability of a building.

The decision whether to incorporate LEED criteria into buildings is contingent on the cost effectiveness of the sustainability-based enhancements. Regrettably, there is limited research on the costs incurred with green design. The green premium refers to the additional expenditures associated with green design. Green design decisions are often not priced out in comparison to nongreen ones, and the relative newness of green technologies results in conservative cost estimates by designers, architects, and their clients. The benefits of green design include cost savings from reduced energy, water, and waste as well as lower operating and maintenance costs. In addition, green design yields enhanced occupant productivity and health. Furthermore, green buildings are 25 to 30 percent more energy efficient and lower peak energy consumption.

The second facet of energy savings most associated with office buildings is the office equipment. This equipment includes personal computers, facsimile machines, photocopiers, telephones, and other instruments designed to facilitate office operations. In 2006, the International Sustainable Development Foundation established the *Green Electronics Council* (GEC) to support the effective design, manufacture, use, and recovery of electronic products. GEC works in conjunction with the electronics industry to recognize and reward environmentally sensitive products. GEC has established the *Electronics Products Environmental Assessment Tool* (EPEAT) to identify electronics that are environmentally preferable. The EPEAT sourcing criteria call for the reduction or the elimination of environmentally sensitive materials (e.g., cadmium and mercury), the use of recycled content, and the implementation of design features that enable recycling at the end of a product's life. Operational criteria include energy conservation concerns (e.g., *Energy Star*), packaging, and upgradeability of products. Products are also evaluated based on corporate environmental performance and whether the corporation has implemented a return policy for obsolete products.[24]

---

[23] Kats, Greg, Leon Alevantis, Adam Berman, Evan Mills, and Jeff Perlman (2003), "The Costs and Financial Benefits of Green Buildings," *California Sustainable Building Task Force*.

[24] Air Pollution Consultant (2007), "Environmental Benefits of Buying Green Computers," *Air Pollution Consultant*, 17 (6), 1.1–1.4.

A-5

Energy Consumption in the Transportation Sector

INTRODUCTION: TRANSPORTATION SECTOR CONTRIBUTORS TO CARBON EMISSIONS

This appendix offers an overview of the role of transportation in global energy consumption. We initially describe the use of energy associated with transportation, and we subsequently outline the use of energy for passenger and freight transportation. In the process, we discuss efforts to enhance the fuel efficiency of alternative modes of transportation. We begin with a description of personal modes of transportation that dominate fuel consumption in this macroeconomic sector. We subsequently describe current and planned levels of mass transit. We also outline energy consumption associated with freight transportation.

The transportation sector accounts for 28 percent of worldwide energy consumption.[1] The United States is the largest transportation energy consumer (26 quadrillion BTU), followed by Europe (19 quadrillion BTU) and China (13 quadrillion BTU). Together, these three areas account for 55 percent of transportation energy consumption. Globally, the transportation sector accounts for 23 percent of total energy-related carbon emissions. Emissions from this sector have increased at a faster rate than any other sector, with emissions doubling since 1970. The increase in carbon emissions correlates with the increase in energy consumption and now stands at more than 7.0 gigatons per year. At 83.2 percent, road travel—for freight and passengers—is the largest user of energy in the transportation sector, and it is the main contributor to increased transportation energy use. Since 1990, energy consumption via other modes of transportation has increased by 13 percent, yet the increase in energy use for road travel over the same period is 41 percent.

Geographic location is significantly associated with the increase in demand for energy. Among Organisation for Economic Cooperation and Development (OECD) nations, the increase in demand for energy use since 1990 has been 30 percent, whereas the increase outside of the OECD has been more than 55 percent. Of the projected 1.4 percent average annual increase in transportation energy consumption between 2012 and 2040, the vast majority (94 percent) of the growth in transportation energy use is expected to come from developing, non-OECD countries.[2] The rapid growth of the economy in several nations has resulted in increased personal income that is associated with higher vehicle ownership. In addition, the rise in income increases the need for freight transportation. The Chinese economy illustrates some of these trends. Although 20 years ago there were virtually no private cars in China, now it is the largest car market in the world, selling 21.1 million passenger cars in 2015 alone.[3] The Chinese began aggressively promoting consumption as a way to balance its export-driven economy in 2000, and the purchase of automobiles continues to be strongly encouraged today.

Interestingly, the Chinese consumer has purchased many types of vehicles, including cars, sport utility vehicles, and pickup trucks. Both government incentives

---

[1] www.ipcc.ch/pdf/assessment-report/ar5/wg3/ipcc_wg3_ar5_chapter8.pdf (February 23, 2017).

[2] www.eia.gov/outlooks/ieo/exec_summ.cfm (February 23, 2017).

[3] http://www.forbes.com/sites/tychodefeijter/2016/05/16/five-things-you-need-to -know-about-the-chinese-car-market/#6ef483a41e73 (February 23, 2017)

and consumer preferences prompt ownership of larger vehicles. Many cities ban cars with engines smaller than 1 liter from entering their downtowns because such cars are typically old and dirty. Some municipalities ban smaller cars from expressways, as they claim these cars endanger their owners when traveling at high speed. Consumer preferences also are associated with bigger vehicles. Because many car owners want to appear wealthy enough to have a chauffeur, Chinese autos tend to be slightly longer than their American counterparts. Consequently, Volkswagen, Audi, Honda, and General Motors have been successful in marketing larger cars, passenger vans, and sports utility vehicles. China is Buick's biggest market, where the company's sales outpace its U.S. sales 8 to 1[4].

Although efforts to economize on the use of energy require consideration of energy use and carbon emissions across the globe, complete data for the transportation sector are not currently available. As the Chinese example illustrates, there is a strong rate of change in consumption habits in emerging economies. Nevertheless, comprehensive data addressing all modes of transportation (other than international air travel) are only available for the 18 countries affiliated with the International Energy Agency. These countries include Australia, Austria, Canada, Denmark, Finland, France, Germany, Greece, Ireland, Italy, Japan, Netherlands, New Zealand, Norway, Sweden, Switzerland, United Kingdom, and the United States.

The transportation sector includes energy associated with *passenger* travel and *freight* travel. Although similar technologies are associated with both transportation needs, the opportunities to realize energy savings vary across transportation sectors.

PERSONAL MODES OF TRANSPORTATION

In 2012, passenger travel accounted for 61 percent of total global transportation energy consumption (about 63 quadrillion BTU).[5] More than 2.1 gigatons of carbon emissions are generated through passenger travel. As Figure A5-1 indicates, light-duty vehicles account for 44 percent of global transportation energy use. Air travel accounts for an additional 11 percent, while buses, two- and three-wheel vehicles, and rail account for the remaining 6 percent. Light-duty vehicles consume more energy than all other passenger transportation combined. Further, light-weight vehicles consume more energy than freight transportation (heavy trucks, marine, and rail), which accounts for 39 percent of global transportation energy consumption.

Figure A5-2 indicates that the high percentage of auto travel is consistent across these mature economies. With the exception of Japan, auto travel accounts for at least 75 percent of passenger travel among countries analyzed by the International Energy Agency (IEA). Across countries in the analysis, auto travel accounted for 82 percent of passenger kilometers in 1990 as well as in 2005. Since 1990, per capita increases in car passenger travel have increased on average 1.1 percent per year, and air travel has increased by 2.7 percent per year. Although there have

[4] www.usatoday.com/story/money/cars/2016/10/18/gms-buick-see-sales-soar----because-china/92363996/ (February 23, 2017).

[5] www.eia.gov/outlooks/ieo/pdf/transportation.pdf (February 23, 2017).

FIGURE A5-1

Passenger transport energy use by mode, USEIA[6]

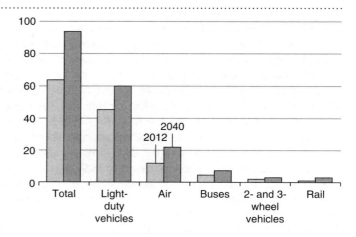

FIGURE A5-2

Share of total passenger travel by mode[7]

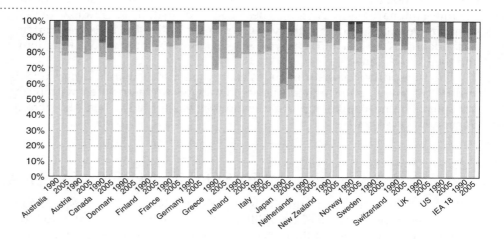

been increases in the amounts of auto travel, these improvements have occurred simultaneously with increases in auto efficiency. Nevertheless, higher passenger transport energy use is associated with a 23 percent increase in auto-related carbon emissions since 1990. Carbon emissions are greatest in Australia, United States, and Canada where vehicles are larger, heavier, and travel distances are longer. In contrast, countries such as the Netherlands and Japan have higher population densities and lower levels of travel per capita.

The amount of energy used has been increasing, yet the energy use per passenger kilometer is declining. People are traveling more, but technology has enabled individual modes of transportation to run more fuel efficiently. *Car ownership* similarly influences energy consumption. In most IEA countries, the percentage of ownership has increased over the past 15 years, and this increased car ownership generally is associated with higher per capita car energy consumption. *Car*

---

[6] www.eia.gov/outlooks/ieo/pdf/transportation.pdf (February 23, 2017).

[7] International Energy Agency (2008), *Tracking Industrial Energy Efficiency and CO2 Emissions*, Paris, France: OECD/IEA.

usage refers to the distance traveled by each car. Car usage has fallen as more households increasingly own more than one car. When homes own multiple cars, journeys are shared between cars, and travel per car declines. Car ownership and usage provide the total distance traveled per capita. In most IEA countries, reductions in the fuel intensity of cars were not sufficient to offset the increases in car ownership and car use. Thus, car energy use per capita increased in most IEA countries. The exceptions to this were Canada, Finland, Germany, Norway, and the United Kingdom.[8]

Efforts to reduce emissions in the transportation sector must recognize that changing transportation energy use takes time.[9] For example, autos and light trucks ordinarily last about 15 years, whereas new aircraft are typically in use for 20 to 35 years. Passenger cars are completely redesigned approximately every eight years, but the essential technologies are in place three years prior to bringing the car to market. New technologies, therefore, often take up to 10 years to be implemented fully into production. In addition, retail marketing must make new fuel technology (e.g., low sulfur diesel fuel) available across a market.

Given that auto-related usage continues to dominate the transportation sector, one must consider ways to reduce consumption. These include changes in personal transportation devices and increased use of mass transit. Personal, motorized modes include diesel, electric, and enhanced gasoline technologies. Other technologies (e.g., natural gas and hydrogen fuel cells) have been proposed as alternatives to gasoline, but these concepts are not currently available at a price level that would capture appreciable market share. The percentage of each diesel, gasoline, and hybrid technology varies markedly from market to market. Although the North American market remains a gasoline market, diesel engines have the dominant market share in Europe.[10] Consider first the use of diesel engines.

Diesel

The diesel engine was invented by Rudolph Diesel in the 1880s as an alternative to steam and gasoline engines.[11] The gasoline and diesel engines developed over time, but for many years, the choice between diesel and gasoline technology was a simple decision. While the diesel engines of 20 years ago offered better fuel efficiency than gasoline engines, these engines produced significant amounts of soot. In addition, these engines were noisy and offered lower pick-up relative to gasoline engines.

In order to appreciate the advantages of diesel over gasoline, it is valuable to examine the basic operation of each motor. Both gasoline and diesel engines are internal combustion devices, and both engines use the standard piston-based cylinder engine block. The combustion process is different for the two engines.

---

[8] International Energy Agency (2008), *Tracking Industrial Energy Efficiency and CO2 Emissions*, Paris, France: OECD/IEA.

[9] Greene, David L., and Andreas Schafer (2003), "Reducing Green Gas Emissions for U.S. Transportation," *Pew Center on Global Climate Change*.

[10] arstechnica.com/cars/2015/10/diesel-how-it-changed-europe-and-how-europe-might -change-back/ (February 23, 2017).

[11] www.turbotraining.com/fliers/MotorArticle.pdf (February 23, 2017).

In a gasoline version, the engine intakes a mixture of gas and air, compresses it, and then ignites the mixture via a spark plug. In diesel motors, no spark plug is required since the fuel is ignited by the high temperature generated during compression. Diesel fuel is a heavier and less volatile mixture of hydrocarbons than gasoline and, therefore, offers more energy per gallon than gasoline. Diesel engines have higher compression ratios, more rapid combustion, and leaner operations. Consequently, diesel engines offer greater thermodynamic efficiency and lower fuel consumption than gasoline engines.[12]

Diesel technology has changed dramatically over the past 15 years, and the changes make these new vehicles viable alternatives to gasoline engines. The first issue with diesel has been the high levels of sulfur produced by the engines. The U.S. EPA mandates of 2006 required oil refiners to produce a clean diesel fuel with sulfur concentrations no greater than 15 parts per billion. This mandate reflects a 98 percent improvement over 1970s era diesel output. The result is substantially lower levels of sulfur dioxide pollutants, and lower sulfur in the air means less acid rain and better engine performance.[13] The exhaust systems also eliminate sulfur and other harmful nitrogen oxide compounds.

A second concern with diesel has been the soot produced by these engines. Diesel soot is *particulate matter*, a mixture of solid and liquid material made up of carbon particles, hydrocarbons, and inorganic material.[14] The American Lung Association reports that short-term increases in exposure to particulate matter have been linked to death from respiratory and cardiovascular causes, including strokes, increased numbers of heart attacks, inflammation of lung tissue, and aggravated asthma attacks. Long-term exposure has been associated with increased hospitalization for asthma, stunted lung function growth in young people, damage to the airways of the lungs, an increased risk of strokes and heart attacks, an increased risk of dying from lung cancer, and a greater risk of death from cardiovascular disease.[15] The U.S. EPA estimates that over 4700 premature deaths occur each year in just nine cities analyzed (Detroit, Los Angeles, Philadelphia, Pittsburgh, St. Louis, Boston, Phoenix, Seattle, and San Jose).[16] The exhaust systems on new diesel motors ensure that limited levels of soot enter the atmosphere. Initially, the exhaust runs through a diesel oxidation catalyst that minimizes hydrocarbons and carbon monoxide. In the next phase, a urea-based solution is sprayed on to the exhaust flow. The hot exhaust air transforms the urea into ammonia and mixes with nitrogen oxides in the selective catalytic reduction (SCR) where the mixture converts to water vapor and harmless nitrogen gas.

One of the advantages offered to diesel is the potential to refine the fuel from a variety of sources. The fuel can be derived from crude oil, but it can also be processed from biowaste. Biodiesel is made through a chemical process in which

---

[12] Sullivan, J. L., et al. (2004), "CO2 Emission Benefit of Diesel (versus Gasoline) Powered Vehicles," *Environmental Science and Technology*, 38 (14), 3217–3223.

[13] Twigg, Martyn V. (2007), "Progress and Future Challenges in Controlling Automotive Exhaust Gas Emissions," *Applied Catalysis B: Environmental* 70 (1), 2–15.

[14] www.dieselnet.com/tech/dpm.php (February 23, 2017).

[15] www.lung.org/our-initiatives/healthy-air/outdoor/air-pollution/particle-pollution. html (February 23, 2017).

[16] Post, Ellen, Kristina Watts, Ed Al-Hussainy, and Emily Neubig (2005), "Particulate Matter Health Risk Assessment for Selected Urban Areas," *U.S. Environmental Protection Agency*.

fat or vegetable oil is separated into methyl esters (biodiesel) and glycerin (a by-product used in soaps and other products). In North America, most biodiesel is made from soybean oil, but in Europe, rapeseed (canola) oil is the most common source. Biodiesel is biodegradable, nontoxic fuel that is essentially free of sulfur and aromatics.[17] The performance advantages of diesel engines are also noteworthy. The higher compression ratios of these motors mean more energy is derived from the air/fuel combination, and the car also enjoys relatively better power than a gasoline engine. Although the higher compression ratio means that engines require heavier crankshafts and connecting rods, the stronger design and the low coefficient of friction result in engines that last longer. It is not uncommon to see these engines operating for well over 200,000 miles.

The new fuel systems, the enhanced exhaust mechanisms, the enhanced fuel injection operations, and the inherent physical advantages have resulted in renaissance for this engine. The initial market for the diesel has been Western Europe. In 2006, diesel engines outsold gasoline engines for the first time in this region. The diesel engine accounted for less than 25 percent of auto sales in 1998, but this market share doubled in less than a decade. Consequently, most European, Japanese, and North American auto producers offer multiple diesel options in Europe, and these new diesel designs are entering into many other markets.

The recent VW scandal involving diesel engines, however, has resulted in a significant reduction in North American diesel sales.[18] VW admitted that 11 million of its vehicles were equipped with software designed to cheat on emissions tests.[19] Nonetheless, manufacturers such as BMW are touting the ecological (low carbon emissions) value of their products as well as the fuel efficiency.

Electric vehicles

Electric vehicles refer to a variety of cars that use electricity to generate movement. These include hybrid electric vehicles, plug-in hybrids, and all electric vehicles. Hybrid electric vehicles run on conventional fuels and an electric motor that uses energy stored in a battery. Regenerative braking and the internal combustion engine charge the battery. Hybrid technology has drawn substantial attention in North America despite modest sales levels. Hybrids account for about 3 percent of the market.[20] Over 4 million hybrid cars have been sold in the United States, making the United States the second largest hybrid market behind Japan.[21] Toyota boasts that 10 percent of its sales are associated with hybrids, but most other manufacturers do not report significant levels of hybrid sales. Estimates indicate, however that hybrid sales will account for 14 percent of the worldwide market for automobiles by 2020.[22]

[17] www.consumerenergycenter.org/transportation/afvs/biodiesel.html (February 23, 2017).

[18] www.wsj.com/articles/diesel-car-sales-slow-significantly-1455825746 (February 27, 2017).

[19] www.nytimes.com/interactive/2015/business/international/vw-diesel-emissions-scandal-explained.html (February 27, 2017).

[20] www.usatoday.com/story/money/cars/2014/06/09/hybrid-cars-market-share-polk/10238155/ (February 23, 2017).

[21] www.hybridcars.com/americans-buy-their-four-millionth-hybrid-car/ (February 23, 2017).

[22] Dolan, Matthew (2009), "Gas Engines Get Upgrade in Challenge to Hybrids," *Wall Street Journal*, January 14, B1.

In order to understand the advantages of hybrid vehicles, it is valuable to examine the manner by which these engines convert and store energy. Hybrid technology includes the standard hybrid engine and the plug-in hybrid. Figure A5-3 illustrates how the gasoline engine powers the wheels and provides energy that is stored in the hybrid batteries. The hybrid system adds two pieces of equipment—an electric motor and fuel cells. At the point of ignition, the engine sends energy to the electric motor and drivetrain. The electric motor sends this energy to the fuel cells. During acceleration, energy is provided to the drivetrain via the electric motor and gas engine. When the vehicle is cruising, the gasoline engine is not in operation, and energy is provided by the fuel cells. Finally, the hybrid engine has the ability to capture the energy from the operation of the brakes and store this energy in the fuel cells.[23]

The standard hybrid offers some advantages and disadvantages relative to the gasoline engines. First, the hybrid uses a much smaller engine than the typical gasoline engine. Larger engines require more fuel to carry them, limit acceleration, and use more energy while idling. The lighter engine is complemented with lighter materials throughout the car, and these lighter materials also reduce energy needs. In addition, the plug-ins take advantage of advanced aerodynamics and low-rolling resistance tires that contribute to fuel efficiency.[24]

The plug-in hybrid has the advantages of the hybrid but also enables the owner to obtain electricity from a power outlet rather than the gasoline engine. The use of the power outlet enables the *charged* hybrid to run for some period of time without using gasoline. For example, the VolvoS90 PHEV plug-in uses a 9.2 kilowatt-hour lithium-ion battery that enable the vehicle to travel up to 35 miles on battery power alone.[25] Plug-in technology is in its infancy, but the fuel efficiency advantages of this technology are noteworthy.

The all electric vehicles use a battery to store the electric energy that powers the motor. These batteries are charged by plugging the vehicle into an electric power source. At the end of 2016, industry records indicated that over one-half million electric cars had been sold in the US market.[26]

Potential buyers of electric vehicles compare the advantages and disadvantages relative to other technologies. Electric vehicles more efficiently convert energy to power at the wheels, and they offer quieter smoother operations. They do not emit pollutants and rely on domestic energy sources. These benefits stand in contrast to the limited range and recharging times endemic to many electric cars.[27]

Enhanced Gasoline

Consumers interested in enhancing fuel efficiency do not necessarily need to move away from gasoline engines. Fuel efficiency can economically be enhanced by buying smaller engine vehicles, using ethanol, and purchasing cars with new

---

[23] auto.howstuffworks.com/hybrid-car.htm (February 23, 2017).

[24] auto.howstuffworks.com/hybrid-car4.htm (February 23, 2017).

[25] www.hybridcars.com/a-dozen-new-plug-in-hybrids-were-looking-forward-to-this -year/ (February 23, 2017).

[26] https://www.recode.net/2016/12/21/14041112/electric-vehicles-report-2016 (May 10. 2017).

[27] https://www.fueleconomy.gov/feg/evtech.shtml (May 10, 2017)

fuel injection systems. Given that government average fuel economy requirements are increasing, most manufacturers are bringing new fuel-efficient gasoline-based cars to market.

A related option is to consider the form of gasoline used by new vehicles. Flex-fuel cars are designed to run on gasoline or a mixture of gasoline and ethanol.[28] Ethanol is a renewable fuel that comes from agricultural feedstocks. Using ethanol results in less pollution and reduces smog-forming emissions by as much as 50 percent relative to gasoline.[29] Despite the limits on emissions, ethanol has a few limitations. Using corn for fuel rather than food reduces the supply of food without complementary increases in the supply of energy. For example, the United States used 40 percent of its 2013 corn harvest to produce ethanol fuel.[30] In some markets, the price of ethanol is greater than gasoline, and it is only widely available in the Midwestern United States. Finally, the mixture of gasoline and ethanol contains less energy than a gallon of gas. Consequently, these engines have 20 to 30 percent lower fuel efficiency when operated using ethanol.

Auto manufacturers are also making improvements in gasoline engines to make them more fuel efficient.[31] Ford Motor Co. introduced an Ecoboost direct-injection technology that offers greater performance and a 20 percent increase in fuel economy over comparable traditional engines. In 2016, sales of the Ford F150 Ecoboost reached 1 million units, and Ford estimates that the F150 Ecoboost will collectively save its owners 110 million gallons in gasoline annually.[32] Ford claims that the premium for Ecoboost—a price Ford has not disclosed—is a better value than a hybrid or a diesel. General Motors is also using new direct-injection engines in about 10 percent of its global production.

One of the simplest and most cost-efficient means by which to save energy in the auto sector is the education of drivers. Although many U.S. state programs instruct new drivers about fuel efficiency, there is substantial degradation of fuel efficiency over time.[33] Table A5-1 outlines a number of strategies that drivers can implement to reduce the amount of gasoline used by their vehicles.

Importantly, the marketing efforts of auto manufacturers and auto dealers and the efforts of government can be focused on the continuous education of drivers regarding fuel efficiency. Estimates developed in the 1980s indicate that a 10 percent savings in fuel efficiency can be realized through proper vehicle

---

[28] Ahn, Kyung-ho, Anna G. Stefanopoulou, and Mrdjan Jankovic (2008), "Estimation of Ethanol Content in Flex-Fuel Vehicles Using an Exhaust Gas Oxygen Sensor: Model, Tuning and Sensitivity," In ASME 2008 Dynamic Systems and Control Conference, pp. 947–954. American Society of Mechanical Engineers.

[29] www.pacificethanol.net/resources/air-quality-ethanol-a-clear-net-benefit (February 23, 2017).

[30] www.forbes.com/sites/jamesconca/2014/04/20/its-final-corn-ethanol-is-of-no -use/#2eb950b32ca2 (February 23, 2017).

[31] Dolan, Matthew (2009), "Gas Engines Get Upgrade in Challenge to Hybrids," *Wall Street Journal*, January 14, B1.

[32] media.ford.com/content/fordmedia/fna/us/en/news/2016/06/29/ford-f-150-ecoboost -hits-1-million-sales--technology-can-save-cu.html (February 23, 2017).

[33] Greene, David L. (1986) "Driver Energy Conservation Awareness Training: Review and Recommendations for aNational Program," ORNL/TM-9897, Oak Ridge National Laboratory, Oak Ridge, TN.

TABLE A5-1.
Efficient Automobile
Operations[34]

Vehicle Operations

a. Observe the speed limit and maintain a steady pace. Excessive speed is inefficient and requires more energy for stopping.

b. Extend one's vision 10 to 12 seconds down the road, and anticipate stops as far ahead as possible.

c. Avoid tailgating as it reduces your chances to alter your path in an emergency.

d. Adjust driving habits to changing road conditions.

e. Use air conditioning at higher speeds and keep the windows closed. Avoid air conditioner use at lower speeds.

f. Instead of heavy braking, take advantage of rolling resistance to help slow down. This technique saves a lot of fuel.

g. Before turning off ignition, turn off all power-consuming accessories. This action minimizes engine load during startup.

h. Avoid revving the engine just before turning off the ignition as its costs extra fuel and can cause engine damage.

i. Limit idling time to 30 seconds, but restarting the engine within 8 to 10 minutes causes little engine wear.

j. Avoid unnecessary steering wheel movement as sideward movements cause fuel-consuming drag.

k. Slowly accelerate on slippery pavement and gravel roads.

l. Avoid quick starts and unnecessary braking.

Vehicle Maintenance

a. Change oil regularly as dirty oil increases friction and engine wear.

b. When possible, use multiviscosity motor oil.

c. Regularly check points and plugs.

d. Upon fill-up, check the engine oil, coolant, transmission fluid, and battery levels.

e. Maintain proper wheel alignment.

f. Maintain tires at maximum pressure, and check pressure when tires are cold.

g. Reduce the engine's idling speed.

h. Regularly replace air and fuel filters.

i. Adjust the automatic choke for proper operation.

j. Monitor the positive crankcase ventilation (PCV) valve regularly.

k. Assess carburetor, fuel pump, gas line, and gas tank for fuel leaks.

l. Regularly lubricate the axle and wheel bearings.

Trip Planning

a. Make sure your vehicle is safe and economically road ready for long trips.

b. Consolidate short trips to avoid as many cold starts as possible.

c. Record and monitor gas mileage.

d. Avoid idling by starting the engine when actually ready to go.

e. Whenever possible, use the telephone rather than making a trip.

f. Plan routes to avoid traffic congestion.

g. Carpool. Multiple parties in the car mean fewer auto trips.

h. Carry as little extra weight as possible in auto's trunk.

i. Park in the first reasonable parking place available.

---

[34] doee.dc.gov/service/fuel-saving-tips-drivers (February 23, 2017).

Vehicle Choice
a. Select a car with a high rear axle ratio and overdrive transmission.
b. Avoid permanent roof racks and wide-tread tires.
c. Consider radial tires.
d. If more than one car is available, use the most economical one as much as possible.
e. Avoid power-consuming accessories.
f. Consider a diesel-powered or an electric hybrid car.
g. Choose a streamlined car with a small frontal area.
h. Use automatic speed control.
Driver Attitude
a. Always consider fuel economy when driving, and drive for fuel economy.
b. Avoid driving when angry or upset.
c. Use public transportation whenever possible.
d. Use a bike or walk for short distances.

operations, selection, and maintenance.[35] Despite recognition of the merits of conservation, large scale efforts at continuing driver education have been absent in many markets.

Another means that drivers can use to enhance fuel efficiency is through global positioning systems (GPS). Drivers equipped with GPS systems input an address and let the GPS systems sketch the route. Although these systems can draw the most efficient route, there is tremendous variability in their operations and routing procedures. Nevertheless, GPS saves energy by indicating wrong turns and highlighting points of interest to consumers.

Another means for saving energy in the auto industry is through ride-sharing and carpool programs. Although there have been appreciable efforts to raise the number of shared rides, more than 10 trillion seats remain empty in car trips, and the average number of passengers per car trip marginally exceeds one passenger. One program that increases auto occupancy is high occupancy vehicle (HOV) lanes. Several states have implemented these HOV on freeways to reduce people-hours of travel without significantly increasing vehicle-hours of travel.

MASS TRANSIT

The use of oil for transportation can be reduced not only through personal modes but also through mass transportation systems. Improvements to mass transit systems are rarely due to progress in one mode of transportation but often involve consideration of the connecting points among alternative transportation modes. Progress, therefore, is not solely due to the advent of new technology. The effectiveness and the performance of these systems are measured in passengers

---

[35] Greene, David L. (1986) "Driver Energy Conservation Awareness Training: Review and Recommendations for aNational Program," ORNL/TM-9897, Oak Ridge National Laboratory, Oak Ridge, TN.

carried, ridership growth, travel speeds, and land development effects.[36] It can take appreciable amounts of time to integrate new technologies into transportation grids. In the following section, we underscore trends in air, bus, and rail technology that have the potential to reduce carbon emissions in the transportation sector. Consider first air transportation.

Air Travel

A recent study from the Intergovernmental Panel on Climate Change (IPCC) estimates that the airline industry accounts for 2 percent of man-made carbon emissions.[37] In the United States, air travel has increased at an average annual rate of more than 5 percent per year since 1970. The passenger miles per gallon for commercial air travel, however, has increased by 150 percent since 1975. The Airbus A320, for instance, can get 77 miles (123.9 kilometers) per gallon (3.8 liters) per person.[38] This increase is primarily due to energy efficiency improvements, but it is also associated with increased occupancy rates. Although local, federal, and international entities pressure the aviation industry to enhance fuel efficiency, most efficiency enhancements have been driven by profit motives rather than regulation.[39]

Peculiarities of air travel contribute to the emissions. Over 90 percent of the exhaust emitted from aircraft is in the form of oxygen or nitrogen. About 7 percent of the exhaust is composed of CO_2 and H_2O, and another 0.5 percent is composed of NO_x, HC, CO, SO_x, other trace chemical species, and carbon-based soot particulates. The combination of these gases is estimated to be a factor of more than 1.5 times that of carbon dioxide alone. The majority of aircraft emissions are injected into the upper troposphere and lower stratosphere at altitudes ranging from 5 to 8 miles above Earth. Consequently, the influence of burning fossil fuels at these altitudes is approximately double that due to burning the same fuels at ground level. Aircraft emissions can impact cloud formation and, therefore, have an indirect effect on climate in addition to the direct effect.[40]

Reductions in climate effects require consideration of the *technological performance* of aircraft as well as the *operational activities*. New technologies from manufacturers have reduced emissions and achieved the largest reductions in energy intensity of any transportation system. These include enhanced engine designs, aerodynamic efficiencies, and structural efficiencies.[41] For example,

---

[36] Zimmerman, Samuel, and Herbert Levinson (2006), "The Facts About BRT," *Planning*, 72 (5), 34–35.

[37] www.boeing.com/resources/boeingdotcom/principles/environment/pdf/2016 _environment_report.pdf (February 23, 2017).

[38] www.wsj.com/articles/SB10001424052748704901104575423261677748380 (February 27, 2017).

[39] Lee, J. J., S. P. Lukachko, I. A. Waitz, and A. Schafer (2001), "Historical and Future Trends in Aircraft Performance, Cost and Emissions," *Annual Review of Energy and the Environment*, 26, 167–200.

[40] www.ipcc.ch/pdf/assessment-report/ar5/wg3/ipcc_wg3_ar5_chapter8.pdf (February 27, 2017).

[41] Lee, J. J., S. P. Lukachko, I. A. Waitz, and A. Schafer (2001), "Historical and Future Trends in Aircraft Performance, Cost and Emissions," *Annual Review of Energy and the Environment*, 26, 167–200.

FIGURE A5-3
Boeing 787 Dreamliner[42]

Boeing's 787 Dreamliner incorporates new engines, increased use of lightweight composite materials, and modern aerodynamics that yield improvements in fuel use and reductions in carbon dioxide emissions.[43]

Operational activities also contribute to an aircraft's carbon emissions. Airlines have increased the number of seats on each plane by over 35 percent since 1950, and they have increased the load factor or percentage of occupancy by 15 percent.[44] In fact, commercial airlines are experiencing historically high load factors, upward of 80 percent. When more people are on a flight, the relative cost of travel is lowered.

Airlines and airports can enhance efficiency by reducing the amount of time that planes are idling on the ground or in holding patterns in the air. The International Air Transport Association (IATA) estimates that air traffic management enhancements could improve fuel efficiency and reduce carbon emissions substantially.[45] Boeing has developed a tailored arrival concept that increases airplane arrival efficiency through continuous versus step-down descent that lowers fuel usage, noise, and emissions.[46] Airlines and airports also benefit from quick turnaround at the gate. Southwest Airlines, for example, uses quick turnaround at the airport terminal as a strategic competitive advantage. Quick turnaround lowers operational costs and raises customer satisfaction.[47]

Enhancements in technology and operations are essential to the future of air travel. Historically, air transportation growth (5.5 percent per year) has outpaced reductions in energy consumption (3.5 percent per year), and research suggests that this trend will continue into the foreseeable future.[48]

[42] www.boeing.com/aboutus/environment/environmental_report/media/pdf/boeing-2008-environment-report.pdf (February 27, 2017).

[43] www.aerospace-technology.com/projects/boeing-787-10-dreamliner/ (February 27, 2017).

[44] Corridore, Jim (2006), "Cleared for Take-off," *Businessweek Online*, June 13.

[45] www.iata.org/Pages/air-traffic-management.aspx (February 27, 2017).

[46] *Machine Design* (2008), "Tailored Arrivals," 80(17), 127.

[47] Hoffer Gittell, Jody (2005), *The Southwest Airlines Way: The Power of Relationships for Superior Performance*, McGraw-Hill Professional.

[48] Lee, J. J., S. P. Lukachko, I. A. Waitz, and A. Schafer (2001), "Historical and Future Trends in Aircraft Performance, Cost and Emissions," *Annual Review of Energy and the Environment*, 26, 167–200.

High-Speed Train

Since the introduction of the Shinkansen high-speed train service between Tokyo and Osaka, Japan, in 1964, the high-speed train (HST) has increasingly become a vibrant part of transportation in many parts of the globe.[49] High-speed trains refers to a family of technologies that provide high-capacity, frequent railway services achieving an average speed of over 200 kilometers per hour (124 miles per hour).[50]

HSTs have been widely used in Asia and Europe but have also been proposed or implemented in the Middle East as well as South and North America. The advent of HST has brought to consideration trade-offs between compatibility and speed. The original Shinkansen HST achieved a speed of more than 200 kilometers per hour, but it required special tracks due to the narrow design of the light rail system. Other systems developed since the Shinkansen have utilized existing track to varying degrees. The ability to use existing track results in lowered costs of implementation but limits the returns from the HST operations.

As we discussed earlier in this section, cost-benefit analysis of a mode of transportation is context specific and requires consideration of the interface between modes of transportation. Nevertheless, there are some notable benefits associated with HST. Since introduction, these systems have been designed to increase capacity. In the short term, the introduction of another mode of transportation increases the opportunities to travel. The costs of alternative reasonable travel modes and travel conditions influence long-term term capacity and acceptance of HST.

A second notable advantage is the reduced travel time relative to other rail systems. The Shinkansen line reduced rail travel between Osaka and Japan to 2-1/2 hours from 7 hours.[51] HST draws travelers from trains, but it also gains travelers from air and car travel. For example, an analysis of the potential of the HST to free runway capacity at London Heathrow indicates that the HST could lead to travel time savings on 10 routes currently served from the airport.[52] If the airport became a rail station, the substitution of HST for air travel would eliminate about 20 percent of its Heathrow's runway capacity

The third important benefit of HST is the safety record of these trains systems. In most markets, these trains offer substantially greater safety records than any alternative mode of transportation. Japan's Shinkansen HST, for example, has not has had a passenger fatality over the 50 years of operation.[53] Although Japan is noted for the high incidence of earthquakes, these catastrophes have infrequently lead to derailments and have never had resulted in fatalities.

---

[49] Miura, Shigeru, Takai, Hideyuki, Uchida Masao, Fukada Yasuto, (1998) "The Mechanism of Railway Tracks," Japan Railway and Transport Review, 15 (March), 38–45.

[50] Givoni, Moshe (2006), "Development and Impact of the Modern High-speed Train: A Review," *Transport Reviews*, 26 (5), 593–611.

[51] Matsuda, M. (1993), "Shinkansen: The Japanese Dream," In: J. Whitelegg, S. Hultén and F. Torbjörn (Eds.) *High Speed Trains: Fast Tracks to the Future*, (Hawes, North Yorkshire: Leading Edge), 111–120.

[52] Givoni, Moshe (2005) *Aircraft and High Speed Train Substitution: The Case for Airline and Railway Integration*. PhD thesis, University College London.

[53] https://www.japantoday.com/category/kuchikomi/view/japans-shinkansen-best-in-world-at-safety-punctuality-tech-but-not-marketing (February 27, 2017).

Although there are substantial benefits to HST, there are some notable environmental outcomes.[54] Because HSTs are predominantly electric powered, emissions are related to sources used to generate the electricity, HST operations increase local air pollution, climate change, noise, and land conversion. The most harmful pollutants related are sulfur dioxide (SO_2) and nitrogen oxides (NO_x). Because the environmental influence of HST and other modes depends on infrastructure and interface to other transportation modes and services, the environmental trade-offs between HST and other modes remains unclear. The merits of HST depend on balance between the number of travelers who substitute HST for air or auto travel versus by the amount of new traffic generated by HST.

Rapid Transit

Between 1995 and 2013, public transit use has increased by 37.2 percent in the United States, a rate higher than the population growth rate, yet only 5 percent of Americans use this form of transportation.[55] One technology that has drawn substantial recent attention is *bus rapid transit* (BRT). BRT is a rubber-tired rapid transit mode that combines stations, vehicles, services, running ways, and intelligent transportation system (ITS) elements into an integrated system.[56] BRT systems and features have been implemented in South America, Europe, and Australia, and BRT systems are integrated into urban planning programs in more than 20 cities in the United States and Canada.[57]

BRT offers several benefits. First, these bus-based systems can be flexibly integrated into existing transportation routes. In congested areas, rapid bus lines can be integrated at relatively lower cost than alternative transit systems such as light rail. Second, the digital operating systems used in BRT systems provide increased service quality in terms of on-time performance and speed. For example, the BRT line on Wilshire Boulevard in Los Angeles operates at speeds that are 75 percent faster than local service.[58] The introduction of BRT systems also has been associated with increased patronage. In Brisbane, Australia, for instance, bus ridership was up 40% in the six months after the introduction of a BRT system[59].

Rapid transit system designers have also benefitted by using some of the attractive components of light rail systems throughout bus routes. Thus, BRT

[54] Givoni, Moshe (2006), "Development and Impact of the Modern High-speed Train: A Review," *Transport Reviews*, 26 (5), 593–611.

[55] www.publictransportation.org/news/facts/Pages/default.aspx (February 27, 2017); and origin-www.bloombergview.com/articles/2016-01-28/cars-are-still-beating-public-transit (February 27, 2017).

[56] Hess D., B. Taylor, and A. Yoh, (2005) "Light-Rail Lite or Cost-Effective Improvements to Bus Service? Evaluating the Costs of Implementing Bus Rapid Transit," *Journal of the Transportation Research Board*, 22–30.

[57] Levinson, Herbert S., Samuel Zimmerman, Jennifer Clinger, and C. Scott Rutherford (2002), "Bus Rapid Transit: An Overview," *Journal of Public Transportation*, 5 (2), 1–30.

[58] Hess D., B. Taylor, and A. Yoh, (2005) "Light-Rail Lite or Cost-Effective Improvements to Bus Service? Evaluating the Costs of Implementing Bus Rapid Transit," *Journal of the Transportation Research Board*, 22–30.

[59] Rathwell, Sean, and Stephen Schijns (2002), "Ottawa and Brisbane: Comparing a Mature Busway System with Its State-of-the-Art Progeny," *Journal of Public Transportation*, 5(2), 163–182.

FIGURE A5-4.
Los Angeles MTA Valley
College stop[60]

systems emphasize simple and direct routes. In addition, they emphasize the permanency of routing and ease of use. Not surprisingly, these features along with speed of transportation increase the attractiveness of BRT to consumers.[61]

Together these benefits yield lower carbon footprints for communities. The carbon footprint per capita for the bus is substantially lower than the footprint for auto travel. Each time someone elects to ride rather than drive, the footprint is lowered.

Due to the popularity of BRT, a number of applications with varying benefits have adopted this term.[62] The Orange Line in Los Angeles is a full-scale BRT because it incorporates all facets of BRT systems, including dedicated bus lanes with intelligent transportation systems, full-scale stations, low-floor/level boarding, branded vehicles, and off-vehicle ticket vending. In contrast, partial BRT systems run part of their routes in city streets and part of their routes in dedicated transit lanes. They offer most of the other amenities and efficiencies of full BRT systems. For example, the Euclid Busway in Cleveland combines in-traffic operations with single bidirectional dedicated lanes. Other rapid bus systems do not employ most BRT benefits but are primarily express buses.[63] Although they may employ intelligent transportation systems, they do not operate via dedicated traffic lanes.

The introduction of BRT must be accompanied by appropriate marketing efforts to ensure patronage.[64] These BRT systems should have a unique and

---

[60] laist.com/2007/07/27/neighborhood_pr_7.php (February 27, 2017).

[61] Carey, Graham N. (2002), "Applicability of Bus Rapid Transit to Corridors with Intermediate Levels of Transit Demand," *Journal of Public Transportation*, 5(2), 97–114.

[62] Hess D., B. Taylor, and A. Yoh, (2005) "Light-Rail Lite or Cost-Effective Improvements to Bus Service? Evaluating the Costs of Implementing Bus Rapid Transit," *Journal of the Transportation Research Board*, 22–30.

[63] www.planetizen.com/node/36406 (February 27, 2017).

[64] Zimmerman, Samuel, and Herbert Levinson (2006), "The Facts About BRT," *Planning*, 72 (5), 34–35.

FIGURE A5-5.
Orlando's LYMMO bus rapid transit[65]

consistent brand image. For example, the LYMMO system operated in downtown Orlando is a BRT system that operates within the city's LYNX transit program. The LYMMO signs use attractive and distinctive lettering that distinguishes the LYMMO system from the rest of transit operations. BRT systems should also promote rider awareness and usage through logos, color combinations, and graphics that are applied consistently to vehicles, stations, and printed materials. Thus, the Orlando LYMMO buses use distinctive colors and the LYMMO logo consistently throughout their routes. Promotional programs also should include public information, service innovation, and pricing incentives. As Figure A5-5 illustrates, Orlando's LYMMO provides information that links the BRT system to points of interest as well as other modes of transportation. In addition, the free cost of this system to consumers is emphasized throughout promotional materials.

The introduction of BRT to Orlando has reaped many benefits. The city enjoys reduced congestion and reduced parking demand in the downtown area. LYMMO has also encouraged more transit use and increased mobility and

---

[65] www.golynx.com/resources/pdf/LYNX-LYMMO-Map-December2016.pdf (February 27, 2017).

accessibility to major downtown destinations. Moreover, BRT has enhanced public perceptions of downtown Orlando and allowed for additional downtown development capacity.[66]

....

FREIGHT TRANSPORTATION

Within the transportation sector, freight accounts for 39 percent of energy consumption. Freight includes the transport of products by highway, air, rail, sea, and pipeline. Freight transport energy use was 40 quadrillion BTU in 2012, and this consumption level was 28 percent greater than the level in 2000.[67] Demand for energy for freight transportation is expected to rise 70 percent between 2010 and 2040.[68]

At 99 percent of total final energy consumption, oil is clearly the fuel of choice for moving freight. Most of this fuel is some form of diesel. Diesel fuel represents 87 percent of trucking and 88 percent of rail transport. Ships use fuel oil (59 percent) and diesel fuel (41 percent) to move products across waterways. Because the movement of freight via rail, water, and pipeline is relatively energy efficient, our analysis focuses on the highway sector.[69]

Movement of freight via highways occurs with light, medium, and heavy-duty trucks.[70] Light trucks include utility vans and step vans, whereas medium-sized trucks include walk-in trucks, city delivery trucks, school buses, and beverage delivery vehicles. Between 1990 and 2000, light truck energy use grew at a faster rate than for any other mode.[71] As Figure A5-6 shows, however, other modes of freight transportation, such as heavy-duty trucks, are expected to experience higher growth through 2040.[72] Heavy-duty vehicles include refuse trucks, dump trucks, cement trucks, and conventional semi-trailers.

Since 1975, the amount of energy required to move a ton of freight has been cut in half.[73] Enhancements in the efficiency of freight transportation are associated with engine systems, heavy-duty hybrids, parasitic losses, idle reductions, and safety considerations.[74] Consider first technological enhancements to engine systems.

---

[66] www.dot.state.fl.us/research-center/Completed_Proj/Summary_PTO/FDOT_BC137_17. pdf (February 27, 2017).

[67] www.eia.gov/outlooks/ieo/pdf/transportation.pdf (February 27, 2017).

[68] www.eia.gov/outlooks/ieo/transportation.cfm (February 27, 2017).

[69] Greene, David L., and Andreas Schafer (2003), "Reducing Green Gas Emissions for U.S. Transportation," *Pew Center on Global Climate Change*.

[70] U.S. Department of Energy (2006), "Roadmap and Technical White Paper," U.S. Department of Energy, Office of Energy Efficiency and Renewable Energy, 21CTP-0003.

[71] Davis, Stacy C., and Susan W. Diegel (2002), "Transportation Energy Data Book: Edition 22," U.S. Department of Energy, ORNL-6967.

[72] www.eia.gov/outlooks/ieo/pdf/transportation.pdf (February 27, 2017).

[73] Davis, Stacy C., and Susan W. Diegel (2002), "Transportation Energy Data Book: Edition 22," U.S. Department of Energy, ORNL-6967.

[74] U.S. Department of Energy (2006), "Roadmap and Technical White Paper," U.S. Department of Energy, Office of Energy Efficiency and Renewable Energy, 21CTP-0003.

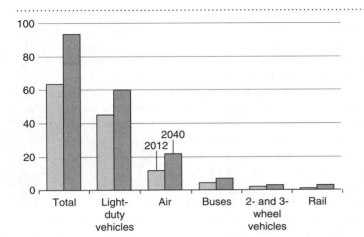

Engine systems are inextricably related to pollution, emissions, oil dependency, and safety. Twin goals of engine systems are to lower emissions and improve thermal efficiency of engine operations. Over the past two decades, NO_x and particulate matter have been decreased 85 percent and 95 percent, respectively. Today's state-of-the-art "super trucks" achieve 50 percent thermal efficiency, thus more energy is being converted to fuel output.[76]

A second initiative associated with engine operations is *hybrid electric vehicle* (HEV). In heavy-duty hybrid trucks, two power sources are combined to obtain the required power to propel the vehicle. HEVs combine the advantages of the electric motor drive and an internal combustion engine to propel the vehicle. The electric traction motor is powered from a battery pack that serves as a secondary energy storage device. The HEV vehicle also has the ability to absorb energy from the operation of the brakes and store this energy in the fuel cells. In a conventional vehicle, only 10 to 15 percent of the energy contained in gasoline is converted to traction, but the hybrid can potentially be improved to 30 to 40 percent. This increase in efficiency reduces emissions and increases fuel economy.[77] Regrettably, the development of heavy hybrid technology has not kept pace with advancements in passenger vehicles.

The operations activities associated with a truck influence the potential to reduce energy consumption. Large trucks are not only the means of transportation for drivers, but they are the homes for drivers on the road. *Parasitic energy losses* are energy losses incurred due to a number of factors that include aerodynamics, auxiliary operations, and other operations. Together these constraints account for 45 percent of the energy used by heavy trucks.[78] Improved technologies that limit

---

[75] www.eia.gov/outlooks/ieo/transportation.cfm (February 27, 2017).

[76] www.trucks.com/2016/10/31/supertruck-program-5-year-phase/ (February 27, 2017).

[77] Emadi, Ali, Kaushik Rajashekara, Sheldon S. Williamson, and Srdjan M. Lukic (2005), "Topological Overview of Hybrid Electric and Fuel Cell Vehicular Power System Architectures and Configurations," *IEEE Transactions on Vehicular Technology*, 54 (3), 763–770.

[78] energy.gov/eere/vehicles/vehicle-technologies-office-parasitic-loss-reduction-research-and-development-rd (February 27, 2017).

energy use contribute to reductions in parasitic energy loss. The aerodynamics and rolling resistance of trucks can be enhanced somewhat, but the rectangular shape of the cargo area is a significant constraint. Auxiliary operations include heating, lighting, and on-board amenities (e.g., computers, entertainment systems, and appliances). These ancillary activities also contribute to energy costs. In many cases, the long-haul trucks stand in the idle position for over six hours per day. This inactive time produces particulate matter, raises the level of noise, and consumes fuel. The energy cost of auxiliary functions can be reduced through technologies that reduce the power requirements associated with these operations. In addition, the time spent idling can be reduced by enhanced freight scheduling, new idling technologies, and turning trucks off.

In order to attract and retain competent drivers, it is essential that safety improvements accompany other efforts to enhance energy efficiency. Crash avoidance and survival is enhanced through advanced braking technologies, stability controls, lane-tracking systems, and video-based visibility systems. The introduction of these technologies can be incompatible with other efficiency goals given that many safety features increase the weight and reduce the aerodynamics of trucks. Therefore, strong coordination between safety and energy efficiency is critical to long-term sustainability concerns.

A-6

Energy Consumption in the Industrial Sector

In this appendix you will learn about:

Primary Industrial Contributors to Carbon Emissions

Carbon Emissions Associated with Steel Production

Carbon Emissions in the Nonmetallic Minerals Industry

Carbon Emissions Endemic to Chemical Production

Carbon Emissions Associated with the Paper and Pulp Industries

PRIMARY INDUSTRIAL CONTRIBUTORS TO CARBON EMISSIONS

In this appendix, we provide an overview of sustainable marketing efforts associated with the industrial sector of the economy. Given that this sector accounts for one-third of all energy consumption, there are important dividends that can be realized from effective management of energy usage and carbon emissions. We, therefore, begin by outlining several industries in this sector that reflect the largest usage of energy as well as the highest potential to reduce carbon emissions. Consider first the leading contributors to climate change in industry.

The International Energy Agency (IEA) recognizes marked potential to reduce emissions in the industrial sector. On a worldwide basis, industry accounts for 37 percent of energy consumption.[1] The use of energy and the amount of carbon emissions varies considerably from one industry to the next. IEA indicates that 70 percent of carbon emissions for the industrial sector are associated with the iron and steel, nonmetallic minerals, and chemical/petrochemical industries. In addition to these industries, there are substantial opportunities to reduce the amount of carbon emissions associated with the paper industry and nonferrous metal sectors. Unlike the household sector, there is not a single indicator associated with emissions across industries. Each industry has different factors that must be considered in effort to reduce emissions. Therefore, we highlight factors associated with enhanced energy efficiency and carbon emissions in each of these industries.

CARBON EMISSIONS ASSOCIATED WITH STEEL PRODUCTION

In 2015, more than 1.6 billion tons of steel were produced in the world.[2] Steel is a seemingly ubiquitous commodity that is incorporated into many final products.[3] Figure AP6-1 indicates that construction is the largest user of steel followed by machinery, metal products, and the automotive sector.

The steel industry and nonmetallic minerals industry are the largest producers of carbon emissions in this economic sector. Figure AP6-2 indicates that more than 83 percent of worldwide production of steel is concentrated in 10 markets. China represents half of global steel production.[4] Over the past two decades, most growth has been in China where the industry is relatively inefficient. In addition, the Chinese market does not have substantial amounts of scrap available for steel recycling.

The production of iron and steel is complex and varies from one country to the next, yet there are similarities in the processes employed across geographic

---

[1] International Energy Agency (2016), *Key World Energy Trends—International Energy Agency*, Paris: International Energy Agency.

[2] www.worldsteel.org/publications/fact-sheets.html (January 4, 2017).

[3] World Steel Assocaition (2008), *2008 Sustainability Report*, Brussells, Belgium: World Steel Association.

[4] edgar.jrc.ec.europa.eu/news_docs/jrc-2016-trends-in-global-co2-emissions-2016-report-103425.pdf (January 5, 2017).

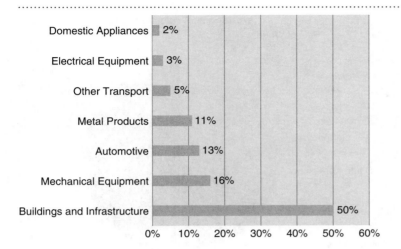

FIGURE AP6-1[5]
Global steel demand by end
use market—2014

regions. In order to gain an understanding of energy consumption, it is necessary to outline the processes endemic to steel production. Figure AP6-3 provides an overview of the essential processes associated with most steel production. Two methods, *basic oxygen* and *electric arc furnaces*, account for the vast majority of steel production. Basic oxygen is ordinarily used for high-tonnage production of carbon steels, and electric arc furnaces are used to produce low-tonnage specialty steels.[6] About 70 percent of production occurs through basic oxygen processes, and 29 percent occurs through electric arc procedures.[7] After one of these processing methods has been employed, the metal is ready for metallurgy and finishing.

Basic Oxygen Furnaces

The production process for steel involves converting raw materials (i.e., iron ore and coal) into iron followed by converting iron into steel. Steel is then transformed via metallurgy and finishing that make the product useful to the construction, automotive, and other industries.

The basic oxygen furnace produces products such as automotive fenders, encasements of refrigerators, and packaging.[8] The production of iron via basic oxygen furnaces involves the introduction of coke, iron ore, and oxygen into a furnace. In order to make coke, bituminous coal is fed into a series of ovens where it is heated at high temperature for 14 to 36 hours in the absence of oxygen.[9] During this process, compounds are driven off and collected. Ammonia liquor is a by-product taken to wastewater facilities, and tar removed during this process is also stored. Light oil taken from the coke ovens becomes benzene, toluene,

---

[5] www.trade.gov/steel/pdfs/07192016global-monitor-report.pdf (January 5, 2017).

[6] www.idaehan.com/en/business/steel/rebar_view?seq=15&keyword=&field = (January 5, 2017).

[7] www.worldcoal.org/coal/uses-coal/how-steel-produced (January 4, 2017).

[8] www.worldautosteel.org/life-cycle-thinking/recycling/ (January 4, 2017).

[9] www.ifc.org/wps/wcm/connect/9ecab70048855c048ab4da6a6515bb18/coke_PPAH. pdf?MOD=AJPERES (January 4, 2017).

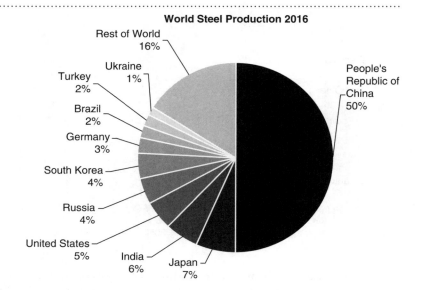

World Steel Production 2016

Rest of World 16%
Ukraine 1%
Turkey 2%
Brazil 2%
Germany 3%
South Korea 4%
Russia 4%
United States 5%
India 6%
Japan 7%
People's Republic of China 50%

and xylene that are useful in chemical production (see petrochemicals below). Naphthalene is also derived as a by-product, and the remaining carbon is coke. The coke is then transferred to quenching tower where it is cooled either by a water spray or circulating an inert gas (nitrogen) in a process referred to as *dry quenching*. Coke making requires 0.75 to 2.0 gigajoules per ton of crude steel and sintering requires 2 to 3 gigajoules per ton.

The production of coke results in several forms of waste. Coke ovens produce air emissions in the forms particulate matter, volatile organic compounds, methane, sulfur oxides, and other pollutants. Wastewater is generated from the cooling of the coke oven gas and the processing of by-products (e.g., ammonia and tar). Coke production generates coke breeze during the quenching process. This compound is used to make sinter or is sold as a by-product. In addition to breeze, coke produces solid waste containing hazardous components such as benzene.[11]

Iron is produced when coke is combined with oxygen, flux, and iron ore in a blast furnace. In hot stoves, compressed air is blended with additional oxygen and heated to 1100°C. Oxygen is then injected at the bottom of the blast furnace. Because hot stoves account for 10 to 20 percent of the total energy requirement in an integrated steel mill, efficient hot stoves can yield substantial energy savings.[12]

Iron ore is ordinarily introduced into the blast furnace in the form of sinter or pellets. Sintering is the more efficient process for making direct feed for blast furnaces, and more than 50 percent of all iron ore is converted into sinter. Sintering

[10] www.worldatlas.com/articles/the-top-10-steel-producing-countries-in-the-world.html (January 4, 2017).

[11] www.ifc.org/wps/wcm/connect/9ecab70048855c048ab4da6a6515bb18/coke_PPAH .pdf?MOD=AJPERES (January 4, 2017).

[12] International Energy Agency (2008), *Tracking Industrial Energy Efficiency and CO2 Emissions*, Paris, France: OECD/IEA.

involves heating fine ore and causing it to agglomerate into larger granules.[13] The heat consumed for sintering reaction is about 33 percent of the total heat input into a steel plant. Since almost half of this energy is released into the atmosphere, waste heat recovery is a key strategy for improved efficiency. Although sintering is more efficient than pellet production, it results in greater amounts of dust levels per ton of steel produced.

Iron is produced in the blast furnace from coke, oxygen, iron ore, and flux. Limestone in the form of flux is added to remove sulfur and other impurities.[14] Impurities in the furnace produce blast furnace slag that rises to the top of the furnace.

Iron that is produced in blast furnaces is then introduced into the basic oxygen furnace. The oxygen steelmaking process converts the molten iron from the blast furnace and steel scrap into steel. High-purity oxygen is introduced that lowers carbon, silicon, manganese, and phosphorous content of the iron, and flux is added to reduce sulfur and phosphorous levels.[15] These impurities are carried off in the slag that floats on the surface of the hot metal. The basic oxygen furnace production of steel requires approximately 1 to 13 gigajoule per ton of crude steel, including the hot stove, blast furnace, and oxygen furnace.

Electric Arc Furnaces

The electric arc furnace (EAF) produces products whose primary requirement is strength. For example, structural beams, steel plates, and reinforcement bars are made via electric arc furnaces.[16] Processing of steel from ore occurs in this manner via direct reduced iron production and electric arc furnace operations. In direct reduced iron production, oxygen is removed from lump iron oxide pellets to produce direct reduced iron (DRI).[17] The electric arc furnace employs this direct reduced iron and scrap to produce steel. Scrap is the most important element, as about 80 percent of the inputs are of this nature.[18] Consequently, it is difficult to control the purity and the quality of the steel produced. Mills that focus on EAF steel production normally concentrate on market segments where steel quality is not as critical.[19] During melting and refining operations, some of the undesirable materials within the bath are oxidized and become electric arc slag. The production of direct reduced iron using natural gas requires about 12 gigajoules per ton of crude steel. Electric arc furnaces use 1 to 1.5 gigajoules of electricity per ton of crude steel.

---

[13] Loo, Chin Eng (2005), "A Perspective of Goethitic Ore Sintering Fundamentals," *ISIJ —International*, 45(4), 436–448.

[14] www.steel.org/making-steel/how-its-made/processes/how-a-blast-furnace-works.aspx (January 4, 2017).

[15] www.911metallurgist.com/blog/wp-content/uploads/2016/03/FLUXES-FOR-METALLURGY.pdf (January 4, 2017).

[16] www.pharosproject.net/uploads/files/sources/573/steel_takes_LEED_011405.pdf (January 4, 2017).

[17] metallics.org.uk/dri/ (January 4, 2017).

[18] World Steel Assocaition (2008), *2008 Sustainability Report*, Brussells, Belgium: World Steel Association.

[19] heattreatconsortium.com/metals-advisor/electric-arc-furnace/ (January 4, 2017).

Metallurgy and Finishing

The use of a basic oxygen or electric arc furnace yields crude steel, but refinement does not end. The liquid steel output from the furnaces is further refined through a series of processes referred to as *metallurgy* . The objectives of these processes are the removal of oxygen, hydrogen, sulfur, and other impurities. After removal of these impurities, the steel is cast into either ingots or cast directly into semi-finished shapes (e.g., slabs). Continuous casting into semi-finished shapes requires less time, labor, energy, and capital than ingot casting.[20] Additional finishing such as galvanization is also incorporated into steel during this final phase.

Sustainability

The steel industry is attempting to enhance environmental sustainability through initiatives associated with *climate change, environmental protection,* and *management of natural resources.*[21] One aspect of climate change efforts focuses on reductions in the amount of carbon dioxide produced for each ton of steel produced. Part of this effort includes investments in technologies that raise the eco-efficiency of production. The International Energy Agency indicates that 3 percent of total sector energy use and CO_2 emissions can be saved through improved efficiency of production processes and better reclamation of by-products of these processes.[22] Improved production processes include application of dry coke quenching in coke making, blast furnace and electric arc furnace enhancements, and steel finishing improvements.[23] The reductions associated with changes in these processes are realized when companies upgrade to best available technologies.

The steel industry efforts to enhance environmental protection focus on monitoring of production and life cycle inventory management. Because the monitoring of operations is essential to this industry, most steel producers operate facilities that are ISO 14001 certified. ISO 14000 refers to a family of management standard established by the International Standards Organization (see Appendix 7). The ISO 14001 standard enables firms to assess the environmental impact of its activities, improve environmental performance, and implement a systematic approach to achieving environmental objectives.[24] More than 85 percent of all employees and contractors in the steel industry operate at ISO registered facilities.[25]

The steel industry also monitors the treatment of natural resources. Material efficiency refers to the amount of material that is not sent for permanent disposal in a landfill or incineration. This efficiency is realized by the familiar reduce,

---

[20] Labson, Stephen, Peter Gooday, and Andrew Manson (1994), *Adoption of New Steelmaking Technologies*, SSRN 2554879.

[21] World Steel Assocaition (2008), *2008 Sustainability Report*, Brussells, Belgium: World Steel Association.

[22] International Energy Agency (2008), *Tracking Industrial Energy Efficiency and CO2 Emissions*, Paris, France: OECD/IEA.

[23] ietd.iipnetwork.org/content/iron-and-steel (January 5, 2017).

[24] Tibor, T., and I. Feldman (1996), *ISO 14000: A Guide to the New Environmental Management Standards.* Chicago: Irwin.

[25] World Steel Assocaition (2008), *2008 Sustainability Report*, Brussells, Belgium: World Steel Association.

reuse, and recycle perspective. Material *reductions* are realized by using coke-less steel production technologies that do not rely on coke production. Marketing the blast furnaces and electric arc furnaces slag to the road construction and cement industries reduces energy costs and overall carbon emissions for the industrial sector.

The *reuse* of material is exemplified by an industry that boasts a 97 percent material efficiency level. The 100 percent efficiency goal is approached by working together with other industries. Efforts to use by-products of steel production more efficiently include coke oven and basic oxygen furnace gas recovery, blast furnace gas use, and slag/steel usage in cement making. Notably, slag marketed to the cement industry has the potential to reduce cement-related CO_2 by 50 percent.

The steel industry is also very active in *recycling*. Virtually all steel is recyclable, and as one of the few magnetic metals, it can easily be separated from waste and other metals. Steel is the most widely recycled material in the world. In 2006, for example, the industry recycled 459 metric megatons, equivalent to 37 percent of the crude steel produced in the year. This recycling reduced carbon emissions by 827 metric megatons and saved the equivalent of 868 metric megatons of iron ore.[26]

CARBON EMISSIONS IN THE NONMETALLIC MINERALS INDUSTRY

Nonmetallic minerals account for 9 percent of industrial energy use but represent 27 percent of carbon emissions.[27] The largest contributor to energy usage in the nonmetallic minerals sector is concrete production, and a central process to this production is the production of *cement*. After water, concrete is the second most consumed product in the world.[28] In 2000, worldwide concrete sales exceeded $97 billion.[29] The production of cement represents about 80 percent of energy use for nonmetallic metals and is an important source of CO_2 emissions. There have been substantial improvements in energy use in this industry over the past 15 years, yet there is potential for additional reduction associated with adoption of best available technologies.

Concrete is a global industry operating in 150 countries with more than 850,000 employees. At 46 percent of global cement production in 2005, China is the largest producer of cement. The top 10 producers (China, India, United States, Japan, Korea, Spain, Russia, Thailand, Brazil, and Italy) account for more than 71 percent of global production. Transportation costs for cement are extensive, and concrete is rarely transported more than 300 kilometers.

---

[26] World Steel Association (2008), *2008 Sustainability Report*, Brussells, Belgium: World Steel Association.

[27] International Energy Agency (2008), *Tracking Industrial Energy Efficiency and CO2 Emissions*, Paris, France: OECD/IEA.

[28] International Energy Agency (2008), Tracking Industrial Energy Efficiency and CO2 Emissions, Paris, France: OECD/IEA.

[29] www.wbcsdcement.org/pdf/agenda.pdf (January 4, 2017).

Concrete production is a relatively simple four-stage process.[30] The first stage is acquisition of raw materials. These materials include limestone, sand, and clay that typically come from quarries located near the cement manufacturing plant. These components provide the four main ingredients for cement: lime, silica, alumina, and iron.[31] In the second stage, these materials are analyzed, blended, and ground for further processing. In the third stage, materials are heated in a very large kiln that is over 200 meters long with a diameter of 3 to 7.5 meters. The kiln reaches temperatures of 1450°C, which turns the material into a marble-sized substance called *clinker*. When the limestone is heated, it undergoes a reaction in which carbon dioxide is released, and calcium oxide is formed. Importantly, about half of the carbon emissions for concrete are associated with this process, and these emissions are unaffected by fuel switching or other efforts to enhance efficiency. In the fourth stage, gypsum is added, and the mixture is ground to a fine powder called **Portland cement**. Although there are other forms of cement, Portland cement is the most common and represents the great majority of cement sales in the United States.[32] Portland cement is marketed in several different compounds that vary based on physical and chemical requirements such as durability and strength.

Cement production can occur via wet or dry processes. The wet process facilitates easier control of chemical activity, but it has higher energy requirements due to the need to evaporate water prior to making calcium dioxide. Because the dry process does not require evaporation or the energy costs associated with wet process cement production, dry processes are replacing wet processes on a worldwide basis.

Sustainability

Due to the amount of carbon emissions associated with the industry, concrete has been implicated as an industry that contributes to global warming.[33] Most of the carbon emissions in concrete production, however, are associated with the production of calcium oxide, a product essential to cement, and most sustainability efforts cannot address this primary source of emissions in the industry. Nevertheless, several strategies have been employed to limit the industry's impact on climate change.

Substantial efforts have been dedicated to reducing the amount of energy employed in the manufacturing process. The size of the kiln used to make cement influences energy costs. In China, the world's largest producer at nearly 50 percent of production, small kilns are being replaced in favor of more efficient larger kilns. Concrete producers are also working with alternative fuels in order to reduce production costs, dispose of waste, reduce carbon emissions, and limit fossil fuel usage. These fuels may include tires, wood, plastics, chemicals, animal carcasses, sewage sludge, and construction waste. The use of alternative

---

[30] www.madehow.com/Volume-1/Concrete.html (January 4, 2017).

[31] International Energy Agency (2008), *Tracking Industrial Energy Efficiency and CO2 Emissions*, Paris, France: OECD/IEA.

[32] pubs.usgs.gov/of/2005/1152/2005-1152.pdf (January 4, 2017).

[33] Rosenthal, Elisabeth (2007), "Cement Industry Is at Center of Climate Change Debate," *The New York Times*, Octoebr 27, 1.

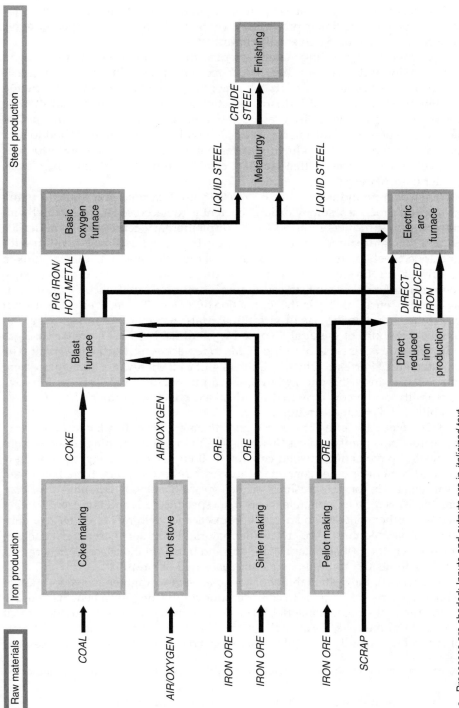

a - Processes are shaded; Inputs and outputs are in *italicized text.*

FIGURE AP6-3 [34]

Steel production processes[a]

Processes are shaded; Inputs and outputs are in italicized text.

[34] International Energy Agency (2008), *Tracking Industrial Energy Efficiency and CO2 Emissions,* Paris, France: OECD/IEA.

fuels varies by country. At one extreme, Germany relies on alternative fuels for about 37 percent of clinker production, yet South Korea, at the other extreme, incorporates less than 5 percent alternative fuels.

The process of grinding materials represents the largest electricity demand in the cement industry. Grinding associated with processing of raw materials and grinding of cement accounts for almost 100 kilowatt hours per metric ton of cement produced. Best industry practice indicates, however, that there is potential to reduce electricity usage by another 20 percent. Despite this potential, over 90 percent of the energy associated with grinding is converted to heat that is not used on the production of cement. Clearly, there are opportunities to develop new processes that facilitate cement production at efficiency levels greater than 10 percent.

The concrete industry relies on *reuse* to limit carbon emissions. In many production processes, some Portland cement is replaced or supplemented with industrial by-products referred to as supplementary cementitious materials (SCMs).[35] Slag procured from the steel industry can be used as a substitute for limestone. Steel slag requires little additional fuel to convert it to cement clinker. As a result, carbon emissions are reduced due to lower energy needs. Fly ash, a by-product of coal burning, and silica fume, a by-product of silicon manufacturing, are also reused as slag in the production of cement. The recovery of industrial by-products avoids the use of virgin materials in cement manufacturing and limits the amount of material disposed in landfills. Moreover, greenhouse gas reductions are achievable by using SCMs to replace some Portland cement. The manufacture of Portland cement requires significant energy use, and replacement with SCMs reduces this energy burden. In addition, reuse of SCMs can improve workability of the concrete mixture, decrease concrete permeability, improve durability, and enhance strength.

Concrete is also one of the most *recycled* materials on the planet.[36] Recycling of concrete pavement involves breaking, removing, and crushing concrete from an existing pavement. Crushed concrete is then used as an aggregate in new Portland cement or other concrete processes.[37] In recent years, there have been advancements in concrete crushing technologies and methods to remove steel from concrete. This recycled concrete meets most specifications and is currently being used with other concrete and asphalt products and yielding better performance over comparable virgin concrete. The material is lighter than other concrete, which lowers the cost of material handling and transportation costs. Furthermore, recycling limits the amount of concrete discarded in landfills.

Analyses of the sustainability of concrete need to augment consideration of reduce-reuse-recycle logic with consideration for the long-term benefits of using concrete as a construction material.[38] The predominant raw material for the cement in concrete is limestone, the most abundant mineral on Earth. Because the materials for concrete are readily available, concrete can be made from local resources and

---

[35] www.concretenetwork.com/concrete/demolition/recycling_concrete.htm (January 4, 2017).

[36] www.pavements4life.com/QDs/Environment_2Recycle.asp (January 4, 2017).

[37] www.concretenetwork.com/concrete/demolition/recycling_concrete.htm (January 4, 2017).

[38] Mehta, P. Kumar (2001), "Reducing the Environmental Impact of Concrete," *Concrete International*, 23(10), 61–66.

processed near a jobsite. Local shipping minimizes fuel requirements for handling and transportation. Concrete also yields durable, long-lasting structures whose life spans can be double or triple those of other common building materials. Finally, homes built with concrete (walls, foundations, and floors) are energy efficient because they take advantage of concrete's inherent ability to absorb and retain heat. Consequently, homeowners can significantly cut their heating and cooling bills and install smaller-capacity HVAC equipment.

CARBON EMISSIONS ENDEMIC TO CHEMICAL PRODUCTION

The chemical industry produces plastics, synthetics, resins, detergents, fertilizers, and many other products on which we rely daily. The industry accounts for 30 percent of industrial energy usage, and this usage rate is growing at 2.2 percent annually.[39] The chemical industry also represents 16 percent of carbon emissions in the industrial sector.

Three types of intermediary products span between raw materials (crude oil, natural gas, coal, and other minerals) and consumer goods. These intermediary products include *olefins*, *aromatics*, and *other intermediates*. Olefins include ethylene, propylene, and xylene. These chemicals are used to make a variety of products such as bottles and trash bags. Aromatics include benzene, toluene, and xylene used to make products such as footwear and car tires. The other intermediaries include synthetic gas production used in ammonia and methanol production. The primary feedstock for olefins and aromatics is crude oil, whereas the primary feedstock for synthetic gas production is natural gas. Within the industry, 75 percent of feedstock is crude oil.

Nine chemical processes account for more than 65 percent of global energy use in the industry. These processes are associated with petrochemicals, inorganic chemicals, and fertilizers.[40]

Petrochemicals

Steam Cracking. Steam cracking is a process in which saturated hydrocarbons are broken down into smaller hydrocarbons. Steam cracking occurs in ovens in which feedstocks are broken down in the presence of steam.[41] This process also results in the removal of by-products such as hydrocarbons, water, and acid gas. Steam cracking accounts for over 39 percent of final energy use in the chemical industry. It is the principal method for producing olefins (ethylene, propylene, and butadiene). This procedure has incurred a 50 percent reduction in energy consumption since the 1970s, yet implementation of improved technologies for the removal of by-products yields greater energy efficiency.

---

[39] International Energy Agency (2008), *Tracking Industrial Energy Efficiency and CO2 Emissions*, Paris, France: OECD/IEA.

[40] International Energy Agency (2008), *Tracking Industrial Energy Efficiency and CO2 Emissions*, Paris, France: OECD/IEA.

[41] Avidan, Amos A., Michael Edwards, and Hartley Owen (1990), "Innovative Improvements Highlight Fcc's Past and Future," *Oil & Gas Journal* 88(2).

Aromatic Extraction. *Aromatic extraction* includes the production of benzene, toluene, and xylene used to make products ranging from medicine to DVDs. Because most energy employed in this process is feedstock, there is limited potential to reduce energy consumption.

Methanol. *Methanol* is a chemical that occurs as a result of biological processes conducted by vegetation, microorganisms, and other living species. It is produced synthetically through the catalytic steam process that typically uses natural gas as the feedstock. Methanol can be produced from natural gas, coal, municipal wastes, landfill gas, wood wastes, and seaweed, and it is used to make a variety of products such as plastics, paints, construction materials, and windshield washer fluid.[42] In 2006, 40 percent of methanol use was for formaldehyde, and another 19 percent was used as a fuel additive. Seventeen countries account for more than 90 percent of methanol production. China is the largest producer and the only one that uses coal as a feedstock. The carbon emission cost associated with natural gas plants are lower that the emissions in coal-based facilities.[43]

Olefin and Aromatic Processing. Olefins are used to make plastics and synthetic rubber. The Unipol reactor process marketed by Union Carbide in 1977 was developed to manufacture polyethylene, while the process for the manufacture of polypropylene was announced in 1983.[44] Polypropylene is the world's most widely used plastic, and Unipol is the most widely used process for making this plastic.[45] The Innovene process developed by British Petroleum (BP) is also widely used.[46] The rights to market Innovene are now owned by Ineos.

Inorganic Chemicals

Chlorine and Sodium Hydroxide. Chlorine is procured when salt is electrochemically decomposed into chlorine and sodium hydroxide. Chlorine is further processed to make polyvinyl chloride (PVC) used in plumbing, whereas sodium chloride is used by the paper, textile, and other industries. At more than 25 percent of total output, the United States is the world leader in production. Chlorine and sodium hydroxide are produced through three processes that vary in their sodium hydroxide concentration. These methods include the mercury, diaphragm, and membrane processes. The greatest potential for energy savings lies in the conversion of mercury and diaphragm process plants to membrane technology.

---

[42] www.methanol.org/chemical/ (January 5, 2017).

[43] International Energy Agency (2008), *Tracking Industrial Energy Efficiency and CO2 Emissions*, Paris, France: OECD/IEA.

[44] www.unioncarbide.com/History (January 5, 2017).

[45] International Energy Agency (2008), *Tracking Industrial Energy Efficiency and CO2 Emissions*, Paris, France: OECD/IEA.

[46] www.ineos.com/businesses/ineos-technologies/technologies (January 5, 2017).

Carbon Black. *Carbon black* is a form of carbon that is primarily used as reinforcement in vulcanized rubber products. The tire industry uses approximately 85 percent of the output of this inorganic compound. In the past decade, there have been efforts to replace some portion of carbon black with silica. Silica tires wear better, offer greater fuel efficiency, and better traction. Nevertheless, the material costs of silica are twice the cost for carbon black.

Soda Ash. *Soda ash* or sodium carbonate is primarily used to make glass, but it is also used in water softeners, detergents, brick manufacturing, and photographic processes. In the United States, the world's largest producer (31 percent share), soda ash is drawn from natural deposits and soda recovery from lakes. In contrast, soda ash is produced through a synthetic process in every other country. This synthetic process is costlier and more energy intensive than natural soda.

Industrial Gases. *Industrial gases* are commonly found in the air and other gases. Nitrogen, the largest selling gas, is used in the food and beverage industry and in multiple manufacturing processes. Oxygen, the second largest selling gas, is used in manufacturing and health care, while nitrogen is used in the food and beverage industry as well as in manufacturing. Carbon dioxide is also used in the food industry, but it is also used in the refrigeration and healthcare industries. Acetylene is the fourth largest selling gas and is used in welding.

Fertilizers

Ammonia is an essential element in fertilizer that is produced by combining hydrogen and oxygen. The nitrogen is procured from the air, whereas the hydrogen is obtained from fossil fuel. Throughout most of the world, natural gas is used to produce hydrogen. Natural gas represents 77 percent of ammonia production. Coal gasification is a different process for hydrogen procurement and represents 14 percent of the world market. Coal is primarily used to produce ammonia in China. The remaining 9 percent of the market relies on partial oxidation of oil to produce hydrogen. This form of production is employed in China and India, the number one and two producers, respectively, of ammonia.

Sustainability

There have been marked enhancements in technology that enable the chemical industry to *reduce* energy consumption. The specific energy consumption associated with steam cracking, for example, has been reduced by 50 percent since 1970.[47] These improvements have occurred through the introduction of enhanced technologies such as process-to-process heat recovery systems. Similarly, application of best practices technologies in the production of olefins and aromatics has the potential to reduce energy efficiency by more than 30 percent. Best practice technologies include the use of improved reactors and enhanced polymerization processes.

---

[47] International Energy Agency (2008), *Tracking Industrial Energy Efficiency and CO2 Emissions*, Paris, France: OECD/IEA.

Among the three processes used to make chlorine, the membrane process requires the least amount of energy. The total energy requirements include electricity used in the decomposition of salt and steam consumption. The membrane process is at least 16 percent more efficient than either other process.[48] Conversion of chemical plants to this procedure results in reductions in the amount of energy consumed in the industrial sector.

Although many chemicals cannot be reused, there are substantial efforts to recycle by-products through the manufacturing of chemicals. In steam cracking, substantial amounts of by-products are recycled, and the form of the by-products varies with the feedstock. For example, for every metric ton of ethane that undergoes steam cracking, 803 kilograms of ethylene is produced. Ethylene is processed into a wealth of products that range from packaging to antifreeze to detergents. The by-products include propylene and butadiene used to produce plastics as well as hydrogen and methane used to fuel the steam cracking furnaces.[49]

CARBON EMISSIONS ASSOCIATED WITH THE PAPER AND PULP INDUSTRIES

At 5.7 percent of total industry energy consumption, the paper and pulp industry is the fourth largest user of energy in the industrial sector. The United States is the largest producer at 24 percent of worldwide output. The top 10 producers (United States, China, Japan, Canada, Germany, Finland, Sweden, Korea, France, and Italy) account for almost 75 percent of output. Since 1990, Chinese production of paper and paperboard has more than tripled.

Approximately one-half of industry production is in the form of packaging, wrapping, and paperboard, and one-third of production is printing and writing paper. Since 1960, the annual growth rate for printing and writing paper has exceeded increases in demand in other sectors of this industry, and the rise in computer and photocopier usage is associated with this increase. The remaining output is newsprint, sanitary paper, and household paper.[50] As the popularity of the Internet and electronic media has increased, the demand for newspapers and periodicals has decreased. The demand for various forms of production is related to Organisation for Economic Cooperation and Development (OECD) membership. Within the OECD, there is a greater demand for paper used for printing and writing. By contrast, paper and paperboard used in packaging fuels demand outside of the OECD.

There are several characteristics that influence the ability to make generalizations about paper production. First, the various producers differ in their access to virgin timber and recycled materials. In addition, energy requirements and

---

[48] Bowen, C. P. (2006), *Development Trends for Ethylene Crackers: Existing Technologies and RD&D*, IEA/CEFIC Workshop Feedstock Substitutes, Energy Efficient Technology and CO2 Reduction for Petrochemical Products, 12–13 December, Paris, France.

[49] International Energy Agency (2008), *Tracking Industrial Energy Efficiency and CO2 Emissions*, Paris, France: OECD/IEA.

[50] International Energy Agency (2008), *Tracking Industrial Energy Efficiency and CO2 Emissions*, Paris, France: OECD/IEA.

plant sizes differ considerably across markets.[51] The paper and pulp industry also differs from other industries because it is a large producer and user of biomass. Across the industry, more than one-third of the energy consumed is biomass. Much of this biomass is black liquor that is produced in the making of pulp. This biomass and other forms of energy are primarily used to generate heat in the production process. Two-thirds of the energy consumed is used to produce heat, while another third is used to make electricity. The biomass use results in relatively low levels of carbon emissions in this industry and suggests that there are modest opportunities to enhance energy efficiency. Estimates from the International Energy Agency, however, indicate significant opportunities to enhance energy efficiency.

In order to understand the potential for savings, it is important to understand the flow of resources in the production process. Raw materials such as logs are cut into wood pulp, and this pulp is processed to separate wood fibers from the *lignin* that binds fibers into solid wood.[52] The processing of pulp either occurs through mechanical pulping or chemical pulping. Mechanical pulping is used for lower grade papers and offers high yields. Chemical pulping is a thermochemical process in which a combination of solvents and heat is applied to separate lignin from wood fibers.[53] The two most common processes are sulfite and sulfate pulping. Sulfate pulping employs the Kraft process whereby sodium sulfate is used to produce a pulp of high physical strength and bulk but relatively poor sheet formation. Sulfite pulping uses sulfurous acid and an alkali to produce pulps of lower physical strength and bulk that offer better sheet formation. These pulps are used in newsprint, printing, bond papers, and tissue.

Approximately 18 percent of energy use is associated with pulping, and most of this consumption (15 percent) is due to mechanical pulping. Chemical pulping produces large amounts of black liquor that is used to generate electricity. Thus, this pulping process produces about one-third of the energy used in the industry.

Once the pulping procedure and energy recovery has occurred, the pulp is bleached and dried to prepare for papermaking. The making of paper includes the blending of pulps and additives, sheet formation, and finishing. The process of papermaking represents 47 percent of total energy use in the industry.

Sustainability

There have been tremendous strides towards sustainability in the industry, yet there are additional measures that would reduce the amount of energy consumption and carbon emissions. These additional measures include advanced pulp drying technologies, enhanced black liquor recovery technologies, and improved heat recovery systems. The International Energy Agency indicates that implementation of best available technologies has the potential to limit final energy consumption.

The reuse of materials in the production process has already posted strong dividends for the paper industry. The reuse of black liquor as a fuel limits reliance on fossil fuel. Moreover, use of this technology has the potential to enable chemical pulp plants to serve as net providers to the electricity grid.

---

[51] www.ilocis.org/documents/chpt72e.htm (January 5, 2017).

[52] www.biocenter.helsinki.fi/groups/HATAKKA/english/background.html (January 5, 2017).

[53] ietd.iipnetwork.org/content/chemical-pulping (January 5, 2017).

Because archival documents, construction materials, and other products cannot be recycled, the theoretcial maximum for recycling of paper is 81 percent. In 2014, recovered paper, including pulp from recovered paper, accounted for 63.9 percent of the raw material for production of new paper in Japan.[54] The average global rate of recylcing is 45 percent, which suggests marked opportunity to recycle. Similarly, The Confederation of European Paper Industries is a colloquim of EU members, Norway, and Switzerland has achieved a 71.7 percent of recycling in 2012.[55]

The effort to promote recycling in the paper industry underscores one of the intriguing challenges of sustainable marketing. There are situations under which one must choose among environmental goals that are somewhat incompatible. For example, the reclamation of recycled paper now accounts for 45 percent of inputs to global production. Note that although recycling results in use of fewer natural resources, the efforts to gather and process recycled materials yields carbon emissions. By contrast, chemical pulping plants that use virgin timber may be carbon neutral. The efforts to yield lower carbon emissions must be viewed simultaneously with the desire to manage natural resources such as timber.

---

[54] www.prpc.or.jp/linkfile/english-paperrecycling.pdf. (January 5, 2017).

[55] www.cepi.org/node/16410 (January 5, 2017).

appendix

A-7

ISO 14000

In this appendix you will learn about:

The International Standards Organization

The Environmental Impact of ISO 14000

The benefits of adopting ISO 14001

Managers of supply chains are increasingly asking suppliers to provide sustainability metrics, and they are requiring third-party certification of major suppliers.[1] In response to these calls for systematic assessment of a firm's influence on the environment, companies of all sizes have implemented *environmental management systems (EMS)*. An EMS is a set of regulations established to achieve environmental goals.[2] The International Standards Organization (ISO) has emerged as a family of standards applied across industries to monitor and control interaction with the environment. The ISO 14000 standards are voluntary standards established by the ISO. ISO has over 100 member countries represented primarily by government and industry standards groups.[3] ISO generates over 1100 new standards every year and currently has developed over 17,500 international standards on a variety of subjects. Given the potential for enhanced performance, many organizations have implanted these standards. The Ford Motor Company, the first automaker to embrace ISO 14000, credits the standard with saving millions of dollars since implementation in 1998.[4]

Two of the primary standards associated in the ISO 14000 family are 14001 and 14004. These standards were updated in 2004.[5] ISO 14001:2004 provides a framework for an organization to control the environmental influence of its activities, products, and services and improve its environmental performance continually. ISO 14001:2004 outlines the guidelines associated with the firm's approach to sustainability, and it provides a strategic approach to the organization's environmental policy. The standard is broad enough to be applied in a variety of contexts that include restaurants, construction firms, hotels, manufacturers and their suppliers, and airports.[6] In addition, small and medium-sized enterprises are also recognizing that they can benefit from ISO 14001:2004 certification.[7]

ISO 14004:2004 provides guidelines on the elements of an EMS, its implementation, and the principal issues involved. The latest (2016) version of ISO 14004 provides a focus on protecting the environment, environmental performance,

---

[1] Hoffman, William (2007), "The Greening of Logistics," *Traffic World*, 271 (25), 10–13.

[2] Syzmaski, Michal, and Piyushi Tiwari (2004), "ISO 14001 and the Reduction of Toxic Emissions," *Policy Reform*, 7 (1), 31–42.

[3] Korul, Vildan (2005), "Guide to the Implementation of ISO 14001 at Airports," *Journal of Air Transportation*, 10(2), 49–68.

[4] *Business & the Environment with ISO 14000 Updates* (2006), "Ford & ISO 14001," *Business & the Environment with ISO 14000 Updates*, 17 (4), 13.

[5] *Business & the Environment with ISO 14000 Updates* (2004), "Improved Versions of ISO 14000 EMS Standards Published," *Business & the Environment with ISO 14000 Updates*, 15 (12), 12–13.

[6] *Business & the Environment with ISO 14000 Updates* (2009), "ISO 14001 for Restaurants? — The Green Restaurant 4.0 Standard (Part 1)," *Business & the Environment with ISO 14000 Updates*, 20 (4), 12–14; Turk, Ahmet Murat (2009), "The Benefits Associated with ISO 14001 Certification for Construction Firms: Turkish Case," *Journal of Cleaner Production*, 17 (5), 559–569; and Chan, Wilco W., and Kenny Ho (2006), "Hotels' Environmental Management Systems (ISO 14001): Creative Financing Strategy," *International Journal of Contemporary Hospitality Management*, 18 (4), 302–316.

[7] Seiffert, Mari Elizabete Bernardini, (2008), "Environmental Impact Evaluation Using a Cooperative Model for Implementing EMS (ISO 14001) in Small and Medium-Sized Enterprises," *Journal of Cleaner Production*, 16 (14), 1447–1461.

leadership and strategic environmental management as well as life-cycle perspectives.[8]

In many cases, organizations desire to make their pursuit of ISO management standards a matter of public record. ISO does not offer certification, but it does provide criteria for determining certification. Certification of ISO 14001:2004 is performed by independent, environmental auditors. The accreditation of these auditors is based on their work experience, education, communication and decision-making skills, and auditor training.[9] External auditors offer consultation over the sustainability efforts of the firm. Certification refers to the auditor's written assurance that it has audited an EMS and verified that it conforms to the standard. Registration, however, occurs when the auditor records the certification in its company register.[10] Certification of ISO 14001:2004 is valid for three years.[11]

Some of the benefits of adoption of ISO 14001:2004 accrue externally. Evidence suggests that, relative to firms with similar assets and performance, companies that implement it realize a competitive advantage over other firms in a market.[12] This advantage is associated with relatively lower toxic emissions among firms that have implemented the standard. The firm also enjoys lowered resource usage, higher energy savings, and lowered costs of waste disposal as a result of ISO 14001:2004 certification.[13] The merits of certification also provide assurance to stakeholders that the firm is committed to sustainability. Certification provides evidence to the local community that the firm is an environmental leader. Government and nongovernment organizations as well as private consumers are more likely to be favorably disposed to firms that adopt the ISO 14000 standards. Adoption of the standard supports the firm's claim about its own environmental policies. Moreover, it illustrates and enumerates plans and action for conformity to environmental guidelines.[14]

Adoption of this standard provides a strong response to customers and suppliers that place environmental demands on the firm. Among U.S. firms, for example, those organizations with capital investments or strong ties to Japanese or European firms are more likely to adopt ISO 14001:2004. Since attitudes associated with sustainability tend to be more pronounced in these geographic markets, U.S. firms with strong relationships with firms in these markets are likely to adopt the standards.[15] In addition, the adoption process, complete

---

[8] www.iso.org/news/2016/03/Ref2052.html (March 2, 2017).

[9] Wilson, Robert C. (2002), "The Professional Credentials for an ISO 14000 Consultant," *Pollution Engineering*, (May), 38–39.

[10] www.iso.org/certification.html (March 2, 2017).

[11] Aravind, Deepa, and Christmann, Petra (2008), "Institutional and Resource-Based Determinants of Substantive Implementation of ISO 14001," *Academy of Management Proceedings*, 1–6.

[12] Corbett, Charles J., and Michael V. Russo (2001), "ISO 14001: Irrelevant or Invaluable? ISO Management Systems, December.

[13] Syzmaski, Michal, and Piysuhi Tiwari (2004), "ISO 14001 and the Reduction of Toxic Emissions," *Policy Reform*, 7 (1), 31–42.

[14] www.iso.org/files/live/sites/isoorg/files/archive/pdf/en/introduction_to_iso_14001.pdf (March 2, 2017).

[15] Gutowski, Timothy, et al. (2003), "Environmentally benign manufacturing: Observations from Japan, Europe and the United States," *Journal of Cleaner Production*, 13 (1), 1–17.

with an assessment of conformity by a third-party auditor, reduces the need for verification among trading partners.

There are appreciable merits of ISO 14001:2004 certification to stakeholders within the firm. Top management gains confidence that it is monitoring and regulating processes within the firm that influence the environment.[16] Consequently, the firm can support claims about sustainability and provide a strong response to criticisms that focus on greenwashing. Employees gain confidence that their firms are environmentally responsible. Given the costs of employee recruitment and turnover,[17] firms that illustrate an empathy for environmental concerns provide additional incentives that attract and retain employees.

---

[16] www.iso.org/files/live/sites/isoorg/files/archive/pdf/en/iso_14001_-_key_benefits.pdf (March 2, 2017).

[17] Townsend, Keith (2007), "Recruitment, Training and Turnover: Another Call Centre Paradox," *Personnel Review*, 36 (3), 476–490.

INDEX